DAY
by
DAY

with the Best of
SPURGEON

*On the love
and loveliness
of Jesus*

Compiled by
Dolores E. Coupland

Deep River
B O O K S

Published by
Deep River Books
Sisters, Oregon
http://www.deepriverbooks.com

ISBN 13: 978-1-935265-13-9

ISBN 10: 1-935265-13-X

Library of Congress: 2010925483

Printed in the USA

Cover design by Joe Bailen

Dedicated to the memory of
Charles Haddon Spurgeon,
who wanted one sole subject for his ministry:
the love and loveliness of his Lord

ABOUT "THE PRINCE OF PREACHERS"

Charles Haddon Spurgeon (1834–1892) was born in Essex, England, and is recognized by all Christendom as "The Prince of Preachers." It is also said that he is the greatest preacher since the apostle Paul. If that is so, we know why. Like Paul, he centered his ministry on "Jesus Christ and him crucified" (1 Corinthians 2:2). The content of his preaching also appears to closely follow that of John the Baptist. Listen to Spurgeon's words: "I desire to be in the same case with John the Baptist. I would have my thoughts of Christ concentrated upon his atoning death, henceforth and evermore. During the little time in which I may be spared to lift my voice in this wilderness, I would bear witness to the Lamb of God. The years may be short in which I may guide this flock, but around the cross shall be to me evermore the place of green pastures, and from the sacrifice of our Lord shall flow the still waters."

This must be the reason why his writings remain popular even today—more than one hundred years after his death. He stated in a sermon published in 1883: "If I had preached any other than the doctrine of Christ crucified, I should years ago have scattered my audience to the winds of heaven." And yes, in the days of his ministry he preached to audiences numbering more than ten thousand.

We are told that even though Spurgeon had no theological schooling, by the age of twenty-one he was the most popular preacher in London. And he remained so until his death thirty-seven years later. Shortly before his death in 1892, over six thousand people were gathering every Sunday to hear him preach in his famous Metropolitan Tabernacle in London.

PREFACE

Although I have been a Christian most of my life, my real spiritual journey began approximately twenty years ago when I picked up Spurgeon's devotional book, *Morning and Evening*. As I read those amazing passages on the love and loveliness of Jesus, my heart was captivated, and since then it has been my passion to share this aspect of Spurgeon's writings with others. This has led to many hours spent going through his sermons, collecting choice thoughts, and assembling them into devotionals. I noticed that this is how Spurgeon prepared some—if not all—of his devotionals in *Morning and Evening*. I have followed his leading in this and believe that he would be pleased with the results.

While updating Spurgeon's language, I have attempted to retain his original wording and appealing style as much as possible. This devotional book is a collection of some of Spurgeon's best thoughts on the love and loveliness of Jesus, but in the preparation of it I have taken a few liberties. When gathering thoughts from various parts of a sermon, it has sometimes been necessary to add a few words as a bridge. Also, because of the format used in these devotionals, I have sometimes added a word or two—or even a sentence—to round out a thought. There were also a few instances when opening or closing statements were needed. Spurgeon, using the King James Version of the Bible, referred to Jesus as "the rose of Sharon" (Song of Solomon 2:1). The newer translations of the Bible indicate that this text refers to the bride, the Shulamite woman. Wanting to remain true to Scripture I have used "Altogether Lovely" in place of "rose of Sharon."

Although most of the meditations in this book have been assembled from choice thoughts gleaned from Spurgeon's sermons, they also include some material from his books *Morning and Evening* and *The Saint & His Saviour*. Since Spurgeon quoted Samuel Rutherford a lot, a few of his quotes have also been included.

Why did some of the messages in *Morning and Evening* strike me so forcefully? I had heard and read about the "love" of Jesus before, but not of his "loveliness." Knowingly or unknowingly, I believe that this is why so many people are drawn to Spurgeon's writings. He not only speaks openly about Christ's loveliness, but he also tries to *portray* it.

A few years ago I came across this statement of his: "Paul did well when he turned ignoramus, and determined to know nothing among the Corinthians save Jesus Christ, and him crucified. As the harp of Anacreon[1] would resound love alone, so would I have but one sole subject for my ministry—the love and loveliness of my Lord. Gladly would I make my whole ministry to speak of Christ and his surpassing loveliness." Yes, this was Spurgeon's main ambition in his ministry, and it is this that draws our hearts.

We also love the eloquence, the fervor, and the passion with which he writes. And when this is centered on Jesus and on his great sacrifice for us, what a powerful combination! Listen to the following words: "O sacred head, once wounded, I could forever gaze, admire, and adore! There is no beauty in all the world like that which is seen in the countenance 'more marred than that of any man.'"

Where do we see most clearly the love and loveliness of our Lord? It is at Gethsemane. It is at Gabbatha. It is at Golgotha. So come. Let us open the pages of this book, day by day, and follow

Charles Spurgeon as he leads us to all those precious places where our Savior lived, suffered, and then died for our redemption.

Dolores E. Coupland

[1]Spurgeon is referring to a poem, "To My Harp," written by Anacreon (570 BC–488 BC), a Greek poet. In this poem, Anacreon tells us about his Harp. He took many desperate measures in order to sing of other things, but he could not move his Harp to sing of anything but Love.

"LOOK" FOR SALVATION

"Look to Me, and be saved, all you ends of the earth!
For I am God, and there is no other."
Isaiah 45:22 nkjv

From the Garden of Gethsemane where the bleeding pores of the Savior sweat pardons,
and from the cross of Calvary where the bleeding hands of Jesus drop mercy,
the cry comes, *"Look to Me, and be saved, all you ends of the earth!"*

But there comes a vile cry from our soul, "No, look to yourself! Look to yourself!"
Ah, as long as you look to yourself there is no hope for you.
It is not what you are, it is what God is—it is what Christ is—that saves you.

There are people who quite misunderstand the gospel.
They think that righteousness qualifies them to come to Christ,
whereas it is sin that is the only qualification.
A sense of sin is what you need.

Look! Do you see that man hanging on the cross?
Do you see his agonized head drooping meekly down upon his chest?
Do you see that blood trickling down his cheeks from the crown of thorns?
Do you see his hands pierced and rent, and his blessed feet supporting the weight of his body,
rent nearly in two with the cruel nails?
And after he dies, do you see the brutal Roman soldier piercing his side with a spear?

Remember, those hands were nailed for you;
those feet gushed blood for you;
that side was opened wide for you.

If you want to know how you can find mercy, there it is: "Look to Me, and be saved."
How simple is the way of salvation, and how instantaneous!
The moment a sinner believes and trusts in his crucified God for pardon he receives salvation.

Take this for a New Year's text, you who love the Lord, and you who are looking for the first time.
In all your troubles look to God and be saved.
In all your trials and afflictions this year, look to Christ and find deliverance.
In all your agony, in all your repentance for your guilt, look to Christ and find pardon.

Now believe on him;
now cast your guilty soul upon his righteousness;
now plunge your dark soul into the bath of his blood;
now put your naked soul at the door of the wardrobe of his righteousness;
now seat your famished soul at the feast of plenty.
Now "look!"

From sermon no. 60, *Sovereignty and Salvation*

SAVING FAITH

By faith in his name.
ACTS 3:16

True faith, the faith that saves, concerns itself wholly with the glorious person
    and the gracious work of him whom God raised from the dead.
Within the compass of Bethlehem, Gethsemane, Gabbatha,[1] Calvary—
    yes, and there at the right hand of the Father—lies the sphere of the sinner's faith.

Faith is where Jesus is,
and she asks no wider range.

Unbelief is always questioning.
    She is so dissatisfied with the simple gospel of Jesus Christ
        that she demands another savior, or no savior, or fifty saviors.
She does not know what she wants.

Unbelief has a very attentive ear to every new notion.
    When this man over here has a novel doctrine and someone over there has another fresh idea,
        unbelief goes helter-skelter—this way and that!
She hears voices crying, "Lo here, and lo there!" and like a silly bird she is lured and snared.

Faith has a different mind, and she takes her stand where Christ is.
She says, "If salvation is anywhere, it is here; it is in him."

She bows before Jesus at Bethlehem and sees hope in his incarnation.
She travels the fields of Judea with him and sees hope in the holy, tenderhearted Lover of souls.
She sees him in Gethsemane covered with the bloody sweat and begins to see her pardon there.
She sees him at Gabbatha and reads hope in the crimson lines engraved on his body by the scourge.
She sees him die on the tree, and she says, "My life is here. If I am saved I must be saved here."
She sees Jesus in the tomb, and as she watches him rise, she sees hope and immortality in him.
She looks up yonder to the throne of the Most High and she sees Jesus interceding for transgressors.

Faith's resolve is to look only to Jesus—her God—for he alone is everything to her.

We are saved when we come to that point.
When Jesus is all our salvation and all our desire, the work of grace has begun in our hearts.

Child of God, Jesus is your Boaz,
and you have come to the right decision
when you are determined to glean in no other field!

You will find satisfaction when you drink water only from his fountain,
and when you eat only of the food at his bountiful table.[2]

[1]The Aramaic name for the paved court where Jesus stood in judgment before the Roman procurator
    Pontius Pilate
[2]From sermon no. 1898, *Mouth and Heart*

CHRIST'S MARVELOUS GIVING

Who gave himself for us.
Titus 2:14

Long ago, before God created man, he foresaw that he would sin,
  but in order to save him he had to find a substitute to bear the penalty of his sin.
In that solemn council chamber when it was deliberated who should be the substitute,
  Christ came forward and offered himself; and in that day he "gave himself for us."

Years later, when the fullness of time had come, a baby was found in a Bethlehem manger.
The One who had given himself as a substitute had come down to earth to be a man.

Follow him for thirty years as he toils amidst the drudgery of a carpenter's shop.
What is he doing? The law needed to be fulfilled and he "gave himself for us" in fulfilling the law.

But now the time comes when the law demands that the penalty be paid.

Do you see him going to meet Judas in the garden with confident but solemn step?
Do you see him bound and taken before Caiaphas, Pilate, and Herod—mocked, insulted, and flogged?
Why does he so passively bear all those insults and indignities? Because he "gave himself for us."

Do you see him being led, a willing captive, up to the hill of Calvary?

Alas! They throw him on the ground!
They drive the accursed iron through his hands and feet!
They hoist him into the air, and there he hangs a naked spectacle of scorn and shame!

Why would the Lord of glory, who made all worlds, be bleeding and dying there?
Why would his lifeless body be buried in the tomb of Joseph of Arimethea?
It was because he "gave himself for us."

What else remains?

He lives again, for on the third day he came out of the tomb.
Yes, he has gone up on high where he is still giving himself for us, for he pleads the sinner's cause.

Now we also expect to go to the realms of the blessed, and what is to be our heaven?
Why, our heaven will be Christ himself, for he "gave himself for us."

> *Oh, he is all that we want; all that we wish for!*
> *We cannot desire anything greater or better than to be with Jesus;*
> *to look into the gleaming of his loving eyes;*
> *to feel him press us to his heart and hear him say that he loved us*
> *even before he laid the foundation of the world.*

From sermon no. 3513, *Christ's Marvelous Giving*

"IN THIS IS LOVE"

*In this is love, not that we have loved God but that he loved us
and sent his Son to be the propitiation for our sins.*
1 John 4:10

Oh, the love of God for us! He "sent his Son."
  He sent his Son to rebels who would not receive him, would not hear him;
    but they spat on him, scourged him, stripped him, slew him!
Yes, God knew how his Son would be treated and yet he sent him.

What must it have cost Jehovah to send his only beloved Son to this earth to die?
Christ is the Father's self; in essence, they are one; there is but one God.
Christ's death was in fact God in human form, suffering for human sin.

God "sent his Son to be the propitiation"—
  that is, to be not only a reconciler, but the reconciliation.

People have questioned God's requirement for a sacrifice before there could be reconciliation,
  as if that were wrong on the part of the Judge of all.
Yes, God required a sacrifice, for he is just and holy; but God found it himself.

Jehovah found the ransom that he demanded.

*It was himself—his own Son—one with himself,
who became the propitiation and the reconciliation.*

It was not that God the Father was unkind and could not be placated unless he smote his Son,
  but that God the Father was so kind that he could not be unjust;
    so supremely loving that he must devise a way by which we could be justly saved.
An unjust salvation would have been none at all.

*"In this is love," that God would send his Son to dwell with sinners,
aye, and to come into contact with their sins,
and thus to take the sword—not only by its hilt, but by its blade—
and plunge it into his own heart and die because of it.*

*O guilty one, even the harps of angels
cannot rise to a higher measure than these glad tidings:*

*The God whom you offended, does not want you to die.
Because he loves you, he opens up a road of reconciliation
through the body of his own dear Son!*

From sermon no. 1707, *Herein Is Love*

PEACE AND GOODWILL

"Glory to God in the highest,
And on earth peace, goodwill toward men!"
LUKE 2:14 NKJV

When the angels sang this song, they sang what they had never sung before.

"Glory to God in the highest" was an old, old song;
    the angels had sung that even before the creation of the world.
But now they sang as it were a new song before the throne of God,
    for they added this stanza: *"On earth peace."*

There had been no peace on earth since the fall of Adam.

But now, when the newborn King made his appearance,
    the swaddling cloth that wrapped him became the white flag of peace.
The manger was the place where the treaty was signed,
    ending the war between man's conscience and God.

It was then—on that day—that the trumpet blew:
    "Sheathe the sword, O man; sheathe the sword, O conscience,
        for God is now at peace with man, and man at peace with God."
Yes, the gospel of God brings peace to the human heart.

And oh, what peace it is!

This sacred peace between the pardoned soul and God the pardoner;
this marvelous at-one-ment between the sinner and his Judge—
this was what the angels sang when they said, "On earth peace."

And then the angels wisely ended their song with a third note: "Goodwill toward men."
    Oh, there can be no greater proof of kindness between the Creator and his subjects
        than when the Creator gives his one and only Son to die for them!
Though the first note is God-like, and the second note is peaceful, this third note melts our hearts.

Now, you who doubt the Master's love, hear the angels' song.

Let your doubts die away in that sweet music,
and let your soul be buried in a shroud of harmony.

God has "goodwill toward men," for he is willing to pardon;
he passes by iniquity, transgression, and sin.

From sermon no. 168, *The First Christmas Carol*

CHRIST'S MEASURELESS LOVE

The love of Christ that surpasses knowledge.
EPHESIANS 3:19

The love of Christ in its sweetness, its fullness, and its faithfulness surpasses all human comprehension.

What language can describe his matchless, his unparalleled love for the children of men?
It is so vast and boundless that, like a swallow skimming the water but not diving to its depths,
words only touch the surface while love beyond measure lies beneath.
A poet has expressed it well: "O love, thou fathomless abyss!"

Before we can have any idea of the love of Jesus,
we must understand his previous glory in the height of its majesty.
And we must also understand his incarnation in all the depths of its shame.

But who can tell us the majesty of Christ?

When he was enthroned in the highest heavens he was very God of very God.
"All things were made through him" (John 1:3).
"He is before all things, and in him all things hold together" (Colossians 1:17).

The praises of cherubim and seraphim perpetually surrounded him.
The full chorus of the hallelujahs of the universe unceasingly flowed to the foot of his throne.
He reigned supreme above all his creatures, "God over all, blessed forever" (Romans 9:5).

Who can tell his height of glory then?
Who can tell how low he descended?

To be a man was something, but to be a Man of Sorrows was far more.
To suffer and bleed and die was much for the Son of God,
but to suffer such unparalleled agony, to endure a death of shame and desertion by his Father—
this is a depth of condescending love that even the most inspired mind utterly fails to comprehend![1]

Would you know how much the Lord loves you?
Would you measure his love?

Go measure heaven with a span;
go weigh the mountains in the scales;
go take the oceans' water and tell each drop;
go count the sand upon the sea's wide shore.

When you have accomplished this,
you will be able to tell how much he loves you![2]

---

[1] *Morning and Evening*, March 28 (M)
[2] Source Unknown

A COLD NIGHT IN GETHSEMANE

Now the servants and officers had made a charcoal fire, because it was cold,
and they were standing and warming themselves.
JOHN 18:18

We note from this incident that it was a cold night in which our Redeemer agonized in Gethsemane.

It was a cold night and yet he sweat—
    not the sweat of a man earning the staff of life, but the sweat of One who was earning life itself:
        "His sweat became like great drops of blood falling down to the ground" Luke 22:44).
It was not the heat outside, but the heat within his soul that distilled those sacred drops.

The throbs of his heart were so mighty; his life-floods rushed with such force
    that the veins, like overfilled rivers, burst their banks
and covered his blessed body with crimson drops!

This great conflict in Gethsemane did not arise through our dear Master's fear of death,
    nor through his fear of the pain and all the shame and disgrace he was about to endure.
This agony was part of the great burden already resting on him as his people's substitute.
    It was this that pressed his spirit down even to the dust of death.

Our Savior bore the full weight of our sin on the cross,
but the Passion began in Gethsemane.

Peter wrote that Jesus "bore our sins in his body on the tree" (1 Peter 2:24).
    This passage is not saying that Christ's substitutionary sufferings were limited to the tree,
        for the original might bear this rendering: "He bore our sins in his body up to the tree."
He came up to the tree bearing that awful load, and still continued to bear it on the tree.

Peter also writes in the same verse, "By his wounds you have been healed."
Jesus bore some of those wounds when he was so cruelly scourged in Pilate's judgment hall.

Our precious Savior was bearing our sins all his life,
    but their terrible weight began to crush him with sevenfold force
when he came to the olive press on that cold and frosty night.

The entire mass, however, rested on him with infinite intensity when he was nailed to the cross.
This caused his agonizing cry, "My God, my God, why have you forsaken me?"

On those cold wintry nights when you are wrapping your garments about you,
remember Gethsemane and the lone Sufferer, who without any shelter,
entered into that awful anguish by which he won our souls from death.

From sermon no. 3181, *A Sermon for a Winter's Evening*, and sermon no. 3190, *Christ in Gethsemane*

THE GLORY OF HIS SACRIFICE

The light of the gospel of the glory of Christ.
2 CORINTHIANS 4:4

Christ's hand is seen in every letter of that wonderful epistle of divine love
   that is called the New Testament, or the New Covenant.
He, himself, is glad tidings to us in every point, and the gospel is from him in every sense.

*Remember, that is not the gospel
that does not relate to Jesus.*

*If there is no blood-mark on it
the roll of tidings may be rejected as a forgery.*

The glory of Christ is best seen in his atoning sacrifice.
But you say, "That was his humiliation and his shame."

Yes, that is true; therefore, it is his glory.
Is Christ not, to every loving heart, the most glorious in his death on the cross?
What garment is more becoming to our Beloved than that robe dipped in his own blood?

*Oh, he is altogether lovely no matter how he is arrayed,
but when our believing hearts behold him
covered with the bloody sweat,
we gaze at him with adoring amazement and rapturous love!*

His flowing crimson adorns him with a robe far more glorious than the imperial purple.
We fall at his feet with sevenfold reverence when we behold the marks of his Passion.

Here lies the heart of the gospel: Jesus Christ suffered in our place.
"He himself bore our sins in his body on the tree" (1 Peter 2:24).

The glory of his cross is the gospel to us,
   for on his cross he bore the whole weight of divine justice in our place.
The iron rod of Jehovah, that would have broken us in pieces, fell on him.

*The glory of Christ's sacrificial death
by which he blotted out our sin and magnified the law —
this is the gospel of our salvation.*

If you dream of preaching the gospel without exalting Christ in it,
   you will give the people husks instead of true bread.
The true gospel is the gospel of the glory of Christ.

From sermon no. 2077, *The Gospel of the Glory of Christ*

SLAYING THE SACRIFICE

"Then he shall kill the bull before the Lord."
Leviticus 1:5

The slaying of the offering was absolutely essential.
The Israelite brought an unblemished bull, but that fact did not make it an atonement for sin.
It must die, and its blood must be sprinkled on the altar in order for it to be an acceptable oblation.

Even so, Jesus must die.
   His perfect nature, his arduous labor, his blameless life, his perfect consecration
      could avail us nothing without the shedding of his blood.
His death is not just the conclusion of his life; it is the most important matter connected with him.

> *We justly value our Savior for his example and for his living intercession,*
> *but in the business of atonement it is absolutely essential*
> *that we always view him as the slain Lamb!*

We are clearly told, "Without the shedding of blood there is no forgiveness of sins" (Hebrews 9:22).
This truth is the subject of all true gospel preaching.
This is what we are called to preach—Christ as crucified; Christ as made a curse for us.

> *Take away the substitutionary death of our Lord*
> *and nothing remains for us but death.*
>
> *Forget the Crucified One,*
> *and you have forgotten the only name*
> *by which we can be saved.*

It is through the blood that the saints enter heaven.
They have "washed their robes and made them white in the blood of the Lamb" (Revelation 7:14).

> *The passport to glory is the precious blood of Jesus.*
> *Access to God is only through the blood of his dear Son.*

Occasionally we meet squeamish people who say, "I cannot bear the mention of the word *blood!*"
   Well, sin is such a horrible thing that God has appointed blood to wash it away
      so that we may have some idea of the terrible nature of sin as God judges it.
It is not without a dreadful blood-shedding that your dreadful guilt could ever be cleansed.

Sin-bearing and suffering for sin can never be pleasant things,
   and neither should the type that portrays it be pleasing to the observer.
On great days of sacrifice the courts of the tabernacle must have been swimming in blood,
   and rightly so, that all might be struck with the deadly nature of sin.

From sermon no. 1772, *Slaying the Sacrifice*

STRICKEN WITH THE SWORD

"Awake, O sword, against my shepherd, against the man who stands next to me,"
declares the Lord of hosts. "Strike the shepherd, and the sheep will be scattered."
ZECHARIAH 13:7

According to the text, the sword was to awake against one who is called by God, "My shepherd,"
giving us to understand that Jesus holds the office of a shepherd.
He is a shepherd appointed by God and sent by him to take care of the sheep.

The text is also clear in the description of Christ's godhead.
The Lord of Hosts says that Jesus is the man who stands next to him; he is God's associate.

Oh, it is a delight to think that he,
who stood in our place and suffered in our stead,
though man, was not merely man!

It was the Infinite who became an infant;
it was the God who became a man
so that he might stand in the sinner's place.

It was God who "bore our sins in his body on the tree" (1 Peter 2:24).
It was God who bled for us on Calvary so that we might live with him forever.

Now think of *the sufferings that our God endured.*
Concerning them, the text says, "Awake, O sword, … strike the shepherd."
The most fatal weapon was used on the perfect Son of Man, the glorious Son of God.
The sword of divine vengeance against sin was plucked out of its scabbard to be used *on him!*

O darling of Jehovah, must you actually bleed?
You who are the fairest among ten thousand, the altogether lovely,
must you be dragged down to the dust of death?

O face, like the noonday sun,
must you be eclipsed in darkness?

O eyes, brighter than the evening star,
must you be sealed in the midnight of death,
after having already been quenched in floods of tears?

It must be so!

The sword that is for criminals;
the sword that is to avenge high treason;
the sword that cannot be quiet as long as there is sin before the throne of God—
that sword must leap out of its scabbard and sheathe itself in the heart of Christ!

From sermon no. 3088, *The Storm and the Shower*

UNPARALLELED SORROW

Is it nothing to you, all you who pass by?
Behold and see if there is any sorrow like my sorrow, which has been brought on me,
which the Lord has inflicted in the day of His fierce anger.
LAMENTATIONS 1:12 NKJV

When we think of Calvary and of our wounded, bleeding Lord,
   we cannot help but think of Jeremiah's words, and we can hear our Lord crying from the cross,
"Is it nothing to you, all you who pass by? Behold and see if there is any sorrow like my sorrow!"

He who bled on Calvary was the Son of the Highest, but he flung aside his divine array
   and he became a man among men, and for men, only to be despised by men!

Instead of receiving him they dragged him to the judgment hall!
They scourged him, spit in his face, blindfolded him, and buffeted him!
They nailed him to the cross and then stood there, mocking and scorning him!

They spared him nothing that shame could invent;
and all this was poured on One
whose feet honored the ground they walked on.

Oh, behold and see if there is any sorrow like his sorrow!

Our Redeemer had no sin, and yet all the sins of humanity were laid on him.

Yes, bring them here—the sins of all ages!
Heap them on his back!

How dreadful is the total sum!
"The Lord has laid on him the iniquity of us all" (Isaiah 53:6)!

Has there ever been dignity that suffered such indignity;
such innocence that has come into contact with such a mass of sin
and suffered for it all?

Oh, behold and see if there is any sorrow like his sorrow!

It seems as if every form of grief was let loose against our Savior;
   from the thorn-crowned head to the bleeding feet, all was wounds and bruises for our sake.
There was also an agony of heart, mind, and soul when God hid his face from him,
   and he was forced to cry, "My God, my God, why have you forsaken me?" (Matthew 27:46).

All the legions from beneath aimed their arrows at his heart;
both heaven and earth stood arrayed against him.

Well does he cry, "Behold and see if there is any sorrow like my sorrow!"

From sermon no. 1620, *Is It Nothing to You?*

LEANING ON OUR BELOVED

Who is that coming up from the wilderness,
leaning on her beloved?
Song of Solomon 8:5

Every soul that journeys towards heaven has Christ's companionship.
No pilgrim is allowed to travel to the New Jerusalem unattended.

Courage, then, ye travelers who traverse the valley of tears!
You come up from the wilderness in dear company,
for one like the Son of God is at your side.

Note the title that is given to the companion of the bride: "Her beloved."
Indeed, he of whom the song speaks is beloved above all others!

He was the beloved of his Father before the earth was created.
He is the beloved of every angel and of all the bright seraphic spirits crowding around his throne.
He is the beloved of every being of pure heart and holy mind.

You are reminded, O pilgrim to the skies,
that you have beside you a companion
whose name is "my beloved."

Rejoice that you are found in such company,
and enjoy the honors and privileges his society gives you.

"Who is that coming up from the wilderness, leaning on her beloved?"
    The bride's posture is that of "leaning"; the beloved's role is that of a divine supporter.
Leaning suggests nearness, and we cannot lean on that which is far away and unapproachable.
    Christ is not only with us, but to an intense degree near us.

Leaning implies the throwing of one's weight on to another,
    and the first act that makes us Christians is when we lay the whole weight of our sins on Christ.
We lay the burden of our sins on our Substitute's shoulder.

We must never try to stand alone by our own strength,
    but make our beloved Lord Jesus, in his manhood and in his godhead,
the leaning place of our whole soul, casting every burden on him.

Even the furnace itself, is as cool and comfortable
as a royal chamber prepared for banqueting with the King
when the soul reclines on the bosom of divine love.

From sermon no. 877, *Leaning On Our Beloved*

MOCKING THE KING

They stripped him and put a scarlet robe on him, and twisting together a crown of thorns,
they put it on his head and put a reed in his right hand.
And kneeling before him, they mocked him, saying, "Hail, King of the Jews!"
And they spit on him and took the reed and struck him on the head.
Matthew 27:28–30

We have before us a king, and such a king as had never been known before!
He is "the Son of the Most High" (Luke 1:32), and yet he became the Son of Man for our sakes.
This is the King who is now before us.

But what an enthronement was accorded to him!

See that scarlet robe; it is a contemptuous imitation of the imperial purple that kings wear.
See that old chair into which the soldiers thrust him so that he might be seated on a mock throne.
See above all that crown on his head. It has rubies in it, but the rubies are composed of his own
    blood, forced from his temples by the cruel thorns.
See, they pay him homage; but the homage is their own filthy spittle that runs down his cheeks.

> *Oh, how could such superlative goodness*
> *be treated with such fiendish malice?*
>
> *How could such grace and majesty*
> *be reduced to such despising?*

We see in our Savior thus mocked and put to shame, the full result of sin epitomized.
   "You will be like God" (Genesis 3:5), said the serpent to Eve in the Garden of Eden;
      and thus tempted, man put out his hand and partook of the forbidden fruit.
He hoped to become like the King of the universe.

> *Ah, foolish man, see what kind of royalty sin brings you!*
> *See how it crowns him with mock dignity and honor;*
> *it makes him look like a king, but it is only a tinsel splendor.*
> *There is a crown on man's head, but it is a crown of thorns!*

This is how sin crowns us, so this is how our Savior was crowned when he stood in our place.
He was mocked, rejected, and crowned with thorns, because this is what we become through sin.
Christ on the cross is a yet fuller type of what man would have become had sin been left alone.

> *"Sin when it is fully grown brings forth death" (James 1:15).*

Sin's only throne is a mock one.
Its only crown is a painful one.
Its only reward is sorrow, shame, and death.

From sermon no. 3138, *Mocking the King*

AN UNBELIEVABLE DECLARATION

The high priest asked him, "Are you the Christ, the Son of the Blessed?"
And Jesus said, "I am, and you will see the Son of Man
seated at the right hand of Power, and coming with the clouds of heaven."
MARK 14:61–62

What do people do with this incident when they deny the deity of Christ?

Christ was put to death on a charge of blasphemy, for claiming to be the Son of God.
Would he not have confessed now if he had not been the Son of God?
Would he have sealed this declaration with his blood?

There is no false religion that would have dared to make such a statement as this man did!

What! That man who speaks not a word;
   that man who is mocked, despised, rejected, made nothing of—
What! *He* is "very God of very God"?

You would never find a false prophet asking anyone to believe such an extraordinary doctrine.
He would never have taught a truth so humbling to himself.
Besides, it is not in the power of any man-made religion to have conceived such an idea.

See deity willingly submitting itself to be spit on
   in order to redeem the ones who are venting the spittle.
Who has ever heard of such a wonder as this?

"The Word became flesh and dwelt among us" (John 1:14).
   He was despised, scourged, mocked, treated as though he were the foulest of all things—
      and all out of pure love for his enemies.
Where have you ever read such a thing as this?

The thought is so great, so God-like; the compassion is so divine, that it *must* be true!
None but God would have stooped from the highest throne of glory to the cross of deepest shame.

Ah! Christ is indeed God!
His declaration is not false.

Who can doubt that he is Messiah?
If God were to send a prophet, would you desire a better one?
Who else could exhibit so completely the human and the divine?
Who could commend himself more fully to the affections of the heart?

He must be the One and Only, with no competitor!
He must be the Messiah of God!

From sermon no. 495, *The Greatest Trial on Record*

THE GREAT ATTRACTION

"And I, when I am lifted up from the earth,
will draw all people to myself."
JOHN 12:32

The cross of Christ, with all its ignominy and shame, is no hindrance to the gospel.
  Indeed, Christ dying for sinners is the great attraction of Christianity!
Thousands upon thousands have been effectually drawn to him
  by seeing how graciously, how readily, how abundantly he pardons as he hangs on the tree.

We expect to receive pardon from that gracious bleeding hand.
We are bold in looking for great pardon from a great Savior suffering so greatly.
We have reason to believe when we hear him saying to the dying thief, "Truly, I say to you,
  today you will be with me in Paradise" (Luke 23:43).

Yes, it is very easy to understand how sin can be forgiven
when we see how it has been avenged in Jesus!

Have not many been wonderfully drawn to the gospel by the intense agonies of Jesus?

Can you see him wrestling in prayer in Gethsemane,
  and view the bloody sweat drops as they fall on the frozen ground,
and not feel invisible, irresistible cords drawing you to him?

Can you see him being flogged in Pilate's hall—
  every thong of the scourge tearing the flesh from his shoulders—
and not feel a desire to fall down and kiss his feet and become his servant forever?

Can you behold him hanging on his cross at Golgotha,
  with his soul overwhelmed with the wrath of God and the bitterness of sin,
and not feel an intense desire to personally see and know this Savior?

You may not feel like kissing the King on his throne,
but what about the King on his cross?

You may revolt from him when he wields a rod of iron,
but what about touching the silver scepter
held in the bloodstained hand that bled for his enemies?

The attractive power in our crucified Lord does not lie in the eloquence of preaching.
  There is power in the cross itself.
The Holy Spirit rests like a dove on that bloodstained tree,
  and through him, constraining grace comes streaming down to human hearts.

From sermon no. 775, *The Great Attraction*

A BLOODSTAINED WAY

"No one comes to the Father except through me."
JOHN 14:6

When we come to God, we must bring only one thing with us, and that is the blood of Christ.
Guilty sinners and saints—both must approach God's throne, pleading Christ's blood and righteousness.

Jesus, Jesus, Jesus—
this is the path for the sinner and the way for the saint.

There is no road to God—even for the holiest person—
no road to God's acceptance, but through Jesus only.

If only we could learn this truth and never forget it:
Our acceptance with God depends on nothing that we can do, or think, or feel, or be.
It depends wholly on what Jesus is, and what he has done, and what he has suffered for us.

You do need a mediator in coming to God, but you do not need one in coming to Christ,
    so go to him just as you are without trying to make yourself better.
Go straight to him with your rags, and sin, and leprosy, and blotches, and sores, and all.
    Do not be afraid that the Father will reject you if you come to him through Christ.

Do you see yonder cross, and that man dying on it in inexpressible agonies?
Do you not think his sufferings are enough to expiate the wrath of God?

Then come boldly to Jesus for he smiles on you. No one has ever been turned away.

Those arms, nailed to the cross, are wide open as if to show you that they are receiving big sinners.
Those feet are fastened to the cross as if they intend to wait there and be gracious to you.
His pierced side seems to say, "My heart is not hard to reach. See, there is a straight road to it, opened
    by the Roman spear. Come, breathe your sighs into my heart and I will hear and answer you."

Come, soul! Come to *this way!*
It is a safe way, for over it hangs the banner of Jehovah's love.
And on the ground is the blood-mark of the Savior's footsteps.

Oh, enter this crimson pathway to the throne of God!
Jesus made it.
Jesus smoothed it.
Jesus dyed it with his blood.

Come, poor soul! Come and put your trust in Jesus alone.
You need not come to the Father with trembling and dismay.

From sermon no. 245, *The Way to God*

A CRY FROM THE CROSS

And about the ninth hour Jesus cried out with a loud voice, saying,
"Eli, Eli, lema sabachthani?" that is, "My God, my God, why have you forsaken me?"
MATTHEW 27:46

Our Lord had trodden the winepress for hours and the work was almost finished.
He had now reached the culminating point of his anguish.
This is his lament from the lowest pit of misery: "My God, my God, why have you forsaken me?"

The records of all time
could not contain a sentence more full of anguish.

Here the wormwood and the gall,
and every other bitterness are outdone.

Here you may look as into a vast abyss
and gaze until sight fails you,
yet you will perceive no bottom.

It is measureless, unfathomable, inconceivable!

This anguish of the Savior on our behalf
is no more to be measured and weighed
than the sin that required it
or the love that endured it.

Our Lord had tolerated pain, loss of blood, scorn, thirst, and desolation,
not complaining about the cross, the nails, and the scoffing.
We do not read of anything more than the natural cry of weakness: "I thirst" (John 19:28).

All the tortures of his body he endured in silence, but when it came to being forsaken by God,
then his great heart burst out, "My God, my God, why have you forsaken me?"
The Father's love was everything to him, and when that was gone, all was gone.

At that moment, the one Mediator between God and man—the man Christ Jesus—
beheld the holiness of God in arms against the sin of man, whose nature he had espoused.
God was with him in a certain sense, but as far as his feelings went, God was against him.
Our Savior had to feel forsaken by God because this is the necessary consequence of sin.

Let us come boldly to the Lord Jesus
and rest in him alone for salvation.

God will never forsake us,
for he has forsaken his Son on our behalf.

From sermon no. 2133, *"Lama Sabachthani?"*

ALL SACRIFICES FULFILLED IN HIM

When Jesus had received the sour wine, he said, "It is finished,"
and he bowed his head and gave up his spirit.
JOHN 19:30

"It is finished." Not only were all types and prophecies and promises now finished in Christ,
   all the typical sacrifices of the old Jewish law were also abolished as well as explained.
They were all finished in him.

Every morning and evening a lamb had been offered.
Great sacrifices were offered on special occasions.

Bullocks groaned.
Lambs bled.
The necks of doves were wrung.

Year after year, the high priest went behind the curtain and sprinkled the mercy seat with blood.

Throughout many years these questions had been asked:
"O Lord, how long?" "Will the bloody sacrifices for sin never be finished?"
"Must there always be a remembrance of sin?" "Will the last High Priest never come?"

But lo, he now comes! He comes who is to close the line of priests.
   There he stands, not clothed now with linen ephod,
      nor with ringing bells, nor with sparkling jewels on his breastplate.
He stands there arrayed in human flesh.

His cross is his altar.
His body and his soul is the victim.
He himself is the priest.

And lo! Before his God
   he offers up his own soul within the curtain of thick darkness—
that darkness that has covered him from the sight of men.

> *Presenting his own blood,*
> *he enters behind the curtain,*
> *sprinkles it there,*
> *and coming forth from the midst of the darkness,*
> *he looks down on the astonished earth*
> *and upward to expectant heaven*
> *and cries, "It is finished! It is finished!*
> *That which you looked for so long*
> *is fully achieved and perfected forever."*

From sermon no. 421, *"It Is Finished!"*

BROUGHT TO THE SHEARERS

Like a sheep that before its shearers is silent, so he opened not his mouth.
Isaiah 53:7

Consider our Savior's patience under the figure of a sheep before its shearers.

Our Lord was brought to the slaughter,
  and brought in another sense by another figure—to the shearers.
He was brought to the shearers so that he might be shorn of his comfort and of his honors,
  shorn even of his good name, and shorn at last of life itself.

> *While he was brought before the **slaughterers**,*
> *he was as quiet as a lamb that is led.*

> *While he was under the hands of the **shearers**,*
> *he was as silent as a sheep that lies down to be shorn.*

You know the story of how patient he was before Pilate, Herod, and Caiaphas, and on the cross.
There is no record of impatience at the pain and shame he endured at the hands of wicked men.

Our Lord "opened not his mouth" against his adversaries,
  and he did not accuse even one of them of cruelty or injustice.
They slandered him but he did not reply; false witnesses arose but he did not answer them.

> *He is silent before the shearers*
> *as they shear away everything from him—*
> *even stripping him of his last rag—and yet he murmured not.*

> *For the joy that was set before him,*
> *he endured the cross, despising the shame,*
> *and not a syllable is uttered that sounds like murmuring or regret.*

In our Savior, there is complete submission.
The sacrifice did not need to be bound with cords to the horns of the altar.
He stands there, willing to suffer, willing to be spit on, to be shamefully abused, and to die.

> *See Jesus like the lamb,*
> *not struggling when the knife is at his throat,*
> *laying down his life willingly for our sakes.*

> *See him lying down,*
> *stretched out in passive resignation beneath the shearers,*
> *as they take away everything that is dear to him,*
> *opening not his mouth.*

From sermon no. 1543, *The Sheep Before the Shearers*

THE SHAME AND SPITTING

I gave My back to those who struck Me,
and My cheeks to those who plucked out the beard;
I did not hide My face from shame and spitting.
ISAIAH 50:6 NKJV

Because our Lord Jesus took our sin, he had to be treated as sin should be treated.

Now of all things that ever existed, sin is the most shameful—
   sin deserves to be *scourged;*
   sin deserves to be *spit on;*
   sin deserves to be *crucified.*
And because our Lord took upon himself our sin, he must be put to shame and scourging.

If you want to see what God thinks of sin,
   see his only Son spit on by the soldiers when he was made sin for us.
In God's sight, sin is a shameful, horrible, loathsome, abominable thing,
   and when Jesus takes it upon himself, he must be forsaken and given up to scorn.

Notice that he willingly submitted to the suffering and the abuse.

He *gave* his back to those who struck him.
He *gave* his cheeks to those who plucked out the beard.
He *did not hide* his face from shame and spitting.

That Christ would stand there, willingly subjecting himself to derision—this is grace indeed!
Surely we will need faith in heaven to believe this fact.

When all heaven lies prostrate at his feet, will it seem possible that he was once mocked?
When angels and principalities and powers are all roused to rapturous music in his praise,
   will it seem possible that once the lowest of men pulled out his beard?
Will it not appear incredible that those sacred hands were once nailed to a gibbet?

We will never cease to wonder that his side was gashed and that his face was spit on.
The sin of humanity, in this instance, will always amaze us!

   As we behold our glorious Redeemer, our hearts will surely exclaim,
   "O ye sons of men, how could you treat such a One with cruel scorn?
   Why didn't you spit on earthly splendors?
   Was there no place for your spittle but his face? His face!
   Woe is me! Woe is me! His face!"

Yet, here is a matter for our faith to rest on.
Our shame and punishment is removed because Jesus has borne it all.
Our dear Redeemer has paid double for all our sins.

From sermon no. 1486, *The Shame and Spitting*

A NIGHT TO BE REMEMBERED

This same night is a night of watching kept to the LORD.
EXODUS 12:42

Of course, this text relates to the Passover.
    The Israelites were directed to never forget that they were once slaves in Egypt,
        and that God had delivered them with a mighty hand.
To assist their memories the ordinance of the Passover was instituted.

The Passover, however, was a type of our Lord's Passion.
He is the true Lamb of God's Passover.

It is by his blood that we are preserved.
It is by virtue of his sacrifice that God passes over us who have received the sprinkling of that blood.

Let us never forget that night that we are urged to remember,
    that dark night when our Lord rose from the table where he had eaten with his disciples,
and went to Gethsemane to begin his sufferings; to be "very sorrowful, even to death" (Matthew 26:38).

Let us remember how he was taken to Pilate, and to Herod, and to Caiaphas …
    to be condemned to death;
    to be lifted high upon the cross;
    to bleed, to suffer physical pain, mental anguish, and spiritual grief.

Oh, it is a night to be remembered in all our generations!
Oh, let it never be forgotten!

We ought to be familiar with every little incident of our Savior's death.
There is teaching in every nail.
There is meaning in the sponge, the vinegar, and the hyssop.
There is instruction in the spear that pierced his side.

If there is any hope for sinners;
if there is consolation for sufferers;
if there is cleansing for the guilty;
if there is any life for the dead,
it is here at the cross.

O believer, dwell at the cross!

Though your mind may forget to consider many things,
let it never leave the meditation of Christ crucified.

From sermon no. 1092, *A Holy Celebration*

WELCOMING OUR BELOVED

I slept, but my heart was awake. A sound! My beloved is knocking.
"Open to me, my sister, my love, my dove, my perfect one,
for my head is wet with dew, my locks with the drops of the night."
Song of Solomon 5:2

Observe the appeals of the Beloved.
He says, "Open to me, my sister, my love, my dove, my perfect one."

O believer, if Christ stoops to enter into such a poor, miserable cottage as our nature is,
    should we not entertain the King with the best that we have?
When he knocks and speaks and pleads with every sweet and endearing title,
    will we refuse to arise and give him the fellowship that he craves?

Did you notice that powerful argument with which the heavenly Lover closed his cry?
He said, "My head is wet with dew, my locks with the drops of the night."

Ah, sorrowful remembrance!

Those drops were not the ordinary dew that falls on the homeless traveler's head.
    His head was wet with scarlet dew.
His locks were wet with the crimson drops of a tenfold night of God's desertion
    when "his sweat became like great drops of blood falling down to the ground" (Luke 22:44).

My heart, how vile you are,
for you are shutting out the Crucified!

Behold the Man, thorn-crowned and scourged, with traces of spittle from unholy mouths!

Can you close the door on him?
Can you grieve the Man of Sorrows?
Can you forget that he suffered all this for you when you deserve nothing at his hands?
After all this, will you give him no recompense, not even admission into your poor heart?

Doors of the heart fly open!

Though rusted upon your hinges,
open ye at the coming of the sorrowful Lover
who was "smitten by God, and afflicted" (Isaiah 53:4).

He whose head is wet with dew, his locks with the drops of the night,
    must not be kept standing in the street.
It behooves us to house him in our hearts and to entertain him with our warmest love.

From sermon no. 793, *Nearer and Dearer*

REASONS FOR LOVING

We love because he first loved us.
1 JOHN 4:19

The logical reason why we love Jesus lies in himself: "We love because he first loved us."

At first we kicked against him and despised him.
   Our language naturally was, "We do not want this man to reign over us" (Luke 19:14),
      and when we heard of him loving us we sneered at him.
He was despised and rejected by men, and we hid, as it were, our faces from him (Isaiah 53:3).

No, we were his enemies! We slew him!

We confess with sorrow that we were the murderers of the Prince of Life and Glory.
   Our hands and our garments were stained with his blood;
      yet, he saw all this through the glass of his foreknowledge and still loved us.
Indeed, our hearts must be harder than stone if they do not respond to such love!

Our Savior so loved us that he stripped himself of his robes of radiance.
He laid aside his scepter and his crown and became an infant in Bethlehem's manger.
The King of heaven spent thirty years in poverty and shame among the sons of men.

> *Jesus, the heavenly Lover, panting to redeem his people,*
> *was content to abide here with no place to rest his head.*

See him yonder in the garden in his agony; his soul very sorrowful, even to death; his forehead—
   no, his head, his hair, his garments—red with the bloody sweat.
See him giving his back to the floggers and his cheeks to those who pull out the beard.
See him as he does not hide his face from shame and spitting, silent like a sheep before its shearers.
See him with the cross on his mangled shoulders, staggering through Jerusalem's streets, unwept,
   unpitied, except by some poor feeble women.
See him, ye who love him, and love him more, as he stretches out his hands and feet to the nails.
See him as he who has power to deliver himself is made a captive.
Behold him as they lift up his cross and dash it down into its place, dislocating all his bones.

Stand if you can, and view that face so full of pain and sorrow.
Look until a sword goes through your heart, even as it went through his virgin mother's very soul.
There are a thousand crimson cords to tie us to the Savior, and hopefully we feel their constraining
   power.

It is his vast love—
   the love that redeemed us;
   the love that suffered in our place;
   the love that pleads our cause before the eternal throne—
it is this love that we give as our reason for loving the Savior, if necessary, even to death!

From sermon no. 636, *The Church's Love to Her Loving Lord*

OUR SYMPATHIZING SAVIOR

He fell on his face and prayed, saying,
"My Father, if it be possible, let this cup pass from me."
MATTHEW 26:39

When you, in your heaviness, shut the door of your room and kneel in prayer;
when that prayer gathers strength and you fall flat on your face in agony;
when you weep and cry before the Most High under a sinking sense of need,
it is hard for you to believe that Jesus ever did the same, but he did.

He asked as really as you ask.
He implored and sought, entreated and wrestled, even as you must do.
He knows the solitary place on Carmel, where Elijah bowed his head and cried out to the Lord.
He knows the weeping and the turning of the face to the wall, even as Hezekiah knew them.

> *Child of sorrow, Jesus can sympathize with you in your loneliness,*
> *in your apparent desertion, your sorrowfulness even to death.*

> *Look to him, then, in your night of weeping and be of good cheer.*

Notice that even as we pray with great intensity in our agonies, so did the Son of God.
   We are told that he expressed himself "with loud cries and tears" (Hebrews 5:7).
He pleaded with God until his pent-up grief demanded audible utterance,
   and he cried, "My Father, if it be possible, let this cup pass from me."

When a man who is as courageous and patient as Jesus is, takes to "loud cries and tears,"
   we may be sure that the sorrow of his heart has passed all bounds.
We know this was so by another sign, for his lifeblood forgot to course in its usual channels
   and it overflowed its banks in a sweat of blood.

This was prayer indeed: Body, soul, and spirit were upon the rack of anguish.
Jesus pleaded with God in a more piteous, painful, and terrible way than we have ever attained.

> *Behold, you are not alone!*
> *Jesus is passing through the deeps with you.*

> *See the bloodstained footprints of your Lord.*

O darkened heart, is there no light here for you?
O child of despair, can you not see in the marred face of your Lord a reason for trusting him?

Since from his lips you hear loud cries, and from his eyes you see showers of tears,
   you may know that his is a sympathetic spirit.
You may run to him in your hour of need, even as the chick seeks the wings of the hen.

From sermon no. 1927, *Our Sympathizing High Priest*

OUR LORD'S INTERCESSION

And Jesus said, "Father, forgive them, for they know not what they do."
LUKE 23:34

Have you noticed when it was that Jesus pleaded?
It was while his enemies were crucifying him.

They had just driven in the nails.
They had just lifted up the cross and dashed it down into its socket, dislocating all his bones.
It was then that this dear Son of God said, "Father, forgive them, for they know not what they do."

While their hands were still imbrued in his blood—
it was then, even then, that he prayed for them!

I also love the *indistinctness* of this prayer.
It is "Father, forgive *them*."

Jesus does not say, "Father, forgive the soldiers who have nailed me here."
He includes them.

Neither does he say, "Father, forgive the people who are beholding me."
He means them.

Neither does he say, "Father, forgive sinners in ages to come who will sin against me."
He means them.

Jesus does not mention them by any accusing names.
He does not say, "Father, forgive my enemies. Father, forgive my murderers."
No, there is no word of accusation upon those dear lips.

"Father, forgive them."
Now I feel that I can crawl into that pronoun *them*.

Oh, by a humble faith appropriate the cross of Christ by trusting in it,
    and get into that big little word *them*!
It seems like a chariot of mercy that has come down to earth, into which we may step,
    and it will bear us safely up to heaven.

Oh, blessed prayer!
The forgiveness of God is deep and broad!

When people forgive,
they leave the remembrance of the wrong behind;
but when God pardons,
he says, "I will remember their sin no more" (Jeremiah 31:34).

From sermon no. 2263, *Christ's Plea for Ignorant Sinners*

A GROSS INSINUATION

They say, "Look at him! … a friend of tax collectors and sinners!"
MATTHEW 11:19

I am going to deny the insinuation intended by the charge brought against our Lord.
Jesus is the friend of sinners, but he is not the friend of sin.

Jesus does forgive sin apart from any human merit,
   but he does not treat virtue and vice as if they were indifferent things.
He does not, in any way, discourage purity and righteousness.

No religion under heaven
is as strong in its denunciation of sin
as is the religion of Jesus Christ!

Some have complained that the gospel makes pardon look too easy.
They say this encourages the thought that sin is inconsequential.

Ah, when the Lord Jesus forgave me, he taught me—at the same time—to dread sin.
I have never had such a sense of the terrible evil of sin as at the very moment of my forgiveness.

Where do you think it was that I read my pardon?
I read it on the cross, written in crimson lines.

I understood that, even though the pardon was free to me,
   it cost my Savior many cries and groans before he could bring me near to God.
It cost his soul inexpressible anguish before even one poor sinner could be redeemed.

It is a gross injustice to say that, in the preaching of the gospel,
   sin is made to appear as only a trifle.
They who know nothing of the sufferings of Christ and of his atoning blood—
   these are the ones who can toy with sin.

The people who gaze on the wounds of Christ cannot help but tremble at sin.
When the substitutionary sacrifice is fully received by the soul, sin appears to be exceedingly sinful.

O sin, I have heard of you by the hearing of the ear,
but at the cross my eye sees you slaying the incarnate God!
Therefore, I turn away from you with abhorrence!

From sermon no. 1319, *The Sinner's Savior*

JESUS IS HEAVEN

Then I looked, and behold, a Lamb standing on Mount Zion.
REVELATION 14:1 NKJV

The apostle John had the privilege of looking inside the gates of heaven,
   and in describing what he saw, he begins by saying, "I looked, and behold, a Lamb!"
This verse tells us that the chief object of heaven is "the Lamb of God,
   who takes away the sin of the world"(John 1:29).

Nothing else attracted the apostle's attention like that Divine Being,
   who has loved us and redeemed us by washing us in his own blood.
He is the constant theme of the songs in heaven.

> *Christian, here is joy for you!*
> *You have looked and you have seen the Lamb!*
> *Through your tears, your sorrowing eyes*
> *have seen the Lamb of God taking away your sins.*

> *Rejoice then, for in a little while,*
> *when your eyes are wiped from tears (Revelation 21:4),*
> *you will see the same Lamb exalted on his throne.*

> *It is now the joy of your heart to hold daily fellowship with Jesus,*
> *and you will have the same joy to a higher degree in heaven.*
> *You will enjoy the constant vision of his presence,*
> *for you will dwell with him forever.*

"I looked, and behold, a Lamb!" Why, that Lamb is heaven itself!
As good Rutherford says, "Heaven and Christ are the same thing."
To be with Christ is to be in heaven, and to be in heaven is to be with Christ.

That prisoner of the Lord very sweetly writes in one of his glowing letters: "O my Lord Christ,
   if I could be in heaven without thee, it would be a hell; and if I could be in hell, and have thee still,
it would be a heaven to me, for thou art all the heaven I want."

Is this not true, O Christian?
All you need to be blessed, supremely blessed, is "to be with Christ."

> *"Not all the harps above*
> *Can make a heavenly place,*
> *If God His residence remove,*
> *Or but conceal His face."*

Morning and Evening, January 17 (M)

LOVELY IN ALL CONDITIONS

Yes, he is altogether lovely.
SONG OF SOLOMON 5:16 NKJV

As a follower of Jesus, walk with those men who accompanied him as he walked among the people, and you will find him to be *lovely in all conditions.*

He is lovely when he talks to a leper, and touches and heals him;
lovely by the bedside when he takes the fever-stricken patient by the hand and heals her;
lovely by the wayside when he greets the blind beggar, puts his finger on his eyes and bids him see;
lovely when he stands on the sinking vessel and rebukes the waves;
lovely when he visits the mourners, goes with the sisters of Bethany to the new grave site, and
    weeps and groans, and—majestically lovely—bids the dead come forth;
lovely when he rides through the streets of Jerusalem on a colt, the foal of a donkey.

> *Oh, had we been there,*
> *we would have plucked the palm branches,*
> *and we would have taken off our garments to strew the way!*

> *Hosanna, lovely Prince of Peace!*

But he was just as lovely when he came from the garden with his face all smeared with bloody sweat;
just as lovely when they said, "Crucify him, crucify him!" (John 19:6);
just as lovely, and if possible more so, when down those sacred cheeks there dripped the cursed
    spittle from the rough soldiers' mouths.

> *Yes, and loveliest—*
> *to my eyes loveliest of all—*
> *when mangled, wounded, fainting, bruised, dying,*
> *he uttered this plaintive cry of utmost grief*
> *from the felon's gibbet whereon he died:*
> *"My God, my God, why have you forsaken me?"*

Oh, view him where you will, in any and every place, is he not—
    I speak to you who know him, and not to those who have never seen him with the eye of faith—
is he not, in night and in day, on the sea and on the land, on earth and in heaven, altogether lovely?

Yes, and he will be lovely forever and ever
    when our eyes will eternally find their heaven in beholding him.
Jesus Christ, "the same yesterday and today and forever" (Hebrews 13:8),
    is always worthy of this word of praise: "Altogether lovely."

From sermon no. 1446, *The Best Beloved*

CARRIED IN HIS BOSOM

He will gather the lambs in his arms; he will carry them in his bosom.
ISAIAH 40:11

Who is he who cares so tenderly for the lambs?

It is he who has "measured the waters in the hollow of his hand" (Isaiah 40:12).
It is he who has "enclosed the dust of the earth in a measure" (Isaiah 40:12).
It is he who has "weighed the mountains in scales and the hills in a balance" (Isaiah 40:12).
It is this same God, who does all these mighty things, who carries the lambs in his bosom.

But *why*? Why does he carry the lambs in his bosom?
Because *he has a tender heart* and any weakness touches him.
If he hears your sigh, or marks your ignorance or your feebleness, his tender heart reaches out to you.

Also, *it is his office to consider the weak; he himself was a lamb once,*
    and someone who has been a lamb, knowing a lamb's weakness, knows how to sympathize with it.
Our Lord Jesus was and is the Lamb of God who takes away the sin of the world,
    so he knows what strong temptation is, for he has felt its power.

There is also another reason why he carries the lambs in his bosom.

He purchased them with his blood.
He sees the marks of his Passion on them so he prizes them and will not allow them to perish.

How precious is the thought of how he carries them!
He carries the lambs—not on his back—but *in his bosom.*

Here is *boundless affection.* Would he put them in his bosom if he did not love them deeply?
Here is *tender nearness.* They are so near that they could not possibly be nearer.
Here is *perfect safety.* Who can hurt them when they are carried in his bosom? An enemy would have
    to hurt the Shepherd first.
Here is *sweet comfort.* What a soft place to ride! How warm! How the warmth of the Shepherd's heart
    cheers his lamb![1]

It makes one wish to be always a lamb
if one could always ride in that chariot.

Delightful is the weakness
that casts us upon such gracious strength.

Rejoice, you lambs, *that you have such a Shepherd to carry you close to his heart!*[2]

[1]From sermon no. 540, *The Lambs and Their Shepherd*
[2]From sermon no. 794, *Jesus and the Lambs*

REMEMBERING JESUS

"Do this in remembrance of me."
1 Corinthians 11:24

Since Jesus must have the chief place in our memories, let us think of him in his daily and hourly trials. Think of the bleak pictures of persecution when he was abhorred and bitten by the foul tooth of envy. Think of how he was accused of having a demon, and of being a glutton and a drunkard.

> *O Son of God, I must remember you*
> *when I think of those years of toil and trouble*
> *that you so graciously lived for my sake!*

Stand here, my soul, in a shady olive garden, and look down—do you see those drops of blood?
 Notice, they are not the blood of wounds, but the blood of a man whose body was unwounded.
Try to picture him as he was kneeling down in agony and sweat, agonizing with his Father,
 and saying, "My Father, if it be possible, let this cup pass from me" (Matthew 26:39).

> *O Gethsemane, your shade is deeply solemn to my soul!*
> *But ah! Those drops of blood!*
> *Surely it is the climax of the height of misery,*
> *the last of the mighty acts of this wondrous sacrifice!*

> *Can love go deeper than this?*
> *Can it stoop to greater deeds of mercy?*

Ah, but I will take you elsewhere, to a place where you will still behold the Man of Sorrows.
 I will lead you to Pilate's hall and let you see him endure the mockery of cruel soldiers,
 the blow of clenched fists, the shame, the spitting, the pulling of the hair, the cruel buffeting.
Can you picture the King of Martyrs stripped of his garments, exposed to the gaze of fiend-like men?

> *O Son of Man! When I see you scourged with rods and whips,*
> *how can I henceforth cease to remember you?*

> *My memory would be more treacherous than Pilate*
> *if it did not forever cry, "Behold the man!" (John 19:5).*

Now finish the scene of woe with a view of Calvary.
See the pierced hands and feet, the scorching sun, the boiling fever and the thirst.
Hear the death cry, "It is finished," and the groans that were its prelude.

> *Oh, that our roving affections would not stray,*
> *but be centered, nailed, fixed eternally to one object—*
> *that of continually contemplating the death and sufferings of our Lord!*

From sermon no. 2, *The Remembrance of Jesus*

BOASTING IN THE CROSS

God forbid that I should boast except in the cross of our Lord Jesus Christ.
GALATIANS 6:14 NKJV

Paul is astounded that anyone would try to set a carnal ordinance ahead of the cross,
by wishing to boast in circumcision or any other outward institution.
The claim that a ceremony was more important than faith in Jesus provoked Paul,
until his heart grew so hot with indignation that he thundered forth the words, "God forbid!"

Paul never used the sacred name lightly, but when the fire was hot within him,
he called on God to witness that he did not and could not boast in anything but the cross!
Indeed, there is to every truehearted believer something shocking and revolting
at the idea of putting anything before Jesus Christ, whatever it may be!

Turning a cold shoulder to the cross of Christ made Paul burn with indignation!
The cross was the center of his hopes, the focus of his affections,
and it was there that he had found peace for his troubled conscience.
God forbid that he would allow it to be trampled on!

Besides, it was the theme of his ministry.
"Christ crucified" had already proved to be the power of God for the salvation of souls.

Would any of you, Paul asks, cast a slur on the cross—
you who have been converted,
you who have seen so clearly Jesus Christ the crucified (Galatians 3:1)?

How his eyes flash!
How his lips quiver!
How his heart grows hot within him!
How he protests: "God forbid that I should boast except in the cross of our Lord Jesus Christ!"

Paul spreads his eagle wing and rises into eloquence,
while his keen eye looks fiercely upon every enemy of the cross.
He burns, he glows, he mounts, he soars; he is carried away completely
when his thoughts are on that meek and patient Sufferer, who sacrificed himself for our sins.

*Oh, may we have something of that glow within our breast
whenever we think of our Lord Jesus!*

God forbid that we should be coldhearted when we come near to him!

*God forbid that we should ever view with heartless eye and lethargic soul
the sweet wonders of that cross on which our Savior loved and died!*

From sermon no. 1447, *Three Crosses*

A PERFECT SAVIOR

God has brought to Israel a Savior, Jesus, as he promised.
Acts 13:23

Our Lord Jesus is a perfect Savior; his very nature fits him for his office.
First, and foremost, he is God.

Who but God could sustain the enormous weight of human guilt?
Who but Deity could bear the awful load of wrath upon his shoulders?
What knowledge but omniscience could understand all the evil, and what power but omnipotence
    could undo that evil?

Yet we know that in order to be a perfect Savior he also needed to be a *man*.
Man had sinned, so man must pay the consequences of his sin.

Only a nature as complex as that of Jesus of Nazareth—
    the Son of God and the Son of Man—
could have worked out our salvation to perfection.

Jesus also became a perfect Savior through his *experiences*.
A physician should have some acquaintance with the disease if he would know the remedy.
Our Savior knew it all, for he "took our illnesses and bore our diseases" (Matthew 8:17).

He did not look at sin from the distance of heaven, but he lived and walked in the midst of it.
    He did not pass hurriedly through the world
        as one might hastily walk through a hospital and not see and understand the disease.
He saw sin in all its forms, having lived more than thirty years in the very midst of it.

Because he took upon himself the nature of the people he came to save,
    every feeling he experienced made him perfect in his work,
    every affliction and pain instructed him,
    every throb of anguish made him wise—
rendering him more accomplished in working out the purposes of God.

No one can have an understanding of Christ's marvelous character
    without saying, "This is *the man* I want as my friend."
If the Lord had given us the ability to create our own Savior—an ideal person to meet our case—
    we would have desired only a person like Jesus.

O Jesus, you are a perfect Savior—
sufferer like ourselves, bearer of all the ills of humanity,
and yet, unlike us, free from sin, holy, harmless, undefiled—
qualified in all respects to undertake and accomplish the great work of salvation!

From sermon no. 478, *Christ—Perfect through Sufferings*

THE THREE HOURS OF DARKNESS

Now from the sixth hour there was darkness over all the land until the ninth hour.
MATTHEW 27:45

Although the Lord had ordered that there be both day and night,
  in this case, he inserts three hours of night into the middle of a day.
Thinking on this miracle, was it not in perfect harmony with *the greater miracle of Christ's death?*

Was the Lord himself not departing from all common rules?
Was he not doing something that had never been done before and would never be done again?

The death of man is a common thing; it is deemed inevitable.
  But that the Son of God, who is equal with God, should die—
    this is beyond all expectation; this is not only above nature, but contrary to it!
The sun darkened at noon would seem to be a fitting accompaniment to such a miraculous death.

This miracle of the darkness was one that would have been pronounced impossible.
It is impossible to have an eclipse of the sun during a full moon, and Passover was at this time.

Ah, when we are dealing with man, and the Fall, and sin, and God, and Christ, and the Atonement,
  we are at home with impossibilities!
We have now reached an area where marvels and surprises are the order of the day.
  Sublimities become commonplace when we come within the circle of eternal love.

> *The way of the cross is ablaze with the divine,*
> *and we soon perceive that "with God*
> *all things are possible" (Matthew 19:26).*

See, then, in the death of Jesus the possibility of the impossible!
Behold how the Son of God can die!

Even as the sun was eclipsed when it was impossible for it to be eclipsed,
  so has Jesus performed on our behalf, in the agonies of his death,
    things that in the ordinary judgment of men must be set down as utterly impossible!
Our faith is at home in wonderland when we observe the ways of our Lord.

And now *this darkness appears to have been very natural and fitting.*
  After realizing that this is indeed the Son of God who stretches his hands to the death of the cross,
    we do not wonder at the tearing of the curtain in the temple.
We are not astonished at the earthquake or at the rising of some of the dead.

These are proper attendants of our Lord's Passion, and so is the darkness.
Where Jesus is present, wonders of power are expected.

From sermon no. 1896, *The Three Hours' Darkness*

HE TROD THE WINEPRESS

"I have trodden the winepress alone,
and from the peoples no one was with me."
Isaiah 63:3

Jesus uses an expressive figure to depict some of the facts in his wondrous feat of conquest.
He says, "I have trodden the winepress."
This figure suggests *toil and labor,* since the fruit of the vine is not bruised without hard work.

So our blessed Lord, though he could have easily crushed the enemies of his church,
    painfully labored to overcome them in the garden.
It was not a light pressing of the foot that was needed when he bruised the old Dragon's head.

> *O my soul, meditate on this glorious Wine-Presser!*
> *Those sins that would have crushed you to pieces,*
> *he had to tread beneath his feet.*

> *How it must have bruised his heel to tread upon those sins!*
> *How it forced from him, not sweat like ours, but drops of blood,*
> *when he could say, "I have trodden the winepress!"*

In the figure employed, there is also an allusion to the staining of his garments:
"Why is your apparel red, and your garments like his who treads in the winepress?" (Isaiah 63:2).

Ah, solemnly contemplate your Savior, sprinkled with his own blood.
Look at him when he is only eight days old, already shedding blood for you.
Go to Gethsemane's garden and mark how he is dressed in a crimson robe of blood.
Go and mark the blood as it flows from his temple where the thorn-crown lacerates his brow.
See the accursed whip of the cruel Romans, tearing off chunks of his quivering flesh.
See him in his weary *via dolorosa*—each stone on which he treads is stained with his precious blood.
Mark how his hands and feet gush with streams of blood as the rough iron tears them asunder.

> *O Jesus, from the crown of your head to the sole of your foot,*
> *you were sprinkled with blood!*
> *Your inward man was stained with blood, and your outward man, too.*
> *You were enveloped in blood, glorious Presser of our sins.*

> *We will not ask again, "Who is this who comes from Edom,*
> *in crimsoned garments from Bozrah,*
> *he who is splendid in his apparel,*
> *marching in the greatness of his strength?" (Isaiah 63:1).*

> *We know why your garments are red.*
> *You have trodden the winepress of the wrath of God.*

From sermon no. 2567, *The Single-Handed Conquest*

JESUS OR BARABBAS?

They cried out again, "Not this man, but Barabbas!"
Now Barabbas was a robber.
JOHN 18:40

Since it was the custom to deliver a prisoner on the Paschal Day,
 Pilate thinks he can allow Jesus to escape without compromising his character with the authorities.
He asks the people which of the two they would prefer—a notorious thief, or the Savior.
 This wretch is brought out and set in competition with Jesus.

Pilate thinks that from a sense of shame the multitude cannot possibly prefer Barabbas,
 but they are so thirsty for Christ's blood, and so moved by the priests,
  that with one consent, they cry, "Not this man, but Barabbas!"
They choose Barabbas, even though they know him to be a murderer, a thief, and a traitor.

Do we not have in this act—
 the deliverance of the sinner and the binding of the innocent—
a type of the great work accomplished by our Savior's death?

Each one of us may take our place beside Barabbas.
 We all have robbed God of his glory,
  and we all have been seditious traitors against the government of heaven.
If he who hates his brother is a murderer, we also have been guilty of that sin.

Here we stand before the judgment seat:
We are allowed to go free while the Prince of Life is bound for us.
God delivers us and acquits us, while the Savior, without spot or blemish, is led forth to crucifixion.

Two birds were taken in the rite of the cleansing of a leper.
 The one bird was killed and its blood was poured into a basin,
  while the other bird was dipped into this blood.
Then, with its wings all crimson, it was set free to fly away into the open field.

The bird slain pictures the Savior,
 and every soul that has by faith been dipped in his blood
flies upward toward heaven, singing sweetly in joyous liberty.

It comes to this—Barabbas must die or Christ must die.
You the sinner must perish, or Christ Immanuel, the immaculate, must die.
He dies so that we might be delivered.

We have been robbers, traitors, and murderers,
 yet we can rejoice that Christ has delivered us from the curse of the law.
He willingly became a curse for us.

From sermon no. 595, *Barabbas Preferred to Jesus*

AMAZING STOOP OF LOVE

Twisting together a crown of thorns, they put it on his head and put a reed in his right hand.
And kneeling before him, they mocked him, saying, "Hail, King of the Jews!"
MATTHEW 27:29

Oh, how low our glorious Substitute stooped for our sake!

In him was no sin, either of nature or of act,
   but he took upon himself our sin and was now regarded as the sinner.
He, who created all things by the word of his power—and by whom all things exist—
   now sat in an old chair to be made a mimic king, to be mocked and spit on.

All other miracles put together are not equal to this miracle!

This one rises above them all and out-miracles all miracles—
that God himself, having espoused our cause and assumed our nature,
would stoop to such a depth of scorn as this!

He voluntarily subjected himself to all the shame and disgrace that base men heaped on him.

Who knows what things were done in that rough guardroom that holy pens could not record!
Who knows what foul jests were made and what obscene remarks were uttered that were even more
   shocking to Christ than the filthy spittle that ran down his cheeks!
You cannot imagine how low your Lord stooped on your account!

How I wish that I could express these words more effectively: See how your Redeemer loved you!
   You know that, when Christ wept at the grave of Lazarus, the Jews said, "See how he loved him!"
Ah! But look at him there among those Roman soldiers—despised, rejected, insulted, ridiculed—
   and you must indeed say, "See how he loved us!"

This love of Jesus is beyond all conception!

If we were to fetch out of heaven all the angelic host before the throne,
and tell them to empty their hearts;
and if we could collect all the love
that ever has been and ever will be in all the saints—
all that would be but a drop in a bucket
compared with the boundless, fathomless love of Christ for us,
that made him willing to be an object of scorn and derision for our sakes.

If we stood in the pillory, and all mankind hooted at us for millions of years,
   it would be as nothing compared with the wondrous condescension of him who is God over all,
stooping as he did for our sakes.

From sermon no. 2824, *Mocked of the Soldiers*

THE LORD OUR RIGHTEOUSNESS

This is the name by which he will be called:
"The LORD is our righteousness."
JEREMIAH 23:6

Christ's life was so righteous that we might say it was righteousness itself.
He is the Law incarnate.

He lived out the law of God to the fullest,
and while you see God's precepts written in fire on Sinai's brow,
you see them written in flesh in the person of Christ.

Our Savior never offended against the commands of the Just One.
　From his eye there never flashed the fire of unhallowed anger,
　　and from his lip there never flowed an unjust or licentious word.
His heart was free of all iniquity; free from the temptations of sin.

The law consists of this: "You shall love the Lord your God with all your heart" *(Matthew 22:37).*
Jesus did that, for it was his food and drink to do the will of him who sent him (John 4:34).
Hunger and thirst and nakedness were nothing to him, nor death itself, in fulfilling his Father's will.

The law also consists of this: "You shall love your neighbor as yourself *(Matthew 22:39).*
　In all that he did, and in all that he suffered, Jesus more than fulfilled the precept,
　　for he saved others, while himself he could not save (Matthew 27:42).
He would rather yield up his spirit in indescribable agonies than to see the souls of men condemned.

Now the core of the title lies in the little word "our"—"Jehovah is *our* righteousness."

Just as the merit of Christ's blood takes away our sin,
　so the merit of his obedience is imputed to us for righteousness.
As soon as we believe, his works are considered to be our works.

When God looks at us, it is as though we were Christ.
He regards *his* life as *our* life.
He accepts, blesses, and rewards us as though all that he did had been done by us.

Now stop a moment and dwell on this title again—"The LORD is our righteousness."
The Lawgiver has himself obeyed the law, so will his obedience not be sufficient?
Jehovah has himself become man so that he may do man's work; has he done it imperfectly?

Let the fact that the Savior is Jehovah strengthen your confidence.
　Look back on your past sins, your present infirmities, and all your future errors,
　　and while you weep the tears of repentance let no fear of condemnation blanch your cheeks.
You stand before God today, robed in your Savior's perfect righteousness.

From sermon no. 395, *The Lord Our Righteousness*

EXTRAORDINARY THINGS

"We have seen extraordinary things today."
LUKE 5:26

If you have beheld Christ's life with the eyes of faith, you have seen many extraordinary things.

First, the Maker of men became a man;
he who fills all space was laid in a manger;
he who is the Son of the Highest was known as the Son of Mary.
We have heard extraordinary things when we have heard of the Incarnation.

Further, he who was the Lord of all became the Servant of all.
"Being found in human form" (Philippians 2:8), he lived a life of perfect obedience to his Father's will.
He went about healing the sick, raising the dead, and ministering to all who came to him.

Best of all, on him who knew no sin, the sin of man was laid,
    and the righteous God meted out to him—the Innocent One—the chastisement due to the guilty.
He was made to be sin "so that in him we might become the righteousness of God" (2 Corinthians 5:21).

What a wonder it is!

The guilty go free
because he who is free from guilt
stands in their place.

Yet, there is more—Jesus died on the cross and loving friends laid him in the tomb.
Death had conquered him; but at that same moment, death was also conquered.
That day, he led death itself captive to its own supremacy.

Wonder of wonders!
Death is put to death by death!

Yet, even that wonder is not the last.
    Jesus lies there for a while, wrapped in grave clothes,
        and death appears to have the mastery over him.
But when the appointed hour strikes, our Savior is up and away!

Jesus left the abode of death, no more to die;
    and by doing so he has also guaranteed our resurrection.
Just as he rose from the grave, so will his people also rise.

If we really understood the history of our Lord Jesus,
we would say concerning every part of it,
"We have seen extraordinary things."

From sermon no. 2614, *Strange Things*

SEEING HIM AS HE IS

We shall see him as he is.
1 John 3:2

Our minds often revert to Christ as he was, and as such we have desired to see him.

How often we have wished to see the Baby who slept in Bethlehem!
How frequently we have wished that we might see the blessed Physician walking among the sick
    and dying, giving life with his touch and healing with his breath!
How frequently, too, have our thoughts retired to Gethsemane!

We will never see him thus, for Bethlehem's glories are gone forever.
Gethsemane's scene is dissolved in the past, and Calvary's glooms are swept away.
We cannot; we must not see him as he was, for we have a larger promise: "We shall see him as he is."

We will never see him mocked by Pharisees and laughed at by Herod's men of war.
We will never see the insulted, the molested, the despised Jesus.
We will never see those sacred cheeks dripping with the spittle, but "we shall see him as he is."

The darkest hour of Christ's life was when his Father forsook him;
    that gloomy hour when his Father's remorseless hand held the cup to his Son's lips,
        and bitter though it was, said to him, "Drink my Son—aye, drink!"
    and when the quivering Savior, said, "My Father, if it be possible, let this cup pass from me."

Oh! It was a dark moment
when the Father's ears were deaf to his Son's petitions;
when the Father's eyes were closed to his Son's agonies!

"My Father," said the Son, "Can you not remove the cup? Is there no other way for man's salvation?"
There is none!

Oh! It was a terrible moment
when Jesus cried, "My God, my God, why have you forsaken me?"

Believer, you will never see that sick face;
you will never see that pale emaciated body;
you will never see that weary, weary heart;
you will never see that sorrowful spirit, for the Father never turns away from his Son now.

What will you see?

You will see your Lord embraced by his beloved Parent;
you will see him sitting at his Father's right hand, glorified and exalted forever;
you will "see him as he is."

From sermon no. 61, *The Beatific Vision*

SORROW AT THE CROSS

"Truly, truly, I say to you, you will weep and lament."
JOHN 16:20

The death of our Lord was, and is, a cause for sorrow.
But during the three days of his burial there was a greater cause for it than now, since he has risen.

To the disciples, the death of Jesus was the loss of his personal presence.
  Do you wonder that they wept and lamented when the Rock of their confidence,
    the delight of their eyes, the hope of their souls, was taken from them?
How would you feel if your best friend was hurried away from you to a shameful death?

Nothing could compensate them for Jesus' absence; he had become their all in all.
For his sake they had left everything and followed him.

They also sorrowed because it was a shattering of all their hopes.

How can a kingdom be set up when the King himself has been slain?
Where is his dominion when he who was to be the King has been nailed up like a felon to the wood?
Who will serve a king who has been cut off from the land of the living?

Poor followers of a dead monarch, how can they have hope for his cause and crown?
How can they be happy when they have seen the end of their fairest life-dream?

Added to this was the sight they had of their beloved Master in his agonies.

Who would not sorrow when Jesus is insulted and reviled and blasphemed by foes?
Who can bear to see the innocent Savior crucified in the midst of a scornful crowd?
Who can listen to his sorrows as they are expressed in the painful cry, "I thirst," and in the
  agonizing question, "My God, my God, why have you forsaken me?"

It is no wonder that his virgin mother was told that a sword would pierce her heart (Luke 2:35),
  for surely there has never been a sorrow like Jesus' sorrow; no grief like his grief.
His heavy woes must have pierced through the hearts of all those who loved him.

Oh, the depths of grief that our Lord endured,
and will there be no answering depths of grief in us?

When all of God's waves and billows flow over you, O Jesus,
will we not be plunged into grief as well?

Yes, we will drink of your cup and be baptized with your baptism.
We will now sit down before your cross and watch with you one hour,
while love and grief occupy our innermost souls.

From sermon no. 1442, *Sorrow at the Cross Turned Into Joy*

SEE HOW HE LOVES!

So the Jews said, "See how he loved him!"
JOHN 11:36

It was at the grave of Lazarus that Jesus wept, and his grief was so obvious to the onlookers,
   that they said, "See how he loved him!"
And we, too, have a share in that special love of Jesus.

As Jesus left heaven's throne for us,
as he came down the celestial hills,
the angels must have said, "See how he loves them!"

When he lay in the manger, an infant,
the angels must have gathered round and said, "See how he loves!"

But when they saw him sweating in the garden,
when he was put into the crucible and began to be melted in the furnace,
then indeed, the angels began to know how much he loves us!

O Jesus! When I see your back torn with knotted whips;
when I see your dear cheeks become a reservoir for the filth and spittle of unholy mouths;
when I behold your honor and your life both trailing in the dust;
when I behold your hands and your feet pierced;
when I behold your body stripped naked and exposed;
when I see you hanging on the cross between earth and heaven, in awful anguish;
when I hear you cry, "I thirst," and see the vinegar thrust to your lips;
when I hear your direful cry, "My God, my God, why have you forsaken me?"
then my spirit is compelled to say, "See how he loves!"

> *Jesus could die,*
> *but he could not cease to love.*

> *He could be torn in pieces,*
> *but he could not be torn away from his people.*

He bled for you.
He gave his whole self for you.

There was not a single nerve in his body that did not thrill with love for you.
There was not a drop of blood that did not have in its red fluid your name.

Oh, how Jesus loved you when he received you all black and filthy to his bosom!
How he loved you when he kissed you and welcomed you as his own fair spouse!

From sermon no. 325, *Constraining Love*

February 11

THE HEART OF JESUS

"I am gentle and lowly in heart."
MATTHEW 11:29

Our Savior says of himself, "I am gentle,"
  because he desired to remove the fears of those who trembled to approach him.
He also says, "I am lowly in heart,"
  which means that he is willing to receive the lowest, the poorest, and the most despised.

So come to him, you who feel like outcasts, for Jesus also was rejected by his people.
You who are despised, come to him who was despised by men.
You who are homeless, come to him who had nowhere to lay his head.
You who are needy, come to him who hungered and thirsted.
You who are lost, come to the Son of Man, who came to seek and to save the lost.

His lowliness also means this: Just as he is willing to receive the lowest,
  so he is willing to do the very lowest and menial service for those who come to him.

He is willing to bear their burdens,
willing to wash their feet,
willing to purge them from their sins in his own blood.

Jesus has performed feats of lowly love for sinners, for he has borne their sin and their shame.
He now delights in saving to the uttermost all who come to God through him (Hebrews 7:25).

"Gentle and lowly"—
as with two masterly strokes of the pencil,
Jesus has given us a perfect picture
of his dear, gentle face—
no, not of his face,
but of his inmost heart.

"Gentle and lowly in heart."

These are two beauties that to a sinner's eyes are the most lovely and fascinating attributes.
They charm our fears and chain our hearts.

Jesus is omnipotent, yet lowly;
he is the Eternal God, yet a patient sufferer;
he is King of kings and Lord of lords, yet "gentle and lowly in heart."

What a divine blending of glory and grace!

From sermon no. 1105, *The Heart of Jesus*

PRECIOUS LORD

To you who believe, He is precious.
1 Peter 2:7 nkjv

Just as all the rivers run into the sea, so all delights center in our Beloved.

The glances of his eyes outshine the sun.
The beauties of his face are fairer than the choicest flowers.
Gems of the mine and pearls from the sea are worthless when compared to his preciousness.

Peter tells us that Jesus is precious, but he did not and could not tell us *how* precious,
      nor can any of us compute the value of God's "inexpressible gift" (2 Corinthians 9:15).
Words cannot depict the preciousness of the Lord Jesus,
      nor can they fully tell how essential he is to our satisfaction and happiness.

Believers experience a sore famine in the midst of plenty if their Lord is absent.
The sun may be shining, but if Christ is hidden, their whole world is dark and it is night.
If the bright morning star is gone, no other star can yield even a ray of light.

What a howling wilderness this world is without our Lord!

If we lose his presence,
      the flowers of our garden wither,
      our pleasant fruits decay,
      the birds suspend their songs,
and a tempest overturns our hopes.

All the lights of earth cannot make daylight if the Sun of Righteousness is eclipsed.
He is the soul of our soul, the light of our light, the life of our life.

O believer, what would you do
with the temptations and cares of this world
if you did not have Jesus?

What would you do when you awaken
and prepare for the day's battle
if you did not have him?

What would you do in the evening
when you arrive home exhausted and weary
if there were no door of fellowship between you and Christ?

Blessed be his name! He will not permit us to face a day without him,
      for his promise is sure, "I will never leave you nor forsake you" (Hebrews 13:5).
Yet, when we think of what life would be like without him, it enhances his preciousness.

Morning and Evening, March 1 (E)

GOD WASHING FEET?

He came to Simon Peter, who said to him, "Lord, do you wash my feet?"
John 13:6

Lord! Master! God! Everlasting Father! Eternal! Almighty! King of kings and Lord of lords!
Do you—do YOU wash my feet?

You call the stars by their names, and they shine by your light (Isaiah 40:26).
You sit above the circle of the earth, and its inhabitants are like grasshoppers (Isaiah 40:22).
You hold the waters in the hollow of your hand and measure heaven with a span (Isaiah 40:12).
Lord, do you wash my feet?

While on earth you trod the waters; the depths knew you and were like marble beneath your feet.
You put fear into Death itself, for Lazarus came forth from the grave at your bidding.
The winds were hushed at your will, and even devils were subject to you.
And do you wash my feet?

> *Remember that no one else could cleanse us;*
> *the infinite God must take away the infinite blackness of our sin.*

> *What a stoop is here, even to washing our feet!*

Now picture before you someone who has walked a great distance and his feet are stained with travel.
   As soon as he steps over the threshold of his host's house, a slave—
      a servant—takes off his sandals.
She brings a basin and some water, and kneeling down washes his feet.

The host does not stoop to this office.
   The master does not wash feet, because it is servile, menial, humiliating work.
Yet this, which was the lowest of all offices in the east, is that which the Savior undertakes—
   not in fiction and metaphor, but in reality—for every one of us.

Truly, this is a subject for wondering;
   yet the wonder is excelled by the fact that he shared a slave's death, as well as a slave's life.
It was a slave's life when he washed our feet,
   and it was a slave's death when they sold him for thirty pieces of silver and then crucified him.

Think of it! The Lord of glory comes down from the grandeur of heaven,
   and from the splendor of infinite honor,
and he washes—in a slave's garb and in a menial manner—the feet of his disciples!

> *O Jesus, I would wash your feet with my tears,*
> *and I would wipe them with the hair of my head,*
> *for I have been a sinner;*
> *but instead, do you wash my feet?*

From sermon no. 612, *Jesus Washing His Disciples' Feet*

PREPARING HIS THRONE OF GRACE

He said to the Jews, "Behold your King!"
JOHN 19:14

Come to Gabbatha and behold your King preparing his throne.
Yes, and making himself ready to sit on it.

When you look in answer to the summons, "Behold your King!" what do you see?

You see the "man of sorrows, and acquainted with grief" (Isaiah. 53:3), wearing a crown of thorns.
You see him covered with an old purple cloak that has been cast over him in mockery.
You see on him the traces of his streaming blood, for he has just been flogged.
You see that his face is blackened with bruises and stained with shameful spittle.

It is a terrible spectacle, but you are actually seeing the establishment of the Redeemer's throne.
He was setting up a new throne so that he might reign as the King of pardoned sinners.

He was already a king before all worlds, and to Pilate's question, "'Are You a king then?'
    Jesus answered, 'You say rightly that I am a king'" (John 18:37 NKJV).
But here before Pilate and the Jews, he was preparing a new throne—a throne of grace.

Mark how he is preparing this throne of grace.

It is by pain and shame endured in our place.
Pain was a great part of the penalty due for sin; therefore, our Substitute must also bear pain.

When Pilate brought forth our martyr Prince, he was the picture of agony;
    he was majesty in misery—misery wrought up to its full height and stature.
The cruel furrows of the scourge and the trickling rivulets of blood adorning his face
    were the signs that he was about to die a cruel death on the cross.

All this he bore, because there could be no throne of grace without a substitutionary sacrifice.
It behooved him to suffer so that he might be a Prince and a Savior.

Behold your King in his pains!
He is laying the deep foundations of his kingdom of mercy.

Many a crown has been secured by blood, and so is this, but it is with Christ's own blood.
Many a throne has been established by suffering, and so is this, but Christ himself bears the pain.

By his great sacrificial griefs,
our Lord has prepared a throne whereon he will sit
until all his people have been made kings and priests to reign with him.

From sermon no. 1353, *Ecce Rex*

LOVE AT ITS UTMOST

"As the Father has loved me, so have I loved you."
JOHN 15:9

Jesus deliberately declares his love, and can you doubt his words?

Do you not answer, "Yes, Lord, it is true indeed!
  There is no need for you to tell me with your lips,
    because you have assured me of it by your wounds.
  I know that you love me!"

Christ loves, not only in word, but in deed and in truth.
  There is a greater force in his deeds of love
    than in all the words that even he could have uttered.
His deeds emphasize his words; he has written out his love in living characters.

*O Master, no man has ever spoken like you,
and yet your most eloquent discourse was when you said little
but stretched out your hands to the cross so they might be nailed there!*

You poured out your heart, not in oratory, but in blood and water.

And all this love is our personal possession.

The great sun shines today on this round earth,
  and while it pours its limitless flood of light on all,
that one tiny daisy as it bathes in the brightness, is able to say, "The sun is all mine."

Though there are myriads of flowers in the meadows and gardens,
  this one flower may freely possess all that the sun can give—
    or rather all that the little flower can receive.
It receives as much as if it were the only flower that blooms.

So Jesus is to each one of us, all our own, even though millions of people also claim him as their own.

In the love of Christ we find our greatest joy.

*The pastures of the Great Shepherd are wide,
but the sweetest grass grows close to his pierced feet.*

*The love of Jesus is the center of salvation;
it is the sun in the midst of the heavens of grace.*

From sermon no. 1982, *Love at Its Utmost*

THE FLOCK OF HIS PASTURE

Tell me, you whom my soul loves,
where you pasture your flock,
where you make it lie down at noon.
SONG OF SOLOMON 1:7

These words express the believer's longing
for present communion with Christ.

Where do you pasture your flock?

In your *house?*
I will go if I will find you there!

In private *prayer?*
Then I will pray without ceasing!

In the *Word?*
Then I will read it diligently!

In your *commandments?*
Then I will walk in them with all my heart!

Oh, tell me where you pasture your flock,
for wherever you stand as the Shepherd,
there I will lie down as a sheep!

I cannot be satisfied apart from you!
My soul hungers and thirsts
for the refreshment of your presence!

Where does your flock lie down at noon?

Whether at dawn or at noon,
my only rest must be where you are
with your beloved flock.

My soul's rest
must be a grace-given rest,
and can only be found in you![1]

Yes, we must have him! "Give me Christ, or else I die" is the cry of our souls.
To be with Jesus is heaven, anywhere on earth or in the skies.
All else is wilderness and desert. Our hearts cannot rest away from him.[2]

[1]*Morning and Evening*, February 3 (E)
[2]From sermon no. 636, *The Church's Love to Her Loving Lord*

THE ROYAL PROCESSION

So they took Jesus, and he went out, bearing his own cross.
JOHN 19:16–17

Soon all eyes will be fixed on a great prince as he rides through the London streets with his royal bride,
  but I invite your attention to another Prince, traveling in another manner through his metropolis.
London will see the glory of the one; Jerusalem beheld the shame of the other.

> *Come hither, ye lovers of Emmanuel,*
> *and we will see this great sight—*
> *the King of Sorrows marching to his throne of grief, the cross!*

There is a great interest in the procession of our Lord—
  greater than in the pageant Londoners are so anxiously expecting.

Will the prince be sumptuously arrayed?
Ours is adorned with garments crimsoned with his own blood.

Will the prince be decorated with honors?
Behold, our King is not without his crown—alas, a crown of thorns, set with ruby drops of blood!

Will the thoroughfares be crowded?
So were the streets of Jerusalem, for great multitudes followed him.

Will there be a chorus of voices, yelling and shouting?
Our Lord had such a greeting, but alas, it was a yell of "Away with him, away with him!" (John 19:15).

> *High in the air, the people will wave their banners;*
> *waving them about the heir of England's throne!*

> *But how can they rival the banner of the sacred cross,*
> *borne that day, for the first time, among the sons of men?*

Thousands of eyes will gaze at the youthful prince, but our Prince has the gaze of men and angels.
All nations gathered about our Lord, and from the sky the angels viewed him with amazement.
Yes, and the great God and Father watched each movement of his suffering Son.

> *Oh, come hither ye people and watch the world's Maker*
> *marching along the way of his great sorrow!*

> *Behold, your Redeemer traverses the rugged path of suffering,*
> *along which he went with heaving heart and heavy footsteps,*
> *in order to pave a royal road of mercy for his enemies!*

From sermon no. 497, *The Procession of Sorrow*

LOVING THE "PERSON"

Love the LORD, all you his saints!
PSALM 31:23

No words can ever express the gratitude we owe to him who loved us
    even when we were dead in trespasses and sins (Ephesians 2:1).
The *love* of Jesus is unutterably precious and worthy of daily praise,
    and the *work* of Jesus in bringing us salvation is glorious and beyond compare.

Yet I do believe that the highest praise of every ransomed soul and of the entire Christian church
    should be offered to the blessed *person* of Jesus Christ, our adorable Lord.
The love of his heart is excelled by the heart that poured out that wondrous love,
    and the wonders of his hand are outdone by the hand that wrought those godlike miracles of grace.

We ought to bless him for what he has done for us;
    but still, the best thing about Christ is Christ himself.
We prize *his*, but we worship *him*; his gifts are valued, but he is adored.

While we contemplate with mingled feelings of awe, admiration, and thankfulness,
    Christ's atonement, his resurrection, his glory in heaven, and his second coming;
        it is he himself, grandly dignified as the Son of God, and superbly beautiful as the Son of Man,
    that sheds an incomparable charm on all those wonderful achievements.

For *him* let our choicest spices be reserved, and to him let our sweetest anthems be raised.
    Our best perfume must be poured on his head, and our alabaster flasks must be broken for him alone.
The time should come when we can heartily say, "I love him because I cannot help it;
    his all-conquering loveliness has completely ravished my heart!"

Oh, that we might love our Lord for his own sake—love him because he is so supremely beautiful!
May a glimpse of him win our hearts and make him dearer to our eyes than light.[1]

> *Your work, Lord, is fair,*
> *but the hand that wrought the work is fairer still.*
>
> *All your designs of love are full of splendor,*
> *but what can we say of the mind that created those designs?*
>
> *The glance, the look of love that you have given me is blessed;*
> *but oh, those eyes of yours,*
> *those eyes that are brighter than the stars of the morning!*
>
> *You are Lord Jesus, better than anything that comes from you.*
> *Since your gifts are infinitely precious,*
> *then what must you yourself be?*[2]

[1] From sermon no. 1446, *The Best Beloved*
[2] Source Unknown

BLOOD ON THE GOLDEN ALTAR

*"The priest shall put some of the blood
on the horns of the altar of fragrant incense before the LORD."*
LEVITICUS 4:7

Through Jesus Christ our Savior, our prayers, our praises, and our service
   are like the mixture of fragrant perfumes that were burnt on the altar before God;
      but it is the blood-mark on the altar that makes the incense acceptable.
Our prayers, praise, and service are acceptable to God because of the atoning sacrifice of Jesus.

It is true that we are to have good works, for faith without works is dead (James 2:17);
   still, the reason for our acceptance with God is not in our good works.
Our acceptance is only in Christ and in his atoning sacrifice.

Let your good works be multiplied, but keep them all at a distance from the sacrifice of Christ.
When you repent of sin, if you begin to trust in your repentance, away with your repentance!
When you serve God, if you begin to trust in your service, away with it!

*Christian, keep your eye fixed on the blood of Jesus.
There is no prayer or praise that comes before God of itself,
for it is imperfect.*

*Keep your eye on Christ's blood
so that even the sin of your holy things
may be put away by the sacrifice once offered on Calvary.*

We would pray a lot better if we thought more of the blood on the altar as *our plea in prayer.*

If we can plead for Jesus' sake and in his name;
if we can plead by his agony and bloody sweat, by his cross and Passion;
then we have found the great secret of prevailing with God.

Should we not also make the precious blood of Jesus *the highest note of our praise?*
Yes, keep your eye on the crucified Christ and then sing as loud as you please.

*Oh, the precious blood,
the atoning sacrifice of our Lord Jesus Christ!*

*The Hallelujah Chorus of all the redeemed
will not have a nobler note than this:
"He loved us and saved us!
He died for us, and we are washed in his blood!"*

There is only one gate of life, and that is sprinkled with the blood of Christ;
   and if you turn away from that door, you have chosen the road leading to death.
There is no hope of entering heaven unless you are resting in the precious blood of Christ.

From sermon no. 2369, *Blood Even on the Golden Altar*

THE FOOD OF LOVE

We love because he first loved us.
1 JOHN 4:19

Love feeds on love.
The constant motive and sustaining power of our love for God is his love for us.

The first thing that our love feeds on, when it is but an infant, is a sense of favors received;
   but when the Christian grows in grace, he loves Christ for another reason.
The disciples did not merely love Jesus because of his gifts.
   Their main reason for loving him was because he had communed with them.

They had walked with him in the villages and had dwelt with him in the mountains.
They loved Christ because he was so glorious!

This, then, is the food of love.
But what if it is not sufficiently nourished and love grows cold as it sometimes does?

Well, if love grows cold, it should go to the place where it was born.

Love was born in the Garden of Gethsemane where Jesus sweat great drops of blood.
It was nurtured in Pilate's hall where Jesus bared his back to the plowing of the lash.
Love was nurtured at the cross amid the groans of an expiring God.
It was beneath the dripping of his blood that love was nurtured.

> *O believer, where did your love spring from,*
> *but from the foot of the cross?*
>
> *Have you ever seen that sweet flower*
> *growing anywhere else?*

It was when you saw "love divine, all loves excelling," outdoing its own self;
it was when you saw love in bondage to itself, dying by its own stroke;
it was when you saw love laying down its life, though it had power to retain it—
it was there that your love was born.

If you wish to recover your love, take it to some of those sweet places.

Make it sit in the shade of the olive trees.
Make it stand at Gabbatha and gaze while the blood is gushing down.
Take it to the cross and bid it look and see afresh the bleeding Lamb.

> *Surely this will make your love spring from a dwarf into a giant,*
> *and this will fan it from a spark into a flame!*

From sermon no. 229, *Love*

"HE HAS RISEN"

"He is not here, for he has risen."
MATTHEW 28:6

Mary Magdalene and the other Mary came to the sepulcher, hoping to find the body of their Lord,
   but the words, "He is not here," must have filled their hearts with utmost grief.
However, their grief was removed when it was added, "He has risen."

"He is not here"—that is sorrowful;
but "he has risen"—this is joyful!

There is probably no fact in history that is so fully proven and corroborated
   as the fact that Jesus of Nazareth, who was crucified and buried, rose again.
And this is the guarantee to every one of us who believe in him of our own resurrection.

The selfsame body that is sown in the earth will rise again from the earth
   in a beauty and glory of which we have not yet known.
The body of that dear child of God to which you bade farewell some years ago will rise again.

Those eyes that you closed—those very eyes—"will behold the king in his beauty" (Isaiah 33:17).
Those ears that could not hear your last tender word—those ears will hear the eternal melodies.
That heart that grew cold and still—that heart will beat again with newness of life.

O believer, do not fear death. What is it?

The grave is but a bath wherein our body, like Esther, buries itself in spices,
   making it sweet and fresh for the embrace of the glorious King in immortality.

It is the wardrobe where we lay aside the garment for a while, and it will come forth purified.
   It was a workday dress when we put it off, but it will be a Sabbath robe when we put it on.
We may even long for evening to undress if there is such a waking
   and such a putting on of garments in the presence of the King.

"He is not here."

Christ is now in heaven, but even as the sun exhales the dew and attracts it upward to heaven,
   so Christ magnetizes and draws our hearts, our thoughts, and our longings up towards him.

"He is not here." Then why should I be here?

Oh, get thee up, my soul, and let all your sweetest incense
go towards him who "is not here, for he has risen."

From sermon no. 1081, *A Visit to the Tomb*

OUR UNFITNESS IS REQUIRED

He delivers the needy when he calls, the poor and him who has no helper.
He has pity on the weak and the needy, and saves the lives of the needy.
PSALM 72:12–13

One said to me lately, "Oh, sir, I am the biggest sinner that ever lived!"
I replied, "Christ Jesus came into the world to save sinners" (1 Timothy 1:15).

"But I have no strength."
"While we were still weak, at the right time Christ died" (Romans 5:6).

"Oh, but," he said, "I have been utterly ungodly!"
"Christ died for the ungodly" (Romans 5:6).

"But I am lost!"
"Yes," I said, "The Son of Man came to seek and to save the lost" (Luke 19:10).[1]

A person is never so "fit for believing" as when, in himself, he is most unfit.
It is unfitness, not fitness, that is really required.

What is fitness for being washed?
Filth, and filth alone.

What is fitness for receiving alms?
Poverty, abject need.

What is fitness for receiving pardon?
Guilt, and only guilt.

If you are guilty; if you are black; if you are foul, you have all the fitness that is required.
So come and find in Jesus Christ all that meets your greatest and most urgent needs.[2]

> *Come ye sinners, poor and needy,*
> *Weak and wounded, sick and sore.*
> *Jesus, ready, stands to save you,*
> *Full of mercy, love and pow'r!*
>
> *Let not conscience make you linger,*
> *Nor of fitness fondly dream.*
> *All the fitness He requireth,*
> *Is to feel your need of Him!*[3]

[1] From sermon no. 2259, *The Simplicity and Sublimity of Salvation*
[2] Source Unknown
[3] Joseph Hart

GRACE NEVER LEADS TO SIN

Sin will have no dominion over you,
since you are not under law but under grace.
What then? Are we to sin because we are not under law but under grace?
By no means!
ROMANS 6:14–15

The doctrine of grace is never dangerous in the hands of an individual
who has been quickened by the Holy Spirit and created anew in the image of God.
The Spirit of God has come and transformed him,
enlightening his understanding, subduing his will, refining his desires, changing his life.

Love for Jesus burns in the pardoned sinner's breast;
therefore, he feels a burning indignation against the murderous evil of sin.
To him all manner of evil is detestable since it is stained with the Savior's blood.

From the death of Jesus, we understand that sin is exceedingly sinful in God's sight.
If eternal justice could not even spare the well-beloved Jesus when sin was imputed to him,
how much less will it spare guilty men?
Something that can cause such terrible suffering, even to the Holy One, must be unutterably evil!

Nothing can have greater power over gracious minds
than the vision of a crucified Savior
denouncing sin by all his bleeding wounds.

What! Live in the sin that slew Jesus?
What! Find pleasure in that which caused his death?
Impossible!

Free grace, handed down *by a pierced hand,* is never likely to suggest self-indulgence in sin.
The very opposite is true.

The tempted soul
looks to the flowing wounds of his Redeemer,
and thus he becomes strong to resist temptation.

The ever-blessed Spirit also leads believers into seasons of prayer,
and what power is found in the child of grace talking with his heavenly Father!
You cannot live on the mount with God and then come down to live like people of the world.

If you have walked the palace floor of glory
and seen the King in his beauty—
until the light of his countenance has been your heaven—
you cannot be content with the gloom and murkiness of the tents of wickedness.

From sermon no. 1735, *The Doctrines of Grace Do Not Lead to Sin*

OUR FIRST SIGHT OF CHRIST

***"When they look on me, on him whom they have pierced,
they shall mourn for him."***
ZECHARIAH 12:10

The first effect on anyone who has a *true sight of Christ* is that it produces sincere sorrow.

They who behold Christ's wounds are themselves wounded.
They who gaze on his pierced heart are themselves pierced in the heart.
They who see the flowing of his precious blood feel their very heart bleed on account of him,
and all that he endured on their behalf.

A sight of his crucifixion crucifies sin.

*A sight of his death—if it is a true sight—
is the death of all love of sin.*

If, then, you have never been affected by the sorrowful spectacle of the bleeding Savior,
you need to look and look—and look again—until you do feel it, for so it will always be:
"When they look on me, on him whom they have pierced, they shall mourn for him."

There will also come over your soul, when you have a true sight of Christ,
much bitterness over the fact that you have slighted Christ's extraordinary love for you.

This truth will come home to your heart with wonderful power:
He loved *me*, and gave himself for *me*;
for *me* he wore that crown of thorns;
for *me* he endured that terrible flogging;
for *me* he suffered even to death.

Above all, there comes to us the black, bitter thought that *our sin caused his death on the tree.*
The awakened soul sighs, "My sins! My sins! My sins!"

This is the terrible character of sin …
it will imbrue its hands in the blood of him who is perfectly innocent and benevolent;
it will take our best Friend by the throat and condemn him as if he were a felon;
it will nail him to a gibbet and then stand and mock his very death-throes.

*There is nothing on earth so devilish as sin!
Oh, to what extremes of atrocity has sin not gone!*

A sight of the cross, therefore, brings grief to the soul because it shows us what sin is
and what are its ultimate issues and true designs if it could carry them out.
Never do we beat our breast so hard as when we see the cross of Jesus!
When we see what our sin did in murdering the Christ of God, we mourn and grieve for him.

From sermon no. 2683, *The Bitterness of the Cross*

THE GRIEF OF FATHER AND SON

Yet it was the will of the Lord *to crush him; he has put him to grief.*
Isaiah 53:10

Jesus had always dwelt at the Father's side.
But "in the fullness of time," God tore his Son from his very heart and delivered him up for us all.

Herein was matchless, peerless love:
The offended Judge permitted his co-equal Son
to suffer the pains of death
for the redemption of a rebellious people!

For a moment, picture in your mind a scene that took place in ancient times
    as a bearded patriarch rises early in the morning and bids his son arise and follow him.
God has commanded Abraham to take his only son and slay him on the mountain as a sacrifice.

Who can picture the father's anguish as he walks with his beloved son to that place of execution?
Who can imagine the father's grief when his son says to him, "Behold, the fire and the wood, but
    where is the lamb for a burnt offering?"(Genesis 22:7).
Who knows the father's emotions as he replies, "God will provide for himself the lamb."

The father communicates to his son the fact that God has demanded his life,
    and Isaac, who might have escaped, declares that he is willing to die if God has decreed it.
Then the father builds an altar, binds his son's hands behind his back, and lays him on the altar.

Now where is the artist who can depict the anguish on the father's face
    as the knife is unsheathed and he holds it up, ready to slay his son?
But here the curtain falls and the black scene vanishes at the sound of a voice from heaven.
    The ram caught in the thicket supplies the substitute.

Ah! What faith and obedience forced man to do, love constrained God himself to do.
    God had but one Son—his own heart's delight—
        but he covenanted to yield him up for our redemption.
He sent his Son to be born of the Virgin Mary, so that he might suffer for the sins of humanity.

Oh, can you tell the greatness of that love, which made the everlasting God,
    not only put his Son on the altar, but to actually thrust the sacrificial knife into his Son's heart?
He completed in act what Abraham only intended to do.

Dear child of God, come and see the place
where God's only Son hung dead on the cross,
the bleeding victim of awakened justice.

Here we indeed see love
and why it was the will of the Father to crush him!

From sermon no. 173, *The Death of Christ*

AWAKE AND SING!

"Awake, awake, Deborah! Awake, awake, break out in a song!"
JUDGES 5:12

Awake ye children of God and bless his dear name, for does not all nature around you sing?

Does the thunder not praise him as it rolls like drums in the march of the God of armies?
Does the ocean not praise him as it claps its thousands of hands?
Do the mountains not praise him when their shaggy trees wave in adoration?

Does the whole earth have a voice, and will we be silent?
Will man, for whom the world was created—will he be dumb?
No! Let man awake and lead the strain!

When people behold a hero like Garibaldi, who emancipates a nation, they revere and honor him.
And will Jesus, the Redeemer of the multitudes, hear no song?
Will he have no triumphal entry into our hearts?
Will the world love its own and the church not honor its own Redeemer?
No! Our gracious, our tender, our faithful God must be extolled! He must have the best of our songs!

Is it not heaven's employment to praise him?
And what can make earth more like heaven than to be employed in the same work?

Come, believer. When you pray, you are but a human,
     but when you praise God in joyful song, you are like an angel.
When you ask for favors, you are but a beggar,
     but when you extol your God, you become next of kin to cherubim and seraphim.

O Christian, do you ask why you should awake this morning to sing to your God?
What! Are you bought with blood, and yet have a silent tongue?
What! Are you an heir of God and joint heir with Jesus, and yet have no notes of gratitude?[1]

Do we sing as much as the birds do?
Yet what have birds to sing about, compared with us?

Do we sing as much as the angels do?
Yet they have never been redeemed by the blood of Christ.

Birds of the air, will they excel me?
Angels, will you exceed me?

You have done so, but I intend to emulate you,
and day by day, and night by night,
pour forth my soul in sacred song.[2]

[1]From sermon no. 340, *Magnificat*
[2]Source Unknown

FRESH VIEWS OF JESUS

Behold, you are beautiful, my beloved, truly delightful.
Song of Solomon 1:16

Our Beloved is inexpressibly beautiful from every point of view.

Our various experiences are given to us by our heavenly Father
    in order to furnish us with fresh views of the loveliness of Jesus.
Even our trials are pleasant when they take us to where we may gain clearer views of him.

We have seen him from the mountaintops—from Amana, Senir and Hermon (Song of Solomon 4:8)—
    and he has also shone on us like the sun at noonday.
But we have also seen him "from the dens of lions, from the mountains of leopards" (Song of
    Solomon 4:8), and he has lost none of his loveliness.

From the languishing sickbed, and from the borders of the grave,
    we have turned our eyes to our soul's spouse, and he has never been anything but "beautiful."
Many saints have looked on him from the gloom of dungeons, and from the red flames of the stake,
    yet they have never uttered a bad word about him, but died extolling his surpassing charms.

What a noble and pleasant occupation it is to be forever gazing at our sweet Lord Jesus!
    Is it not an unspeakable delight to view the Savior in all his offices
        and to perceive that he is matchless in each?
It is like shifting the kaleidoscope, as it were, and finding fresh combinations of matchless grace.

> *In the manger and in eternity,*
> *on the cross and on his throne,*
> *in the garden and in his kingdom,*
> *among thieves or in the midst of cherubim,*
> *he is everywhere "altogether lovely."*
>
> *Carefully examine every little act of his life*
> *and every trait of his character,*
> *and you will find him as lovely in the minute,*
> *as in the majestic.*

Judge him as you will, you cannot criticize him.
Weigh him as you please, and he will not be found wanting.

Eternity will not discover the shadow of a spot in our Beloved,
    but rather, as ages revolve, his hidden glories will shine forth with even more splendor.
His inexpressible loveliness will more and more ravish all celestial minds.

Morning and Evening, May 22 (E)

HEAVEN'S GREATEST JOY

"Father, I desire that they also, whom you have given me,
may be with me where I am."
JOHN 17:24

That for which Jesus prayed is heaven's *greatest joy.*
Notice that he does not pray that his people might be "where I am," but, *"with me* where I am."
His desire is not for them to just be in heaven, but for them to be *with him* in heaven.

The very heart and core of heaven is to be with Christ.

Heaven without Jesus would be an empty place;
it would be a harp without strings,
a sea without water.

Oh, how we long for that day when we will not see Jesus at a distance, but face to face!
    If it is so wonderful to get even a glimpse of him now and then,
        what will it be to gaze on that blessed face forever?
And we will never have to turn our eyes away from him to look on a world of weariness and woe.

We will not even have weeping eyes to blind us in our vision.
We will have no distractions, since we will have no fields to till and no garments to spin.
We will have no tired feet, no dark distress, no burning thirst, no pangs of hunger.

We will have nothing to do or to think upon,
but forever to gaze on that Sun of Righteousness
with eyes that cannot be blinded,
and with hearts that can never be weary.

Yes, John, you laid your head on your Savior's bosom,
    and I have often envied you,
but I will have your place by-and-by.

Yes, Mary, it was your sweet delight to sit at your Master's feet
    while Martha was cumbered with her much serving.
I, too, am too much cumbered with this world,
    but I will leave my Martha's cares in the tomb and I will sit to hear your Master's voice.

Yes, O bride, you had asked to be kissed with the kisses of his lips,
    and what you asked for, poor humanity will yet experience.
We will place our lips on our Savior—not as Judas did, but with a true, "Hail, Master!"

And then, wrapped in the beams of his love even as a dim star is eclipsed in the sunlight,
    so we will sink into the sweet forgetfulness of ecstasy,
which is the best description we can give of the joys of the redeemed.

From sermon no. 188, *The Redeemer's Prayer*

GRACE ABOUNDING

But where sin increased, grace abounded all the more.
ROMANS 5:20

The place called Calvary is the spot where sin increased, yet it is where grace abounded all the more.

Look in at the council chamber of the Sanhedrin and hear them charge the Son of God with blasphemy. See him hurried away to Pilate's hall and to Herod's judgment seat, "despised and rejected by men."

Behold how they mocked him and how they pulled out his hair!
See how they defiled his face with their accursed spittle and crowned him with thorns!
Observe how they assailed him with insult upon insult and cruelty upon cruelty!
Can you not say that sin increased there?

See him toiling painfully through the crowded streets, ridiculed by the multitude!
Watch him as at last he ascends the hill of doom!
Behold him hanging on the cross in indescribable agony while the heartless spectators jeer!
Can you not say that sin increased there?

What foaming billows of iniquity rolled up around that accursed tree,
swelling and rising until they completely immersed the Lord in their horrible depths!

Yet "where sin increased, grace abounded all the more."

Oh, for an angel's tongue to tell of the wondrous mystery!

How does one describe the grace that so gloriously abounded in our Lord on the cross?—
the grace that flashed so favorably from those languid eyes,
the grace that fell in cleansing drops from those opened veins,
the grace that fell in torrents from that pierced side,
the grace that heaved and tossed and struggled convulsively in those tortured limbs,
the grace that fought and wrestled and at last conquered in that anguished spirit,
the grace that interceded for the transgressors, as Jesus prayed, "Father, forgive them,"
the grace that cried with a mighty voice, "It is finished," before the Savior bowed his head and died.

May it be your happy lot to sail upon that sea of grace,
for it can never be fathomed.

May you drink from that fountain of grace,
for you will never be able to drink it dry.

May God give you the bliss of knowing in your own experience
how much grace abounds through the atoning sacrifice of Christ.

From sermon no. 3304, *Grace Abounding*

A COMPELLING QUESTION

When he entered Jerusalem,
the whole city was stirred up, saying, "Who is this?"
MATTHEW 21:10

I can imagine that memorable night when the angels came to Bethlehem's manger,
    looking with wondering awe upon the newborn child, and whispering, "Who is this?"
Knowing that he was the ever-glorious Son of God, whom they had obediently served,
    they must have marveled to find him there—now an infant—sleeping where the cattle feed.

I can imagine them following him throughout those twelve years of his childhood,
    and during those years when he worked in the carpenter's shop, using the saw and the hammer.
The supernal excellence of his secret life must have compelled them to ask, "Who is this?"

I can imagine them following him throughout the three years of his public ministry …
    seeing him in the wilderness, tempted by the Devil, though he is Lord of all;
    watching him in his sleepless nights on the mountainside, praying;
    beholding him and strengthening him in his agony and bloody sweat in Gethsemane.

I can imagine them gathered around the cross with all its terrors,
    and if their eyes could have known tears, sobbing out the words, "Who is this?"
When he was buried, and after three days rose again from the grave,
    all the angelic host must have been filled with great amazement.

When our Lord ascended on high, leading captivity captive, and clothed with great glory;
    and the angels met him, joined in the triumphal procession and approached the golden gates;
there must have been a lingering wonder among the watchers at the portal of heaven.

They asked, *"Who is this* King of glory?"
    and the answer was, "The LORD, strong and mighty, the LORD, mighty in battle!" (Psalm 24:8).
When they repeated the question, "Who is this King of glory?"
    they received the reply, "The LORD of hosts, he is the King of glory!" (Psalm 24:10).

The angels must marvel, even now …
    that their glorious Lord would have gone down to earth to be born of a woman;
    that he would have actually been tempted by the Devil;
    that he would have known poverty, and nakedness, and death itself.

As the angels observe Jesus with his wounds—his scars—still visible;
    and with his humanity in union with his godhead,
they must still look on him with joyous astonishment, and ask, "Who is this?"

> *If we would spend time in reviewing our Savior's life and death,*
> *we, too, with holy wonder, would be compelled to ask, "Who is this?"*

From sermon no. 3394, *Who Is This?*

GIVING HIS LIFE FOR THE SHEEP

"I am the good shepherd.
The good shepherd lays down his life for the sheep."
JOHN 10:11

Christ has laid down his life for us many times over.

He dwelt as God, inhabiting the praises of eternity, but he laid down that life for us.
To leave heaven's glories for the sorrows and sins of earth—this was laying down his life for the
  sheep.

All the while he lived on earth, Jesus laid down his life for the sheep.

Those prayers on the cold mountainside at night were for his people.
Those earnest pleadings in the midst of the crowd by day were for them.
Those weary journeys, the hunger and the thirst were for them.

Then, *one dark night he laid down his life for his sheep* in the sense, no doubt, intended here.
It was on that dreadful night—you know it!—that night of God's Passover.

The Shepherd went around his flock and the sheep were sleeping,
  but then the howling wolf came and startled the sheep and they all were scattered.
They forsook the Shepherd and fled.

That night, the Good Shepherd confronted the grim monster,
  who had leaped into the fold, thirsty for the blood of the sheep.
The Shepherd caught him to his breast and there was a desperate struggle.

Our Great Shepherd was wounded in his head, his shoulders, his hands, and his feet,
  and one awful fang tore open his side.
But he held the wolf—held him until he had slain him.

Then, dashing his body to the ground and putting his foot on him, he shouted, "It is finished,"
  but at the same moment the Great Shepherd fell.
In slaying our foe, he had himself been slain.

But scarcely had the Shepherd touched the earth than he sprang up again, and he said,
  "The Father loves me, because I lay down my life that I may take it up again" (John 10:17).

Oh, how can you not love him?
Do you not wish to kiss forever those dear wounds?

We must worship this blessed Shepherd who has conquered our foe,
and has delivered us from the jaw of the lion and from the paw of the bear,
and has set us safely forever in his fold.

From sermon no. 2919, *Whose Goodness Faileth Never*

THE GREAT SUBSTITUTION

**For our sake he made him to be sin who knew no sin,
so that in him we might become the righteousness of God.**
2 CORINTHIANS 5:21

Oh, how heaven wondered, how the stars stood still with astonishment,
    and how the angels stayed their song for a moment,
when for the first time, God showed how he might be just and yet be gracious!

*"O sinner," he said, "My heart has devised it!
My Son, the pure and perfect,
will stand in your place and be accounted guilty,
and you, the guilty,
will stand in my Son's place and be accounted righteous!"*

It would make us leap to our feet with astonishment if we understood this thoroughly—
    the wonderful mystery of the transposition of Christ and the sinner!
He came into the world to live as a man, and to die as God.

Now remember the *consequences of this great substitution.*
    The Son of God agreed to be the substitute,
        and God begins with him at his birth by putting him in a manger.
Because he is taking the sinner's place, he is subjected to woe and poverty, from beginning to end.

See him when he has grown to manhood: Grief pursues him and sorrows follow him.
Guilt is imputed to him, and that brings grief with all its horrible reality.
And at last, see death coming with more than its usual horrors.

Mark the grim Prince of Darkness, with all his cohorts, besetting the Savior!
Notice their terrible war on him in the garden as he lies there wallowing in his blood!
See him in Pilate's bar where he is mocked and spit on, tormented, abused, and blasphemed!
Behold him nailed to the cross, while the mocking is continued and the shame unabated!
Mark him crying for water and is given vinegar to drink!

*O God, where are you, that you permit the oppression of the innocent?
Have you ceased to be King of Justice, not shielding the Perfect One?*

*"Be still!" says God, "He is perfect in himself, but he is the sinner now;
he stands in the sinner's place with the sinner's guilt on him.
Therefore, it is right; it is just; it is what he has himself agreed to,
that he should be punished as if he himself were a sinner;
that he should die—unblessed, uncomforted, unowned!"*

Yes, Christ indeed suffered the consequences of that great substitution!

From sermon no. 141, 142, *Substitution*

PRIEST AND VICTIM

He has no need, like those high priests, to offer sacrifices daily,
first for his own sins and then for those of the people,
since he did this once for all when he offered up himself.
HEBREWS 7:27

Here is *the Priest:* "He offered up himself."

Jesus Christ, the Son of God, came into the world and "offered up himself" as a sacrifice for sin.
The Great High Priest, who officiated on the occasion of that unique sacrifice, was Christ himself.

There were wicked men who were the instruments employed in accomplishing his death,
    but after all, the great hand that presented the Lamb of God as the one sacrifice for sin
was the hand of the Christ of God: "He offered up himself."

Our High Priest was not just a delegated or elected priest,
    he was Christ Jesus himself, in whom "the whole fullness of deity dwells bodily" (Colossians 2:9).
Christ—who "is the radiance of the glory of God and the exact imprint of his nature" (Hebrews 1:3)—
    stood at the altar presenting "himself" to God as the one and only sacrifice for sin.

O sinful people, come hither, for here is a sacrifice
that must fully satisfy the demands of the divine law
since Christ himself puts on the priestly garments and offers it to God!

"He offered up himself." That is to say, he voluntarily agreed to be the victim for this sacrifice,
    since Pilate's servants and Herod's soldiers could not have slain him without his own consent.
He, who caused the earth to quake and open when he died, could have buried them in it while he lived.

Our Lord was strong and vigorous, even at the moment of his death.
That glorious shout, "It is finished," came from One who was still in the vigor of his strength.
When he bowed his head it was because he chose to do so: "He offered up himself."

Oh, this makes the sacrifice of Christ so blessed and glorious!

They dragged the bulls and they drove the sheep to the altar;
they bound the calves with cords to the horns of the altar;
but it was not so with the Christ of God.

No one compelled him to die;
he voluntarily laid down his life.

"He offered up himself."

From sermon no. 2693, *Priest and Victim*

WRITTEN WITH TRANSGRESSORS

He poured out his soul to death and was numbered with the transgressors.
ISAIAH 53:12

Our Lord died for sinners; but who would expect that he would be written in the sinners' register? He was not and could not be a sinner; yet it is written that he was numbered with the transgressors.

O sinner, see how close Jesus comes to you!

Is there a census taken of sinners?
Then, in that census, the name of Jesus is written down.

Because Jesus was "numbered with the transgressors,"
   he was treated in the providence of God as transgressors are treated.
Transgression often brings on us poverty, sickness, reproach, and desertion;
   and Jesus had to take his share of all of these with sinful men.

No winds were tempered for this shorn Lamb.
No winter's frost was stayed.
No night dews were dried to comfort his secret agonies.

All things in this world that are so terrible to man, because he is guilty, were just as terrible to Jesus.

The nails that pierced him tore his tender flesh, just like they would have torn that of the sinful.
All his bones were put out of joint by the jolting of the cross when it was uplifted and dashed into
   the earth.
The sun shone on him until his tongue was dried up like a potsherd, and he cried, "I thirst."

There was no softening of the laws of nature for this man, even though he had never offended.
   He had to stand as a sinner—where sinners stand—
      to suffer from the common laws of a sin-cursed world.
In him was no sin, yet he "was numbered with the transgressors."

Sinking and anguish of spirit, and death itself, cannot come upon those who are perfectly righteous.
Because Jesus voluntarily put himself in the sinner's place, he had to bear the sinner's doom.

Being numbered with the transgressors, the justice that smites sin smote him.
The frown that falls on sin fell on him.
The darkness that comes over human sin gathered in sevenfold night about his sacred brow.

Oh, we ought to feel a mingling of grief and joy
when we think of our Lord putting his name down with transgressors!

He took our place so that we might take his place;
he took our sin so that we might take his righteousness.

From sermon no. 2070, *Christ's Connection with Sinners the Source of His Glory*

PRECIOUS WOUNDS

I saw a Lamb standing, as though it had been slain.
REVELATION 5:6

Why will our exalted Lord appear in glory with his wounds?
Because his wounds are to him what they are to us—his glories, his precious jewels.

To the eye of the believer, Jesus is never so precious, never so utterly beautiful,
as when he can say of him, "My beloved is radiant and ruddy" (Song of Solomon 5:10)—
radiant with holiness and ruddy with his own blood.

We may talk of Christ in his beauty as he raised the dead and stilled the tempest,
but oh, nothing can ever match the beauty of Christ as he hung on the cross!
There we behold all his attributes developed, all his love drawn out, and all his character expressed.

His character is expressed in letters so legible
that even a poor stammering heart
can read and speak out those lines
as he sees them written in crimson on the bloodstained tree.

The wounds of Jesus are far more beautiful than all the splendor and pomp of kings!

He no longer wears a thorn-crown, but it was a glorious diadem, such as no monarch has ever worn!
He no longer bears a scepter of reed, but it was far more glorious than a scepter of gold!
He is no longer buffeted and spit on, but he never seems so lovely as when we see him maltreated
for our sakes, enduring all manner of grief, bearing our iniquities, and carrying our sorrows!

Because Jesus finds such beauty in his wounds
he will never renounce them.

He will wear the flesh
in which he courted and wooed our souls,
and he will also wear the royal purple of his atonement
throughout all eternity.

Yes, we will see the man who hung on Calvary's cross;
and though we may occasionally envy the disciples who beheld that sight,
we will have the privilege of seeing our Lord in glory with his wounds still visible.

Oh, what a delight it will be
to behold his face and to lie in his bosom
and to see those dear pierced hands and the wide-open side!

When we have been in heaven for countless ages we will still have the death of our Lord before us.
This will constantly stir up our holy hearts to fresh outpourings of grateful praise.

From sermon no. 254, *The Wounds of Jesus*

OUR SAVIOR'S THIRST

After this, Jesus, knowing that all was now finished, said ... "I thirst."
JOHN 19:28

From the moment that Jesus rose from the Communion Supper,
he had no further refreshment, either of food or of drink.
Yet certainly he needed drink, for all through that long night in Gethsemane he sweat—
we know what kind of sweat—"like great drops of blood falling down to the ground" (Luke 22:44).

He then was hurried away to Caiaphas, and afterwards to Herod and to Pilate,
encountering the terrible accusations, the torture, and the insults of his enemies.
There was a strain put on his system, such as none of us have ever had to endure and never will.
Yet, not one morsel of bread or one drop of water crossed those blessed and parched lips.

You remember, also, the peculiar way in which our Lord was put to death.
Jesus had a double cause for thirst—long fasting without drink, and then the bitter pangs of death.

Now remember that all this was for you;
the nails were driven for you, and he thirsted for you.

Think again of *who* it was, who said, "I thirst." Who was it?

It was he who balanced the clouds and filled the channels of the mighty deep.
He said, "I thirst," and yet in him was a well of water springing up to eternal life.

Yes, he who guided every river in its course, and watered all the fields with grateful showers—
the King of kings and Lord of lords, whom heaven adores and all eternity worships—
he it was who said, "I thirst."

Matchless condescension—from the infinity of God to the weakness of a thirsting, dying man.
He was the perfect and ever blessed God, who stooped so low as to cry as we have done, "I thirst."

Underlying those words, "I thirst," *there is something more than a mere thirst for drink.*
Once, when he sat on the well of Samaria, he said to a poor prostitute, "Give me a drink" (John 4:7).
And he got drink from her—drink that the world knew nothing about when she gave him her heart.

Yes, Christ is always thirsting
for the salvation of precious souls.

He thirsted to redeem mankind;
he thirsted to accomplish the work of our salvation.

This very day, he still thirsts.

From sermon no. 3385, *The Savior's Thirst*

OUR SOUL'S THIRST

After this, Jesus, knowing that all was now finished, said ... "I thirst."
JOHN 19:28

Do you know that we are crucified together with Christ? Well, then, consider his cry, "I thirst."
Does this not mean that we should thirst as well?

Yes, but we do not thirst in the old way wherein we were bitterly afflicted,
for Jesus says that whoever drinks of the water that he gives will never thirst (John 4:14).
Now we covet a new thirst—a refined and heavenly appetite—a craving for our Lord.

O thou blessed Master,
if we are indeed nailed to the tree with you,
give us a thirst that can only be satisfied
by the cup of the New Covenant in your blood!

Next to the actual enjoyment of our Lord's presence, we love to hunger and thirst for him.

Rutherford once said, "I thirst for my Lord and this is joy; a joy which no man takes from me.
Even if I may not come at him, yet shall I be full of consolation, for it is heaven to thirst for him,
and surely he will never deny a poor soul liberty to admire him, adore him, and thirst for him."

As for myself, I would grow more and more insatiable for my divine Lord,
and when I have much of him I would still cry for more, and then for more, and still for more.
My heart will not be content until he is all in all to me, and I am altogether lost in him.

"I thirst"—aye, this is my soul's word with the Lord.
Borrowed from his lips, it also suits my mouth.[1]

Oh, it is a sweet thing to be panting for closer fellowship, for a fuller enjoyment of Jesus' love!

Long ago, someone said, "I have been sinking my bucket down into the well full often,
but now my thirst for Jesus has become so insatiable,
that I long to put the well itself to my lips, and drink right on."[2]

Oh, what a life to sit beside this Well of love,
and drink and sing, and sing and drink!
And then to have desires and soul faculties stretched and extended out
many thousand fathoms in length and breadth
to take in seas and rivers of love.[3]

[1]From sermon no. 1409, *The Shortest of the Seven Cries*
[2]*Morning and Evening*, October 6 (M)
[3]Samuel Rutherford

A WILLING SUFFERER

"Do you think that I cannot appeal to my Father,
and he will at once send me more than twelve legions of angels?"
MATTHEW 26:53

Jesus says, when about to be arrested and bound, "I can presently call down twelve legions of angels."
He had influence with the Father, who would have immediately sent him the inhabitants of heaven.

Think of seraphs at the beck and call of the Man of Sorrows!

He is despised and rejected by men,
and yet angels that excel in strength await his bidding.

There can be no limit to the available resources of the Christ of God.
The band that Judas led would have been swallowed up at once if Jesus had summoned his allies.

Behold, dear saint, the glory of your betrayed and arrested Lord!
    Bear in mind that Jesus in his humiliation was still the Lord of all.
The more clearly you perceive this, the more you will be compelled to admire
    the all-conquering love that took him to the death of the cross.

Our Lord was betrayed into the hands of sinners, but he went with them willingly.
    They flogged him, but they could not have lifted the whip if he had not permitted it,
        and when he died he did not die through the failure of his natural strength.
He died because he had surrendered himself to death as our atoning sacrifice.

A single prayer would have brought our Lord deliverance from his enemies,
    but he was so perfectly submissive, yes, so eager to accomplish our salvation
that he would not pray to avoid the cruelty of his enemies and the bitterness of death.

Our Lord had such a desire for our salvation,
    such a thirst to honor and glorify his Father in the work he had given him to do,
that he would not even prevent his sufferings by a prayer.

Jesus was willing, from beginning to end, to be our suffering Savior.

He was willing to be born at Bethlehem,
    to work at Nazareth,
    to be mocked at Jerusalem,
and at last to die at Calvary.

Jesus—the willing Sufferer—must be a willing Savior.
If he willingly died, he must with equal willingness be ready to give us the fruit of his death.
If he was so willing to become a sacrifice, how willing he must be to share the glorious results of his
    sacrifice with you, and with all who come to God by him.

From sermon no. 1955, *Jesus Declining the Legions*

THE SON GLORIFIED

When Jesus had spoken these words, he lifted up his eyes to heaven, and said,
"Father, the hour has come; glorify your Son that the Son may glorify you."
JOHN 17:1

Christ's petition that he might be glorified was answered during his sufferings.

But was there not ignominy? Yes, he died a felon's death.
Was there not shame? Yes, he was spit on and derided.
Was there not weakness? Yes, he slept in a grave.

It is in his ignominy, shame, and weakness that Jesus is the most honorable, adorable, and strong.
Faith sees a splendor in her crucified Lord that outshines all the previous glories of his eternal
   throne.

The Son of God was glorified in the manner in which he bore our guilt.

He made no angry speeches when he was blindfolded and buffeted and spit on.
He displayed nothing but gentleness, even when his enemies had pierced his hands and feet.
He showed nothing but triumphant pity and almighty love when they mocked his agonies.
He did not free a hand from the cruel tree to crush the scorners, when they cried, "Let him come
   down now from the cross, and we will believe in him" (Matthew 27:42).

The Father glorified his Son by making him—even during his Passion—victorious over all his enemies.

That nailed foot bruised the Serpent's head so that he could never resume his former power.
That nailed hand grasped the serpent of sin and strangled it.
That dying head, as it bowed itself, smote death with its own sword, for by dying he slew death.

O glorious Lord, you have led captivity captive,
making a show of your adversaries openly, even on your cross!
Yes, the Father glorified you while you were suffering the agonies of death.

Besides this, there were some outward signs of Christ's glory in his death.

Did the temple not tear her curtain?
Did the sun not conceal his face?
Did the rocks not open and the dead arise?
Did the centurion not cry, "Truly this was the Son of God!" (Matthew 27:54)?

Yes, the Father glorified his Son even when it was his will to crush him and put him to grief.
With one hand he smote and with the other hand he glorified.
There was a power to crush, but there was also a power to sustain.

The Father glorified his Son.

From sermon no. 1465A, *The Son Glorified by the Father and the Father Glorified by the Son*

A MEMORIAL OF CHRIST

"Do this, as often as you drink it, in remembrance of me."
For as often as you eat this bread and drink the cup,
you proclaim the Lord's death until he comes.
1 Corinthians 11:25–26

This feast of the Lord's Supper is a memorial of Christ, and as such, *it is simple and very significant.*
How clearly it depicts Christ's incarnation!
We take the bread, and that bread which we eat and which becomes assimilated with our flesh,
is the type of the incarnation of the Savior who veiled his glory in our human clay.

The same bread, broken, becomes the type of that body—
that precious body of the Savior, rent and torn with anguish.

We have there the scourge, the nails, the cross—
all set forth by that simple act of breaking the bread.

The wine represents the blood of him who took blood in order to become one blood with us.
Then, being a man, he became "obedient to the point of death, even death on a cross" (Philippians 2:8).

Just as the wine is pressed from the cluster
and poured into the cup,
so Christ's blood was pressed from him in the winepress of divine wrath,
and poured out to make atonement for our sins.

A child, standing by the communion table and asking, "What does this ordinance mean?"
may simply be told, "My child, we break this bread to show how Jesus Christ's body suffered;
and we pour out this wine, illustrating how he poured out his blood for the sins of humanity."

When I take that bread and eat it, and take that cup and drink from it,
I bring to remembrance not only the fact that Christ suffered,
I also remember that he suffered *for me*—that he had an interest *in me.*

The Lord of glory loved *me*, and gave himself *for me.*
That head, now crowned with glory, was once crowned with thorns *for me.*
He whom all heaven worships and adores once hung on the cross in extreme agony *for me.*

Oh, that I could have the cross painted on the pupils of my eyes,
so that I could not see anything
except through the medium of my Savior's Passion!

O Jesus, set yourself as a seal on my hand, as a signet on my arm,
and let me wear the pledge forever
where it is conspicuous to my soul's eye!

From sermon no. 3151, *The Lord's Supper, Simple but Sublime!*

THE BATTLE AS SEEN IN HEAVEN

Then I saw heaven opened, and behold, a white horse!
The one sitting on it is called Faithful and True,
and in righteousness he judges and makes war.
And the armies of heaven, arrayed in fine linen, white and pure,
were following him on white horses.
REVELATION 19:11, 14

The beloved John, above all others, was familiar with the humble Savior.
He had leaned his head on his bosom, and knew the painful beatings of his sorrowful heart.

He could never erase from his memory the suffering image of his Master.
He had seen him that dreadful night when he was covered with a gory sweat in Gethsemane.
He had seen him after he had been buffeted and scourged in Herod's palace and in Pilate's hall.
He had even stood at the foot of the cross and seen him in the extreme agonies of death.

Truly, if John had spoken to us in vision, in symbolic terms,
    regarding what he had seen of his Lord and Master here on earth,
        he would have described him as a footman going forth to fight alone.
No armies would have been following him, because all his disciples had forsaken him and fled.

He would have told us that he wore no glittering armor,
    but with his garments dipped in blood, and with his face smeared with shame,
the solitary Champion fought alone amidst the dust and smoke of the battle.

He would have told us that he fell and bit the dust, causing his foes to rejoice,
    but of how he afterwards leaped up from the grave
and trod down all his adversaries, taking captivity captive.

But now in the passage before us a door was opened in heaven,
    and John saw something he had never seen before or even imagined.
He saw the same warrior Lord, but in a completely different manner.

If John had continued to look at Christ and his followers with the eye of sense,
    viewing the battle on earth as it is seen in history,
he would have said that he saw the same despised and rejected One heading a band of people
    who are equally despised and rejected—leading them into prison and to death.

He would have told us of how the banner of the gospel is borne aloft amid smoke and dust,
    and of how Christ crucified is proclaimed amid contention and ridicule.
But now a door was opened in heaven, and John saw the scene as God sees it.

He looked at it from heaven's point of view,
    and saw the conflict between good and evil, between Christ and Satan, between truth and error.
He saw it in heaven's own clear light, and wrote the vision so that we might also see it,
    and thus our hands might be strengthened for the conflict, our hearts for the fight.

From sermon no. 1452B, *The Rider on the White Horse and the Armies with Him*

WHERE TO LEARN HUMILITY

He humbled himself by becoming obedient to the point of death,
even death on a cross.
PHILIPPIANS 2:8

Jesus is the great Teacher of true humility; we must daily learn from him.
See the Master taking a towel and washing his disciples' feet (John 13:5).

Follower of Christ, will you not humble yourself?
When you see him as the Servant of servants, how can you be proud?

> *The sentence, "He humbled himself,"*
> *offers a summary of Christ's life on this earth.*

> *He stripped off one robe of honor,*
> *and then another,*
> *until naked,*
> *he was fastened to the cross.*

> *There he emptied his innermost self,*
> *pouring out his lifeblood for us all.*

> *Finally, they laid him penniless in a borrowed grave.*

> *How low was our dear Savior brought!*
> *How then can we be proud?*

Stand at the foot of the cross.

Count the purple drops by which you have been cleansed.
See the thorn-crown and Jesus' scourged shoulders gushing crimson.
See his hands and feet given up to the rough iron.
See him mocked and scorned.
See the bitterness, the pangs, and the throes of inward grief shown in his body.
Hear the chilling cry, "My God, my God, why have you forsaken me?" (Matthew 27:46).

If you do not lie prostrate before the cross, you have never seen it.
You were so lost that nothing could save you but the sacrifice of God's only beloved Son.
Think of that, and as Jesus stooped for you, bow in lowliness at his feet.

May the Lord bring us in contemplation to Calvary.
    There our position will no longer be that of pompous pride,
        but we will take the humble place of one who loves much because much has been forgiven.
Pride cannot live beneath the cross, so let us kneel there and learn.

Morning and Evening, June 3 (E)

THE OBJECT OF FAITH

*If you confess with your mouth that Jesus is Lord
and believe in your heart that God raised him from the dead, you will be saved.*
Romans 10:9

It is evident that Jesus Christ, dead and risen, is the foundation of faith.
The *object of faith* is the most important subject for our contemplation.

There are many who think too much of their faith
    and too little of the object of their faith.
They question whether their faith is strong enough,
    instead of looking to see whether their faith is resting on a right foundation.

The whole foundation upon which faith rests is …
    Christ living in the flesh,
    Christ dying in that flesh,
    Christ rising from the dead,
    Christ pleading in glory on behalf of sinners.

Not even a hairbreadth of faith's foundation is found outside of Jesus Christ.

Faith does not build on its own experience.
It does not build on any merit that it fancies it has procured by long and ardent service.
It does not rest on any of its own graces, raptures, fights, or prayers.
Its cornerstone is Christ Jesus.

Mainly, Faith looks to Christ offering himself up for us on the tree.

She stands at the foot of the cross,
    watching that mysterious, that matchless spectacle—God made flesh, bleeding and dying.
She sees the Son of God enveloped in pain, rent with agony, obedient even to death.

She watches him with the expectancy of hope and the emotion of gratitude,
    both of which bring the tears streaming down her cheeks.
She hears the expiring Sin-Bearer cry with a loud voice, "It is finished," and she adds a glad amen.

She believes there is …
    enough in those wounds to wash away her sin,
    enough in that sacrifice to avert the thunders of an angry God,
    enough in that righteousness to cover her from head to foot and win the smile of infinite Justice.

*Oh, blessed cross, you are the one pillar of our consolation!
Faith builds her all on this cornerstone.*

From sermon no. 519, *Believing With the Heart*

OUR LORD'S PRIVATE THOUGHTS

He took the twelve disciples aside, and on the way he said to them,
"See, we are going up to Jerusalem.
And the Son of Man will be delivered over to the chief priests and scribes,
and they will condemn him to death and deliver him over to the Gentiles
to be mocked and flogged and crucified, and he will be raised on the third day."
MATTHEW 20:17–19

We will not be presumptuous if we humbly ask, "What were Christ's private thoughts at that time?"
We may be sure that what he shared with his disciples was the outcome of his innermost meditations.

Our Lord was forecasting his death in all its mournful details,
    and it is frequently more painful to anticipate death than it is to actually die.
Yet Jesus dwelt upon his sufferings even to the minute details.

The shadow of his death was upon him before he reached the tree of doom.
In his thoughts he was already enduring the agonies of the cross.
Yet he did not put away the thought, but dwelt upon it as one who tastes a cup before he drinks it.

He knew that the Father would bruise him and put him to grief in the approaching day of his anger.
He knew that the wicked would pierce his hands and feet.
He knew all that would occur, but he did not back away from the pledge he had given in the council
    chamber of eternity that his life would be rendered up as a ransom for sinful men.

While our Lord was thinking of his death, *he also had an eye on those for whom he would suffer.*
    Out of his strong love for us—even for us—he determined to pay our ransom price in death,
        but he made a voluntary offering of himself even before he died.
He surrendered himself in purpose before his body was actually offered up on the cross.

Then there naturally came into his mind *the grand sequel of it all: He would rise again!*
On the third day it would all be over and the recompense would begin.

A few hours of bitter grief—
    a night of bloody sweat,
    a night and a morning of mockery when he would be flouted by the profane,
    a direful afternoon of deadly anguish on the cross and of dark desertion by Jehovah—
and then the bowing of the head and rest in the grave for his body, and on the third day the light
    would break upon mankind, for the Sun of Righteousness would rise with healing in his wings!

Oh, what must have been the meditations of our Lord!

How precious are your thoughts toward us, O Christ!
How great is the sum of them!
Wonderful things you pondered in your soul
on those dark days of your approaching agony!

From sermon no. 2212, *The Private Thoughts and Words of Jesus*

ABIDING IN FELLOWSHIP

"Abide in me."
JOHN 15:4

What is the true position of a believer?

It is that of a sheep abiding close to its shepherd.
It is a state of perpetual communion with our Lord Jesus.

We need fellowship with Jesus, not as a luxury for red-letter days and Sabbaths,
    but as the necessary provision for every day of our lives.
"Abide in me" is his word to us for all seasons and we should strive to realize it.
    Always, by night and by day, on the Sabbath and on the weekdays, we should abide in him.

In wondrous love Jesus has called himself our husband and has taken us to be his bride,
    and would that not be a strange love—or lack of it—
that would allow a married couple to walk together day by day without the fellowship of affection?

If we wish to have happiness,
where is it to be found but in walking close to Jesus?

Heaven on earth is nearness to Christ.
Fellowship with him is paradise without a serpent in it;
    it is Canaan itself without the Canaanitish foe.

Communion with Jesus is the porch of glory,
    the dawn of the heavenly day.

Communion with Christ—if it is not actually heaven—
    is certainly the choicest suburb of the New Jerusalem.[1]

Oh, the joy of entering into fellowship with Christ in such a way that we never lose his company!

His shadow may fall on us as we rest in the sun or walk in the garden.
His voice may cheer us as we lie down on the seashore and listen to the murmuring waves.
His presence may glorify the mountain solitude as we climb the hills.
Jesus may be to us an all-surrounding presence, lighting up the night, perfuming the day,
    gladdening all places, and sanctifying all pursuits.

Our Beloved is the inseparable Companion of his loving disciples,
    so let fellowship with him be the atmosphere of your life, the joy of your existence.
This will give you a heaven below and prepare you for a heaven above.[2]

[1]From sermon no. 1149, *My Restorer*
[2]From sermon no. 3295, *Communion with Christ and His People*

ONLY ONE TRUE KING

Your eyes will behold the king in his beauty;
they will see a land that stretches afar.
ISAIAH 33:17

"The king"—a sweet title that belongs to our Lord Jesus Christ as his exclusive prerogative.
Yes, there are other kings now, but theirs is only a temporary title.
Our Lord Jesus is the real King—the King of kings—the King who reigns forever and ever!

Oh, tell us not of emperors! There is but one Imperial brow!
Tell us not of monarchs, for the crown belongs to the blessed and only Potentate!
He alone is King! As such we think of him and long for his appearing!

Note well the promise, "Your eyes will see the king in his *beauty*."
Does this not suggest to us that the King has been seen, though not in his beauty?

Yes, he was seen on earth as the prophet foretold: "despised and rejected by men; a man of sorrows,
    and acquainted with grief" (Isaiah 53:3).
It was also said of him: "He had … no beauty that we should desire him" (Isaiah 53:2).
Many were astonished, for his appearance was "marred, beyond human semblance" (Isaiah 52:14).

Oh, that was in the day of his humiliation, but we are yet to see the King in his beauty!
What grandeur to behold! The sight will overwhelm us!

No doubt the words of this text originally had a timely, and a strictly literal meaning for the people
    of Jerusalem. When the city was besieged by Sennacherib, the inhabitants saw Hezekiah in garbs
    of mourning. How he had rent his clothes in grief and sorrow!

But the day would come, according to prophecy, when Sennacherib must fall and then there would
    be a time of liberty. The people would be able to travel to the utmost ends of Palestine and see a
    land that stretches afar. Hezekiah would come out in his robes of majesty on a joyful occasion to
    praise the Lord, and thus the people would see the king in his beauty.

That was the original meaning of the text, but it bears an even greater meaning for all people.

By faith, have we not seen our King in his robes of mourning?
Have we not seen Jesus in the sorrowful weeds of affliction and humiliation?

Our faith has gazed on him in the rent garments of his Passion.
We have beheld him in his agony and bloody sweat, in his crucifixion and death.

Well, now, another and brighter view awaits us:
Our eyes will one day see the King in a more glorious array.
We will behold the King in his beauty, and then we will enter and enjoy "a land that stretches afar."

From sermon no. 3542, *A Precious Promise for a Pure People*

STRONGER THAN DEATH

Love is as strong as death.
SONG OF SOLOMON 8:6 NKJV

What a well-chosen comparison! Other than love, what is stronger than death?
With steadfast foot Death marches throughout the world.

> *Everywhere and in every place beneath the moon you have full sway, O death!*
> *None among the sons of Adam can withstand your insidious advances.*

> *The most ardent prayers cannot move the flinty stroke of death.*
> *That scythe is never blunted; that hourglass never ceases to flow.*

But Christ's love is as strong as death, for who can stand against the strength of his love?

When the bride says that Christ's love is as strong as death,
   she may have foreseen that it would one day be tried as to which was the strongest.
These two once entered into a desperate struggle—a struggle that angels gazed on in amazement!

Jesus, incarnate Love, at first seemed to be overcome by Death.
You remember how "his sweat became like great drops of blood falling down to the ground."
You remember how his back was plowed, his hands were pierced, and his side was opened.

Oh! Death thought that it had gained the victory, but Jesus triumphed gloriously!
Love reigned, while Death lay prostrate at his feet.

Jesus' love was indeed as strong as Death, for he swallowed up Death in victory;
   he not only overcame it, but seemed to devour it!
"O Death," said Love, "I will be thy plague! O grave, I will be thy destruction!"
   And Love has kept its word and proved itself to be "as strong as Death."[1]

> *Oh! Christ's love was indeed stronger than the most terrible death,*
> *for it endured the trial of the cross triumphantly!*

> *It was a lingering death, but love survived the torment!*
> *It was a shameful death, but loved survived the shame!*
> *It was an unrighteous death, but love bore our iniquities!*
> *It was a forsaken and lonely death from which the Father hid his face,*
> *but love endured the curse and triumphed over all!*

> *Never has there been such love; never such death!*
> *It was a desperate duel, but love was victorious!*[2]

[1]From sermon no. 364, *The Shulamite's Choice Prayer*
[2]*Morning and Evening*, October 13 (E)

HOW TO SEE CHRIST'S GLORY

And the Word became flesh and dwelt among us,
and we have seen his glory.
JOHN 1:14

But you answer, "How can we see Christ's glory now, today?"

Well, faith sees it.
Faith looks back to the man who lived and died for us, and sees glory in his shame, honor in his disgrace, riches in his poverty, triumph in his conflict, and immortality in his death.

And faith is also assisted by communion.

Hopefully, you know what it means …
to be alone in your room with Christ, with your eyes beholding him alone;
to kneel down, taking the same position he took as he agonized in Gethsemane;
to see by fellowship the sweat of blood as it streams from every pore of his body;
to see him rise as men carrying swords and clubs approach him, seize him, and bind him;
to see him ridiculed and hounded through the streets as he is taken to Calvary to die.

Communion gives us some understanding …
of the bitterness of that cup which the Savior drank;
of the sharpness of those nails that pierced his hands and feet;
of the agonies of that death which he endured for our sakes.

Yes, communion can show us Christ's glory, even in his shame,
and then it can take to its wings and show us his glory beyond the skies.
Each one of us may behold his glory, past and present.

Ah, these eyes of mine have never seen the Savior, but my heart has seen him.
These lips have never kissed his cheek, but my soul has kissed him.

In the spirit, I may have the same access to Christ as did John the beloved;
and this rich enjoyment may be obtained by all who seek it.
This very day, we may have actual fellowship with the Father and with his Son Jesus Christ.

Oh, this is a joy worth worlds!

O pleasures of the world, ye would cease your endeavors to tempt us
if you knew—as we do—the sweeter pleasures of Christ's face!

O thunders of the world, ye would cease your attempts to frighten us
if you knew—as we do—the sweet solace that is found in Christ!

Yes, we have seen Christ's glory, though not as fully as those who are kneeling before his throne.

From sermon no. 414, *The Glory of Christ Beheld!*

A PERSONAL TESTIMONY

***And the Word became flesh and dwelt among us, and we have seen his glory,
glory as of the only Son from the Father, full of grace and truth.***
JOHN 1:14

We who have seen Christ's glory have a testimony to bear,
   so let me bear my testimony of what my own eyes have seen, of what my own ears have heard,
and of what my own heart has tasted—that Christ *is the only Son from the Father.*

He is divine to me even if he is only human to the rest of the world.
He has done for me what only a God could do.

He has subdued my stubborn will and has melted my heart of stone.
He has broken my prison bars and has set this captive free.
He has turned my mourning into laughter and my desolation into joy.

I also bear testimony that he is *full of grace.*

He drew me when I struggled to escape from his grace,
      and when at last I came trembling like a condemned culprit to his mercy seat,
         he said, "Your sins which are many are all forgiven you. Be of good cheer."
Oh, let others despise him, but I bear witness that he is full of grace!

And as he is full of grace, so he is *full of truth.* Not one of his promises has failed.

I bear witness that …
      a servant has never had a better master than I have;
      a bride has never had such a husband as Christ has been to my soul;
      a sinner has never had a better Savior;
      a mourner has never had a better comforter than Christ has been to me.

I want no one but him.

In life, he is my life;
in death, he will be the death of death;
in poverty, Christ is my riches;
in sickness, he makes my bed;
in darkness, he is my star;
in brightness, he is my sun.

He is my manna as I camp in the wilderness,
   and he will be my new corn when I come to Canaan.
He is the Rock on which I now rest, and he is the Rock in which I will dwell forever.

From sermon no. 414, *The Glory of Christ Beheld*

MAJESTY IN MISERY

Now the men who were holding Jesus in custody were mocking him as they beat him.
They also blindfolded him and kept asking him, "Prophesy! Who is it that struck you?"
LUKE 22:63–64

Here we see perfect, infinite, unutterable goodness beaten, bruised, assailed, assaulted!

The blessed Son of God who stood there
    had within his soul that mercy which endures forever;
yet these men mocked him!

He did not come here on an errand of vengeance,
    but to bring peace and goodwill to men, and to set up a kingdom of joy and love;
yet they beat him!

His eyes flamed with love,
    and there gleamed in them bright diamonds of pity for all the sorrows of humanity;
        yet those cruel men hid those precious eyes of his.
They blindfolded the Christ of God!

His face is far brighter than the sun that lights up the world.
    There is nothing under heaven, or in heaven itself,
        that can rival the face of the Well-beloved.
Yet these men struck it!

How the angels must have quivered with horror
    when hearing for the first time that men had struck the face of their Lord!
It was but his human face, it is true, but therein they struck at all of Deity.
    It was man hitting God in the face!

It is not within the compass of lips of clay to describe the condescending sufferings of him who,
    though he was called "Mighty God, Everlasting Father, Prince of Peace" (Isaiah 9:6),
nevertheless stooped so low as to be mocked, beaten, and blindfolded for our sakes!

What a marvel it is that the God, who had reigned in glory over myriads of holy angels,
    would allow himself to be mocked by vile wretches who could not have lived
        an instant longer in his presence if he had not permitted them to do so.
He who was the Creator of all things allowed himself to be treated with the utmost cruelty.

This is one of those great mysteries of the faith that will always stagger us.

We believe it without the slightest hesitation;
yet, the more we try to grasp it, the more it eludes us.

From sermon no. 2825, *Majesty in Misery*

LOVING A REAL CHRIST

You whom my soul loves.
Song of Solomon 1:7

When we read this text, we are struck with the reality of this love.

Did you notice that the bride is addressing Christ, not as an abstraction, but as a person? He is a real person to her: "You whom my soul loves."

These seem to be the words of someone …
    who is pressing her beloved to her bosom;
    who sees him with her eyes;
    who tracks him with her feet;
    who knows that he is, and that he will reward the love that diligently seeks him.

Yes, we must realize the person of Christ.

We must view our Lord as being as real a person as we are ourselves—
    very man—
    a man who could suffer;
    a man who could die;
    substantial flesh and blood.

We fail in our love because Christ is not as real to us as he was to the early church.
    They preached Christ more than they preached doctrine.
They did not dwell on the truths about Christ, but on Christ himself—his hands, his feet, his side, his eyes, his head, his crown of thorns, the sponge, the vinegar, the nails.

Oh, for the Christ of Mary Magdalene
rather than the Christ of the critical theologian!

Give me the wounded body of divinity
rather than the soundest system of theology.

We want Christ—not an abstract, doctrinal, pictured Christ, but a real Christ.

Until we can feel that he is a real man, a real person, really present with us,
    and that we may speak to him, telling him of all our wants and desires,
        we will not readily attain a love like that of the text.
We will not be able to say to our Lord, "You whom my soul loves."

O believer, pray that you may know a love which realizes Christ,
and that can address him as "you whom my soul loves."

From sermon no. 338, *Love to Jesus*

CONSOLATION IN HIS SORROWS

A man of sorrows, and acquainted with grief.
Isaiah 53:3

Look at the term, "a man of sorrows."
Now in the Bible there is the expression, "the man of sin."
What does "the man of sin" mean, but that a man is made up of sin—one who is all sin.

Well, then, "a man of sorrows" means a man made up of sorrows—
    sorrows from the crown of his head to the sole of his foot.
He has sorrow without and sorrow within.

Take the next expression, "and acquainted with grief."

When you see our Lord in Gethsemane, pressed by the strong arm of grief
    until he is covered all over with a gory shirt of bloody sweat,
then you know that he has been acquainted with grief's desperate tugs.

When you see him bleeding at his hands and feet and side,
    with his spirit crushed as his Father leaves him in the thick darkness,
then you know that he was indeed acquainted with grief![1]

Yet, as great as our Lord's sufferings were, they are to be looked upon with sacred triumph.

Our Savior is no longer in Gethsemane, agonizing, or on the cross, dying.
The crown of thorns has been replaced by many crowns of sovereignty.
The nails and the spear have given way to the scepter.

> *The suffering is ended, but the blessed results never end.*
> *Our Redeemer now beholds the success of all his labors.*

Let it never be forgotten that the subject of our Savior's sorrows
    has brought more comfort to mourners than any other theme in revelation.
Even the glories of Christ do not afford such consolation to the afflicted as the sufferings of Christ.

There is no remedy for sorrow beneath the sun like the sorrows of Emmanuel.
Even as Aaron's rod swallowed up all the other rods, so Christ's grief makes our grief disappear.
We can bear poverty, slander, contempt, or bodily pain, or death itself, because our Lord has borne it.

> *If there is consolation anywhere,*
> *surely it is to be found in the delightful presence of the Crucified![2]*

[1]From sermon no. 2573, *Unparalleled Suffering*
[2]From sermon no. 1099, *The Man of Sorrows*

A PRESENT JUSTIFICATION

Whoever believes in him is not condemned.
JOHN 3:18

You are aware that in our courts of law, a verdict of "not guilty"
    amounts to an acquittal and the prisoner is immediately discharged.
So it is in the gospel: The words "not condemned" imply the justification of the sinner.
    It means that the believer in Christ receives a *present* justification.

Faith does not produce this fruit in the future, but right *now*.
Justification is the result of faith and is given the very moment you accept Christ as your all in all.

The thief on the cross was justified the moment he turned the eye of faith to Jesus.
Paul, the aged, after years of service, was no more justified than was the thief with no service at all.

Today we are accepted in the Beloved.
Today we are absolved from sin.
Today we are innocent in the sight of God.

Oh, ravishing, soul-transporting thought!

There are some clusters of Eshcol's vine (Deuteronomy 1:24-25)
    that we will not be able to gather until we enter heaven;
    but this is a bough that runs over the wall to us now.

This is not like the corn that cannot be eaten until we cross the Jordan.
Justification is part of our manna in the wilderness.
It is a portion of our daily sustenance as we journey on our way to heaven.

We are *now*—even *now*—pardoned.
Even *now* our sins are put away.
Even *now* we stand in the sight of God as though we had never sinned.

We are as innocent as father Adam before he had eaten the forbidden fruit.
We are as pure as if we had never received the taint of depravity in our veins.

"There is therefore *now* no condemnation for those who are in Christ Jesus" (Romans 8:1).

Even *now* there is not one sin in the Book of God against any of his people,
    for it is written, "Who shall bring any charge against God's elect?" (Romans 8:33).
In the sight of the Judge of all the earth, there is neither speck, nor spot, nor wrinkle,
    nor any such thing remaining on any believer.

From sermon no. 362, *None But Jesus—Second Part*

DRINKING OF THE MUDDY WATERS?

"What do you gain by going to Egypt to drink the waters of the Nile?"
JEREMIAH 2:18

Jehovah had proven to be worthy of Israel's trust, yet they forsook him to follow after false gods. The Lord frequently reproved them for this infatuation.

Our text contains but one instance of God earnestly reasoning with them. It may be translated: "What do you gain by going to Egypt to drink the waters of the muddy river? Why do you leave that which is good and healthy to follow after that which is evil and deceitful?"

O true believer, called by grace and washed in Christ's precious blood,
why are you going to Egypt to drink of the muddy waters?

Swine eat husks and sinners wallow in sin,
but what are you doing who are renewed in the image of God?

Oh look! There is a crowd yonder! They have evidently assembled for a riotous purpose. Yes, they are attacking a man! Pressing through the crowd, I see that the man's appearance is "marred, beyond human semblance" (Isaiah 52:14). It is indeed he! It is the Crucified One! It is none other than Jesus, the Savior!

Listen to the blasphemies that are poured in his ears!
See how they spit in his face and hold him up to contempt!
Hear them cry, "Crucify him, crucify him, crucify him!"

They are doing it! They have nailed him to the tree! Standing over him is a man with the hammer in his hand, who has just now driven in the nails. Looking around at the mob, I see all manner of people of infamous reputation. But oh, there is one man over there whose face looks very familiar. Ah yes! I have seen him before. I have seen him on his knees in prayer, pleading what he called "the precious blood." What is he doing here in this unparalleled scene of sin and crime?

Are you sickened at heart at such a spectacle—a Christian crucifying Christ? Whenever you turn your back on him, you are crucifying him once again, and holding him up to contempt (Hebrews 6:6).

O Christian, you have tasted a much better drink
than can be had from the muddy waters of this world's pleasure!

You have had precious fellowship with Jesus;
you have had the joy of seeing him,
and of leaning your head on his bosom.
Can the trifles, the songs, and the laughter of this world
satisfy you after that?

You have eaten the bread of angels,
and can you now live on husks?

From sermon no. 356, *Words of Expostulation*

WHO CAN DESCRIBE LOVELINESS?

Yes, he is altogether lovely.
SONG OF SOLOMON 5:16 NKJV

Loveliness—we feel its power and we become its slaves,
  but we cannot write, even with a pen of lightning, a description of what it is.
How, then, can I—enamored, entranced, enraptured with him who is altogether lovely—
  how can I find words, terms, expressions that will adequately portray him?

Besides, were I baffled by nothing else, there is this: The beauty of Christ is mysterious.
It surpasses all the comeliness of human form.

Have you ever gazed with complete satisfaction on the work of any painters
  who have tried to picture the loveliness of our Lord Jesus Christ?
How can they photograph the sun?

When the brightness of the Father's glory is the subject, the canvas glows in vain.
Who can ever depict Immanuel, "God with us" (Matthew 1:23)?[1]

Yes, the person of Christ strikes eloquence dumb when it would describe him.
It paralyzes the artist's arm when with fair colors he would portray him.
It is beyond the sculptor to carve his image even in a massive block of diamond.

There is nothing in nature comparable to him;
  before his radiance the brilliance of the sun is dimmed.
Nothing can compete with him, and heaven itself blushes at its own plainness of countenance
  when his "altogether lovely" person is beheld!

Ah, you who pass him by without regard, it is well said by Rutherford:

> *Oh, if ye knew him, and saw his beauty,*
> *your love, your heart, your desires*
> *would close with him and cleave to him.*

> *Love by nature, when it sees,*
> *cannot but cast out its spirit and strength upon amiable objects,*
> *and good things, and things love-worthy;*
> *and what fairer thing is there than Christ?*[2]

[1]From sermon no. 1446, *The Best Beloved*
[2]*The Saint & His Saviour*

HIS THRONE ENDURES FOREVER

His throne shall be established forever.
1 CHRONICLES 17:14

Monarchs may die and crumble back to dust, and their empires with them,
but the throne of the Son of David will endure forever and ever.
No acts of senators, nor decrees of tyrants, nor raging of the multitude, nor foaming of rebels
can interfere in the least degree with the supreme power of Jesus of Nazareth.

His very cross proclaimed him King, and King he is!

*He who suffered death for our sakes
is now crowned with supreme glory and honor.*

All things this day bow before the Lord Jesus, willingly or unwillingly.
That heel that once was bruised when the Serpent wounded it
has crushed the Dragon's head, and he now holds it down upon the earth.
Life and death and worlds unknown lie in subjection to him who lives but who once was dead.

*Great princes have their heralds
who with blasts of trumpet proclaim their honors and dignities;
but who will proclaim the glories of the Son of Man
who once laid down his life for our sins?*

We have heard of wounded men, crushed amid a heap of bleeding bodies, lying on the battlefield,
rousing all the life that remained when they saw the great Napoleon come riding over the plain.
With their legs gone they raised themselves upon their arms in order to salute their captain.

If such poor souls could pay such homage to the one who shed their blood like water,
then how much greater should be our homage to the One who purposely shed his blood for us?[1]

*Oh, let us praise him! Let us extol him!
Down with all our idols! Up with the Lord Jesus!
Let the standards of pomp and pride be trampled underfoot,
but let the cross of Jesus be lifted on high!*

*Oh, for a throne of ivory for our King!
Let him be set on high forever,
and let my soul sit at his footstool
and kiss his feet, and wash them with my tears!*[2]

[1]From sermon no. 1928, *Our Ascended Lord*
[2]*Morning and Evening*, September 29 (E)

WHO IS THIS?

Who is this who comes from Edom, in crimsoned garments from Bozrah,
he who is splendid in his apparel, marching in the greatness of his strength?
ISAIAH 63:1

The prophet beholds in vision the Captain of our salvation returning from battle.
He beholds the majestic march of this mighty Conqueror, and he cries, "Who is this?"

"Who is this?" is a question we all may ask, for none of us fully know our Lord Jesus.
Paul, after he had known Christ for fifteen years, still desired that he might know him.

Now if this passage does indeed refer to our Savior's resurrection,
    it is a remarkable truth that even his disciples did not know him after he had risen.
Mary Magdalene ought to have known him, but she thought he was the gardener,
    and the two disciples who walked with him to Emmaus did not know him either.

Would it not have been marvelous, if discerning him, they had said:

"Who is this? Behold him marching in the greatness of his strength, and yet just a few hours ago we
    saw him dead and helped to lay his lifeless body in Joseph's tomb!"

"Who is this? We just saw him stripped! They took his garments from him at the cross, and now he
    is 'splendid in his apparel.'"

"Who is this? His enemies spit in his face and nailed him to the tree, but now his garments are
    crimsoned with the blood of his foes, and he comes back as a conqueror!"

The question ends, "Who is this, *marching in the greatness of his strength?*"

Our Lord did not come back feeble and wounded from slaughtering our enemies.
He returned in a majestic march.
He returned as a victor who would have everyone know that his force is irresistible.

The earth shook beneath Christ's feet at his resurrection, for there was a great earthquake.
The Roman guards "became like dead men" (Matthew 28:4) at his appearing.

O sinner, the Lord Jesus Christ is no petty, puny Savior!
He is marching to meet poor sinners,
but he is marching in the greatness of his strength!

As he marches through the nations, it is as a strong man,
mighty to rescue every soul that puts its trust in him!

From sermon no. 1947, *Who Is This?*

WHY IS HE RED?

Who is this who comes from Edom, in crimsoned garments from Bozrah,
he who is splendid in his apparel, marching in the greatness of his strength? ...
Why is your apparel red, and your garments like his who treads in the winepress?
ISAIAH 63:1–2

In vision, the prophet observes the color of the Conqueror's garments.

Originally, red was not Christ's color,
     for we are told that his garments are "radiant, intensely white" (Mark 9:3).
Hence the question arises, "Why is your apparel red?"

The glory of Christ's purity is such that we say to ourselves:

"Red—why, that is the color of Edom, the adversary."
"Red—that is the color of the earth, of our humanity."
"Red—that is the color of our scarlet sins."

Why is he red?

Although the text indicates that he is red with the blood of his adversaries,
     we must also think of our Lord as being red with the literal shedding of his own blood.
It was in this way that his victory was accomplished.

The text depicts the result of that blood-shedding in the overthrow of his enemies and ours.
     When our Lord's own blood was shed,
          sin and death and Hades were trodden down and destroyed like grapes in the winepress.
When he was suffering, he was striking down his enemies.

By the shedding of his own blood, he was shedding the blood of his foes.
     The life of the powers of darkness was taken away by his blood.
When we see Jesus coming back—literally covered with his own blood—
     we discern him spiritually as crimsoned with the slaughter of evil and its abettors.

Oh, our Lord never looks so lovely as when he appears as "a Lamb that has been slain"!
In his red colors he is in the prime of his beauty.
Of all his royal garments, that crimson vest is the most kingly.

Glory to the bleeding Christ!
If there is one hallelujah louder than any other,
let it be to him who wears the garment dipped in blood!

Behold the colors of atonement,
for they are the ensigns of eternal victory!

From sermon no. 1947, *Who Is This?*

WHY IS HE RED?

FATHER AND SON ARE FOR US

If God is for us, who can be against us?
ROMANS 8:31

It is impossible for us to express the full meaning of this delightful phrase, "God is for us."

He was for us before the worlds were made.
He was for us or he would not have given us his well-beloved Son.
He was for us when he struck his Son and laid the full weight of our penalty on him.
He was for us or he would not have brought us humbly to seek his face.

> *Arrayed in all the attributes that make him God,*
> *he is always for us,*
> *and "if God is for us, who can be against us?"*

And oh, how sweetly God the Son has been for us!

We see him lifting that face all covered with bloody sweat
  and saying to us, "I am for you. I am sweating these great drops of blood in order to redeem you."

We see him carrying the cross upon his raw, bleeding shoulders,
  and every painful step he takes is to the tune, "I am for you, poor sinner."

We behold him bleeding on the tree with outstretched hands,
  and all his wounds dripping with blood, are saying, "Christ is for you."

Today as Christ pleads before the eternal throne,
  this is the tenor of his plea: "I am for you."

When he comes a second time to receive his children home,
  the mighty Advent trumpet will ring out, "Christ is for you, O ye blood-bought saints!"

> *Believer, Christ cannot be against you.*
> *You cannot look into that dear face of his*
> *and think that he would ever leave you.*
>
> *Would he have bought you at such a price;*
> *would he have suffered so much for you and yet forsake you?*
>
> *So Christian, whoever may be against you, here is comfort:*
> *God the Father and God the Son can never be against you.*
> *They are eternally and immutably for you,*
> *and if that is so, who can be against you?*

From sermon no. 580, *God Is With Us*

"JESUS ONLY" IS OUR HEAVEN

Jesus only.
MARK 9:8

What do I hope to have in heaven?
I may answer in the words of my text, "Jesus only."

"Whom have I in heaven but you?
And there is nothing on earth that I desire besides you" (Psalm 73:25).

Do not be deceived by the poet's visionary heaven
    where he tells you of a heaven of the intellect; a heaven of imagination.
Do not be carried away like children by such a fictitious paradise
    for the heaven of your heart, and the only heaven that can satisfy it, is "Jesus only."

To lie in his embrace,
to be forever steeped in the ocean of his grace,
to know his heart,
to behold his countenance,
to admire his beauties,
to be swallowed up in his glory—
this is the highest ambition of the believer.

There is nothing in heaven that is equal to Christ.

There is no flower in all the gardens of paradise
    that blooms with such loveliness as the Altogether Lovely.

There will be no gem adorning the crowns of the glorified
    that will glisten so gloriously as the eye of Christ.

There is no splendor in the realms of paradise, however godlike and divine,
    that is half as majestic as that head of his,
that head with its locks that "are wavy, black as a raven" (Song of Solomon 5:11).

O sinner, are you panting for this heaven?

Remember, there is only one ladder that can take you there,
and that ladder is called Jesus.
The foot rests on the earth in his humanity,
and the top leans in heaven on his godhead.

"Jesus only" is our one hope of heaven.

From sermon no. 2634, *Jesus Only—A Communion Meditation*

ENGRAVED IN HIS HANDS

"Behold, I have engraved you on the palms of my hands."
ISAIAH 49:16

"Behold," *is a word of wonder,* and its intention is to excite admiration.
Here indeed is a theme for marveling!

Heaven and earth may well be astonished
    that a holy God would have engraved on his hands the names of sinners,
        that rebels would attain such a closeness to his heart
    as to actually be written on the very palms of his hands!

The word "engraved" depicts the perpetuity of the inscription.

It is engraved, not into the hand of man, but into the hand of God.
It is engraved, dug into that immortal and eternal hand.

Our engravers press down on their tools,
    saying how stern the labor is that cuts each mark into the hard metal.
And God—with the whole strength of omnipotence—
    has leaned down on the tool in order to cut our names into his own flesh.

Was there not such an engraving at Calvary?
Is it not written, "It was the will of the LORD to crush him; he has put him to grief" (Isaiah 53:10)?[1]

Yes, the engraver's tool was the nail, backed by the hammer.
Jesus had to be fastened to the cross so that his people might be engraved on the palms of his hands.

There is much consolation here.
We know that what a man has won with great pain,
he will keep with great tenacity.

Child of God, you cost Christ too much for him to forget you.

He recollects every pang that he suffered in Gethsemane
and every groan that he uttered for you on the cross.
The engraving on his hands brings to his remembrance
the redemption price he has paid to set you free.

What better proof do you have that Christ remembers you, than this:
He loved you and gave himself for you (Galatians 2:20).[2]

[1]From sermon no. 512, *A Precious Drop of Honey*
[2]From sermon no. 3441, *God's Memorial of His People*

MISSION ACCOMPLISHED

"The Son of Man came to seek and to save the lost."
LUKE 19:10

Survey the sufferings of Jesus Christ, and you will never imagine that he died in vain.

Come, place yourself in the Garden of Gethsemane and listen to yonder man in his agony.
Do you hear those groans? They are the groans of an incarnate God.
Do you hear those cries? They come from one who is the Father's equal, but he stooped to become a man.

Now rise, for he has risen; Judas has betrayed him and is taking him away.
Now look down. Do you see that blood staining the ground?
It is the sweat of the man, Christ Jesus.
Can you imagine this: Blood falling from the veins of incarnate Deity and failing in its purpose?

But now, come to the judgment hall and see your Master in the midst of a cruel band of soldiers.
Do you see how they spit on those sacred cheeks, how they pull his hair, how they strike him?
Do you see the crown of thorns with its ruby drops of blood?

And can you now stand there and look at this man whom Pilate is bringing forth,
still bleeding from the lash and covered with spittle, and believe that he—the incarnate God—
will be made such a spectacle to men, to angels, and to devils, and yet fail in his design?
Can you imagine that even one lash of that whip will have a fruitless aim?

Will Jesus Christ suffer this shame and spitting and torture
and yet endure what is far worse—a disappointment in the fulfillment of his intentions?
No, by Gethsemane and Gabbatha, we know that what he designed by his death must be accomplished!

Then again, see him *hanging on his cross.*
The nails have pierced his hands and feet, and there he hangs in the broiling sun.
His bodily pains increase, while his soul's anguish is even worse—even to death!

Can you still believe that Christ's blood was shed in vain?

*Can you look at even one of those precious drops
as it trickles from his head or his hands or his feet
and imagine that it will fall to the ground and perish there?*

*No, the waters may fail from the sea, and the sun grow dim with age,
but the value, the merit, the power of the blood of Jesus
will never die out or fail in its purpose!*

The design of the Savior's death must be fulfilled!

From sermon no. 204, *The Mission of the Son of Man*

A GOOD HOPE

*Hope does not put us to shame, because God's love
has been poured into our hearts through the Holy Spirit who has been given to us.*
ROMANS 5:5

God gives us, even here, a foretaste of heaven's supernatural enjoyment
in the forms of peace, calm, bliss, exultation, and delight.
When God's love is poured into our hearts, it produces hope, and this hope is never ashamed.

O reader, what is your hope? What are you resting on?
Do you have hope because God's love is flooding your heart through the Holy Spirit?
If your hope is centered on what you have done for yourself, you are resting on a false hope.

Your hope will only be true and genuine …
    if it is fixed on the Rock of ages;
    if it is built on the substitutionary sacrifice of Jesus Christ.

O self-righteous one, you must stop building on the sand of your own doings.

You must build on the rock of what Christ has done.
You must build with a humble faith and with an earnest love.
You must build with the precious stones of love, trust, and holy fear.
Then when the deluge comes you will laugh at it, and will sing in the midst of the storm.

O sinner, if you would like to enter such a bright hope and enjoy such a love, *behold the open door!*

The entrance into a good hope is by the door of divine love,
    and there it shines in all its resplendence on yonder cross!
Your hope is where the Son of God made flesh gave his hands and feet to the cruel nails.

There where every nerve is a road for the hot feet of pain to travel on,
there where Christ's whole body is tortured with inexpressible anguish,
there where his soul is pressed as beneath the feet of Deity;
there, sinner, there is your hope!

Your hope is not in your tears, but in his blood;
not in your sufferings, but in his woes;
not in your penance, but in his agonies;
not in your life nor your death, but in his life and death.

O sinner, look to him! There is life in a look at the Crucified One.

*Look through the mist of Satan's temptations and the dew of your tears.
Look to Jesus dying on Calvary and you will live.*

From sermon no. 829, *The Perfuming of the Heart*

CRIES GOING UP TO HEAVEN

*To Jesus, the mediator of a new covenant,
and to the sprinkled blood that speaks a better word than the blood of Abel.*
HEBREWS 12:24

The first shedding of human blood was a terrible experiment.
Can you see Cain, stiff with fright, standing there by the corpse, awestruck at the sight of blood?
But then some comfort arises in his mind when he sees the crimson lifeblood soaking into the earth.

Perhaps he also felt a momentary joy, thinking that he was now rid of the one who troubled him,
    and since the earth had swallowed up the blood, and his deed was speechless and silent,
he could just go on his way as though nothing had happened.

It was not so, however, for though that blood was silent in the seared conscience of Cain,
    it had a voice elsewhere, reaching the ear of the invisible God, who said to Cain, "What have you
    done? The voice of your brother's blood is crying to me from the ground" (Genesis 4:10).

Then Cain knew that blood could not be idly spilt and that murder would be avenged.
He knew there was a tongue in every drop of spilt blood, which prevailed with God.

*Now you must remember the terrible experiment tried at Calvary
when not only a man, but the Son of God himself, was slaughtered!*

It was a dreadful experiment ...
    when they actually dared to take the nails and fasten the Son of God to the accursed tree;
    when they lifted up his holy body and watched his griefs until they ended in his death;
    when they pierced his side and blood and water flowed out.

Pilate, who had washed his hands in water, thought there would be no consequences to his actions,
    and the scribes and Pharisees thought, *We have silenced him. There will be no voice to that blood.*
But the cry of Jerusalem went up to heaven: "His blood be on us and on our children!" (Matthew 27:25).
    This cry was registered in the books of justice, and Jerusalem soon became a den of misery.

But there was also another cry that went up to heaven that day.
It was a cry that came from the cross of Calvary.
It was a cry resounding from the wounds of Immanuel: "Father, forgive them" (Luke 23:34).

The blood of Abel was not voiceless, and neither was the blood of Jesus.
The blood of Jesus cried, so as to be heard in heaven.
It spoke, not worse things, but better things than that of Abel.
It did not demand fiercer vengeance than that which fell on Cain.
It did not ask that we be fugitives on this earth, banished from God forever,
    but it cried, "Father, forgive them," and it prevailed; the curse was removed and a blessing given.

From sermon no. 708, *The Blood of Abel and the Blood of Jesus*

FORGETTING OUR SAVIOR

"My people have forgotten me days without number."
JEREMIAH 2:32

It would seem almost impossible for those who have been loved with an everlasting love,
   and who have been redeemed by the blood of the dying Lamb,
to ever forget their all-loving, all-gracious Savior.

Forget him who never forgot us?
Forget him who poured out his blood for our sins?
Forget him who loved us even to death?
Is this possible?

Yes, it is not only possible, but it is too sadly a fault with all of us.

Do you not have to admit that this is true? Do you not at times find yourself forgetting Jesus?
Some creature comes along and steals your heart and you neglect communion with him.

We must be determined that whatever else we let slip through our fingers and from our minds,
   we will hold fast to Jesus.
And the best way to do this is to go directly to his cross.

Let us view the blood flowing from those many wounds that he received on our behalf.
Let us look into that dear face of his, the image of matchless misery and majesty combined.
Let us note the thorn-crown and all the marks of shame and disgrace that cruel men heaped on him.
Let us hear him cry, "My God, my God, why have you forsaken me?" (Matthew 27:46).

> *O Christian, if you have lost your first love,*
> *the best place to get it back is at the place where it was first born;*
> *and since it was born at the cross, that is where you must go.*

> *Now and forever, dear Christian, you must keep very close to the cross*
> *for it is impossible to forget your Savior there.*

It seems to be a surprise to David that the Lord would think of man, for he wrote,
   "When I look at your heavens, the work of your fingers, the moon and the stars, which you have
      set in place, what is man that you are mindful of him?" (Psalm 8:3–4).
Yet the Lord is mindful of man, and it grieves him when man is not mindful of him.

He wants us to remember him, to think of him, and to trust and love him;
   and when we do not, he cries out, "My people have forgotten me;
they have forgotten their Maker, their best Friend, and their greatest Helper!"

From sermon no. 2, *The Remembrance of Christ*, and sermon no. 2975, *Forgetting God*

DISTINGUISHED BY HIS STAR

Now after Jesus was born in Bethlehem of Judea in the days of Herod the king,
behold, wise men from the east came to Jerusalem,
saying, "Where is he who has been born king of the Jews?
For we saw his star when it rose and have come to worship him."
MATTHEW 2:1–2

See the glory of our Lord Jesus Christ—even in his state of humiliation.
　　He is born of lowly parents, laid in a manger, and wrapped in swaddling cloths,
　　　　but, lo, the principalities and powers in heavenly places are in commotion!
A host of angels descend to proclaim the Advent of the newborn King and to sing glory to God.

Then, behold! A star appears!

This star is commissioned to wait upon the Lord;
to be his herald to men far away and to usher them into his presence;
to be his bodyguard, watching over his cradle.

Earth, too, is stirred for simple shepherds come to pay homage before the mysterious child,
　　and after them, coming from afar, are the most studious minds of the age.
Lo! These wise men offer gifts—gold, frankincense, and myrrh—as they bow down before him.

　　　　　Christ, though a child, is still King of kings;
　　　　though among the oxen, he is still distinguished by his star.

If wise men of old came to Jesus and worshiped, should we not also come?
　　Let us who are now worshiping, come and worship with greater reverence and intense affection.
And may we who are far away from him spiritually—just as the Magi were far away physically—
　　come and ask, "Where is he who has been born king of the Jews? For we have come to worship him."

　　　　　Oh, it was well for them to come to the baby Jesus,
　　　　　　led by the feeble beams of a star!

　　　　Yet, we will find it even more blessed to come to him now;
　　　　　　for now he is exalted in the highest heavens,
　　　　and by his own light reveals his own perfect glory.

　　　　　Oh, let us hasten to bow down and worship
　　　where shepherds and wise men and angels have led the way!

　　　　If you have neither gold, nor frankincense, nor myrrh,
　　　　　bring your faith, your love, and your repentance;
　　　　　　and falling down before the Son of God,
　　　　pay him the homage and reverence of your heart.

From sermon no. 1698, *The Star and the Wise Men*

BELONGING TO ONE ANOTHER

My beloved is mine, and I am his.
Song of Solomon 2:16

"My beloved is mine."

The bride makes this the first of her joy notes, the cornerstone of her peace.
It is no small thing to claim God as ours, to claim Jesus the beloved as ours.
Yes, to put it in the singular and call him *mine!*

We do not rejoice in our spiritual privileges as much as in the One from whom they come.
   We have received righteousness, sanctification, and redemption;
     we have both grace and glory secured to us,
  but we prefer to claim the fountain rather than the streams.

What would all the treasures of the covenant be to us without Christ?
We have all things in him; therefore, our main treasure—yes, our sole treasure—is our Beloved.

O ye saints of God, has there ever been a possession like this?

You have your beloveds, ye daughters of earth,
but what are they compared with our Beloved?

Jesus is the Son of God and the Son of Man;
he is the darling of heaven and the delight of earth.
He is such a lover that all earthly loves put together
are not worthy to touch the hem of his garment
or to loosen the strap of his shoe.

O worldling, you cannot hold your treasures as we hold ours.
You cannot say of anything, "It is mine," for your holding is too precarious.
Your treasures are only temporary, terminable at the end of one frail life;
but we have an eternal, an everlasting possession.

"I am his."

This is as sweet as the former statement.
These two are joined together with diamond rivets: "My beloved is mine, and I am his."
Put the two together and you have reached the summit of delight.

That we are his is a fact that is very clear to us.

We are his because he bought us with his blood and has called us by his grace.
We are his because he is married to us and we are his bride.
We are his because we have heartily given ourselves to him, bound to him by love forever.

From sermon no. 1190, *A Song Among the Lilies*

THE AGONY IN GETHSEMANE

And being in an agony he prayed more earnestly;
and his sweat became like great drops of blood falling down to the ground.
LUKE 22:44

All his life our Lord scarcely uttered an expression of grief,
    and yet here he says, not only by his cries and by his bloody sweat,
but also in so many words, "My soul is very sorrowful, even to death" (Matthew 26:38).

What was the cause of this overwhelming grief in Gethsemane?
It was now that our Lord had to take a certain cup from the Father's hand.

It was not from the Jews,
not from the traitor Judas,
not even from Satan,
that the trial came now.

It was a bitter cup appointed to him by his Father.
It was a cup that especially amazed his soul and troubled his inmost heart.

Jesus shrank from it; therefore, be assured that it was a potion ...
    more dreadful than physical pain because he did not shrink from that;
    more dreadful than reproach because he did not turn aside from that;
    more dreadful than Satanic temptation because *that* he had overcome.
It was something inconceivably terrible, amazingly full of dread that came from the Father's hand!

The following verses remove all doubt as to what it was:
"It was the will of the LORD to crush him; he has put him to grief" (Isaiah 53:10).
"The LORD has laid on him the iniquity of us all" (Isaiah 53:6).
"For our sake he made him to be sin who knew no sin" (2 Corinthians 5:21).

> *The great and fathomless ocean of inexpressible anguish,*
> *dashing over our Savior's soul when he died,*
> *is inconceivable!*

Even the spray from that great tempestuous deep, as it fell on him, baptized him in a bloody sweat.
    He had not yet come to the raging billows of the penalty itself,
        but his soul was weighed down with intense grief and anguish,
    even while standing on the shore and hearing the awful breaking at his feet.

It was the shadow of the coming tempest;
it was the prelude of the Father's desertion while he bore our sin and paid our debt—
it was this that laid him low!

From sermon no. 1199, *The Agony in Gethsemane*

ABOVE HIS COMPANIONS

God, your God, has anointed you with the oil of gladness
beyond your companions.
PSALM 45:7

Who are Christ's companions?

Perhaps his companions are the kings and princes of this world,
    since the psalm is descriptive of Christ in his royalty.
Well, is he not anointed with gladness beyond them all?

Kings rejoice in their dominions, their extent and population;
    but our King looks from shore to shore, and of his dominion there is no end.

Kings like to rejoice in the victories they have achieved;
    but he "who comes from Edom, in crimsoned garments from Bozrah" has more joy than they.

Kings like to boast in the sureness of their throne;
    but "your throne, O God, is forever and ever" (Psalm 45:6).

Kings of the earth, you may take off your crowns, and remain uncrowned,
for on the head of King Jesus there are many crowns!

O ye lords and rulers, you may lay down your dignities and honors,
for you are undignified in the presence of him who is beyond his companions!

Ah, where will his companions be found?

Search among the wise, and who will match the gladness of incarnate wisdom?
Search out the mighty and you will find no arm like his.
Go and travel among the famous, and who will compare with his illustrious name?

Standing as high above all men
as the heavens are above the earth,
Jesus is, indeed, anointed with the oil of gladness
beyond his companions!

As people always take a deep interest in that which has *cost them dearly,*
    so Christ finds infinite solace and delight in his people.
He purposely stretched out his hands for them on the bloodstained tree.

He beholds the reward of his soul's travail in every regenerate heart,
and as he looks on the purchase of his blood
his heart is filled with gladness.

From sermon no. 498, *The Gladness of the Man of Sorrows*

A KING SENT IN LOVE

Then Hiram the king of Tyre answered in a letter that he sent to Solomon,
"Because the Lord loves his people, he has made you king over them."
2 Chronicles 2:11

I am going to take our text away from Solomon, for true as it was in his case,
it is more emphatically true in reference to our King.
God has been pleased to make Christ our King, so our text will read like this:
"Because the Lord loves his people, he has made Jesus to be King over them."

There was an urgent necessity for us to have Jesus as our King.
We are such poor creatures that we cannot live without a form of rule and government,
and he who takes the Lord Jesus Christ to be his master will be rightly and wisely guided.
But to my mind, the bliss of being under the dominion of Christ lies in the character of Christ.

If I must have a master, let me have ...
the Christ of Bethlehem,
the Christ of Nazareth,
the Christ of Calvary,
the Christ of heaven.

If I must submit my mind and will to another—
and surely I must do so, or else I must submit it to the dominion of my own lusts and passions—
if I must have a king, let it be Jesus Christ whose head was crowned with thorns.

Who would not gladly serve him who permitted the little children to come to him?
Who would not willingly serve him who sat on the well at Sychar and talked with a poor, sinful
woman until he had won her soul and made her into a zealous and successful missionary?
Who would not freely serve him to whom tax collectors and sinners drew near, forsaking their sins?

He is so divinely royal, so affable, generous, humane, benevolent, gracious, godlike,
that to serve him is to serve one who is "distinguished among ten thousand" (Song of Solomon 5:10).
He not only reigns over us, he also loves us with such love that he even died for us,
and where can you find another monarch who has done that for his subjects?

We have seen portraits of kings holding the globe and the scepter in their hands,
wearing a crown—perhaps adorned with a wreath in token of their victories—
but when our King puts on his royal regalia,
what are the chief ensigns of his sovereignty, the tokens of his universal dominion?
They are the wounds in his hands, and in his feet, and in his side.

Oh, we rejoice that the Father has so loved us
that he sent the Savior to redeem us and to be our King forever and ever!

From sermon no. 2760, *A King Sent in Love*

SAVED BY A MAN

He is the Son of Man.
JOHN 5:27

Although there is nothing new about the doctrine of Christ's manhood, it is very important.
   It is one of those provisions of the Lord's household that, like bread and salt,
      should be placed on the table at every spiritual meal.
We can never meditate too much on Christ's blessed person as God and as man.

It would not have been consistent with divine justice
   to accept any other substitute for us except that of a man.
The breach of the law was caused by man, and by man it must be repaired.

Oh! Glory be to his blessed name!

The man, the matchless man, the representative man—
by right of kinship allowed to redeem—
stepped in and suffered what was due to us,
made amends to injured justice and set us free.

And now, because of Jesus, we may draw near to God,
   not trembling to approach the One whom we have so grievously offended.
There is a man ordained to mediate between us and God, the man Christ Jesus.

A holy God will by no means spare the guilty, but come and look at the Son of Man!

He is a man whose hands are full of blessing;
whose eyes are wet with tears of pity;
whose lips are overflowing with words of love;
whose heart is melting with tenderness.

Do you see the gash in that man's side?
   Through that wound there is a highway to his heart,
      and whoever needs his compassion will soon excite it.
Yes, the way to the Savior's heart is open, and penitent seekers will not be denied.

O sinner, place yourself beneath the cross of Jesus!
Look up and say, "Blessed Physician, your wounds can heal me.
You are a man and you know what man suffers."

He waits to save; to receive sinners and reconcile them to God.

From sermon no. 1099, *The Man of Sorrows*

POURING OUT HIS SOUL

He poured out his soul to death.
Isaiah 53:12

Notice the expression: "He poured out his soul to death."
It is deliberate.
It is a libation presented with thought and care.

It is not only the spilling of Christ's blood,
it is the resolute pouring out of his whole life to its last drop—the pouring it out to death.
Jesus was practically pouring out his life from the day his public ministry commenced, if not before.
He was always dying by living at such a rate that his zeal consumed him (John 2:17).

> *Deliberately—and as if it were drop by drop—*
> *he was letting his soul fall upon the ground,*
> *until at length, on the tree of doom,*
> *he emptied it all out*
> *as he cried, "It is finished,"*
> *and gave up his spirit.*

And as it was deliberate, so it was very *real*.

His was *real* suffering, *real* poverty, *real* weariness.
When he came to his last agony, his bloody sweat was no fiction.
His great sorrow, even to death, was no fancy.

When the scourges fell on his shoulders, it was *real* pain that he suffered.
The nails, the spear, the sponge, and the vinegar—these tell of a *real* Passion.

The sufferings of his death are beyond us.
Certainly, we will never experience that pouring out of soul to death that was peculiar to Jesus,
in which he went far beyond the martyrs in their most extreme griefs.
There were points of anguish regarding his death that were for him alone.

"He poured out his soul to death."
See how complete it was.

Jesus gave poor sinners everything.
His every faculty was laid out for them.
To his last rag he was stripped on the cross.

No part of his body or of his soul was kept back from being made a sacrifice.
He made no reserve.
He did not even keep back his innermost self—"he poured out his soul to death."

From sermon no. 2070, *Christ's Connection with Sinners the Source of His Glory*

HEAVEN ON EARTH

Our citizenship is in heaven,
and from it we await a Savior, the Lord Jesus Christ.
PHILIPPIANS 3:20

It is a very blessed experience to be able to walk on earth and look up to heaven,
   but it is a higher experience to live in heaven and look down on earth.
And this is what the believer may do; he may sit "in the heavenly places" (Ephesians 2:6).

Oh, to live in heaven, to dwell there,
to let the heart be caught up from this poor life
into that rich life that is above!

This is where we should be, where we may be
if we are quickened by the divine life.[1]

Turn to the biographies of eminent saints and you will find instances recorded there
   in which Jesus has been pleased, in a very special manner, to speak to their souls;
      to unfold the wonders of his person and the matchless glories of his office.
Their souls were so steeped in happiness that they thought themselves to be in heaven.

Though they were not actually in heaven, they were on the very threshold of it,
   for when Jesus manifests himself to his people it is a young heaven on earth.
It is paradise in embryo; it is the beginning of the bliss of the glorified.[2]

Heaven itself, although it is a fertile land, flowing with milk and honey,
cannot produce a flower as beautiful as the Altogether Lovely.

Its highest joys mount no higher than the head of Jesus;
its sweetest bliss is found in his name alone.

If we would know heaven, let us know Jesus;
if we would be heavenly, let us love Jesus.

Oh, that we were perpetually in his company,
that our hearts might be satisfied with his love![3]

Heaven on earth is abounding love to Jesus.
To love Jesus is another name for paradise.[4]

[1]From sermon no. 2267, *Life from the Dead*
[2]From sermon no. 29, *Christ Manifests Himself to His People*
[3]*The Saint & His Saviour*
[4]Source Unknown

TREATED WITH CONTEMPT

And Herod with his soldiers treated him with contempt and mocked him.
LUKE 23:11

Why did these men treat our Lord with such contempt?
No doubt, part of the reason was because of his patience and gentleness.

His face was not like the face of a man of war.
It was marred with grief but not with anger.
It was worn with sorrow but not with battle.

He was the lamb—not the lion.
He was the dove—not the eagle.

Jesus stood before them unarmed, and when "reviled, he did not revile in return" (1Peter 2:23).
For this reason, those fighting, mean-spirited men despised him.

Furthermore, our Lord was ridiculed by Herod because he refused to gratify his curiosity
    and perform miracles, signs, and wonders for his amusement.
The wicked Herod virtually said to the holy Jesus, "Come, work us a miracle. We hear that you
    have delivered from death, so now release yourself from our hands."

> *There stands our Lord with all power in his hands,*
> *but he will not lift a finger for his own deliverance*
> *or for Herod's amusement.*

> *O blessed Jesus, it is still the same,*
> *for you will not dazzle nor amuse!*
> *That is why men prefer any charlatan to you.*

The royal claims of Jesus also excited their scorn.
    You can almost hear the "Aha! aha! aha!" of Herod as he says, "Call him a king? Go to the Pool of
        Bethesda and fetch up some poor wretch who lies there and call him a king! Here, put the white
    robe on him; let him at least look like a monarch. Is he not every inch a king?"

Then the soldiers took up the jest.
How bitterly, how derisively they made his royalty the football of contempt!

Thus even today, the world despises the royalty of King Jesus.
Those who would lie in the dust before the meanest prince have no esteem for the King of kings.

> *O Lord Jesus, in our eyes you are all the more dear and honored*
> *because you were greatly despised!*
> *Though you were charged with sedition,*
> *we fall at your feet and proclaim you King of kings!*

From sermon no. 2051, *Setting Jesus at Naught*

THE REJECTED STONE

The stone that the builders rejected has become the cornerstone.
PSALM 118:22

All the details of Christ's life corresponded with the prophecies.
    If the Jews had willed to see it, they would have perceived
        that Jesus was anointed to be the Cornerstone of the spiritual temple.
Yet they persistently rejected him.

His rejection was even more remarkable and sorrowful,
    because he was rejected by the builders or leaders of the Jewish nation.
And this rejection was not a common one: It was a violent, an indignant rejection!

This precious Stone was kicked and rolled about with violence,
    and all kinds of ridicule and slander were poured on it.
Nothing would satisfy the Jewish leaders but the blood of the man
    who had disturbed their consciences and questioned their pretensions.

They slandered him in life and mocked him in death.
They spat accusations at him when he was free and defiled him with spittle when he was bound.
They made him live an outcast's life and then hung him up to die a felon's death.

They willfully and resolutely rejected him, partly, because of blind prejudice.
They expected a king surrounded with earthly pomp and girded with strength to break the Roman yoke.

Because he came as the son of a lowly virgin,
because he came dressed as a peasant and humbly dwelt among the common people,
they rejected him.

His humble life should never have been a cause for rejection
    for was it not prophesied that he would come in such a manner?
He agreed with the prophecies, but not with their prejudices;
    therefore, they cried, "Away with him, away with him!" (John 19:15).

They had eyes but would not see;
the light was around them but they did not comprehend it.

The pride of their hearts kept them in ignorance.

The Pharisee, supremely righteous in himself, did not want a man who taught him that he was lost.
He did not want the man who had come to be the Savior of sinners.

Thus the Ever-blessed was chased out of the world by the pride that scorns all excellence except its own.
Men flung away God's dearest jewel because it outshone their own counterfeit jewelry.

From sermon no. 1420, *The Head Stone of the Corner*

THE CORNERSTONE

The stone that the builders rejected has become the cornerstone.
PSALM 118:22

Christ now has the chief place of honor in the building of God.
He has become the Head over all things to his church.

Glory be to his blessed name!
In the midst of his people he is above all and over all.

We worship with rapture the King of kings and Lord of lords!
There is none like him among the sons of men,
and in all things he has the preeminence.

He who was crucified is now enthroned;
he who lay in the grave now reigns in glory!

This precious Cornerstone binds God and man together in wondrous unity, for he is both in one.
He joins earth and heaven together, for he participates in both.
He joins time and eternity together, for he was a man of a few years, yet is the Ancient of Days.
He joins Jew and Gentile together, for they are one in him.

Wondrous Cornerstone!
You bind together all who are in you,
and they are being built together into a holy temple.

Our Lord Jesus Christ has risen from the depths of degradation and shame to a place of honor,
    to become the greatest Being on the face of the earth.
Our Savior has lost nothing because of his enemies.

They scourged his back, but they did not rob him of that imperial purple that now adorns him.
They crowned him with thorns, but those thorns have increased the brilliance of his diadem of light.
They pierced his hands, preparing them to sway an irresistible scepter of love over men's hearts.
They crucified him, but his crucifixion led him to greater honor since he therein finished the work
    given him to do, and now God has exalted him and given him a name that is above every name.

Jesus has ascended from all the maltreatment of Gabbatha to the seat of infinite majesty.
He has gone from the bar to the throne and there he sits in glorious splendor.

The eternal purposes of Jehovah will be fulfilled.
    Our enemies may mine and undermine, they may openly oppose and secretly assail,
        but on this Rock—even on Christ Jesus—
    the truth and the church will rest forever and no harm will come to it.

From sermon no. 1420, *The Head Stone of the Corner*

MORE BEAUTIFUL THAN EVER

"The Son of Man will be delivered over to the chief priests and scribes,
and they will ... deliver him over to the Gentiles
to be mocked and flogged and crucified."
Matthew 20:18–19

The chief theme that our Lord dwelt on was his own sufferings, even to death.

Our Lord Jesus said many delightful things;
    and in everything he said, his voice is like angels' music to our ears.
But it is from the trials of the cross that his voice is richest in consolation.

We draw a lot closer to him when we gaze on his bloody sweat,
    or see him robed in shame, crowned with thorns, and enthroned on the cross.
Our Lord's incomparable beauties are always most visible amid his griefs.
    When we see him on the cross, we feel like borrowing Pilate's words: "Behold the man!"

We do not have a real knowledge of Christ until he puts on his crimson garments.
    We do not know our Beloved when we only see the purity of the snow-white lily;
        but we do perceive him when—in his wounds—he is red like the rose.
Then we can truly say, "My beloved is radiant and ruddy, distinguished among ten thousand."[1]

Do you remember the Scottish woman's response after Claverhouse[2] murdered her godly husband?

"Ah!" Claverhouse said, "What do you think of your bonny husband now?"

She answered, "I always thought my man was very beautiful, but I never saw him look better than he does now since he has died for his Master."

Now can you say the same of Christ?

Oh, he has ever been precious to me!

I love him in every shape and form,
but when I see him put on his crimson robe
and bleed at every pore for me;
when the rubies are in his hands and on his feet,
and I see him still despised and rejected by men,
I love him more than ever!

I love his shame and I love his reproach,
and I count it greater riches than all the treasures of this world![3]

[1]From sermon no. 2212, *The Private Thoughts and Words of Jesus*
[2] John Graham of Claverhouse (1648–1689) was employed by the government of King Charles II to enforce Episcopacy upon Scotland. He engaged in persecuting the Covenanters, a group that resisted the government of Charles II and fought and suffered for adherence to their own form of worship.
[3]From sermon no. 2368, *The Living Care of the Dying Christ*

THE WONDER OF ANGELS

Though he was rich, yet for your sake he became poor.
2 CORINTHIANS 8:9

How surprised the angels were when they learned that Christ, the Prince of Light and Majesty,
intended to shroud himself in clay and become a baby, to live as a man and die!

When the rumor surfaced we can only imagine their wonderment.

What! Would he who wore a crown bedecked with stars—would he lay that crown aside?
What! Would he who wore the purple of the universe—would he be dressed in a peasant's robe?
What! Would he who was everlasting and immortal—would he one day be nailed to a cross?

Can you imagine their wonder when the deed is actually being accomplished?
Can you conceive their wonder when Christ said to them, "I will not disdain the virgin's womb;
I am now going down to earth to become a man"?
Can you picture them as they declared that they would follow him?

Yes, they followed him as closely as they were allowed,
nor would they leave him until they had also brought wonderment to the shepherds
and had hung up new stars in honor of the newborn King.

And now wonder, ye angels …
that the Infinite has become an infant;
that he who "hangs the earth on nothing" (Job 26:7) now hangs at his mother's breast;
that he who bears up the pillars of creation is now so weak that he must be carried!

> *Oh, wonder ye who knew him in his riches,*
> *while you now admire him in his poverty!*
>
> *Where does the newborn King sleep?*
> *Does he have the best room in Caesar's palace?*
>
> *Has a cradle of gold been prepared for him*
> *and pillows of down on which to rest his head?*
>
> *No, it is where the cattle feed—in the dilapidated stable—*
> *it is in a manger that the Savior lies.*

He who had placed the stars on high and had made them glisten in the night,
did not have even one star of glory upon his brow.
We may indeed say, "Though he was rich, yet for our sakes he became poor."

From sermon no. 151, *The Condescension of Christ*

STRICKEN BY GOD

Yet we esteemed him stricken, smitten by God, and afflicted.
ISAIAH 53:4

Our Savior had to consciously stand before God as the Sin-Bearer,
    according to that ancient prophecy: "The LORD has laid on him the iniquity of us all" (Isaiah 53:6).
Then it was true: "He made him to be sin who knew no sin" (2 Corinthians 5:21).

Sin, sin, sin was everywhere around and about Christ.
He had no sin, but he appeared as "the Lamb of God, who takes away the sin of the world" (John 1:29).
He had to feel the weight of sin and the turning away of that holy face that cannot look on it.

Jesus was hung up as an accursed thing on the cross, because he became "a curse for us—
    for it is written, 'Cursed is everyone who is hanged on a tree'" (Galatians 3:13).
And that is why the Lord God did not own him as his before all the people.

God might have sent him twelve legions of angels, but not even one angel came after he left Gethsemane.

His despisers might spit in his face, but no swift seraphs came to avenge the indignity.
They might bind him and scourge him, but none of the heavenly host would interpose to screen his
    shoulders from the cruel lash.
They might fasten him to the tree with nails and lift him up and scoff at him, but no cohort of
    ministering spirits hastened to drive back the rabble and release the Prince of Life.

> *He appeared to be forsaken by God,*
> *smitten by him, and afflicted,*
> *delivered by him into the hands of cruel men*
> *who unleashed indescribable misery upon him.*

His Father also dried up that sacred stream of peaceful communion and loving fellowship
    that had flowed between them throughout his whole earthly life.
He was not smiled on, not allowed to feel that he was close to God;
    and this, to his tender spirit, was grief of the keenest kind.

Our Lord suffered to the extreme point of deprivation.
We can only faintly guess his sorrow when he felt forsaken by his Father.
Well might he cry, "My God, my God, why have you forsaken me?" (Matthew 27:46).[1]

> *Oh, it was an anguish never to be measured,*
> *an agony never to be comprehended!*
>
> *It is to God, and to God alone, that his griefs are fully known![2]*

[1]From sermon no. 2133, *"Lama Sabachthani?"*
[2]From sermon no. 873, *Christ Made a Curse for Us*

WHITE AND RUDDY

My beloved is white and ruddy,
Chief among ten thousand.
SONG OF SOLOMON 5:10 NKJV

This text appears to be calling our attention to two chief characteristics of our Lord.

Solomon had often seen the snow-white lambs—the emblems of purity—
    brought up to the temple to be offered in sacrifice.
Perhaps this is why he says, "My beloved is white."

He had also seen the uplifted knife in the priest's hand
    and then the ruby stream as it flowed down at the foot of the altar,
until the lamb was stained crimson in its own blood.

Here we see the two together:
    the white—the immaculate purity,
    the red—the sacrificial blood-shedding.
These are the two essentials of the Christian faith concerning our Savior.

Our Lord is in himself, white. That is, *he has immaculate perfection of character.*
    In his godhead, Jesus Christ is perfection itself.
As to his humanity, the term whiteness describes him very well,
    because he was born without natural corruption or any taint of hereditary depravity.

> *He is the Lamb of God without spot or blemish,*
> *"the radiance of the glory of God*
> *and the exact imprint of his nature" (Hebrews 1:3).*

Jesus came into this world as the Substitute for sinners.
He suffered death so that all who trust in him might have eternal life.

> *Our Lord Jesus is "white" in his spotless innocence,*
> *and he is "ruddy" in his sacrificial sufferings.*

> *He is not only sinless, he is also the chief of martyrs.*

He is called the "chief among ten thousand"—
    that is to say, Christ is higher, better, lovelier, and more excellent than all who are around him.
Whatever excellencies there may be in others, they are all eclipsed when he comes near.

If you find one, a hundred, a thousand, ten thousand—all excellent—
    they must all give way when Jesus appears,
just as the stars are forgotten when the sun arises in his strength!

From sermon no. 2478, *Christ's Perfection and Precedence*

LOVE'S CROWNING DEED

"Greater love has no one than this,
that someone lays down his life for his friends."
JOHN 15:13

This is the ultimate act of love. Self-denial can go no further.
What more can love do, than to lay down its life for another?

Yes, people dying for their friends—this is superlative love.
But Jesus dying for us is even greater than this!

Jesus was immortal, hence the special character of his death.
    A substitutionary death for love's sake, in ordinary cases,
        is but a slightly premature payment of that debt which must be paid by all.
But such is not the case with Jesus because he did not need to die at all.

There was no reason why he should die, apart from laying down his life for his friends.
    In heaven he was the Son of God, forever with the Father—eternal and everlasting—
        but he came to earth and assumed our nature so that he might be capable of death.
Yet remember, though becoming capable of death, his body need not have died.

Our Lord Jesus—and none but he—could stand at the brink of the grave and say, "I lay down my
    life that I may take it up again. No one takes it from me, but I lay it down of my own accord.
I have authority to lay it down, and I have authority to take it up again" (John 10:17–18).

We poor mortals only have power to die,
but Christ had power to live.

That splendid, immortal Being chose to become mortal,
yielding himself up to death's pangs without necessity,
except for the necessity of his mighty love.

Herein is the greatness of Jesus' love—
    though he called us "friends," the friendship was all on his side.
He called us friends, but our hearts called him enemy for we opposed him.

Oh, the enmity of the human heart toward Jesus!
    Of all the enmity that has ever come from the bottomless pit,
        this enmity toward the Christ of God is the strangest and the most bitter of all.
And yet for these very people Jesus Christ gave himself up to suffer and die.

Monarch of misery and Lord of love,
never has there been love like yours!

From sermon no. 1129, *Love's Crowning Deed*

NEARNESS TO JESUS

But for me it is good to be near God.
PSALM 73:28

Gracious souls can never be perfectly at ease unless they are in a state of nearness to Jesus.
    When they are away from him, they lose their peace.
The nearer to Jesus, the nearer to the perfect calm of heaven;
    and the further away from him, the nearer to that troubled sea of unrest that plagues the wicked.

We have learned through experience—through divine grace—
    that none but Jesus can ever give happiness to our souls.
Peace, liveliness, vitality—all depend on enjoying constant communion with him.
    We will never know the true meaning of *joy* unless we sit like Mary at Jesus' feet.

One who has tasted communion with Jesus will be dissatisfied with everything else.
    He will find that music has lost its melody and light its brightness,
        and life itself will be darkened with the shadow of death if his Lord is absent.
Nearness to Jesus is his soul's desire.[1]

Oh, how precious is Jesus!
How can I go elsewhere for joy or comfort
when he is so full, so rich, so satisfying?

I would live in Christ's heart.
In the clefts of that rock
my soul would eternally abide.

"Even the sparrow finds a home,
and the swallow a nest for herself,
where she may lay her young,
at your altars, O LORD of hosts,
my King and my God" (Psalm 84:3).

And I, too, would make my nest, my home, in you.
Never from you, may my soul depart again,
but may I nestle close to you,
O Jesus, my true and only rest![2]

Yes Lord, we your children can say that you have been our home, our safe dwelling-place.
Oh, what joy, what peace we have found in your sacred bosom!
There is no home like the breast of the Lord, to which, in all generations, true believers fly.[3]

[1]From sermon no. 539, *Heavenly Love-Sickness!*
[2]*Morning and Evening*, September 29 (E).
[3]From sermon no. 59, *Watch-Night Service*

REMEMBERING THE PRICE

You were bought with a price. So glorify God in your body.
1 Corinthians 6:20

I would seek to refresh your memory with this fact: "You were bought with a price."

There in the midnight hour amid the olives of Gethsemane, the Son of God kneels,
groaning, pleading in prayer, wrestling.
See the beady drops of sweat standing on his brow.

Ah! That sweat is blood—big crimson drops of blood!
They are so big they are even falling down to the ground!

> *O soul, your Savior speaks to you from Gethsemane,*
> *"It is here that I bought you with a price."*

Track him in his path of shame and sorrow until you see him at Gabbatha.
Mark how they bind his hands and fasten him to the whipping post.
See them laying on the scourges and the cruel Roman whips, tearing his flesh. The plowers make
deep furrows on his blessed body and the blood gushes forth in purple streams.
Notice the rivulets that join those purple streams, coming from his temples where the crown of
thorns has pierced them.

> *From beneath the scourges,*
> *Jesus speaks to you with accents soft and low,*
> *"My child, it is here that I bought you with a price."*

But see him on the cross itself.
See how his hands and feet are fountains of blood.
See how his soul is filled with anguish.

> *And there, before the soldier pierces his side with a spear,*
> *Jesus bows his head and whispers,*
> *"It was here that I bought you with a price."*

Oh, by Gethsemane, by Gabbatha, by Golgotha,
by every sacred name collected in the Passion of our Lord,
by sponge and vinegar and nail and spear,
by everything that increased the pain and anguish of his death,
I conjure you to remember that you were "bought with a price" and "are not your own."

From now on let it be said of you,
that you are not only a person of good morals and respectable conduct,
but that above all, you are a person who is filled with love for the One who bought you.
You are a person who lives for Christ and knows no other passion.

From sermon no. 1004, *"Bought With a Price"*

"LOOKING TO JESUS"

Looking to Jesus, the founder and perfecter of our faith.
HEBREWS 12:2

It is the work of the Holy Spirit to turn our eyes away from self to Jesus;
    so we might expect Satan's work to be the exact opposite.
He is constantly trying to make us regard ourselves instead of Christ.

Satan insinuates …
    your sins are too great for pardon;
    you have no faith;
    you do not repent enough;
    you will never be able to endure to the end;
    you do not have the joy of God's children;
    your hold on Jesus is too weak.

All these thoughts are centered on self,
    and we will never find comfort or assurance in this way.
The Holy Spirit turns our eyes entirely away from self.
    He tells us that we are nothing, but that "Christ is all, and in all" (Colossians 3:11).

Remember, it is not *your hold* on Christ that saves you—it is Christ.
It is not *your joy* in Christ that saves you—it is Christ.
It is not even *your faith* in Christ, though that is the instrument—it is Christ's blood and merits.

So, do not even look at your hand as it is grasping Christ; look at Christ.
Do not look to your hope, but to Jesus, the source of your hope.
Do not look to your faith, but to Jesus, the founder and perfecter of your faith.

We will never find happiness by looking at our prayers, our works, or our feelings.
It is what *Jesus is,* not what we are, that gives rest to the soul.

Dear reader, if you want to overcome Satan and have peace with God, you must be "looking to
    Jesus."
Simply keep your eye on him.
Keep his death, his sufferings, his merits, his glories, and his intercession fresh on your mind.

When you awake in the morning, look to him.
When you lie down at night, look to him.

O child of God, do not let your hopes or fears
come between you and your Savior!

Stay close to him, for he will never fail you.

Morning and Evening, June 28 (M)

DILIGENT DEALINGS WITH THE BLOOD

"These are the ones coming out of the great tribulation.
They have washed their robes and made them white in the blood of the Lamb."
REVELATION 7:14

What is the lesson taught in this passage?
In times of tribulation we must have diligent dealings with the blood of the Lamb.

We should diligently *meditate on it.*
A sight of Christ in his agony is a wondrous cure for our agonies.

> *That crown of thorns about thy head, O bleeding Lamb,*
> *quickly eases my aching and throbbing brow.*
> *And oh, how those eyes of yours, red with weeping,*
> *have looked with consolation into my grieving soul!*
>
> *Seeing your holy cheeks so stained with spittle*
> *makes me forget the reproach I am bearing.*
> *And when I see you stripped naked and hung up on the cross,*
> *I think very highly of enduring persecution for your sake.*

The chief thing is this—that the blood is *actually applied to the soul.*

If you lie soaking in the Atonement;
    if you are putting your broken heart to sleep on the breast of Christ, close to his wound,
        you will have sweet peace and rest in times of tribulation.
When the blood is applied to the conscience it breathes peace through the soul.

Oh, for a little of Christ's blood sprinkled in the chambers of the soul!

If sin is pardoned, we are secure.
If Christ stands in our place and his precious blood pleads for us, we are content to lie down
    at his feet and say, "Do what you will, Lord, for we are forgiven."

When the blood of Christ is applied to the soul, we are assured that the end will be glorious.
We are content to bear a cross now since we will soon wear a crown.

> *O sinner, the fountain is still open for iniquity and sin;*
> *you have but to wash and you will be clean.*
>
> *A simple faith will obtain complete purification from all sin.*

From sermon no. 1316, *Why the Heavenly Robes Are White*

OUR LORD'S PREACHING

"The Spirit of the Lord is upon Me,
because He has anointed Me to preach the gospel to the poor;
He has sent Me to heal the brokenhearted."
Luke 4:18 nkjv

The purpose of our Lord's anointing was so that he might preach.
It was his business to preach, and he did preach; he was always preaching.

He preached when he was on the mountain, and he preached when he sat at the Pharisee's table.
He preached when he did not speak, for his silence was as eloquent as his words.
He was preaching when he lent his feet to the woman, so that she might wash them with her tears,
    just as much as when he was dividing the loaves and the fishes and feeding the hungry multitude.
He preached from the bloodstained tree; with hands and feet fastened there he delivered the greatest
    sermon on justice and love, on vengeance and grace, on death and life, that has ever been preached.

Oh, yes, always a preacher, our Savior preached wondrously!
If he walked the streets, he preached as he walked.
If he sought rest and the people thronged him, he did not send them away without a gracious word.

But now, notice the people to whom he especially preached the gospel.

They were "the poor," the meek, "the brokenhearted"—
    a people who are not lofty in their own thoughts, because they have been broken down.
They seek no high honors and desire no praises but bow down before the Lord in humility.

If you think that you are keeping God's laws perfectly and hope to be saved by your works,
    you must remember that the whole have no need of a physician.
Jesus did not come on such a needless errand as that of healing people who have no illnesses,
    but the sick need a doctor and he has come in great compassion to heal their wounds and diseases.

So, if you are sick, you may be sure that the Savior has come to heal you.
If you are poor, you may be certain that Christ has come to enrich you.
If you are sad and sorrowful, you may be sure that Christ has come to comfort you.

You nobodies—you who have been turned upside down and emptied right out—
you who are bankrupt and beggars;
you who feel like you are clothed with rags and covered with wounds, bruises, and sores (Isaiah 1:6);
you who are utterly bad through and through, and know it, and mourn it, and are humbled by it;
you may know that Christ was anointed in order to give mercy to such poor creatures as you are.

Oh, how we ought to rejoice in the anointing of Jesus
since it benefits such poor, sinful objects!

From sermon no. 3237, *Our Lord's Preaching*

MURDEROUS SINS

O you who love the Lord, hate evil!
Psalm 97:10

You have a friend, the best friend you have ever had. I know him and have loved him, and he has loved me. But there was a day when I took my walks abroad that I came upon a spot forever engraved on my memory, for there I saw this friend—my best, my only friend, *murdered.*

I stooped down with great sadness and looked at him and saw that he was cruelly murdered.

I saw that his hands and feet had been rent with rough iron nails.
I saw misery in his dead countenance, so terrible that I hardly dared look at it.
His body was emaciated with hunger, and his back was red with bloody scourges.
His brow had a circle of wounds about it, indicating that it had been pierced by thorns.

I shuddered, for I had known this friend very well. He had no faults; he was the purest of the pure, the holiest of the holy. All his life he "went about doing good" (Acts 10:38). He had healed the sick, fed the hungry, and raised the dead. For which of these deeds did they kill him?

As I looked into that poor sorrowful face, I wondered who could have been a wretch so vile as to pierce such hands. I said to myself, *Where do these traitors live? Who are these people who could have smitten someone like this?*

Had they murdered an oppressor, I might have forgiven them.
Had they slain one who had indulged in vice or villainy, it might have been his just deserts.
Had it been a murderer and a rebel, or one who had committed sedition, I would have said, "Bury his corpse for justice has at last given him his due!"

Oh, where are the traitors lodged? Oh, what jealousy, what revenge I felt! If only I might find these murderers, what would I do with them! As I continued to observe that corpse, I heard a footstep and wondered where it was. Listening, I perceived that the murderer was close at hand. Because it was dark, I groped about to find him. I found that somehow or other, wherever I put my hand, I could not meet with him, for he was nearer to me than I realized. At last, I put my hand on my breast.

"I have you now!" said I; for lo, he was in my own heart. The murderer was hiding within my own bosom, dwelling in the recesses of my inmost soul. Then I wept. Here I was standing in the very presence of my murdered Master, and it was I who was harboring the murderer. Guilty, I knelt over his corpse and sang that plaintive hymn:

> 'Twere you my sins, my cruel sins,
> His chief tormentors were;
> Each of my crimes became a nail
> And unbelief the spear.

Revenge! Revenge! You who fear and love the Lord take vengeance on your sins and hate all evil!

From sermon no. 208, *Righteous Hatred*

"THE LAMB OF GOD"

The next day he saw Jesus coming toward him, and said,
"Behold, the Lamb of God, who takes away the sin of the world!"
JOHN 1:29

In describing our Lord Jesus in his sacrificial character,
    John was very explicit in declaring him to be the sacrifice of God.
He says, "Behold, the Lamb *of God."*

Did the Baptist thus recall the day when Abraham walked with his son to the mount of sacrifice,
    and Isaac said, "Behold, the fire and the wood, but where is the lamb for a burnt offering?"
And Abraham replied, "God will provide for himself the lamb for a burnt offering" (Genesis 22:8).

Centuries later, John seems to say, "That saying of the father of the faithful is now fulfilled. Behold,
    how God provides! Behold, the Lamb of God!"

> *Oh, is it not wonderful that he against whom all sin was leveled*
> *would himself provide the sacrifice for sin?*
>
> *Behold the sin **of man** and the Lamb **of God!***
> *Jesus is the Father's best beloved, his choice one, his only one,*
> *and yet he delivered him up for us all!*
> *God's Son became God's Lamb!*
>
> *O my Father, my Father, do I sin and do you find the sacrifice?*
>
> *But if a sacrifice must be found by the Father,*
> *why must it be found so close to his heart?*
>
> *He could find the sacrifice for sin only in his own bosom;*
> *he had only one Son and he gave him up for us.*

Who sacrificed the Lamb of God? Who was the priest on that dreadful day? Who put him to grief?
Who caused him the direst pang of all when he cried, "Why have you forsaken me?" (Matthew 27:46).
Was it not the Father himself?

This was the hardest point of Abraham's test: "Take your son, your only son Isaac, whom you love,
    and go to the land of Moriah, and offer him there as a burnt offering" (Genesis 22:2).
He himself must officiate at the sacrifice.

This the great Father did!

Today, this truth remains: Jesus is the Lamb that God always accepts, must accept, glories to accept.
Bring Jesus with you when you approach God, and you have brought an acceptable sacrifice.
You cannot fail to be forgiven when you come pleading the name of Jesus.

From sermon no. 1987, *"Behold the Lamb of God"*

DELIGHTING IN THE KING'S GLORY

The LORD of hosts, he is the King of glory!
PSALM 24:10

Do we not delight in our King's present glory and in the glory yet to be revealed?

That he rules us is delightful;
that he rules all worlds is also inspiring;
that he has power to execute his righteous will is also pleasant;
but oh, what a joy it is to think of his own great glory!

You who have followed him through the streets of Jerusalem in all his shame
and then stood with weeping eyes at Calvary as you watched him in the bitter pangs of death,
let your hearts be joyful in knowing that the cross and the thorn-crown are now in the past.

Oh, come and behold him now in his Father's courts!
Like the sun in the firmament his glory flames forth!
Angels and principalities and powers are all lost in the blaze of his brightness!

Listen to their hymns!
They are all for him.

Behold them as they bow!
They bow before the Lamb once slain.

> *Unto him who lives, and was dead,*
> *and is alive forevermore (Revelation 1:18),*
> *the song of cherubim and seraphim ascends.*

> *All harps praise and all hearts adore*
> *the King of Glory in the midst of Zion.*

Blessed be his name!

Oh, that I had permission to bow so near to him that I might kiss his blessed feet;
or at least be able to steal into the lowest seat in heaven
and but for a moment gaze on that godlike face that was stained with spittle for my sake!

I would ask for no higher joy than to look on that glorious Being
who was once despised and rejected on my account
but who is now adored by angels and worshiped by all the saints.

Our King's substitutionary death of sorrow has won the deepest admiration of my heart.

From sermon no. 963, *Our King Our Joy*

THE HEAVEN OF HEAVEN

They will see his face.
REVELATION 22:4

It is the chief blessing of heaven, the cream of heaven, the heaven of heaven, to see Jesus.

Who will speak lightly of the streets of glassy gold and the gates of pearl?
Who would forget that we will see angels, and seraphim, and cherubim?
Who would fail to remember that we will see apostles, martyrs, and confessors?
Who would not long to see again his departed loved ones who now sleep in Jesus?
But still, the main thought we now have of heaven is that we will see Jesus.

Heaven would not be a desirable place if Jesus were not there,
   or, if being there, we could not enjoy the nearest and dearest fellowship with him.
Christ is all in all to us here, and so we pant and long for a heaven
   in which he will be all in all to us forever.

A distant sight of him has turned our sorrow into joy.
Communion with him lifts us above our present cares, and strengthens us to bear our heavy burdens.
What then, will heavenly communion be?

Oh, to literally see his face;
to see the very flesh and blood that suffered on Calvary;
to see the hand that was pierced with the nail, now grasping the scepter of all worlds;
to see the very head that was bowed down with anguish, now crowned with a royal diadem;
to see that face, so marred, now resplendent amidst the thrones of heaven!

Into that selfsame countenance
we will be permitted to gaze.

Oh, what a sight!

Yes, we will see his face as it is now in all its glory, with no traces of his former anguish.

He looks like a Lamb that has been slain, and he still wears his priesthood;
   but all that has to do with the shame, and the spitting, and the slaughter,
      has been so transformed that the sight is all blissful, all comforting, all glorious.
In his face there is nothing to excite a tear or to cause a sigh.

Roll by, ye years; hasten on, ye laggard months and days,
so that we may behold our Beloved—
the One who has redeemed us to God by his blood,
the One whom we love with such a passionate desire
that we would suffer ten thousand deaths to be in his embrace!

From sermon no. 824, *The Heaven of Heaven*

BEDS OF SPICE

His cheeks are like beds of spice yielding perfume.
SONG OF SOLOMON 5:13 NIV

Lo, the flowery month has arrived!
March winds and April showers have done their work
and the earth is now clothed with beauty.

Come my soul, put on your best clothes
and let us go and gather a bouquet of heavenly thoughts.

You know where to go, for the "beds of spice" are well-known
and you have often smelled their sweet perfume,
so you will go at once to your Well-beloved
and you will find all loveliness, all joy in him.

That cheek once so cruelly beaten with a rod,
so often bedewed with tears of sympathy and then defiled with spittle—
that cheek as it smiles with mercy is a fragrant aroma to my heart.

You did not hide your face from shame and spitting, O Lord Jesus;
therefore, I will find my dearest delight in praising you!
Your cheeks were furrowed by the plow of grief
and crimsoned with blood from your thorn-crowned temples;
and these marks of boundless love attract my soul
far more than beds of scented herbs.

Oh, if I may not see the whole of his face,
then I would behold his cheeks,
for the slightest glimpse of him is exceedingly refreshing,
and it yields to my spirit a variety of delights!

In Jesus I find not only fragrance but beds of spice,
not one flower but all kinds of sweet flowers.
He is my rose and my lily, my violet and my cluster of henna.

When he is with me it is May all year round
and my soul goes forth to wash its happy face in the morning dew of his grace
and to find solace in the birds who are singing his promises.

Precious Lord Jesus, let me truly know the blessedness
that dwells in abiding, unbroken fellowship with you.
I am a poor, worthless one, whose cheek you have stooped to kiss,
so let me kiss you in return with the kisses of my lips.

Morning and Evening, May 1 (M)

THE THEME OF SCRIPTURE

"Search the Scriptures because … it is they that bear witness about me."
John 5:39

Jesus Christ is the Alpha and Omega of the Bible.
He is the constant theme of its sacred pages; from first to last, they testify of him.

At the Creation we discern him as one of the sacred Trinity (John 1:1–3).
We catch a glimpse of him in the promise of the woman's offspring.
We see him typified in the ark of Noah.
We walk with Abraham as he sees the Messiah's day.
We hear the venerable Israel talking of Shiloh.
In the numerous types of the law, we find the Redeemer foreshadowed.

Prophets and kings, priests and preachers, all look one way.
They stand as the cherubs did over the ark of the covenant, desiring to look within
and read the mystery of God's great atonement.

In the New Testament, our Lord is the one pervading subject on every page.
The whole substance of the New Testament is Jesus Christ crucified.

What would be left of the Evangelists if you removed Christ from them?
What would be left of Paul's epistles if Jesus were taken away?
What have Peter, James, Jude, or John to write about, but the same subject?

Even the closing sentence of Scripture is bejeweled with the Redeemer's name:
"Come, Lord Jesus! The grace of the Lord Jesus be with all. Amen."

We should consider the Word to be like a mirror into which Christ looks down from heaven;
and then, we looking into it, see his face reflected as in a glass—darkly, it is true—
but still a blessed preparation for when we will see him face to face.

The Bible contains Jesus Christ's letters to us,
perfumed by his love.

These pages are the garments of our King,
and they all smell of myrrh, aloes, and cassia.

Scripture is the golden chariot in which Jesus rides,
and it is filled with love for all his people.

The Scriptures are the swaddling bands of the holy child Jesus;
unroll them and you will find your Savior.

Morning and Evening, June 10 (E) and sermon no. 546, *Alpha and Omega*

PERFECT THROUGH SUFFERINGS

For it was fitting that he, for whom and by whom all things exist,
in bringing many sons to glory,
should make the founder of their salvation perfect through suffering.
HEBREWS 2:10

Christ was not made perfect in character through his sufferings;
   he was always perfect—perfect God and perfect man.
But as the founder of our salvation he was made perfect through his sufferings.

It was necessary for Christ to suffer in order for him to sympathize with us.
You cannot cast human suffering into any shape that is new to him.

If you feel a thorn in your foot,
remember that it once pierced his head.

If you have an obstacle to overcome,
you may see there the mark of his hands,
for he has climbed that way before you.

The path of sorrow
has blood-marked footprints all along the way,
for the Man of Sorrows has been there,
and he can now sympathize with you.

Besides receiving his atoning blood, it is also necessary to follow Christ's example;
   and had Christ not suffered, he could not have been *an example* to us.
We would have said, "Yes, he may be an example to unsuffering angels,
   but not to those who have to tread the hot coals of the furnace."

He could never have shown us how to be patient if he had never suffered.
He could never have taught us to forgive if he had never been injured.
He could never have trained us in holy courage if he had never fought a battle.
He could never have shown us hope in tribulation if he had not waded to his throne through
   tribulation.

Our Savior met all the experiences of life.

He was in the company of all types of people.
He was shot at from all quarters of the earth.
He was in every respect tempted as we are (Hebrews 4:15).

If we know our Savior in the sweetness of his sympathy
and in the perfection of his example,
we will know him to the joy of our hearts forever.

From sermon no. 478, *Christ—Perfect Through Sufferings*

A HEAD WITH MANY DIADEMS

On his head are many diadems.
REVELATION 19:12

Yes, you know whose head this is and you have not forgotten its marvelous history—

a head that in infancy had reclined on the breast of a woman,
a head that had meekly bowed in obedience to a simple carpenter,
a head that had sweat "great drops of blood falling down to the ground" (Luke 22:44),
a head that had been spit on and whose hair was pulled,
a head that in the grim agony of death, crowned with thorns, gave utterance to the terrible cry,
    "My God, my God, why have you forsaken me?" (Matthew 27:46),
a head that afterwards slept on the pillow of the grave,
a head that rose again from the tomb and looked with eyes of love on the women waiting there.

Who would have thought that a head "so marred, beyond human semblance" (Isaiah 52:14)—
    a head that suffered more from the tempests of heaven and earth than any other mortal brow—
would now be surrounded with many diadems, with many star-studded crowns!

Oh, let every believing eye look through the thick darkness
and behold Jesus as he sits this day on the throne of his Father,
and let every heart rejoice at the many crowns of dominion on his head!

First and foremost, there sparkles about his brow the everlasting diadem of the King of heaven.
The angels are his; the cherubim and seraphim continually sing his praise.
The mightiest spirit delights to carry his commands to the most distant world.

This earth is also a part of his wide domain so on his head is the crown of creation: "All things
    were made through him, and without him was not any thing made that was made" (John 1:3).
You see his works when you lift your eye to the upper spheres and behold the starry worlds.

On his head is the crown of providence,
    and next to this, there also glitters the thrice-glorious crown of grace.
The river of God's mercy flows from his throne and he sits as Sovereign, dispensing mercy.

I pause here, overcome by the majesty of the subject,
and instead of attempting to describe that brow and those glittering diadems,
I will act the part of a seraph, and bow before that well-crowned head, and cry,

"Holy, holy, holy, art thou Lord God of hosts!
Thou art supreme, and unto thee be glory forever and ever!"

From sermon no. 281, *The Savior's Many Crowns*

QUIET AND UNOBTRUSIVE

He will not quarrel or cry aloud,
nor will anyone hear his voice in the streets.
MATTHEW 12:19

This passage wonderfully depicts the Redeemer's gentleness.
What a quiet, unobtrusive life was that of him whom they called "the carpenter's son"!

It is true that he was very energetic; he fought against sin even to agony and blood.
   With thrilling eloquence and many tears he cried out against evil and warned people to escape.
This passage teaches us that while others were contentious for power and notoriety, Jesus was not.
   He raised no party; he incited no strife; he sought no honor; he courted no popularity.

He left the arena of this world's contests to others.
His was another field of conflict.

His first labors were very private and his kingdom was not very obvious.
He went about healing and teaching, calling John and James and Peter and Andrew and Matthew.
He spent a whole day talking with a woman at a well, doing what we call ordinary mission work.

Our King came among us in meek and lowly guise,
and so he continued among us.

Gently gliding through the world,
he is seen by his light rather than heard by his sound;
content to shun fame and avoid applause.

He could not help being popular; as a speaker he was sure to attract thousands,
   for "no one ever spoke like this man!" (John 7:46).
And as a miracle worker, many people followed him in order to witness his wonders
   and to eat of his loaves and fishes.

With such a generous spirit, it is not surprising that the people tried to make him a king;
   but he tore away from them, stepped into a boat and passed over to the other side.
Rough waters were more to his liking than hot-blooded mobs of transient admirers
   who could be bought with bread and fish.

He came to endure, not to enjoy;
to be despised, not to be crowned.

His design was not to be the idol of the people,
but to break the idols and lead their hearts back to God.
Hence he did not quarrel or cry aloud or run in the world's race.

From sermon no. 1147, *The Gentleness of Jesus*

CHRIST IN THE COVENANT

"I will ... give you as a covenant to the people."
ISAIAH 49:8

Jesus Christ himself is the sum and substance of the covenant and is the property of every believer.
You know his attributes as God; you know that he is omniscient, omnipresent, omnipotent,
and all these great and glorious attributes that belong to God are yours.
You may put your hand on any characteristic of Christ as the Son of God and say, "It is mine."

Your arm, O Jesus, that upholds the pillars of the earth—that arm is mine.

Those eyes, O Jesus, that pierce through the thick darkness and behold futurity—
those eyes are mine to look on me with love.

Those lips, O Christ, that sometimes speak words louder than ten thousand thunders
or whisper syllables sweeter than the music of harps—those lips are mine.

You must also consider his attributes as man. All that Jesus possesses as *perfect man* is yours.
As a perfect man he stood before his Father, full of favor, and accepted by God as a perfect being.

O believer, God's acceptance of Christ is your acceptance.
The love that the Father sets on a perfect Christ, he sets on you now.
His perfect righteousness, his stainless life that kept the law and made it honorable, is yours.

You must remember that Christ is also yours *in all his offices.*
In every name he bears and in every crown he wears he is the believer's own.

Do you see him on earth?
There he stands, *the Great High Priest* offering his bloody sacrifice.

See him on the tree:
His hands are pierced, his feet are gushing blood.

Do you see that pallid countenance and those languid eyes flowing with compassion?
Do you behold that mightiest of sacrifices—the sum and substance of them all?

Believer, that is *yours.*
Those precious drops plead and claim *your* peace with God.
That open side is *your* refuge; those pierced hands are *your* redemption.
That cry of a forsaken heart was uttered for *you*; that death was for *you*.

Come, consider Christ in any one of his various offices;
but when you have considered him lay hold of this thought—
in all these things he is *your* Christ, given to *you* as the eternal covenant,
to be *your* personal possession forever.

From sermon no. 103, *Christ in the Covenant*

THE CURSE REMOVED

Christ redeemed us from the curse of the law by becoming a curse for us—
for it is written, "Cursed is everyone who is hanged on a tree."
GALATIANS 3:13

How humbling this truth is to our pride …
    that the curse of God is on everyone who is the offspring of Adam;
    that every child born in this world is born under the curse, since it is born under the law.

Then, in addition to the curse that rests on us because we are children of Adam,
    there is also the curse that comes through our own transgression.
The first moment that we sin we come beneath the curse quoted in the text, "Cursed be everyone
    who does not abide by all things written in the Book of the Law, and do them" (Galatians 3:10).

It is a dreadful thought …
    that the trail of the Serpent is over the whole earth;
    that the poison of sin is in the fountain of every human heart;
    that the blood in all our veins is corrupt;
    that all of us are under the curse unless we have been redeemed from it by Christ.

Oh yes, there is redemption for sinners,
but "the curse of the law" was not easily taken away!

The thunderbolts had been in God's hand, needing to be launched!
The sword was unsheathed, for divine justice had to be satisfied!
Vengeance had to fall!

So how could the sinner be saved?

The Son of God appeared and he said:
"Father, launch your thunderbolts at me!
Here is my breast; plunge the sword of justice in here!
Here are my shoulders; let the lash of vengeance fall on them!"

Thus Christ our substitute came forth and stood for us,
"the righteous for the unrighteous,
that he might bring us to God" (1 Peter 3:18).

Jesus Christ, our Savior, drank the veritable cup of our redemption to its very dregs.
    He suffered beneath the crushing wheels of divine vengeance
        the selfsame pains and sufferings that we ought to have suffered.
Divine justice is satisfied because Christ has endured the full penalty of all his people's guilt.

From sermon no. 3254, *The Curse Removed*

THE ETERNAL NAME

His name shall endure forever.
PSALM 72:17 NKJV

No one needs to be told that this is the name of Jesus Christ that "shall endure forever."
The proud works of man will pass away, but the honor of Christ's name will last forever.

Ah! As long as there is a sinner on earth
who has been reclaimed by Omnipotent grace,
Christ's "name shall endure."

As long as there is a Mary who is ready to wash his feet with tears;
as long as there breathes a chief of sinners who has washed himself in the fountain opened for sin;
as long as there exists a Christian who has put his faith in Jesus and found him to be his delight,
there will be no fear that Jesus' name will cease to be heard.

As long as true Christians live;
as long as we have manifestations of Christ's love, sights of his face, whispers of his mercy;
as long as we have assurances of his affection, promises of his grace, hopes of his blessing,
we cannot cease to honor his name.

But if *we* were to cease singing his praises *would Jesus Christ's name be forgotten?*
No. The stones would sing and the hills would be an orchestra.
The mountains would skip like rams and the little hills like lambs, for is he not their Creator?

If the lips of all mortals were dumb, there are enough creatures in this wide world to sing his praise.
The sun would lead the chorus and the moon would sweetly sing as she plays on her silver harp.
Stars would dance in their measured courses and the immense void would burst out in a shout,
"Thou art the glorious Son of God! Great is thy majesty, and infinite thy power!"

Can Christ's name be forgotten? No. It is painted on the skies and it is written on the waters!
The winds whisper it, the seas chant it, the beasts low it, the thunders proclaim it, the earth shouts it!

If this great universe should subside, would Christ's name be forgotten?
No. For yonder stand the angels; they, too, sing his glory.
Cherubim and seraphim cry unceasingly, "Holy, holy, holy, is the Lord God Almighty" (Revelation 4:8).

If the universe vanished, Christ's name would still be heard,
for the Father would hear it and the Spirit would hear it;
and deeply engraved on the immortal rocks of ages it would stand—
Jesus, the Son of God, co-equal with his Father!

"His name shall endure forever."

From sermon no. 27, *The Eternal Name*

ABOUT HIS FATHER'S BUSINESS

"Did you not know that I must be about My Father's business?"
LUKE 2:49 NKJV

Behold the condescension of Jesus, that he would become the servant of the Father,
    to do not his own business, but the Father's business.
See how he stoops to become a child subject to his mother.
    Though he was equal in power with God, he took "the form of a servant" (Philippians 2:7).

Note that as Christ goes about his Father's business,
    he always sets before us a *perfect example for our imitation.*
You never find him doing anything that you may not imitate.

You see him healing the sick to teach us benevolence.
You see him enduring temptation to teach us steadfastness.
You see him forgiving his enemies to teach us the grace of meekness and forbearance.
You behold him giving up his very life to teach us how we should surrender ourselves to God
    and to give up ourselves for the good of others.

Put Christ at a funeral and there you may imitate him—"Jesus wept" (John 11:35).
Put him on the mountaintop; he will be there alone in prayer and you may imitate him.
Put him with enemies; he so confounds them that he is a great model for you to copy.
Put him with friends and he will be "a friend who sticks closer than a brother" (Proverbs 18:24).

Despise and spit on him, and you will see him bearing contempt
with the same evenness of spirit that characterized him when he was exalted.

Not even once did he swerve from that bright, true mirror of perfection.
He was in everything an example, always doing his Father's business.

And ah! When he came to the climax of his labors, how thoroughly he did it!

It was his Father's business that made him sweat great drops of blood.
It was his Father's business that plowed his back with many gory furrows.
It was his Father's business that pricked his temple with the thorn-crown and caused him to be
    mocked and spit on.
It was his Father's business that made him despise the shame when, naked, he hung on the tree.
It was his Father's business that took him up to heaven where he sits at the right hand of God,
    still doing his Father's business.

Oh, glory to thee, Christ Jesus! You have done it.
You have done your Father's business well.

From sermon no. 122, *Christ about His Father's Business*

ALWAYS THE LAMB

Then I saw a Lamb, looking as if it had been slain,
standing in the center of the throne,
encircled by the four living creatures and the elders.
REVELATION 5:6 NIV

Our Savior always was, and is now, acknowledged to be Lord and God.

All the church worships him.
All the myriad of angels cry aloud in praises to him.
All knees will bow before him "in heaven and on earth and under the earth" (Philippians 2:10).

When you call him King of kings and Lord of lords, these lofty titles fall far below his glory and majesty.
    If we stood up with all the millions of the human race
        and with one voice lifted up a shout of praise to him,
    our highest honors would scarcely reach the lowest step of his all-glorious throne.

Yet, in all the glory of his deity
our Lord still appears as the Lamb that was slain.

This is still his chosen character.

The story is told of a great warrior, who on the anniversary of his most renowned victory,
    would always put on the coat in which he fought the fight, adorned with the marks of the battle.
Our Lord today, and every day, still wears the human flesh in which he overthrew our enemies,
    and he appears as one who has just recently died, since by death he overcame the Devil.

Always and forever he is the Lamb.
Even as God's prophet, priest, and king, he remains the Lamb.

When you will see him at last, you will say as John did, "Then I saw a Lamb, looking as if it had been
    slain, standing in the center of the throne, encircled by the four living creatures and the elders."
The Lamb is the center of the wonderful circle that makes up the fellowship of heaven.

Oh, write the Passion of your Lord on the tablet of your heart
and let nothing erase the treasured memory!

Think of him mainly and chiefly as the sacrifice for sin.
Set the Atonement in the midst of your mind
and let it tinge and color all your thoughts and beliefs.

Jesus bleeding and dying in your place
must be to you as the sun in your sky.

From sermon no. 2095, *The Lamb in Glory*

ASSURANCE IN CHRIST'S RESURRECTION

Who is to condemn? Christ Jesus is the one who died—more than that, who was raised—
who is at the right hand of God, who indeed is interceding for us.
ROMANS 8:34

What does Christ's resurrection from the dead have to do with the justification of a believer?

God held as it were a bond against us that we could not pay;
    and if it had remained unpaid we would have been sold forever under sin.
We would have had to pay the penalty of our transgressions.

By his death, however, Jesus paid the whole debt that was due from us to God.
But the bond was not cancelled until the day he rose from the dead.

On the cross we see Jesus dying for our sins as an expiating sacrifice,
    but in the Resurrection we see God acknowledging the death of Christ
and accepting what he has done for our indisputable justification.

This truth may be represented in another way:

Christ's death was the digging of the well of salvation.
Stern was the labor; toilsome was the work!

He dug on, and on, and on, through rocks of suffering,
    into the deepest caverns of misery;
but the Resurrection was the springing up of the water.

Christ dug the well to its very depths, but not a drop of water sprang up.
The world was still dry and thirsty.

Then on the morning of the Resurrection, a voice was heard: "Spring up, O well!" (Numbers 21:17);
    and Christ came forth from the grave—and with him came the resurrection and the life.
Pardon and peace for all souls sprang up from the deep well of his misery.

We do see ground for hope when Christ is bound, for he is bound for us;
we do see reason for rejoicing when he dies, for he dies for us;
we do see a theme for solid satisfaction in his burial, for he is buried for us;
but when he comes from the grave, having swallowed up death in victory, our hope bursts into song!

He lives, and because he lives, we also will live.
He is delivered from death and we are delivered too.
Death no longer has dominion over him and it no longer has dominion over us.

His deliverance is ours.
His freedom is ours.

From sermon no. 256, *The Believer's Challenge*

NO TOOLS ALLOWED

*"If you make me an altar of stone,
you shall not build it of hewn stones,
for if you wield your tool on it you profane it."*
Exodus 20:25

God's altar was not to be built with hewn stones,
  because no trace of human skill or labor was to be seen on it.

Human wisdom delights in trimming and arranging the doctrines of the cross
  into an artificial system that is more congenial to the depraved tastes of the fallen nature.
But instead of improving the gospel, carnal wisdom invents another gospel.
  Any alteration or amendment to the Lord's own Word profanes it.

The proud heart of man is eager to have a hand in the justification of his soul.
  Preparations for Christ are planned, humility and repentance are trusted in,
    good works are celebrated, and natural ability is flaunted.
Through these exercises we are placing human tools on the divine altar.

The Lord alone must be exalted in the great work of atonement.
Not a single mark of a human chisel or hammer is allowed.

There is an inherent blasphemy in attempting to add to what Christ Jesus,
  in his dying moments, declared to be finished.
There is a sacrilege in trying to improve on that which the Lord Jehovah finds perfect.

*Trembling sinner, put away your tools
and fall on your knees in humble supplication.*

*Accept your Lord and Savior Jesus Christ
as the altar of your atonement,
and rest in him alone for salvation.*

Today's text should be used as a warning to believers.
  There is far too much inclination among Christians
    to adjust the truths of Scripture according to their own way of thinking.
This is a form of irreverence and unbelief.

Let us strive against this, and receive truth as it is found in God's Word—
  rejoicing that the doctrines of Scripture are unhewn stones.
They are suitable material for building an altar for the Lord.

Morning and Evening, July 14 (M)

GREAT DROPS OF BLOOD

His sweat became like great drops of blood falling down to the ground.
LUKE 22:44

You will notice that Jesus not only sweat blood, but it was *great drops* of blood.
They not only coated the surface of his skin and were absorbed by his garments
until he became like the red heifer that was slaughtered on that very spot (see Numbers 19:2–3),
but the drops even fell down to the ground.

Here he stands unrivaled.

He was a man in good health, only about thirty years of age,
yet the mental pressure arising from our Lord's agony
forced the pores of his body to sweat great drops of blood.

> *Oh, how tremendous must have been the weight of sin
> that it could crush out of our Savior great drops of blood!*
>
> *What a demonstration of the mighty power of his love!*

Isaac Ambrose observed that the sap which flows from the tree that is uncut is always the best.

This precious Tree yielded sweet spices …
when it was wounded by the knotty whips;
when it was pierced by the nails on the cross;
but see, it pours out its best spice when there is no whip, no nail, no wound!

This reveals to us that the sufferings of Christ were voluntary.

There is no need for him to be lanced for the blood flows freely.
There is no need to apply the knife for his blood flows spontaneously.
Of itself, his blood flows in crimson torrents!

If people suffer great pain of mind, apparently the blood rushes to their heart;
their face becomes pale and frequently they faint.
The blood has gone inward as if to nourish the inner being.

Now look at our Savior in his agony.

He is so utterly oblivious of self,
that instead of his agony driving his blood to his heart to nourish himself,
it drives it outward to bedew the earth and thus minister to us.

> *The awful agony as his blood is poured out on the ground
> pictures the fullness of the offering Christ made for us.*

From sermon no. 493, *Gethsemane*

CROSSING THE BROOK KIDRON

The king crossed the brook Kidron.
2 SAMUEL 15:23

The brook Kidron was an insignificant but very filthy ditch outside the walls of Jerusalem;
   and it was into this brook that the filth of the sacrifices of the temple were thrown.
If it was not as some have called it—the open town sewer—it was certainly close to it.

Crossing over that foul and black brook
   has therefore become the symbol of a deep time of sorrow and acute distress;
      and so we are told that "the king crossed the brook Kidron."
The way—even for kings—is by the brook of grief and shame.

Now a greater king than David has crossed the brook Kidron;
   and since all the people wept as David crossed over it,
let us also weep as we remember how Zion's greater king passed over that black brook.

Oh, there has never been such a king as he, so glorious and so fair;
   his eyes were the suns of heaven and his presence was its glory!
But he came down among his creatures, who were fallen, seeking to help them.

He raised their dead and healed their sick.
When they were hungry, he fed them, and when they were fainting, he refreshed them.
His words were full of love and his teachings full of wisdom and grace.

But now they seek his blood! Yes, they seek his blood!
In the night they are pursuing him!

They will overtake him!
They will haul him away to the judgment seat!
They will put him to death!

> *O cruel world, not to know its greatest benefactor!*

Surely you remember the awful agonies by which he purchased our redemption.
There is this concerning our Lord that is not matched by David: He was truly slain!

The foes who pursued him overtook him.
They pierced his hands and his feet.
They lifted him up, a spectacle of scorn, and there he died.

But his cross was his triumph. Calvary was the battlefield on which he won the victory.
He rose from the grave and so he came back to Jerusalem again just like David did.

From sermon no. 3431, *The King Passing Over Kidron*

THE BRIEF INTERVAL REVEALED

Then those who had seized Jesus led him to Caiaphas the high priest,
where the scribes and the elders had gathered.
MATTHEW 26:57

After the mob had dragged our Lord from the house of Annas, they reached the palace of Caiaphas,
and *a brief interval* occurred before the high priest came to question the prisoner.

How were those sad minutes spent there?
Was the poor victim allowed to get some rest?
Was he allowed to collect his thoughts before having to face his accusers?
Far from it!

Luke tells the pitiful story:

"Now the men who held Jesus mocked Him and beat Him.
And having blindfolded Him, they struck Him on the face and asked Him, saying,
'Prophesy! Who is the one who struck You?'
And many other things they blasphemously spoke against Him" (Luke 22:63–65 NKJV).

The officers were waiting until the chairman of the court would come to interview the prisoner,
but instead of allowing the accused to take a short rest before such an important trial,
they spent all that time in venting their bitter malice on him.

Observe how they insult his claim to the Messiahship.
They bind our Savior's eyes and then, striking him, one after another,
they bid him exercise his prophetic gift for their amusement.
They tell him to prophesy as to whom it was who struck him.

Oh, shameful question!

How gracious was the silence,
for an answer might have withered them forever!

The day will come when all who have struck their Lord
will realize that he has seen them,
though they thought his eyes were blinded.

Yes, the day will come, blasphemer, worldling, careless one,
when everything you have done against Christ's cause and Christ's people
will be published before the eyes of men and angels,
and Christ will answer your question.
He will tell you who struck him!

From sermon no. 495, *The Greatest Trial on Record*

NOTHING UNLOVELY

Yes, he is altogether lovely.
SONG OF SOLOMON 5:16 NKJV

In describing a friend, have you sometimes been obliged to omit a prominent characteristic
  when you wished to make a favorable impression?
You have had to paint him as the artist once painted Oliver Cromwell
  with the great wart over his eyebrow purposely left out of the portrait.

We feel that it is kind to leave out the warts when describing the people we esteem.
  But when it comes to describing our Lord and Savior,
    there is nothing to leave out, nothing to guard or extenuate.
You never need to put a finger over the scar in his case as Apelles did when he painted his hero.[1]

No, tell it all!
Reveal the details of his private life and of his secret thoughts.
They need no concealment.

Lay bare the very heart of Christ, for that is the essence of love and loveliness.
  Speak of his death-wounds, for in his scars there is more beauty
    than in the uninjured beauty of another.
Even when he lies dead in the tomb he is more comely than the highest angels of God.

Nothing about our Lord needs to be concealed.
Even at his cross, where his enemies stumble, his choicest beauties are seen.

> *Oh, it is a great mystery, but a sure fact,*
> *that in our Lord's marred countenance*
> *his beauty is best seen!*
>
> *Anguish gave him a loveliness*
> *that could not have been reached otherwise.*
>
> *His Passion put the finishing touches*
> *upon his unrivaled loveliness.*

No one has ever been able to uphold an accusation against Jesus.
The sharp arrows of slander fall blunted from the shield of his perfection.

Yes, he is altogether lovely, meaning that there is nothing in him that is unlovely.
You may look and look again, but there is nothing in him that will not bear the closest scrutiny.

[1]Apelles was a 4th century BC Greek painter whose portrait of Alexander the Great showed him covering
  the scar on his cheek.
[2]From sermon no. 1446, *The Best Beloved*

CHRIST'S SUFFERINGS FORETOLD

*"We are going up to Jerusalem, and the Son of Man
will be betrayed to the chief priests and the teachers of the law.
They will condemn him to death and will turn him over to the Gentiles
to be mocked and flogged and crucified."*
MATTHEW 20:18–19 NIV

With these words our Lord gives the details of his sufferings.

He says first of all, that he "will be betrayed."
    Betrayed! That means sold by cruel treachery!
It means that one who eats bread with him will lift the heel against him.
    It means that a man who is his familiar acquaintance will sell him for a paltry bribe.

Jesus adds that he "will be betrayed to the chief priests and the teachers of the law."
    The priests ought to have been his greatest defenders for they were the spiritual guides of Israel,
        yet these were our Lord's bitterest enemies.
It was through their malice that he was condemned and crucified.

In our Master's death, all men conspired—not half the world, but all of it—
    the Gentile takes his share in this iniquity for Pilate condemns him to the cross.
The priests hand him over to Pilate, who commits him to the Roman soldiers to perform the cruel deed.

What dreadful scorning our Lord endured at the hands of the Jews
    when they spit in his face, blindfolded him and struck him!
And he was also scorned by the Gentiles when they put on him a scarlet robe,
    thrust a reed in his right hand, and then kneeling before him, cried, "Hail, King of the Jews!"

Yes, they pulled his hair!
They struck his cheeks!
They spit in his face!
They flogged him!
They crucified him!

Oh, behold him! Behold him!

See how his hands are extended and cruelly nailed to the wood.
See how his feet are fastened to the tree, and his hands and feet must bear the weight of his body.
See how the nails tear through his flesh as the weight drags his body down.
See how a fever causes his mouth to become like an oven and his tongue cleaves to its roof.

Crucifixion was an inhuman death,
    yet the Savior was "obedient to the point of death, even death on a cross" (Philippians 2:8).
The wonder is that he could foresee all this and yet speak of it so calmly.

From sermon no. 2212, *The Private Thoughts and Words of Jesus*

THE BETRAYAL

Jesus said to him, "Judas, would you betray the Son of Man with a kiss?"
LUKE 22:48

Perceive how black the treason was: Judas was Christ's servant
  and as such had been treated with utmost confidence.
But Judas was even more than this; *he was a friend—a trusted friend.*

> *This is vile indeed: to be installed as purse-bearer to the King of kings*
> *and then turn around and sell the Savior!*

> *This is treason in its highest form!*

Remember that the world saw Judas as a colleague and partner of our Lord,
  and when such an association has been established and there is treachery,
    it is as though our arm committed treason against our head, or as if our foot deserted the body.
Nothing can cause greater anguish than to be sold to destruction by one's bosom friend.

Notice the calm and gentle way in which our Lord *met this affliction.*
  Observe the first word he said to Judas after he had polluted his cheek with a kiss: "Friend."
He said, "Friend, do what you came to do" (Matthew 26:50). *Friend?*
  Then our Lord added, "Judas, would you betray the Son of Man with a kiss?"

I can imagine his tears and his faltering voice when he thus addressed his own familiar friend:

> *"Judas, would you betray the Son of Man?"—*
> *the suffering, sorrowing Friend whom you have seen naked and poor*
> *and without a place to lay his head?*

> *"Judas, would you betray the Son of Man?"—*
> *prostituting the fondest endearing sign, a kiss?*

> *"That which should be a symbol of loyalty to the King,*
> *will it be the badge of your treachery?*

> *"That which has been reserved as the best symbol of affection,*
> *will you make it the instrument of my destruction?*

> *"Would you betray the Son of Man with a kiss?"*

This also must have aggravated the woe of our beloved Savior
  when he saw the final impenitence of the traitor and read his tearful doom.
He had once said of Judas that it would have been better for him if he had not been born.

From sermon no. 494, *The Betrayal*

A SACHET OF MYRRH

My beloved is to me a sachet of myrrh.
Song of Solomon 1:13

The soul clings to Christ and she has good reason for doing so,
    for her own words are, "My beloved is to me a sachet of myrrh."
Myrrh may be compared to Christ for its *preciousness*,
    since myrrh is always spoken of in Scripture as being a rich, rare, and costly substance.

But then no myrrh could ever compete with Jesus Christ!

He is so precious
that even if heaven and earth were put together,
they could not buy another Savior.

When God gave his Son to the world,
he gave the best that heaven had.

Take Christ out of heaven,
and there is nothing for God to give.

Christ was God's all, for we read, "In him the whole fullness of deity dwells bodily" (Colossians 2:9).
Oh, precious gift of the whole of deity in the person of Christ!

How inestimably precious is that body of his that he took of the substance of the virgin!
Well might angels herald the coming of this immaculate Savior.
Well might they watch over his holy life for he is precious in all his actions.

How precious he is—as myrrh—in the offering of his great atonement!
What a costly sacrifice that was!
At what a price we were redeemed!—not with silver or gold, but with the precious blood of Christ.

And how precious he is in his resurrection!
Rising from the dead, that glorious Sun scatters all the nights of all his people by one rising.

How precious today are those incessant pleadings of his through which the mercies of God
    come down like the angels on Jacob's ladder to our needy souls!

Yes, Christ is to the believer,
in every aspect,
like myrrh for rarity and excellence.

From sermon no. 558, *A Bundle of Myrrh*

A DESCENT IN HUMILITY

And being found in human form, he humbled himself
by becoming obedient to the point of death, even death on a cross.
PHILIPPIANS 2:8

How can we measure Christ's descent when we do not know what it is to be equal with God?

Our text, however, is not actually speaking of Christ's humiliation in becoming a man.
It is speaking of his humiliation *after* he took upon himself our nature.

My gracious Lord,
you have already descended far enough!
Will you descend even further?
You were in the form of God; now you are in the form of man!

That is an unspeakable stoop!
Will you still humble yourself?

Surely he is brought low enough!
He was the Creator who made heaven and earth, yet he lies in a virgin's womb,
and after he is born he is cradled where the horned oxen feed.
Now the Creator is also a creature; the Son of God is also the Son of Man.

Could there be a greater condescension than this?

The Infinite is joined to the infant,
the Omnipotent to the feebleness of a newborn baby.

Yes, this was not all.
Throughout his whole life on earth Christ humbled himself.
In his body he suffered weakness, hunger, thirst; in his mind he suffered rebuke, slander, lies.

Where did he finally arrive in that dreadful descent?
What was the bottom of the abyss?

It was death, "even death on a cross."

That was the worst kind of death. It was also an extremely painful death of lingering agony.
It was a shameful death, for the cross was reserved for slaves and the lowest of felons.
It was a penal death, for he died as a criminal.
It was an accursed death, for "cursed is everyone who is hanged on a tree" (Galatians 3:13).

Our Lord humbled himself, even to this lowest point of all,
"even death on a cross."

From sermon no. 2281, *Our Lord in the Valley of Humiliation*

FAITH'S SURE FOUNDATION

"Whoever believes in him will not be put to shame."
1 PETER 2:6

The foundation of the believer's faith is Jesus Christ: "Whoever believes in *him*."
We place our trust in him when we see that he has suffered the consequences of our sin.

So, if we wish to have faith, we must accompany our Lord Jesus to Gethsemane
    where we will hear every drop of his blood pleading with us that we should trust him.
There his sighs and cries and throes of anguish all plead with us to rely on him.

Regarding him as the Son of the Highest, we see here an overwhelming argument for faith.
Who can doubt the merit of that work, beginning with the holy Son lying prostrate in Gethsemane,
    "very sorrowful, even to death" (Mark 14:34)?

Then, we trace him as he is seized and hurried away to the high priest, to Herod, and to Pilate.

How they pour contempt on him!
How the floggers scourge him!
How the degraded mock him!

His lowest shame,
his worst desertion,
his bitterest griefs—
    all say to us, "Can you not trust him?"

Then comes the death scene.
    With tears in our eyes we stand at the cross and see those blessed hands and feet nailed to the tree
        so that our Lord might be made a curse for us.
Can unbelief live after this?

Even before Christ's heart is opened by the spear thrust,
    we perceive that he is bleeding in every part of his body and soul,
for he is a mass of anguish.

> *O Son of God, if ever it were treason to doubt your power to save*
> *it must be so when we see you hanging on the cross!*
> *You have triumphed over our unbelief on the bloodstained tree!*
>
> *We feel constrained to cry, "I must believe!*
> *Those nails have crucified my unbelief!*
> *That spear has slain my doubts!"*

From sermon no. 1429, *Faith's Sure Foundation*

THE TEARING OF THE CURTAIN

And Jesus cried out again with a loud voice and yielded up his spirit.
And behold, the curtain of the temple was torn in two, from top to bottom.
MATTHEW 27:50–51

Through the death of Christ, the curtain of the temple was torn
  and the mysteries that had been concealed in the Most Holy Place were laid open to the gaze of all.
This was the first miracle of Christ after his death, and there is a singular sacredness surrounding it,
  for it was a deed of wonder done in that awful and mysterious place that was the abode of God.

See! He dies, and at the very door of God's high sanctuary,
Jesus tears the curtain in two!

There is an awful solemnity about this miracle,
for it is wrought before Jehovah himself!

At the same moment that his spirit departed from his body,
  our blessed Lord took hold of the great curtain of his Father's symbolic house and tore it in two!
All types and shadows of the ceremonial law then vanished.
  They vanished because they were fulfilled and explained in the death of Christ.

We also see here the great Opener into the presence of God,
  for there was no way into the Most Holy Place until Jesus, dying, tore the curtain.
So if you desire to approach God, Christ's death is the way to him.
  Jesus not only says, "I am the way" (John 14:6), but in tearing the curtain he makes the way.

Stop a moment and adore your dying Lord.

Does he, with such a miracle, signalize his death?
Does this not prove his immortality?

And see what power he possessed!
  His hands and feet are nailed to the cross,
    and as he hangs there he cannot protect himself from the insults of the soldiers.
But in his utmost weakness he is so strong that he tears the heavy curtain of the temple in two!

Now if Jesus does this for us in his death,
surely we will be saved by his life.

Jesus who died, is yet alive, and we must rely on him
to lead us into the holy places "not made with hands" (Mark 14:58).

Our Savior performed a miracle when he died,
opening the way for sinners to draw near to God.

From sermon no. 2059, *The Miracles of Our Lord's Death*

MEDITATING ON THE LAMB

"Behold, the Lamb of God!"
JOHN 1:36

Jesus Christ, as the atoning sacrifice, should be the principal object of every believer's thoughts. This one subject should engross our innermost souls.

> *Yes, this should be the main topic of each day's consideration*
> *and the favorite topic of each night's reflection.*

No theme for contemplation can equal this noblest of all topics—

God allied to human nature;
God in union with humanity, taking human sin;
God's stupendous love in condescending to be numbered with transgressors
   and suffering for sin that was not his own.

O believer, this is indeed the most needful subject for contemplation!
   You may forget many other things without suffering serious consequences,
      but you must live upon Christ; you must meditate on him.
Otherwise, you have missed the bread from the feast and the water from the well.

The crucified Savior is as needful for our meditation as is the air for our breathing.
There is no subject in the world so vast, so sublime, so pure, so elevating, so divine!
Let us behold Jesus Christ, the Lamb of God, and our eyes have seen all that is precious.[1]

> *Even when we get to heaven*
> *we will want no subject for meditation, except Jesus Christ.*

> *We will want little else in heaven besides him;*
> *he will be our bread, our food, our beauty, and our glorious garment.*

> *The atmosphere of heaven will be Christ;*
> *everything in heaven will be Christ-like.*

> *Yes, Christ is the heaven of his people!*[2]

Oh, go and live on Calvary, ye saints,
   for better air cannot be found beneath the scope of heaven!
As you linger there in meditation, your thoughts of the Savior will be sweet.[3]

[1]From sermon no. 1060, *Behold the Lamb*
[2]From sermon no. 2690, *Meditation on God*
[3]From sermon no. 2403, *The Sweet and the Sweetener*

PRAYERS OF SWEET INCENSE

Golden bowls full of incense, which are the prayers of the saints.
REVELATION 5:8

That prayer is pleasing to God is not due to any merit believers possess in themselves.
    In the best prayer, offered by the holiest saint,
        there is enough imperfection to render it a polluted thing.
By themselves, our prayers would be an offense to divine holiness, rather than a sweet fragrance.

Our consolation lies in our beloved Intercessor who stands before God for us, even Christ Jesus.
    He possesses such an abundance of precious merit
        that he imparts a delicious odor to our supplications and prayers.
Through his merit our intercessions are acceptable to the Majesty of heaven.

It was the early church father, Ambrose, who used a wonderful illustration concerning believers'
    prayers. He said we are like little children who run into the garden to gather flowers to please
    their father, but we are so ignorant and childish that we pluck as many weeds as flowers, and
    some of them are very noxious. We carry this mixture in our hands thinking that it is acceptable
    to him.

The mother meets the child at the door and says, "Little one, you don't know what you have gathered."

She unbinds the mixture and takes from it all the weeds, leaving only the sweet flowers, and then
    she takes other flowers—sweeter than those the child plucked—and inserts them in place of the
    weeds. Then she puts the perfect bouquet into the child's hand and he runs with it to his father.

Jesus Christ, in more than motherly tenderness, thus deals with our supplications. If we could see
    one of our prayers after Christ Jesus has amended it, we would hardly recognize it.

Even our good flowers
grow fairer in Jesus' hand.

We clumsily tie them into a bundle,
but he arranges them into a fair bouquet
where each beauty enhances the charm of its neighbor.

If I could see my prayer after the Lord has prayed it,
    I would discover much missing, and much there, that had nothing to do with me.
His boundless sweetness lends to me and my poor prayer a sweetness not my own.

The prayers of God's saints are as precious incense
because they are accepted in the Beloved.

From sermon no. 1051, *Golden Vials Full of Odors*

MOCKINGLY HONORED

O men, how long shall my honor be turned into shame?
PSALM 4:2

The honor that Christ ought to have received among men was rendered to him only in shame. The following is an outline of someone's insight into how they mockingly honored our Lord.

First of all, they gave him a procession of honor.

When a victorious general returns from the war, he rides through the streets of the city;
    applauded by the crowds gathered there to welcome him.
And when Jesus Christ, the Son of God, was to be honored by the world, he also had a procession.

See the Man of Sorrows bearing his cross as he is led to the place called Calvary.
    See him painfully toiling on and then sinking beneath the burden of his load,
        while all around him the clamorous multitude is crying, "Away with him! Crucify him!"
That was the procession of honor that men gave to the Lord Jesus Christ.

Next, they gave him a cup of honor.

When a person of distinction comes to visit from a foreign country he is given hospitality,
    but when Christ came to this earth on a mission of mercy, what was he given?
He was given a stupefying drink that he refused to take, since it would deaden his powers;
    and then, when he was so parched that he cried, "I thirst," he was given vinegar to drink.

Then they gave him a seat of honor.

It is the custom to conduct noble visitors to the most honorable position available;
    and the world conducted its honored Guest along the *Via Dolorosa*.
It led him right up to the seat of honor. There it is—the accursed tree!

He will have little rest there, for the nails will be roughly thrust through his hands and feet,
    and then they will brutally jerk the cross down into the hole prepared for it.
His whole body will be so jarred and shaken that he will cry out,
    "I am poured out like water, and all my bones are out of joint" (Psalm 22:14).

They also gave him a title of honor.

When the Queen wishes to honor any of her subjects, she makes them knights or baronets or peers,
    but the world thought that Christ was only worthy of the title "the King of thieves."
Pilate called him "the King of the Jews," but the others practically called him "the King of thieves,"
    for they crucified him between two thieves as if to say that he was the worst of the three.

Oh, let us try to realize the feelings of our blessed Savior
when men turned his honor into shame, even in the very throes of death!

From sermon no. 3276, *Christ's Glory Turned to Shame*

MORE LOVE DESIRED

Rightly do they love you.
Song of Solomon 1:4

Believers love Jesus with a deeper affection than they dare give to any other being.
They would rather lose father and mother than part with him.

They hold all earthly comforts with a loose hand,
    but they carry Jesus locked fast in their hearts.
They voluntarily deny themselves for his sake,
    but they will not be driven to deny him.

People have tried to separate the faithful from their Master,
    but their attempts have been fruitless in every age.
Neither crowns of honor nor frowns of anger have untied this Gordian knot.

This is no ordinary attachment that the world's power can dissolve,
    for neither man nor devil has been successful in doing so.
Satan's craftiness has been proven to be weak indeed
    when it comes to tearing apart two divinely welded hearts.

It is written, and nothing can blot out the sentence, "Rightly do they love you."

However, the intensity of the love of the upright
    is not to be judged so much by what it appears
as by what the upright long for.

It is our daily lament that we cannot love Jesus enough.
We wish that our hearts were capable of holding more and of reaching further.

Like Samuel Rutherford, we sigh and cry,
    "Oh, for as much love as would go round about the earth, and over heaven—
        yea, the heaven of heavens, and ten thousand worlds—
    that I might let all out upon fair, fair, only fair Christ."

Alas! Our longest reach is but a span of love,
    and our affection is but a drop in a bucket compared with his love.
But measure our love by our intentions, and it is high indeed!
    We trust that this is how our Lord judges it.

Oh, that we could give all the love in all hearts
in one gigantic bundle
to him who is altogether lovely!

Morning and Evening, August 7 (M)

THE SIGN OF TRUE JOY

*"This will be a sign for you: you will find a baby
wrapped in swaddling cloths and lying in a manger."*
LUKE 2:12

The shepherds did not ask for a sign, but one was graciously given to them.
　　The sign that the joy of the world had come was this: they were to go to the manger
　　　　and they would find the Christ in it, and he was to be the sign.
So the shepherds went and found the Baby "wrapped in swaddling cloths."

Now as you look at this infant, you will not notice even a meager amount of *temporal power.*
Observe the two little arms of a little baby who must be carried wherever he goes.

> *Alas, the nations of earth look for joy in a strong military power,
> but Jesus establishes his eternal empire, not on force, but on love.*

> *O ye people, see your hope in the mild and gentle Prince!
> He whose glory is his self-sacrifice, is our true benefactor.*

Look again, and you will see *no pomp* to dazzle you.

Is the child wrapped in purple and fine linen?
Ah, no!

Does he sleep in a cradle of gold?
No, the manger alone is his shelter.

There is no crown on the Baby's head,
　　nor is there a coronet surrounding the mother's brow.
A simple maiden from Galilee and a little child in ordinary swaddling cloths is all you see.

> *Alas, the nations are dazzled by a vain show!
> The pomp of empires and the pageantry of kings are their delight.*

> *O ye people, true joy lies in truth and righteousness, in peace and salvation,
> of which yonder newborn Prince, in the garments of a peasant child, is the true symbol!*

Neither was there *wealth* to be seen at Bethlehem.
Here in the cradle of the world's hope at Bethlehem, we see far more poverty than wealth.

> *O ye people, your joy will never lie in your gold,
> but in the gospel enjoyed by all classes!*

> *Jesus, by raising us up to spiritual wealth,
> redeems us from the chains of Mammon, and in that liberty gives us joy.*

From sermon no. 1026, *Joy Born at Bethlehem*

"IN-DOOR" RECEPTION

"This man receives sinners."
Luke 15:2

This man who towers above all other men,
    who is holy, harmless, undefiled, and separate from sinners—
this man receives sinners!

This man who is none other than the Eternal God
    before whom angels veil their faces—
this man receives sinners!

That we would be willing to seek the lost is nothing special, for they are of our own race.
    But that he—the offended God—against whom the transgression has been committed,
        would take the form of a servant and bear our sins,
    and would then be willing to receive the vilest of the vile—this is indeed marvelous!

We must take note that "this man receives sinners"—not for them to remain sinners.
    He receives them in order to pardon their sins, to cleanse their hearts with his purifying Word,
        and to preserve their souls by the indwelling of the Holy Spirit.
He enables them to serve him, to praise him, and to have fellowship with him.

When he has cleansed sinners he receives them, not only as disciples, but as companions.
No, more! He receives them as friends.

He receives sinners into his heart's love.
He takes them from the trash heap and makes them his "treasured possession" (Malachi 3:17).
He snatches them like an iron brand from the fire and preserves them as costly monuments of
    his mercy.
None are as precious in his sight as the sinners for whom he died!

When Jesus receives sinners,
    he does not do it at an "out-door" reception
where he charitably entertains them for a while as great men do with passing beggars.

No, he opens the golden gates of his royal heart
    and he receives the sinner right into himself.
Yes, he admits the sinner into personal union with himself
    and makes him a member of his body, of his flesh, and of his bones.

Oh, there has never been a reception like this!

Today, this man is still receiving sinners.
If only sinners would receive him.

From sermon no. 665, *Open House for All Comers*

LOOKING AT THE PIERCED ONE

"I will pour out on the house of David and the inhabitants of Jerusalem
a spirit of grace and pleas for mercy,
so that, when they look on me, on him whom they have pierced,
they shall mourn for him."
ZECHARIAH 12:10

This tenderness of heart and mourning for sin
   is actually wrought by a faith-look at the pierced Son of God.
True sorrow for sin does not come without the Spirit of God;
   but the Spirit only works sorrow by leading us to look to the crucified Savior.

There is no true mourning for sin until the eye has seen Christ.
   As someone has said, "Eyes are made for two things at least—
      first, to look with, and next, to weep with.
   The eye that looks to the pierced One is the eye that weeps for him."

> *O soul, when you look where all eyes should look,*
> *even to him who was pierced,*
> *then your eye weeps for that for which all eyes should weep,*
> *even the sin that slew your Savior.*

Saving repentance is only within sight of the cross.
Faith and repentance are born together, live together, and thrive together.
No one can repent of sin without believing in Jesus, nor believe in Jesus without repenting of sin.

How wonderful it is that all our evils can be remedied by that sole prescription: "Look to Me,
   and be saved, all you ends of the earth!" (Isaiah 45:22 NKJV).
Jesus was lifted on a cross to be looked at; he was nailed there in order to be a perpetual spectacle.

> *The more you look at Jesus crucified,*
> *the more you will mourn for sin.*

> *The cross is God's hammer of love*
> *wherein he smites the hearts of men with irresistible blows.*

Books that speak of the Passion of our Lord, and hymns that sing of his cross,
   have always been precious to saintly minds and have a holy influence on heart and conscience.

> *Christian, live at Calvary, for there you will live at your best!*
> *Live at Calvary, and love at Calvary,*
> *until live and love become the same thing.*

> *Or as one ancient writer stated:*
> *"Look at the cross until all that is on the cross is in your heart."*

From sermon no. 1983, *How Hearts Are Softened*

THE UNDESERVED GIFT OF GOD

Thanks be to God for his inexpressible gift!
2 CORINTHIANS 9:15

Our Lord Jesus must come to us humans by way of a gift.
We could never have deserved such a sacrifice—Christ's own life for our salvation.

We can imagine a man meriting this or that honor among his fellow men;
   but when we think of the King of kings and Lord of lords giving himself up to die for us,
      we are amazed at those who think they can make themselves deserving of such a sacrifice.
How can they imagine that by living a good life they can actually deserve the gift of Christ!

If we had ever been able to keep God's law perfectly;
if there had been no omission of duty and no commission of sin;
if we could have taken the compound merits of a perfect world and laid them at the feet of God,
they would never have deserved the inexpressible sacrifice that our Lord Jesus made for us!

There would have been no need for Christ's death if man had not sinned;
   but had there been a supposable need, Christ's sacrifice would never have been deserved,
even if we had remained innocent like our first parents in the Garden of Eden before the Fall.

> *Who can tolerate, even for a moment,*
> *the thought that any human merit could deserve*
> *the incarnation of God and his shameful death on the cross?*

It is clear from the Scriptures that Christ was given for the undeserving.
   "Christ Jesus came into the world to save sinners" (1 Timothy 1:15).
He took upon himself, not our righteousness—for there was none for him to take—
   but "the LORD has laid on him the iniquity of us all" (Isaiah 53:6).

The prominent idea of Christ in the Scriptures is that of a priest offering a sacrifice;
   but the priest is for people who need atonement for their sins.
The expiation, the sacrifice, the sin-offering is for guilty people.

> *Why would Christ die on the cross for deserving people?*
> *A Savior is for sinners;*
> *a dying Savior is for those who deserve to die.*

> *Christ does not come to us as deserving him,*
> *but he is God's inexpressible gift!*

The poorest person in the world may accept a gift; a trembling hand may receive a gift.
   He who is a thief and a robber, yes, a murderer doomed to die, may accept a gift
      if it does not come by merit or by way of reward, but entirely of the generosity of the bestower.
Do not insult God by bringing your poor merits as the purchase price of his free gift of Christ.

From sermon no. 2290, *God's Unspeakable Gift*

OUR EYES WILL SEE HIM

I myself will see him with my own eyes—I, and not another.
How my heart yearns within me!
JOB 19:27 NIV

I have heard of him, and though I have not seen his face, unceasingly I have adored him.
But I will see him!

Yes, we will actually gaze at the exalted Redeemer!

We will see the hand that was nailed for us.
We will see the very lips that said, "I thirst."
We will see the head that was crowned with thorns, and bow with all the blood-washed throng.

Faith is precious, but what will sight be?

Viewing Jesus through the glass of faith
makes the soul rejoice with inexpressible joy!

But oh, to see him face to face,
to look into those dear eyes,
to be embraced by those divine arms—
rapture begins at the very mention of it!

Oh, what will the vision be when the veil is taken from his face and the dimness from our eyes,
and we will talk with him even as we talk with a friend!
Yes, it is not only vision, it is also communion.
We will have all that the bride desired in the Song of Solomon—and ten thousand times more!

Then Jesus will tell us of his love, rehearsing the ancient story of the everlasting covenant
and of his purchase of us by his rich compassion.
And then we will tell him of our love, pouring into his ear our song of gratitude—
a song never sung before, pure and undefiled, full of serenity and joy.

O Christian, anticipate heaven!

Within a short while you will leave all your troubles and trials behind,
and your poor panting heart will find its rest as it beats on the breast of your Beloved.
Your eyes, now suffused with tears, will weep no longer.

Oh rejoice! You will gaze in ineffable rapture upon the splendor of him who sits on the throne—
no, more!—you will sit on his throne, for he is King of kings and you will reign with him.
The triumph of his glory will be shared with you—his crown, his joy, his paradise.
These will be yours, because you will be co-heir with him who is the heir of all things.

From sermon no. 274, *Paul's Desire to Depart*

MAKING LIGHT OF CHRIST

*"But they made light of it and went their ways,
one to his own farm, another to his business."*
MATTHEW 22:5 NKJV

According to the parable these people made light of a marriage banquet a king had provided.
They were freely invited, but they willfully absented themselves.
They *despised the feast!*

Ah sinner, you are despising the feast when you make light of God's gospel,
    and when you make light of that, you are far more foolish than he who sees no light in the sun,
or who beholds no fairness in the moon or brilliancy in the starry firmament.

Trample if you please on God's lower works, but remember, when you make light of the gospel,
    you are making light of the masterpiece of your great Creator—
that which cost him more than the creation of all worlds—the bloody purchase of Christ's agonies.

The people in the parable also *made light of the king's son* when they absented themselves.
It was *his* marriage and they dishonored the glorious one in whose honor the feast was prepared.

And when we make light of the gospel, we are making light of Christ;
    of the One before whom glorious cherubim and seraphim bow themselves;
    of the One who is "God over all, blessed forever" (Romans 9:5).
It is a solemn thing to despise our Lord Jesus Christ and to treat him with cruel scorn.

Oh, when I see him wrestling in Gethsemane
    with his body enveloped in a shirt of blood,
I bow over him, and say, "O Redeemer, bleeding for sin, can any sinner make light of you?"

When I behold him with rivers of blood rolling down his shoulders,
    beneath the cursed flogging of Pilate's whip,
I must ask, "Can a sinner make light of such a Savior as this?"

When I see him yonder, nailed to a tree,
    expiring in torture and crying, "My God, my God, why have you forsaken me?" (Matthew 27:46),
I ask myself, "Can anyone make light of this?"

*Remember, if you are making light of Christ,
you are insulting the only One who can save you,
the only One who can bear you across the Jordan,
the only One who can unbolt the gates of heaven and give you welcome.*

*O sinner, think of your sin if you are making light of him,
for you are making light of the King's only Son!*

From sermon no. 98, *Making Light of Christ*

OUR ASCENDED LORD

Who has gone into heaven and is at the right hand of God,
with angels, authorities, and powers having been subjected to him.
1 PETER 3:22

By going into heaven, our Lord has gone into the place of perfect happiness and glory.
No weariness, no mockery, no sinking of heart, no bearing of reproach remains.

The man Christ Jesus is now blessed forever!
He is now filled with ineffable satisfaction,
the reward of his Passion and death.

Let us reflect that nothing could stop him from going there.
Death bound him with the strongest cords, but he could not be held by them.
He has also gone into heaven despite the designs of malicious men.

Have you ever wondered why these men did not attack Jesus when he showed himself openly
and when he had led his disciples to the Mount of Olives?
They were as still as stones while he passed over to take possession of the inheritance.

As death could not hinder him, and the malice of men could not detain him,
neither could the forces of Satan block his way.
We see no trace of the archenemy after Christ had risen from the dead.

O Prince of Darkness, you met him in the wilderness at the beginning,
so why did you not go and approach him at the end?
Why not assail him by the sea when he stood there with bread and fish?

Prince of Darkness, why not hasten to shoot one last arrow at him?
Why did you not summon all your allies to block his passage to the Golden City?

No, the powers of darkness were silenced.
They could only gnash their teeth with rage, but they could not even make a hiss at him.
Jesus had so thoroughly cowed and subdued them in Gethsemane and on the cross
that nothing remained but to triumph over them and lead captivity captive.

O thou blessed Conqueror, your warfare was accomplished,
and the road to your Father's capital lay open before you!
In peaceful triumph you passed beyond the clouds.

Troops of angels met you on the road with joyful songs;
the heir of all things was returning to his home, none disputing his passage.

From sermon no. 1928, *Our Ascended Lord*

KNOWING THE LOVE OF CHRIST

To know the love of Christ that surpasses knowledge.
EPHESIANS 3:19

Realizing personally and vitally the love of Christ is the privilege of the child of God.

I once heard words at a prayer meeting that struck my mind, and they still abide in my memory. A brother had been praying, and asked a very great favor:

"O Lord," said he, "give me Mary's place!
Lord, I would sit at your feet and hear what you have to say
and receive it as a willing scholar receives his master's words."

I thought he would stop there, but he added:

"No, Lord, I have not asked enough!
I have not asked according to the royalty of your nature.
Lift me higher! Lift me higher!
Not at your feet would I sit, but I would lean on your breast.

"Oh, put me where John was, that I may lean my head on your bosom!
Let me not merely learn the truth you teach,
but may I feel your heart beat and know your love for me."

Well now, I thought that second prayer was a noble one; but he had yet a third one to offer:

"No, Lord, no! That is not enough!
I have not asked yet according to the tenor of your promise.

"You have lifted me from your feet to your breast,
now lift me higher, even to your lips!"

And then he quoted these words: "Let him kiss me with the kisses of his mouth! For your love is better than wine" (Song of Solomon 1:2), and he very beautifully paraphrased it:

"Lord, let me give to you the tokens of my love
and receive from you the present tokens of your love for me;
and not only to know it, and to feel your very heart beat,
but to receive the token of it as my lip of prayer meets your lip of blessing,
and my lip of thanksgiving touches your lip of benediction."

From sermon no. 455, *The Love of Jesus, What It Is, None But His Loved Ones Know*

OUR SUBSTITUTE

He himself bore our sins in his body on the tree.
1 Peter 2:24

There is a *substitution for our sins*, and by that substitution believers are saved.
A substitute intervened and bore the sins that would have crushed us.

Remember, he who bore our sins in his body was "God over all, blessed forever" (Romans 9:5).
  This is a truth scarcely to be declared in words!
It wants flame and blood and tears with which to tell this story of an offended God
  stooping from his glory in order to save the very ones who had rebelled against his glory!

Oh, let us love and adore him!

*Let your soul climb up to the right hand of the Majesty above
and bow there in lowliest reverence and adoring affection,
seeing that he, the God over all, whom you offended,
has himself bore our sins!*

As stated in the text, *this substitution was carried out by Christ personally,* not by proxy.
"He himself bore our sins in his body."

The Old Testament priest brought a substitution, but it was a lamb;
  he struck the knife, and the warm blood flowed from it.
But our Lord Jesus Christ had no substitute for himself.

*O thou Priest of God!
The pangs are to be your own pangs!
The knife must reach your own heart!*

*No lamb for you!
You are the Lamb!*

*The blood that streams at your feet
must be your own blood!*

*Wounds there must be,
but they must be wounds in your own flesh!*

Turn your loving eyes to your Lord and behold that everything he did for you he did himself.
The heart that was broken for our sin was his own heart, and the life given up was his own life.

From sermon no. 1143, *Death for Sin, and Death to Sin*

CHRIST SUFFERED

Christ also suffered once.
1 PETER 3:18

There is compassed within this expression a summary of the whole life and death of Christ.

We cannot tell how much our Lord suffered, even during the brightest moments of his career,
 for he was always "despised and rejected by men; a man of sorrows, and acquainted with grief."
We do not have all the details of his life, but Peter sums it up well when he says, "Christ suffered."

When he came to Gethsemane, shall I speak of the bloody sweat and the groans that startled angels?
No, I need not say more than this: "Christ suffered."

Shall I tell of his betrayal by Judas and of his being hurried from bar to bar—
 falsely accused, beaten, bruised, flogged, and made nothing of?
Truly, I may sum it all up by saying that he suffered.

As for all the rest—
 that march along the *Via Dolorosa,* and the fastening to the wood;
 the wounds, the cruel fever, the direful thirst, the mockery, the scorn;
 the desertion by his Father when he must at last yield himself up to death itself—
what better summary could even an inspired apostle give than to say, "Christ also suffered once"?

This expression sums up the whole of his life.

He suffered, but he did not even complain.
 Isaiah's prophecy was literally fulfilled: "Like a lamb that is led to the slaughter, and like a sheep
  that before its shearers is silent, so he opened not his mouth" (Isaiah 53:7).
Having undertaken to suffer for sins, he silently went forth to meet it.

When he stood before Pilate and his enemies flogged him, what did he do? *He suffered.*
When they bound his eyes and struck him, what did he do? *He suffered.*
When they spit in his face, what did he do? *He suffered.*
When they nailed him to the cross, what did he do? *He suffered and prayed, "Father, forgive them."*

He suffered; and there was nothing to take away from the completeness of that suffering.
 The Lord had laid on him the iniquity, and consequently, the suffering of us all,
  and he silently accepted it at the Father's hand without a complaint or a murmur.
You can sum it all up without a single word added: "Christ also suffered once."

So, when next you are called to suffer,
let this text whisper in your ear,
"Christ also suffered once."

From sermon no. 2573, *Unparalleled Suffering*

OUR KING OUR JOY

Let the children of Zion rejoice in their King!
PSALM 149:2

There must be certain principles indwelling our hearts before we can rejoice in our King.

The first is our loyalty.
The children of Zion are loyal to their King.

As loyal subjects we not only submit to those decrees that are pleasing in themselves,
    but we unwaveringly submit to the entire administration of our King.
His throne and dynasty are paramount to us, and in all his actions we take delight.

No people anywhere have ever had such a monarch.
    No rule has ever been so good, so kind, so loving.
Every day we elect him anew in our heart's warmest love,
    and we sing again and again:

> *"Crown him, crown him, King of kings, and Lord of lords."*

Apart from the throne and crown of the Lord Jesus, we feel a devout attachment to *him*.

As the Son of God, we worship him and adore him, and our hearts reverently confide in him.
    But as bone of our bone and flesh of our flesh, our Brother, our Redeemer,
        who has purchased us with his own heart's blood,
    he is the beloved of our souls, the focus of our hearts, and none can ever rival him!

The sweetness of his name has often revived our fainting spirits,
    and a sense of his presence has filled us with the new wine of holy exultation.
He is all in all to us. His offices, his works, his honor—
    all these are as garments perfumed with myrrh and aloes, but *he himself is fragrance.*

Nothing grieves us so much as when people speak lightly of him.
Nothing so excites our indignation as when they disdain his cross and his crown.

There has never been anyone like him!
No other love could be compared with his for a moment!
He is "distinguished among ten thousand" (Song of Solomon 5:10) and altogether lovely.

> *None can ever extol him too much!*

> *Our hearts are never overloaded with his glories;*
> *our ears are never weary of hearing his praises!*

From sermon no. 963, *Our King Our Joy*

SEE HIS GREATNESS

See how great this man was.
HEBREWS 7:4

Let us consider how great our Lord Jesus Christ is by looking at the surroundings of his First Advent.

Thousands of years before his birth, holy men were already discussing him.
Think of that system of types and symbols that God had ordained by his servant Moses.
This system was a revelation of the Messiah, who would yet appear in the fullness of time.

Yes, "see how great this man was," for when he came many were watching for him.

Simeon and Anna could not depart until he appeared.
Humble shepherds as they watched their flocks waited for the signal to hasten to adore him.
The wise men forgot the weariness of a long journey so they might lay their gifts at his feet.

"See how great this man was."

When he was born and laid in a manger
the whole earth was moved by his appearing.

The life of Jesus Christ is great throughout, no matter how you view him.

View him in the wilderness, and you see that he is grandly victorious over temptation.
View him in the crowd, and you see that he is greatly wise in answering those who would entrap him.

Behold him in his agony in the garden.
Has there ever been such an agonizer?

Behold him as the Crucified.
Has a cross ever held such a sufferer?

Yes, come and "see how great this man was!"

In death he destroys death!
In the grave he bursts the sepulcher!

Oh, "see how great this man was!"
Yet we can only touch the fringe of this subject.

We see but the skirts of our Lord's garments.
His actual glory is unspeakable, unsearchable!

Oh, the depths! Oh, the depths!

From sermon no. 1835, *The Man Christ Jesus*

A FINISHED WORK

When Christ had offered for all time a single sacrifice for sins,
he sat down at the right hand of God.
HEBREWS 10:12

We are taught here the completeness of the Savior's work.
He has done all that was necessary to be done to make an atonement and an end of sin.
He has done so much that it will never be necessary for him to be crucified again.

His side, once opened, has sent forth a deep stream—
deep enough and precious enough to wash away all sin.

Never again will his side need to be opened;
never again will his hands need to be nailed to a cross.

It is inferred that Christ's work is finished, because he is described here as sitting down.
He would not sit down in heaven if he had more work to do, for sitting down is the posture of rest.

Jesus seldom sat down to rest during the years of his public ministry,
    for he said, "I must be about My Father's business" (Luke 2:49 NKJV).
His life was one of incessant toil—traveling, healing, teaching, and preaching.

He may have sat down for a moment on a well; but even there he preached to the woman of Samaria.
He went into the wilderness, but not to sleep; he went there to pray.
His midnights were spent in labors as intense as those of the day—labors of agonizing prayer,
    wrestling with his Father for the souls of men.

His was a life of continual labor—
bodily, mentally, and spiritually—
but now he rests; there is no toil for him now.
There is no sweat of blood, no weary foot, no aching head.

Do you think our Savior would sit at his Father's right hand if he had not finished all his work?

Ah no, the fact that the Father allowed him to ascend into heaven,
    and that he said to him, "Sit at my right hand" (Psalm 110:1),
        proves that he had perfected his Father's work.
This shows us that Christ's sacrifice was completed and accepted by the Father.

Oh, glorious work of salvation!
This man has done it! This man has finished it!

Rejoice Christian! Your salvation is a finished salvation.
You are accepted perfectly in Christ's righteousness.

From sermon no. 91, *Christ Exalted*

DESPISING SHAMEFUL MOCKERY

Who for the joy that was set before him endured the cross, despising the shame.
HEBREWS 12:2

Behold the Savior despising shameful mockery!

From Herod's hall, right down to his death, he faced various mockers.
In the first place, they mocked his person, for they stripped him of every garment he possessed.

Jesus was stripped twice; and though our painters for obvious reasons cover him on the cross,
    there he hung—the naked Savior of a naked race.
He who had clothed the lilies of the field with great beauty
    did not even have a rag to conceal his nakedness from a staring, mocking, hard-hearted crowd.

He made coats of skins for Adam and Eve when they were naked in the garden,
    and took from them those poor fig leaves with which they sought to hide their nakedness.
But now they divide "his garments among them, by casting lots" (Matthew 27:35),
    while he himself, exposed to the pitiless storm of contempt, has nothing to cover his shame.

Besides his person, these mockers also mocked Christ's office as king.
He was indeed a king—and what a king! He was King of kings and Lord of lords!

So did the people bring crowns with which to honor him?
Did the nobility of earth cast their robes beneath his feet to carpet his footsteps?

No, they deliver him up to rough and brutal soldiers . . .
    who place him on a mimic throne,
    who replace his robes with an old soldier's cloak,
    who place a crown of thorns about his brow,
    who place in his hand a scepter of reed,
and then bow the knee before him and "honor" him with their mimic homage.

Think of the King of kings and Lord of lords …
    having for his adoration the spittle of guilty mouths,
    having for his homage the striking of filthy hands,
    having for his tribute the jests of brutal tongues!

> *O thou King of kings, has there ever been shame like yours—*
> *flouted by soldiers, and stricken by their vulgar hands?*
>
> *O earth, how could you endure this iniquity?*
>
> *O ye heavens, why did you not fall in mighty indignation*
> *to crush the men who thus blasphemed your Maker?*

From sermon no. 236, *The Shameful Sufferer*

THE SIN OFFERING

"All the rest of the bull—he shall carry outside the camp to a clean place,
to the ash heap, and shall burn it up on a fire of wood."
LEVITICUS 4:12

The one who brought the sin offering has been forgiven.
He has been accepted at the brazen altar and his prayers have been heard at the golden altar.
The curtain has also been sprinkled with blood on his behalf.

Yes, but what about the victim itself?
Draw near and learn with holy wonder!

The priest took the bull, and gathering up all the innards, the skin, the dung—
   all this to teach us the horribleness of sin, and what the Substitute had become when he took our sin—
he took it all up, and either himself personally, or assisted by others, took it outside the camp.

Perceive the sad procession: The priest all smeared with blood, carrying away the carcass of the bull.
   It was killed at the altar of burnt offering, but it could not be burned there.
That altar was holy, and when the sin was laid on the bull, it ceased to be looked on as a holy thing.
   It could not, therefore, be burned in the holy place and must be taken completely away.

Now try to grasp the idea of Jesus being put away from God.
Hear the air pierced with the awful cry, "My God, my God, why have you forsaken me?"
It was not possible for God to look upon sin, even when it was laid on Christ.

> *How could our iniquities and transgressions be better displayed*
> *than by that bleeding, mangled mass,*
> *which the high priest had to carry away from the camp*
> *as though it were a thing to be abhorred!*

> *It is your Savior made sin for you, and put away on your behalf!*

After the removal, they kindled the fire and burned it all.
See here a faint image of the fire that consumed the Savior upon Calvary.

> *As you see Jesus scourged by Pilate,*
> *and afterwards bleeding on the accursed tree,*
> *you see the fire of divine wrath consuming the sin offering.*

> *The angels say, "Holy! Holy! Holy! Lord God of hosts!"*
> *What did they say when he, whom they hymned as "glorious in holiness,"*
> *bowed his head and died because he was "made sin for us"?*

> *O blessed Son of God, where we cannot understand, we will adore!*

From sermon no. 739, *The Sin Offering*

VISITATIONS FROM GOD

Because of the tender mercy of our God,
whereby the sunrise shall visit us from on high.
Luke 1:78

In what ways has the Lord shown his tender mercy in purposing to visit us?

God's greatest visit to us was in *the incarnation of our blessed Lord and Savior Jesus Christ.*
Scripture records many visits of God to men, but the most wonderful visit of all
    was when he came to live here for some thirty years or more and worked out our salvation.

What but "tender mercy," hearty mercy, intense mercy,
    would bring the great God to visit so closely that he actually assumed our nature?
Kings visit their subjects, but they do not take on their poverty, sickness, or sorrow,
    but our Lord came into our flesh; he veiled his godhead in a robe of our inferior clay.

O children, the Lord so visited you that he became a baby, and then a child,
    who lived in obedience to his parents and grew in stature as you must do!

O working people, the Lord so visited you that he became a carpenter's son
    and thus knows all about your toil and weariness!

O people of all ages, Jesus Christ so visited you
    that he was tempted in every respect as you are, yet without sin (Hebrews 4:15)!

But we must remember that Christ's visit was not merely to teach us and set us a divine example.
He visited us so completely that he even took upon himself our condemnation.
He stood in our place and paid the price of our redemption.

Yes, our Lord so visited us
that he actually became our ransom!

This was tender mercy indeed!
It excels all conception and speech!

Since this first visit by the Lord, we have often had special visits from him,
    bringing with them rapturous joys, singular deliverances, and countless blessings.
We have enjoyed near and dear communion with the Father and with his Son.

When we have been burdened with unusual cares, or weeping over heartbreaking situations,
    the Sunrise from on high has visited us with tender, loving mercy.
Our lives are as bright with these visits as the sky is with stars.

Yes, God's visits to us are proofs of the intensity and the tenderness of his mercy.

From sermon no. 1907, *The Tender Mercy of Our God*

A FULFILLMENT OF PROPHECY

"I gave my back to those who strike,
and my cheeks to those who pull out the beard;
I hid not my face from disgrace and spitting."
Isaiah 50:6

Of whom does the prophet speak? Does he speak of himself or of someone else?
We cannot doubt that Isaiah is writing here about the Lord Jesus Christ.

Surely this is one of the prophecies to which our Lord himself referred to when he said to his disciples,
   "See, we are going up to Jerusalem, and everything that is written about the Son of Man by the
   prophets will be accomplished. For he will be delivered over to the Gentiles and will be mocked
   and shamefully treated and spit upon. And after flogging him, they will kill him" (Luke 18:31-33).

Isaiah's remarkable prophecy of flogging and spitting must indeed refer to the Lord Jesus.
Its highest fulfillment is found in him alone.

Who else could the prophet be speaking of when you read the whole chapter?
Who else could say with the same breath: "'I clothe the heavens with blackness and make sackcloth
   their covering.' I gave my back to those who strike, and my cheeks to those who pull out the
   beard" (50:3, 6)?

What a descent from the omnipotence that veils the heavens with clouds
   to the gracious condescension that does not veil its own face, but permits it to be spit on!
He is God, and yet—at the same time—he must be "a man of sorrows, and acquainted with grief."

We must believe that the speaker in our text is none other than Jesus, the Son of God and the Son of Man.
   We have before us the language of prophecy,
      but it is as accurate as if it had been written at the very same moment as the event.
Isaiah might have been one of the Evangelists, since he describes so accurately what our Savior endured.

If you wish to have more confirmation regarding the accuracy of this prophecy
   read those passages in the Gospels that describe the sufferings of our Lord and Savior.
Matthew, one of the four gospel writers, says, "Then they spit in his face and struck him. And some
   slapped him, saying, 'Prophesy to us, you Christ! Who is it that struck you?'" (26:67-68).

Dear reader, come and gaze reverently and lovingly
upon the most despised and rejected of men.
The sight demands adoration!

I would remind you of what Moses did when he saw the bush that was burning, but was not consumed—
   a fit emblem of our Lord on fire with grief, yet not destroyed.
I urge you to turn aside and see this great sight, but first attend to the mandate—
   "Take your sandals off your feet, for the place on which you are standing is holy ground" (Exodus 3:5).

From sermon no. 1486, *The Shame and Spitting*

ALPHA AND OMEGA IN RANK

"I am the Alpha and the Omega, the first and the last, the beginning and the end."
REVELATION 22:13

The thoughts presented here, if not the intended meaning of the text, are closely related to it.

Our Lord may very well be described as the Alpha and the Omega *in the sense of rank.*
He is *Alpha, the first*, the chief, the foremost, the firstborn of every creature, the Eternal God.

Alpha was frequently used by the Hebrews to signify the best,
    just as we are accustomed to using the letter A, saying that something is "A1."
So we may say that Jesus Christ is the Alpha—the first—in this sense.
    Call him by whatever title Scripture has given him, he is always the first in it.

But though our blessed Lord is thus Alpha—the first—
    he was once in his condescension made *Omega—the last.*
How can we describe the mighty descent of the Son of God?

From the loftiness of his Father's glory, and from his own divine grandeur,
    our Lord actually stooped to become a man.
There is a vast difference between being God and being man, but to this he came.

But this is not enough.
He stoops even lower than man!

Yes, there is a verse in which he seems to put himself on a level with the least of all creatures,
    for he says, "I am a worm and not a man, scorned by mankind and despised by the people" (Psalm 22:6).
His Father forsook him; the wrath of heaven rolled over him.
    He was utterly crushed and broken, poured out like water, and brought to the dust of death.

Place all the creatures of God in their order,
    but in that dreadful day when Jesus hangs on the cross,
you must put him for misery, for weakness, for shame, as the last—the Omega.

How marvelous is this tremendous sweep of his humiliation!
From the highest throne in glory, he descended into the lowest depths of the tomb.
Death brings the creature to its very lowest degradation and makes it as though it were nothing.

Yes, our gracious Lord Jesus died,
and as we see the incorruptible body lying in Joseph's sepulcher,
we can but marvel that the great Alpha
would come so low as to yield up his spirit,
being subjugated beneath the power of the last adversary.

From sermon no. 546, *Alpha and Omega*

FAIRER THAN MEN

You are fairer than the sons of men.
PSALM 45:2 NKJV

There is a thing called beauty that wins the hearts of men,
    and strong Samson is weak as a child before its enchantment.
Mighty men, not a few, have bowed before it and paid it homage.

But if you want real beauty, look into the face of Jesus
    for that marred countenance has more loveliness than any fabled beauty.
There is no beauty anywhere but in Christ.

O sun, you are not fair when compared with him!
Ye stars, you are not bright when set side-by-side with his eyes!

O fair world and grand creation of a glorious God,
you are but a dim and dusky blot
compared with the splendors of his face!

When the clouds are finally swept away and you behold your Savior,
    you will be compelled to say that you had never known what true loveliness is.
Yes, when the curtains that hide him from your view are drawn aside,
    you will find that nothing you had ever seen will stand a moment's comparison with him.

You will be ready to exclaim,
"O black sun, black moon, dark stars,
as compared with my lovely Lord Jesus!"

If you want someone to love who is fairer than all the children of men, then love Jesus.
He does not have the excellence of one man, but of all men—without the faults of any.[1]

In all beings there is something lacking,
but in Jesus there is all perfection.

Even the best of his saints
have had stains on their garments and wrinkles on their brow.

All earthly suns have their spots,
and this fair world has its wilderness,
but Christ Jesus is gold without alloy,
light without darkness, glory without cloud.[2]

[1]From sermon no. 325, *Constraining Love*
[2]*Morning and Evening*, March 9 (M)

A WITNESS OF CHRIST'S SUFFERINGS

*I exhort the elders among you, as a fellow elder
and a witness of the sufferings of Christ.*
1 PETER 5:1

Peter was what we have not been: *an eyewitness of the sufferings of Christ.*

He could never forget the sight of the Lord Jesus in his awful agony in the garden.
He remembered seeing him rise from prayer, and saying, "My betrayer is at hand" (Matthew 26:46).

He could not fail to remember the look on his Master's face
    when he who had eaten bread with him lifted his heel against him (John 13:18),
and the Son of Man was betrayed with a kiss from the apostate apostle (Luke 22:48).

He was also an eyewitness of our Lord being hurried away to the bar of Annas.
He remembered seeing someone strike him on the mouth.
He could recall how they charged him with blasphemy.
He could recollect how, after the first examination was over, Annas sent him bound to Caiaphas.

It was in the palace of Annas that Peter denied his Master.
    He could never forget that gaze of concentrated agony and pity when Jesus looked at him,
        not so much reproachfully, perhaps, as mournfully.
A spark from that torch of anguish set his heart ablaze, and he went out and wept bitterly.

We believe—we cannot help believing—that Peter quickly rallied from his fit of cowardice.
We believe that he came to the forefront again and saw the Master in Pilate's judgment hall.
We believe that Peter and the other apostles were eyewitnesses of his sufferings.

They may have seen him when he was being flogged.
They observed him as he was being ridiculed and flouted and mocked.
They saw him as the cross-bearer.

They watched him as he went in awful anguish along the *Via Dolorosa* to the mount of crucifixion.
They saw him nailed to the tree to die there like a felon with no relief or assistance.
They heard his bitter cry, "My God, my God, why have you forsaken me?" (Matthew 27:46).

*Yes, Peter was an eyewitness of Christ's sufferings,
and when he was writing to these elders, he seemed to say to them:
"Feed the flock of God, for I saw the Great Shepherd when he bought that flock.
I was there when he purchased the sheep with his own blood."*

*O my brethren, by Christ's agony and bloody sweat, by his cross and Passion,
by his precious death and burial, by his glorious resurrection and ascension,
I beseech you to feed the flock of God that he has purchased with his own blood!*

From sermon no. 2610, *A Witness and a Partaker*

FAITH WITNESSES OF CHRIST'S SUFFERINGS

I exhort the elders among you, as a fellow elder
and a witness of the sufferings of Christ.
1 PETER 5:1

Peter was a witness of Christ's sufferings, and as far as possible let us be witnesses with him.

We, never having seen Christ in his sufferings,
    might never have had any participation in this part of our text
if there had not been another kind of witnessing, namely, *the faith-witness.*

Thousands were eyewitnesses of our Lord's sufferings, yet they did not see their true meaning.
They saw the dear Sufferer besmeared with his blood, but they did not look into his wounds by faith.
They saw him die—some of them beating their breasts—but did not know why he died.

Dear reader, are you a faith-witness
of the sufferings and agonies of Christ?

Well do I remember that day when by faith I saw Christ Jesus dying on the cross.
It was then that I perceived who he was, and why he died, and what he accomplished by that death.

I understood that he took my place so that I might take his place.
I understood that he took my sin so that I might take his righteousness.
I understood that he bore my woe so that I might share his joy.

And when I saw all that with my soul's inner eye
    and perceived my share in my Savior's sacrifice, and believed in him to the saving of my soul—
oh, it was a blessed and happy day for me!

There are some who depreciate this faith-witness, but it is faith that saves.

You may be an eyewitness and yet perish as Judas did.
You may be an eyewitness and still hate Christ as Caiaphas did.
But if you become a faith-witness you will receive hope, love, and salvation.

Peter was an eyewitness, but better still, he was a faith-witness.
This is the reason why he went on to be *a testifying witness.*

The chief business of any minister of Christ, or of any elder of the church of Christ,
    is to bear testimony to the sufferings of Christ.
If the atoning sufferings of Christ are left out of the ministry, that ministry is worthless.

We are all to be constantly bearing our witness of Christ,
saying, "Behold, the Lamb of God,
who takes away the sin of the world!"(John 1:29).

From sermon no. 2610, *A Witness and a Partaker*

THE TOUCH OF A MAN'S HAND

One having the appearance of a man touched me and strengthened me.
Daniel 10:18

Daniel fell on his face and was cast into a dead swoon,
   because he was unable to bear the sight of the man clothed in linen
whose "body was like beryl, his face like the appearance of lightning" (Daniel 10:6).

It appears from our text that, when weighed down under a sense of the divine presence,
   the readiest method of consolation is found in the touch of a certain mysterious human hand.

*Comfort is best brought to man by a man,
and if we are to be strengthened,
the touch of "one having the appearance of a man" is needed.*

It is ever the richest and highest comfort to us, as believers in Christ, that the Lord Jesus is a man;
   and when he strengthens us it is often by laying his human hand on us.
He reveals his kinship with us, and we are consoled and strengthened by a sense of his union with us.

Jesus is God; but Jesus was born, Jesus lived, Jesus died, Jesus rose again,
   and Jesus is now in heaven *as a man*.
He is God and man in one person.

Oh, how the touch of the hand of Jesus—the man—strengthens us in our earthly sorrows!
The choicest consolation for sorrow is the fact that Jesus knows all about it.
There is no abyss of grief into which Jesus has not descended.

Sickness of body and pangs of soul, bereavement, poverty, desertion, treachery—he knows all these.
Malice, envy, contempt, slander, and deadly hate—all shot their darts at him.
He has sounded the depths of the ocean of sorrow.

Well may we be satisfied to go through the valley of tears, for it is "the King's dale"
   and all along it we can track his footprints.
We know them, for we can see the marks of the nails; they are the footprints of the Crucified.

He carried up to heaven the selfsame human heart that was pierced below,
   and there he remembers Calvary and all the griefs he suffered on our behalf.
He sympathizes with us still.

*Jesus puts his hand on us, and says,
"Fear not; I am with you in your sorrows.
My heart is like your heart; therefore, be of good cheer."*

From sermon no. 1295, *Our Lord's Humanity a Sweet Source of Comfort*

CHRIST LIFTED UP

"And I, when I am lifted up from the earth, will draw all people to myself."
JOHN 12:32

Jesus uses the words "lifted up" to express the manner of his death.
Notice that he does not say, "I, when I am crucified," or "I, when I am hanged on the tree."
He says, "I, when I am lifted up," which in the Greek means exaltation.

Christ's cross is Christ's glory.

Man seeks to win his glory by the slaughter of others—Christ, by the slaughter of himself.
Man seeks a crown of gold—Christ sought a crown of thorns.
Man thinks his glory lies in being exalted over others—Christ thought his glory lay in becoming
   "a worm and not a man" (Psalm 22:6), a scoff and a reproach among all who beheld him.

He stooped when he conquered.
He won more love by the cross than anywhere else.

O Lord Jesus, you would never have been loved so much
if you had sat in heaven forever,
as you are now loved since you stooped to death!

You won more love by the nail than by the scepter.
Your pierced side brought you no emptiness of love,
for your people love you with all their hearts.

Yes, Christ won glory by his cross.
   He was never so lifted up as when he was cast down.
The Christian will bear witness that though he loves his Master everywhere,
   nothing moves his heart to rapture like the story of the Crucifixion and the agonies of Calvary.[1]

There is an attractive power about our Lord's person,
   and about his life,
   and about his teaching,
but still, the main attraction lies in his death on the cross.

When he became "obedient to the point of death, even death on a cross" (Philippians 2:8),
   shame cast no shame on his cause, but gilded it with glory.
Christ's death threw no weakness into Christianity, but rather, it is the right arm of its power.

*A living Savior people **may** love,*
*but a crucified Savior they **must** love.*[2]

[1]From sermon no. 139, *Christ Lifted Up*
[2]From sermon no. 1717, *The Marvelous Magnet*

STRIPES ON BODY AND SOUL

With his stripes we are healed.
Isaiah 53:5

The body of our Lord and Savior was bruised because he was scourged by Pilate,
  and the scourging of the Romans was peculiarly brutal.
They did not have a law like the Jews that stopped at thirty-nine stripes, but they smote at random.

Our Savior endured a scourging that was intended to be a substitute for death.
"I will … punish him and release him" (Luke 23:16), said Pilate.
But instead of it being a substitute for death, it became a prelude to it.

Most people would prefer to die rather than to be scourged according to the system of the Romans.
  Sinews of oxen were intertwined with knuckle bones of sheep, and with small slivers of bone,
    so that every stroke gashed the flesh deeply, causing fearful wounds and tearing.
Our Savior's back was plowed and furrowed deeply in the day of his scourging (Psalm 129:3).

Now you may look at Jesus, covered with the livid bruises, and say, "With his stripes we are healed,"
  but you must not stop there and think that flesh wounds were his only stripes.
The stripes that our Lord bore in his soul were even more terrible.

Think of God smiting! God must smite sin wherever he sees it.
  It is just as essential for God to crush sin as it is to love;
    and indeed, it is love in another form that makes him hate that which is evil.
So when God saw our sin laid upon his Son he smote him.

Yes, the angels worship him, and yet Jehovah smote him!

Nothing looks especially beautiful to the eye that has once gazed on Christ;
  and yet men spit in his face and marred his lovely countenance with cruel blows of brutal fists.
No curses fell from his dear lips—he only had words of pity and of sweet intercession—
  and yet they wounded, and buffeted, and blasphemed him!

O grief, far deeper than the sea! O woe immeasurable!

They despitefully abuse him
who came on errands of pure mercy and grace!

O cruel whips and cruel hands,
and yet more cruel hearts of wicked men!

Surely we can never read such words as these without feeling that they call for sorrow—
  sorrow, which if mingled with spiritual repentance, will be a suitable anointing for Christ's burial,
or at least a bath in which to wash away the bloodstains from his dear, mangled flesh.

From sermon no. 1068, *A Simple Remedy*

THE KNOCK!

"I have loved you with an everlasting love;
I have drawn you with loving-kindness."
JEREMIAH 31:3 NIV

The thunders of the law are used to bring us to Christ, but victory is achieved by loving-kindness.

The Prodigal Son returned to his father's house out of his sense of need;
    but "while he was still a long way off, his father saw him and felt compassion,
and ran and embraced him and kissed him" (Luke 15:20).

The prodigal's last steps up to his father's house
    were with the loving kiss still warm on his cheek
and with the words of welcome still ringing like music in his ears.

> *"Law and terrors do but harden,*
> *All the while they work alone;*
> *But a sense of blood-bought pardon*
> *Will dissolve a heart of stone."*

One night the Master came to the door and knocked with the iron hand of the law
    until the door shook and trembled on its hinges!
But the sinner barricaded the door, saying, "I will not admit that man!"

The Master turned away, but by-and-by he came back,
    and with his own hand, using especially the part softened by the penetrating nail,
he knocked again—oh, so softly and tenderly.

This time the door did not shake, but strange to say, it opened,
    and there on his knees the once unwilling host was found rejoicing to receive his guest.
"Come in, come in. Your knock has moved my heart, and I could not think of your pierced hand
    leaving its blood-mark on my door, and of you going away homeless."

So in every case loving-kindness wins the day.
What Moses with the tablets of stone could never do, Christ does with his pierced hand.[1]

> *Hearts are tender things*
> *and are not to be forced open with crowbars.*
>
> *The doors of the heart open gently to him who holds the key;*
> *and who is that but he who made the heart*
> *and bought it with his precious blood.*[2]

[1]*Morning and Evening*, February 29 (M)
[2]From sermon no. 1717, *The Marvelous Magnet*

A FORETASTE OF HEAVEN

**Sealed with the promised Holy Spirit,
who is the guarantee of our inheritance.**
EPHESIANS 1:13–14

The Holy Spirit is more than a "guarantee of our inheritance."
He is also a sweet foretaste of heaven.

They who possess the Spirit of God have reaped the firstfruits of the eternal harvest.
They have beheld the first rays of the rising sun of eternal bliss.

By the Holy Spirit there is given to the people of God—even now—
experiences, joys, and feelings that prove they will be in heaven.
Heaven is brought down to them, helping them to understand in some measure what heaven is like.

There is one foretaste of heaven that the Spirit gives that is always the most precious.
These are the moments when the child of God has real fellowship with the Lord Jesus.
His eyes can actually look on *him*—not with these human optics, but with the eyes of the soul.

> *Today, your head may lean on the Savior's bosom.*
> *Today, he may be your sweet Companion.*
>
> *The world then recedes and disappears,*
> *and the things of time are covered with a pall of darkness.*
>
> *Christ only stands out before the believer's view.*

Do not tell us of feasts, ye children of mirth!
Do not tell us of music, ye who delight in melodious sounds!
Do not tell us of wealth, and honor, and the joys of victory, ye who are engrossed in such things!
One hour with Christ is worth an eternity of all earth's joys!

> *May I but see him,*
> *may I but see his face and behold his beauties;*
> *this joy alone will content my soul.*
>
> *Let the hot sun of tribulation dry up all the water brooks,*
> *but this fresh spring will fill my cup to the brim.*
> *Yes, it will make a river of delight wherein my soul shall bathe.*

To be with Christ on earth is the best, the surest, the most ecstatic foretaste of the joys of heaven.

If you *know* Christ, you may know that heaven is yours.
If you *enjoy* Christ, you are learning a little of the bliss of heaven.

From sermon no. 358, *The Earnest of Heaven*

THE RED HEIFER

This is the statute of the law that the LORD has commanded:
"Tell the people of Israel to bring you a red heifer without defect,
in which there is no blemish."
NUMBERS 19:2

The sacrifice here is a *red* heifer, and these animals were rare,
   because it was very difficult to find one that was all red and without any blemishes.
If it had even one white or black hair it was rejected.

The heifer had to be wholly and entirely red,
   bringing to the minds of the Israelites the idea of blood,
      which was always associated with atonement and the putting away of sin.
And when we think of Christ we always associate him with his sacrifice.

Oh, there is nothing about Jesus
that the trembling conscience loves to rest upon so much
as his red cleansing blood!

Our beloved Master—
   with bloody sweat covering his face;
   with ruby drops surrounding his thorn-crowned head;
   with his back flowing with rivers of blood where the whips have scourged him;
   with his hands and feet streaming with founts of crimson;
   with his side giving forth a rich cataract of his heart's blood—
never seems so lovely as when thus "clothed in a robe dipped in blood" (Revelation 19:13).

"Who is this who comes from Edom,
in crimsoned garments from Bozrah,
he who is splendid in his apparel,
marching in the greatness of his strength?

"'It is I, speaking in righteousness, mighty to save.'

"Why is your apparel red,
and your garments like his who treads in the winepress?" (Isaiah 63:1–2).

Oh, this is the glorious Savior, mighty to save,
and never seen so mighty to save
as when he is robed in crimson!

The red heifer was *without blemish*, denoting the perfection of Christ's character.
He was born without any human defilement, conceived immaculately through the Holy Spirit.

From sermon no. 527, *The Red Heifer*

REMEMBERING CHRIST'S PERSON

"Do this in remembrance of me."
1 CORINTHIANS 11:24

Christians have many treasures to lock up in the cabinet of memory.

They ought to remember all the mercies and blessings bestowed on them;
　　but there is *One* whom they should embalm in their souls with the most costly spices,
　　　　One who, above all other gifts of God, deserves to be kept in perpetual remembrance.
His portrait should be framed in gold and hung up in the stateroom of the soul.

We should be earnest students of all the *deeds* of the conquering Messiah,
　　and we should be conversant with the *life* of our Beloved,
but we must not forget his *person,* for the text says, "Do this in remembrance of me."

It is Christ's glorious person
that should be the object of our remembrance.
It is his image that should be enshrined
in every temple of the Holy Spirit.

But some will say:
"How can we remember Christ's person when we have never seen it?
We did not see his feet as they trod the journeys of his mercy.
We did not see his hands as he stretched them out in loving-kindness.
We did not hear the wondrous intonation of his voice as he awed the multitudes.
We cannot picture the sweet smile that always lingered on his lips.
We cannot remember him in his sufferings and agonies for we have never seen him."

Well, it may be true that you cannot remember his visible appearance,
　　because you were not born then, but even the apostle Paul said, "Even though we once
regarded Christ according to the flesh, we regard him thus no longer" (2 Corinthians 5:16).

So even though you do not know your Savior according to the flesh,
　　you may know him according to the spirit.
In this manner you can remember Jesus just as much as those favored ones
　　who had once trod in his footsteps, walked by his side, or laid their heads on his bosom.

Memory annihilates distance and overleaps time,
and it can behold the Lord,
even though he is now exalted in glory.

The newborn creature loves to remember Christ. He cannot help it!
Who can resist the matchless charms of Jesus Christ?
Who can refuse to adore the King of Glory, the majestic Son of God?

From sermon no. 2, *The Remembrance of Christ*

OUR SOUL'S LOVE

I found him whom my soul loves. I held him, and would not let him go.
SONG OF SOLOMON 3:4

With full assurance we must grasp the Savior and have daily communion with him.
With our inmost soul we must so love Jesus that we cannot live without him.

The words are very strong, "him whom my soul loves," as if the bride ...
    might love the daughters of Jerusalem,
    might love the watchmen of the city,
    might love them all in their place,
yet her soul's love, her deepest, fondest, purest love, is only for him.

Ardent lovers of Jesus must diligently seek him.

The chapter before us says that the bride ...
    sought him on her bed,
    sought him in the streets,
    sought him everywhere that he was likely to be found.

Yes, we must enjoy the perpetual fellowship of Jesus.
If we love him with our soul's love, we cannot rest until we know that he is with us.

> *O Lord, give us fellowship with you!*
> *We are often led to see you through the word proclaimed,*
> *but, O Lord, it is no outer court worship that will satisfy us!*
>
> *We want to come into the Holy of Holies and stand at the mercy seat itself.*
> *Seeing you afar off and hearing about you will not content our spirits;*
> *we must draw near to you and behold you as the world cannot.*
>
> *Like Simeon, we must take you in our arms or we cannot see your salvation.*
> *Like John, we must lean our head on your bosom or we cannot rest.*
>
> *Your preachers are wonderful, but oh, we feel constrained to go beyond them*
> *for we thirst for fellowship with you, dear Savior!*

We must leave no stone unturned; we must search to the very uttermost until we find our Beloved.

If any sin obstructs the way, it must be rigorously given up.
If there is any neglected duty, it must be earnestly discharged.
If there is a higher walk of grace necessary for continuous fellowship, we must ascend it.

We have no peace or joy until we can say, "I found him, I held him, and I would not let him go."

From sermon no. 1035, *The Real Presence, the Great Want of the Church*

"BEHOLD THE MAN"

So Jesus came out, wearing the crown of thorns and the purple robe.
Pilate said to them, "Behold the man!"
JOHN 19:5

If there is one place where our Lord Jesus most fully becomes the joy and comfort of his people,
it is where he plunged deepest into the depths of woe.

Come hither, gracious souls, and *behold the man* in the Garden of Gethsemane.
Behold his heart so brimming with love that he cannot hold it in, so full of sorrow that it must find a vent.
Behold the bloody sweat as it distills from every pore of his body and falls to the ground.

Behold the man as they drive the nails into his hands and feet.
Look up, repenting sinners, and see the sorrowful image of your suffering Lord.
Mark him as the ruby drops stand on his crown of thorns, adorning it with priceless gems.

Behold the man when he is poured out like water and brought to the dust of death.
Behold and see! Has there ever been sorrow like his sorrow?

All you who pass by, draw near and look on this spectacle of grief.
It is unique, unparalleled, a wonder to men and angels, a prodigy unmatched.

Oh, behold the Emperor of Woe,
who had no equal or rival in his agonies!

Gaze on him, ye mourners,
for if there is no consolation in a crucified Christ,
there is no joy in earth or heaven.

If there is no hope in the ransom price of his blood,
then there is no pleasure at the right hand of God.

We have but to sit at the foot of the cross to be less troubled with our doubts and woes.
We have but to see *his* sorrows and *our* sorrows we will be ashamed to mention.
We have but to gaze into his wounds and our own will be healed.

If we would live holy lives, it must be by the contemplation of his death.
If we would rise to dignity, it must be by considering his humiliation and his sorrow.[1]

O child of God, when you are troubled,
take your rest by looking to Calvary!
And if the first glance does not quiet you, look, and look again,
for every grief will die where Jesus died.[2]

[1]*Morning and Evening*, July 22 (E)
[2]From sermon no. 1717, *The Marvelous Magnet*

TRUE REPENTANCE

For godly grief produces a repentance that leads to salvation.
2 Corinthians 7:10

True repentance always involves the Lord Jesus, because you cannot repent without looking to him.

A person may hate sin, just like a murderer hates the gallows, but this does not prove repentance.
   If I hate sin because of the punishment, I have not repented of sin; I merely regret that God is just.
But if I see sin as an offense against Jesus Christ and loathe myself because I have wounded him,
   then my heart has truly been broken.

My repentance of sin is in accordance with God's Spirit if I believe …
   that those thorns on my Savior's head were plaited by my sinful words;
   that those wounds in his heart were placed there by my heart-sins;
   that those wounds in his feet were made by my wandering steps;
   that those wounds in his hands were made by my sinful deeds.

Only under the cross can you repent.

Repentance elsewhere is remorse clinging to sin
and only dreading the punishment.

Seek under God a hatred of sin,
caused by a sight of Christ's love.

True sorrow for sin is eminently practical. No one will say he hates sin if he lives in it.
It will make us watchful over our daily actions lest we offend in anything.

Sincere repentance is continual; believers repent until their dying day.
Other sorrows yield to time, but repentance grows with spiritual growth.[1]
The more we love Jesus, and the nearer we come to perfection, the deeper will be our lamentation.

Yet this is a sweet sorrowing—sweet, sweet sorrow—
   to creep to the cross-foot and lie there,
sorrowing over our sin against such a Savior, but still rejoicing that it is all forgiven.

Oh, this is joy, rest, bliss—just to lie there and weep and wash with tears
the feet that came on that errand of love and mercy for us!
And still to weep, and look, and love, and long,
and weep again, and kiss again and again
the blessed feet of him who has redeemed us to God by his blood!

Oh, may the Lord keep us there forever![2]

[1]From sermon no. 575, *The Pierced One Pierces the Heart*
[2]From sermon no. 2691, *Sorrow and Sorrow*

DECLARING THE FATHER'S NAME

"I will tell of your name to my brothers;
in the midst of the congregation I will sing your praise."
HEBREWS 2:12

In the words of our text, we have the last thoughts of our Lord and Master,
and they beautifully illustrate the fact that he was governed by one ruling passion.
That ruling passion most strong in death was the glory of God.

Our Lord probably declared the Father more by his acts than by his words,
because the life of Christ is a discovery of all the attributes of God.

If you would know the gentleness of God, observe Jesus receiving sinners and eating with them.
If you would know his condescension, see Jesus taking little children in his arms and blessing them.
If you would know whether God is just, hear the words of a Savior as he denounces sin.
If you would know the mercy of God, see it manifested in the ten thousand miracles of the Savior's hands,
and in the constant sympathy of the Redeemer's heart.

The life of Christ is a perpetual unrolling
of the great mystery of the divine attributes,
and you may rest assured that what Jesus is, that the Father is.

Our Lord made the grandest declaration of the godhead in his death.
There at Calvary, where the Righteous One suffered for the unrighteous,
in order to redeem them and bring them back to God,
we see the godhead resplendent in noonday majesty.

Would you see stern justice such as the Judge of all the earth perpetually exhibits?
Would you see the justice that will not spare the guilty, which smites and will not endure it?

Then behold the hands and feet and side of the Redeemer welling up with crimson blood.
Behold his heart broken as with an iron rod, dashed to shivers as though it were a potter's vessel.
Listen to his cries; mark the lines of grief that mar his face.
Behold the turmoil, the confusion, the whirlwinds of anguish that seethe like a boiling caldron in
his soul.

At the same time, if you would see the grace of God, where will you discover it as in the death of Jesus?
Thoughtful minds will readily discover all of the great qualities of deity in our dying Lord.
Linger amidst the wondrous scenes of Gethsemane and Gabbatha and Golgotha,
and you will observe how power and wisdom, grace and justice strangely combine.

None of the harps of angels, or the fiery, flaming sonnets of cherubs
can glorify God as did the wounds and pangs of the great Substitute
when he died to make his Father's grace and justice known.

From sermon no. 799, *Jesus, the Example of Holy Praise*

A PRECIOUS MOTTO

And David said, "There is none like it; give it to me."
1 SAMUEL 21:9 NKJV

I am not going to spiritualize this text, but use it as a motto: "There is none like it; give it to me."

All who are acquainted with the salvation that is in Christ will confess that "there is none like it." Look at the root of the gospel, *the precious blood of Jesus*. Where is there blood that equals it? There is no blood like the blood of the Son of God, shed in so remarkable a manner.

This blood, when sprinkled on us, enables us to enter boldly into the inner sanctuary. This blood, when sprinkled on our doorposts, preserves us from the destroying angel. This blood, when we are washed in it, leaves us whiter than snow.

> *O Lord, here I am, sinful and black; but you have precious blood.*
> *Give it to me, that I might be made pure and white.*

Then, *as for his righteousness*, which is also involved in our salvation, "there is none like it."

The righteousness of Adam in the garden, with all its perfection, was still liable to come to an end, but the righteousness of Christ can never be altered.
In heaven, we will sparkle like the sun when we put on this glorious array.
Christ, on Tabor's mountain, did not shine more lustrously than will poor sinners.

> *O Lord, here I am, naked; but you have a perfect robe.*
> *Give it to me, that I might be covered.*

Where the blood of Christ has washed, and where the righteousness of Christ is imputed, there comes "the peace of God, which surpasses all understanding" (Philippians 4:7). Those who are in the enjoyment of this peace will tell you "there is none like it."

The peace that comes from the world is without a foundation;
the peace that comes from ceremonies soon departs in the day of trouble;
the peace that rests upon self-righteousness is based upon the sand;
but the peace that rests upon the blood and righteousness of Jesus Christ will outlast all time.

> *O Lord, here I am bowed down with grief, but you have peace to give.*

> *Here is my heavy heart, like a broken lily, withered and dying,*
> *but you can freshen it up and give me joy instead of sorrow.*

> *O Lord, give it to me!*

From sermon no. 3122, *Craving the Best Things*

"THIS SAME JESUS"

"This same Jesus, who has been taken from you into heaven,
will come back in the same way you have seen him go into heaven!"
ACTS 1:11 NIV

Notice how these bright spirits describe our Lord: "This same Jesus."
This description *came from those who really knew him.*
They watched him all his life, and when they said of him, "This same Jesus,"
then we know by an infallible testimony that he really was—and is still—the same Jesus.

Yes, Jesus is gone, but he still exists.
He has not dissolved into nothing like the mist of the morning.
"This same Jesus" has gone up to his Father's throne; and he is there today,
as certainly as he once stood at Pilate's judgment bar.

The Christ they hung on the cross is the selfsame man who now sits on the throne of God.
The Christ they spit on is the same Christ who is worshiped by angels, day and night.
The Christ they scourged is he before whom principalities and powers delight to cast their crowns.

"This same Jesus"—I love that word—for "Jesus" means *a Savior!*

This is he who opened the eyes of the blind and brought the prisoners out of the prison-house.
This is he who touched the lepers, and who raised the dead;
and he is the same Jesus today, bearing the same tender love for guilty men.
He is the same in his readiness to receive and to cleanse all who come to him by faith.

"This same Jesus." This must also mean that *he who is to come*
will be the same Jesus who went up into heaven.
There is no change in our blessed Master's nature, nor will there ever be.

> *Yes, he will possess the same tenderness when he comes to judge;*
> *the same gentleness of heart when all the glories of heaven and earth gird his brow.*

> *Our eyes will see him in that day, and we will recognize him,*
> *not only by the nail prints, but by the very look of his countenance*
> *and by the character that gleams from that marvelous face.*

> *We will say, "It is he! It is he! He is the selfsame Christ,*
> *who went up from the top of Olivet, from the midst of his disciples!"*

Yes, he is always the same Jesus,
so look forward to his second coming without fear or dread.
Look for him with that joyous expectancy with which you would welcome Jesus of Bethany—
the One who loved Mary, and Martha, and Lazarus.

From sermon no. 1817, *The Ascension and the Second Advent Practically Considered*

NO LONGER SEEN DIMLY

For now we see in a mirror dimly, but then face to face.
1 CORINTHIANS 13:12

We see Jesus Christ now, but it is dimly—not as we will see him soon.

We now see him by faith …
    bearing all our heavy burdens on his omnipotent shoulders;
    carrying away all our iniquities into the wilderness, where, if they are sought, will never be found.

We now see enough of Jesus …
    to know that "he is altogether lovely" (Song of Solomon 5:16 NIV);
    to say of him: "This is all my salvation and all my desire" (2 Samuel 23:5 NKJV).

*Sometimes, when he has thrown up the lattice
and we have seen him through those windows of agate,
his beauty has so entranced us that our hearts have been ravished!*

Yet, all we have ever seen of him
    is something like the report given by the Queen of Sheba regarding Solomon's wisdom.
When we see the Great King we will be compelled to say, "Not even half was told" (1 Kings 10:7 NIV).

Many suggestions have been made of what we will do and enjoy in heaven,
    but they are all wide of the mark compared with this one—
    we will be with Jesus and will behold his glory (John 17:24).
This is the heaven of heaven: "In my flesh I shall see God " (Job 19:26).

We will see the feet that were nailed and will touch the hand that was pierced.
    We will see the gracious head that wore the thorns,
        and will bow before him who is ineffable love, inexpressible condescension, infinite tenderness.
Oh, what will it be to bow down before him and kiss that glorious face!

*O Jesus, what more do we want
than to see you by your own glorious light;
to see you and to speak with you as with a dear friend?*

It is pleasant to talk about this, but what will it be like when the pearly gates actually open?
The streets of gold will hold little attraction for us, compared with the King in the midst of the throne.

*He it is, who will rivet our gaze,
absorb our thoughts, enchain our affections,
and move all our sacred passions
to their highest pitch of celestial ardor!*

We will see Jesus!

From sermon no. 1002, *Now, and Then*

THE SUBSTITUTE HAS APPEARED

He has appeared once for all at the end of the ages
to put away sin by the sacrifice of himself.
HEBREWS 9:26

In order to save us, *Christ appeared*—
appeared as a baby at Bethlehem, swaddled like any other child.
This baby is "Mighty God, Everlasting Father, Prince of Peace" (Isaiah 9:6), appearing in human form.

He remained in obscurity for thirty years, probably toiling as a carpenter in Nazareth.
Three more years rolled by—years of toil and suffering as he ministered in public.

And then, the great debt was to be paid! The bill was presented! The charge was laid!
Would Christ be there to answer it?

He is there—there among those olives in Gethsemane!
He is there in prayer, but what prayer! Never has earth heard such groans and cries!
He is there wrestling, but what wrestling! He sweats "great drops of blood falling down to the ground."

The sinner is called for, and the sinner's Substitute has appeared!
He has appeared on the sinner's behalf in the Garden of Gethsemane—
a garden that is so rightly named "the olive-press"!

But now comes that darkest hour of all—that awful scene at Calvary!
Listen to the dreadful artillery of heaven as the Father thunders forth his wrath against sin!
Behold the flames of fire, the forked lightning of God's anger against all iniquity!

Who is there to bear this?
In whose breast will the fire of God's wrath and anger be quenched?

He comes! On yonder tree he presents himself!

He did not hide his face from shame and spitting;
and at last—on the cross—he does not hide himself from divine desertion.
Hear his piteous cry, "My God, my God, why have you forsaken me?" (Matthew 27:46).

Then was fulfilled the prophecy given by the mouth of Zechariah, "'Awake, O sword, against my
shepherd, against the man who stands next to me,' declares the Lord of hosts" (Zechariah 13:7).

That sword is sheathed in Christ's heart!
Yes, Christ appeared! He was visibly crucified among men!
He appeared on that dreadful day of judgment and of vengeance!

So it was, and only so, that he was able to put away sin!

From sermon no. 2283, *Christ's One Sacrifice for Sin*

HIS CAPTIVITY SETS US FREE

"If you seek Me, let these go their way."
JOHN 18:8 NKJV

These words of Jesus were like coats of armor that concealed the wearers from their enemies.
Under the shield of these words the disciples walked securely through the midst of the boisterous
mob that was gnashing their teeth at Christ and laughing at him, revealing their savage malice.
The disciple John, standing at the foot of the cross, did not have even a hair on his head touched.

The word of Jesus proved to be a royal word—a divine word—and men were constrained to obey it.
It was a word, not only guarding the disciples at that time,
but since no Scripture is of private interpretation
it was also a royal passport given to all Christ's people in the ways of providence.

However, mystically understood, the words have a far deeper meaning.

The true seizure of Christ was not by the Romans nor by the envious Jews, *but by our sins.*
The true deliverance given to the disciples was not from Roman weapons, *but from the penalty of our sins.*

O Christian, if your sins are tormenting you, hear the voice of Jesus:
"If you seek Me, let these go their way."

The law of God comes out to seek us who have violated it;
and it has many and just demands against us.
But Jesus, who stood in our place, puts himself before the law, and says, "Do you seek me? Here it am,
but when you take me prisoner, let these—in whose place I stand—go their way."

When the law met with the Lord Jesus and made him its servant
and constrained him to bear its penalty,
all of Christ's people were absolutely and forever set free.

Jesus Christ then, as he stands before the law,
and is bound by the law,
and is flogged by the law,
and is crucified by the law,
and is buried by the law,
says to you who trust in him, "Go your way, the law cannot touch you. It has smitten me instead."

O Christian, since Christ has obeyed the law
and has also suffered its penalty,
you may now rejoice in the law as a gracious rule of life.

It is not a yoke of bondage to you,
for you are not under the law, but under grace.

From sermon no. 722, *The Captive Savior Freeing His People*

GOD'S HIGHEST GLORY

*"Glory to God in the highest, and on earth peace
among those with whom he is pleased!"*
LUKE 2:14

The angels had been present on many grand and glorious occasions,
    and they had joined in many a solemn chorus to the praise of their Almighty Creator.
But now—when they saw God stooping to become a baby—they lifted their notes even higher.

Reaching to the uttermost stretch of angelic music, they gained the highest notes of divine praise
    as they sang, "Glory to God in the highest," for they felt that God could go no higher in goodness.
Thus they gave to him their highest praise in the highest act of his godhead.

What is the lesson to be learned from this first syllable of the angels' song?
Why this, that salvation is God's highest glory!

God is glorified in every dewdrop that twinkles in the morning sun.
He is magnified in every flower that blooms in the forest, though it lives to blush unseen.
He is glorified in every bird that warbles on the limb, in every lamb that skips in the meadow.

Do the stars not exalt him when they write his name on the azure of heaven in their golden letters?
Do the lightnings not adore him when they flash his brightness in arrows of light, piercing the darkness?
Do the thunders not extol him when they roll like drums in the march of the God of armies?

*But, O universe! You may sing and sing
until you have exhausted yourself,
yet you will never create a song
as sweet as the song of Incarnation!*

Though creation may be a majestic organ of praise,
    it cannot reach the compass of that golden canticle—Incarnation.
There is more in that than in all creation; there is more melody in Jesus in the manger
    than there is in worlds on worlds rolling their grandeur around the throne of the Most High.

Pause Christian, and consider how every attribute is magnified.

Lo! What *wisdom* is here! God becomes man so that God may be just and the justifier of the ungodly.
Lo! What *power*! Where is power so great as when it conceals power? What power, that the godhead
    would unrobe itself and become man!
Lo! What *love*! Jesus becomes a man in order to die for us!

Name one attribute of God that is not manifest in Jesus.
    The whole of God is glorified in Christ.
And though a portion of the name of God is written in the universe,
    it is best read here—*in him who was the Son of Man, and yet, the Son of God.*

From sermon no. 168, *The First Christmas Carol*

THE LOWLY KING

Rejoice greatly, O daughter of Zion! Shout aloud, O daughter of Jerusalem!
Behold, your king is coming to you; righteous and having salvation is he,
humble and mounted on a donkey, on a colt, the foal of a donkey.
ZECHARIAH 9:9

Whenever God would have his people especially happy, it is always in himself.
If it is written, "Rejoice greatly," then the reason is, "Behold, your king is coming to you!"
Our chief source of rejoicing is the presence of King Jesus in our midst.

Whether it is his First or his Second Advent, Christ's very shadow is a delight;
   his footstep is sweet music to our ear.
That delight springs from the fact that he is ours: "Behold, *your* king is coming to you."
   Dear saint, whatever he may be to others, he is your King, and he comes to *you.*

The verse goes on to tell us why the Lord is such a source of gladness.
   It is because he is righteous and is bringing us salvation.
He has worked out the stern problem of how God can be just, and yet save the sinful.
   He has borne the penalty of our sin, and now we are saved in him.

Moreover, it is written of him that he is humble.
His outward state portrays the lowliness and the gentleness of his character.

At the height of his grandeur he is not like the proud monarchs of earth.
   He prefers the patient donkey to the noble charger;
      and he is more at home with the common people than with the great.
In his grandest pageant in his capital city he came "mounted on a donkey."

> *He rode through Jerusalem in state;*
> *but what lowliness marked the spectacle!*

Instead of officials in their robes, he was surrounded by common peasants and children.
Boughs of trees and garments of friends strewed the road, instead of flowers and costly tapestries.

> *Our Lord gave himself no grand airs,*
> *but was natural, unaffected, and free from all vain-glory.*
> *His greatest pomp went no further*
> *than riding through Jerusalem on a colt, the foal of a donkey.*

> *He is your King, O Zion!*
> *Shout, to think you have such a Lord!*

> *Where the scepter is love and the crown is humility,*
> *the homage should be bright with rejoicing.*
> *None will groan or ever complain beneath such authority.*

From sermon no. 1861, *The Lowly King*

LONGING FOR THE CROSS

"I have a baptism to be baptized with,
and how great is my distress until it is accomplished!"
Luke 12:50

Christ longed for the cross, because it was the goal of all his exertions.
It was the place where he could say, "It is finished" (John 19:30).
He could never have said that on his throne, but he cried, "It is finished" while on his cross.

He preferred the sufferings of Calvary to the honors of the multitude,
    for preach as he might,
    and bless them as he might,
    and heal them as he might,
his work was still incomplete; the baptism he had to be baptized with was not yet accomplished.

He longed for his cross, because it was the top-stone of his labor.
He longed for his sufferings, because they were the completion of his great work of grace.
He looked on his crucifixion *as the hour of his triumph.*

His disciples thought the cross would be a degradation.
Jesus, however, looked through the outward and the visible—and beheld the spiritual.

"The cross," said he, "the gibbet of my doom may seem to be cursed with degradation.
My name may be dishonored as one who died on the tree,
        but I do not look at the cross as you do.
    I know its disgrace, but I despise the shame.
I look on the cross as the gate of triumph, as the portal of victory.

"Oh, shall I tell you what I will behold from the cross?—

    just when my eye is swimming with its last tear,
    just when my heart is palpitating with its last pang,
    just when my body is rent with its last thrill of anguish,
        then my eye will see the head of the Dragon broken.
        My eye will see my offspring eternally saved,
and I will behold the ransomed coming from their prison houses.

"In that last moment of my doom,
when my mouth is just preparing for its last cry of 'It is finished,'
        I will behold the year of my redeemed.

"Yes, I will behold in vision the glories of the latter days
when I will sit on the throne of my father David and judge the earth,
    attended with the pomp of angels and the shouts of my beloved!"

From sermon no. 139, *Christ Lifted Up*

DYING FOR THE UNGODLY

While we were still weak, at the right time Christ died for the ungodly.
ROMANS 5:6

The apostle Paul was deeply affected by the fact that God gave his Son to die for the ungodly.
We can understand God loving those who love him;
those who are renewed in his image and striving for holiness.
But it is an overpowering thought that he loved us when there was nothing good in us at all.

God even loved us before he laid the foundation of the world.
Seeing us as fallen and lost, he resolved to send his Son to die for us.

Jesus came, not because we were good, but because we were evil.
He gave himself, not for our righteousness, but for our sins.

The moving cause of love in God
was not in our excellence, but in himself.

He loved us when we hated him and when we opposed him,
when we cursed him, persecuted his people, and blasphemed his ways.

That Christ loved us in heaven was a great thing;
that he then came down to earth to be born in Bethlehem was a greater thing;
that he lived a life of obedience for our sakes was a wonderful thing;
but that he died for us—this is the climax of love's sacrifice, the summit of the Alp of love!

Some sights astonish us for a while and then grow commonplace, but the cross of Christ grows on us.
The more we know of it, the more it surpasses knowledge.

That God himself would take our nature,
and then in that nature die on a cross in order to save us who were his enemies,
is something that could only be believed on no less authority than the divine.
It is altogether miraculous, and there is nothing worth knowing or admiring compared with this!

Nothing can ever rival in interest the cross of Christ.

Study whatever books you may,
the knowledge of a crucified Savior
will still remain the most sublime of all the sciences.

The apostle then goes on to say that the Lord must ever love us, now that we are reconciled.

If God loved us when we were enemies, surely he will continue to love us now that we are friends.
If he died for us when we were rebels, surely he will refuse us nothing now that we are reconciled.
If Jesus reconciled us by his death, surely he can and will save us by his life.

From sermon no. 1904, *The Personal Pentecost and the Glorious Hope*

WORKERS WITH GOD

We are God's fellow workers.
1 CORINTHIANS 3:9

In Christ's church, the useful, untiring laborers who are toiling for him
    are the very people who have the most fellowship with him.
In their toil they have him working side by side with them, and thus are God's fellow workers.

When we as a church, and each of us as individuals,
have anything to do for Jesus,
we must do it in communion with him.

A vision of the Crucified is what we need.

When we are toiling in his harvest field, we sometimes grow very weary
    because the harvest is plentiful, but the workers are few.
We often feel that the edge of our sickle is growing very, very blunt,
    and we wish we could lie down beneath the shade of a tree and toil no longer.

Ah, but just then we see the Crucified One
coming forward with his mighty sickle!

As we mark the blood drops streaming from his brow;
as we see the nail print in the hand with which he grasps the sickle;
when we see how he toils and how he labors;
when we see the awful love with which he sacrifices himself—
he has stripped off his very garments and in all the nakedness of self-denial
gives himself up that he may save others, while himself he cannot save—
then we pluck up heart again and take hold of our sickle.

Oh, for a vision of the Savior's face covered with the spittle!
See him marred and bruised by the rough Roman soldiers!
See him as Pilate brings him forth, and cries, "Behold the man!" (John 19:5).
See him while they lift him up on high and dislocate all his bones!

Why, what can you not endure compared with this?

You only sip at that cup which the Savior drained to the dregs.
You only feel a scratch from those nails that went right through his hands.

Courage, thou solitary worker!
Let Christ's griefs solace you.

From sermon no. 605, *Good Works in Good Company*

WHY PETER'S FALL IS RECORDED

The Lord turned and looked at Peter. And Peter remembered the saying of the Lord,
how he had said to him, "Before the rooster crows today, you will deny me three times."
And he went out and wept bitterly.
LUKE 22:61–62

Peter's fall is recorded four times at considerable length.
Is this telling us that we should give it fourfold attention?

It deserves special mention because it must have greatly increased our Lord's grief,
     knowing that while he was enduring untold indignities on man's behalf
        his most prominent disciple was denying him with oaths and curses.
Surely none of the tortures he endured from his enemies would have caused him such pain!

> *Blessed Master, there is not one tint of all the colors of grief*
> *that is lacking in the picture of your Passion.*

> *It is not possible to depict sufferings more acute and intense than yours*
> *when you died—"the righteous for the unrighteous"—to bring us to God.*

I also believe that Peter's fall and restoration are fully recorded
     in order to depict the greatness of our Redeemer's saving power.
This is especially so in the immediate prospect of his cruel death on the cross.

Is it not wonderful to think that, before he dies, Jesus restores this great backslider?
And what about the dying thief? Does he not represent another class of sinners?

Yes, Peter is the backslider restored.
The dying thief is the sinner saved at the eleventh hour.

I cannot imagine any incidents during Christ's Passion that reveal greater grace than these two.
They so richly adorn and embellish the cross.

> *O Christian, do you not think that there is in this fourfold record*
> *an instructive lesson for you concerning the frailty of the best of humans?*

> *Does Peter's fall not tell you that you are also weak*
> *and that you will fall if left to yourself?*

> *You must look to your Master and trust wholly in him.*
> *Never rely on your own experience or on the firmness of your resolutions,*
> *or you will surely fall just as Peter did.*

From sermon no. 2771, *Peter's Fall and Restoration*

THE CROWN OF THORNS

Twisting together a crown of thorns, they put it on his head.
MATTHEW 27:29

As we press into the guardroom, what do we see when we behold our Savior crowned in this way?

We see here the Christ—the generous, loving, tender Christ—treated with indignity and scorn.
We see the Prince of Life and Glory made an object of derision by rough and brutal soldiers.
We see the lily among thorns, purity lifting itself up in the midst of opposing sin.
We see here the sacrifice caught in the thicket—and held fast there as a victim in our place—fulfilling the ancient type of the ram held in the thicket, which Abraham slew instead of his son Isaac.

We see here Christ's *lowliness and weakness triumphed over* by the lusty legionaries.
When they brought him into the guardroom, they felt that he was entirely in their power and that his claims to be a king were so absurd as to be only a theme for contemptuous jest.

He was poorly dressed since he wore only the clothing of a peasant—was he a claimant of purple?
He held his peace—was he the man to stir up a nation to sedition?
He was all wounds and bruises, fresh from the scourger's lash—was he the hero to inspire an army's enthusiasm and overturn old Rome?

So they mocked his claims to be a king,
    but it was not merely mockery, for their *cruelty added pain to insult.*
If they had intended to only mock him, they might have twisted together a crown of straw,
    but they meant to pain him; therefore, they fashioned a crown of thorns.

They had scourged him until there was no part of his body that was not bleeding beneath their blows,
    except for his head, and now that head must be made to suffer too.
Alas, our whole head was sick, and our whole heart faint (Isaiah 1:5),
    so he must be made in his chastisement like to us in our transgression.

There was no part of our humanity without sin,
so there must be no part of his humanity without suffering.

If we had escaped in some measure from iniquity,
so might he have escaped from pain,
but since we had worn the foul garment of transgression,
and it covered us from head to foot,
even so he must wear the garments of shame and derision
from the crown of his head,
to the very sole of his foot!

Oh, dive as we may, we cannot reach the depths of this abyss of woe and shame!
Oh, mount as we may, these storm-swept hills of agony are still above us!

From sermon no. 1168, *The Crown of Thorns*

THE UNKNOWN WAYS OF LOVE

"What I am doing you do not understand now,
but afterward you will understand."
JOHN 13:7

These words were spoken to Peter after his exclamation of surprise, "Lord, do you wash my feet?"

This was a very natural expression of astonishment, yet unwise.
    Although it was a marvelously condescending action for Jesus to wash his disciples' feet,
        he had already performed a greater condescension by coming to earth in the form of a man.
It was a far greater marvel for the Son of the Highest to dwell among mortals in a human body.

Had Peter also understood what Jesus had prophesied concerning his sufferings and death,
    he would have seen that it was a very small thing for his Master to take a towel and a basin.
It was indeed small in comparison to having our iniquities laid on him!

If it surprises you to see the Lord of glory wear a towel,
    does it not amaze you even more to see him clad in the purple robe of mockery?
And think of how he was stripped of his clothing at the cross and left with nothing to wear.

It is wonderful that he would take the basin in the Upper Room,
    but surely it was even more extraordinary that he would take the cup in the garden,
and drink in its full bitterness until "his sweat became like great drops of blood" (Luke 22:44).

It was a surprising action when he washed the disciples' feet with water,
    but it was a far greater marvel when he poured out his heart's blood in order to wash every part of us.

In our Lord's doings there is much that we cannot understand.
Our text relates to everything that he does: "What I am doing you do not understand now."

You may know something of what Jesus does,
yet the mystery is not completely laid bare to your eyes.
There are folds of his manifold grace that are as yet unopened.

The work of Jesus is beyond you.
It surpasses you, for it cannot be measured.

If his work was small, we could measure it;
if his love was scanty, we could know it;
if his wisdom was finite, we could judge it;
but where everything is beyond comprehension, who can pretend to know?

We must remember that in our salvation, Christ himself is the sum and substance.
In it, every attribute of his divinity is employed to the full.
It is therefore not at all surprising that we cannot know what he does.

From sermon no. 1293, *The Unknown Ways of Love*

INNOCENT AND SPOTLESS

You were ransomed ... not with perishable things such as silver or gold,
but with the precious blood of Christ, like that of a lamb without blemish or spot.
1 PETER 1:18–19

If there had been even one sin in Christ, he would not have been capable of being our Redeemer;
   but he was without spot or blemish—without original sin and without practical transgression.
The reason why his blood is able to save is because it is the blood of an innocent victim.

When the Israelite struck the knife into the poor innocent lamb,
   we can imagine him thinking, "Ah, this poor creature dies, not because of its own guilt,
but to show me that I am guilty and that I deserve to die like that!"

Turn, then, your eyes to the cross, and see Jesus bleeding and dying there for you.
Remember, "For sins not his own, he died to atone."

> *O guilty one, the blood of Jesus is able to save you,*
> *because he was perfectly innocent himself;*
> *and he died, the righteous for the unrighteous, to bring us to God.*

Christ's blood has power to save, not only because God appointed that blood—
   and because it was the blood of an innocent and spotless being—
      but because Christ himself was God, and the blood that he shed was godlike blood.
Can you imagine the value of the blood of God's own dear Son?

> *It was the wonder of angels that God would condescend to die.*
> *And it will be the unceasing wonder throughout eternity*
> *that God would become a man in order to die.*

> *Oh, when we stop to think that Christ was the Creator of the world,*
> *and that the universe was upheld by his all-sustaining shoulders,*
> *we cannot wonder that his blood is able to cleanse from sin!*

Come, my soul; come and stand with all saints and sinners at the cross,
   and see this man overcome with weakness, fainting, groaning, bleeding, dying.
This man is also "God over all, blessed forever" (Romans 9:5).
   Can you doubt the power of such blood to save you?

Can you see any stretch of sin out-measuring the power of Deity,
   any height of iniquity outdoing the topless steeps of the divine?
Can you imagine a depth of sin deeper than the Infinite,
   or a breadth of iniquity broader than the Godhead?

From sermon no. 228, *The Blood*

VOLUNTARY POVERTY

Though he was rich, yet for your sake he became poor.
2 CORINTHIANS 8:9

How was our Savior poor in the ordinary sense?

He was born of humble parents, the son of a carpenter.
He took a lowly place even in his birth for he was laid in a manger.
His intimate acquaintances were fishermen.

When he died, his only possessions were the garments he wore,
    and even those were taken away from him by the soldiers.
There he was—naked, dead, and indebted to charity!
    He did not even have a sepulcher of his own, for he was laid in a borrowed tomb.

He thus became poor outwardly, but was that all?
No, he was also poor regarding his friends.

Judas betrayed him.
Peter denied him.
All the disciples forsook him and fled.

He was so poor that even the comforts that are left to the most degraded were taken away from him.
    He was even forsaken by his Father.
"Eli, Eli, lema sabachthani?" (Matthew 27:46) indicated an inward poverty,
    even deeper than that naked and mangled body indicated an outward poverty.

He had given up all; laid aside everything—

His crown of glory was exchanged for the thorns of shame;
his imperial mantle of dominion was cast aside so that he might wear his own blood.

He was no longer adored, but spat upon;
he was no longer revered, but despised.

He did not have a throne, but a cross;
he did not have the brightness of glory, but the blackness of midday-midnight;
he did not have life and immortality, but "it is finished," and the giving up of his spirit.

"Though he was rich, *yet for your sake* he became poor."

For you, those drops of crimson sweat as they stained the cold earth;
for you, the cruel lash that pitilessly plowed those holy shoulders;
for you, each of those cruel nails and the spear that pierced his side.

From sermon no. 3380, *Our Lord's Voluntary Poverty*

ALWAYS WITH OUR LORD

So we will always be with the Lord.
1 THESSALONIANS 4:17

The chief blessedness of heaven lies in this: We will *always* be with our Lord.
No break will ever occur in the intimate communion of the saints with Christ.

Here, our high days and bright Sabbaths, with their sweetest joys, must have their evenings,
    and then come the workdays with the burdens of the week upon them.
But there the Sabbath is eternal, the worship endless, the praise unceasing, the bliss unbounded.

There can come no end to us and no end to our bliss,
since there can be no end to our Lord.

What will it mean to be forever with the Lord?

A notable preacher explained it this way:
"Forever life, forever light, forever love, forever peace, forever rest, forever joy."

As great as this is, recollect that these are only the fruit and not the root of the joy.
Jesus is better than all of these; his company is more than the joy that comes from it.
It is not "life forever," nor "light forever," but "forever with the Lord" that we desire.

Oh, to be with him! I ask for no other bliss
and cannot imagine anything else more heavenly!

Why, touching the hem of his garment healed the sick woman,
and seeing him was enough to give life to us when we were dead.
What is it then to be with him actually, consciously, and always?

We love to think of being forever with the Redeemer, not only as Jesus the Savior, but as *the Lord*.

Here we have seen him on the cross and have lived thereby.
We are with him now in his cross-bearing and shame, and it is well.
But our eternal companionship with him will enable us to rejoice in him as Lord.

Oh, how we will delight in obeying him as our Lord!
How we will triumph as we see what a Lord he is over the whole universe!
How we will adore him in his glory and forever hail him as King of kings and Lord of lords!

Yes, we will always be with the Lord,
and his Lordship will be most on our minds.
He has been raised into glory and honor
and never again needs to suffer shame.

From sermon no. 1374, *Forever With the Lord*

ONLY ONE REDEMPTION

For you were bought with a price.
1 Corinthians 6:20

It is a high honor to our poor fallen race that man is the only redeemed creature in the universe.
He alone has cost the Lord his life.
The blood-mark of the Son of God is found nowhere else.

Even the rebellious angels have not been redeemed by blood.
God has spent more on us than on the whole universe.

The Lord could speak worlds into existence,
    or mold massive orbs as one rolls clay in his hands.
But in order to erect the new creation of redeemed people
    he had to endure the loss of his own dear Son.

Yes, God had to resign his Beloved to death.

In the person of his one and only Son
he had to ransom men by his own sufferings.

Think of yourself, dear reader, as being totally unique—a special wonder in all creation.
You alone can say, "I know that my Redeemer lives" (Job 19:25).

Neither in the earth nor in the stars, nor in yonder golden streets
    will there ever be beings—other than humans—
    who have "washed their robes and made them white in the blood of the Lamb" (Revelation 7:14).
How great a value we ought to place on ourselves since we are bought with such a price!

O God, "what is man that you are mindful of him,
and the son of man that you care for him?" (Psalm 8:4).

Yes, our Lord does indeed care for us.
He cared for us when he took our nature into union with the divine.
He cared for us when he redeemed us with inexpressible pain and anguish.

Dear child of God,
if you want to know your true value,
see Christ on the cross and mark his wounds.

Do not think so cheaply of yourself, stooping to live only for the pleasures and riches of this earth.
You are too precious to waste yourself on fading flowers.
Use yourself only for honorable purposes; for eternal realities.

From sermon no. 1554, *Redemption by Price*

VOLUNTARY CONDESCENSION

"I gave my back to those who strike,
and my cheeks to those who pull out the beard;
I hid not my face from disgrace and spitting."
ISAIAH 50:6

Behold the Messiah as the peerless sufferer,
   and this sufferer on whom man spat was the Eternal God.
He who was a prisoner in Pilate's hall—accused of sedition—was the King of kings.

He who gave his shoulders to the cruel whip of the Roman scourge
   until the plowers made deep scarlet furrows down his blessed back (Psalm 129:3)—
      he was that God who created and sustains the heavens and the earth and all things that exist.
He was a suffering man, but at the same time he was the Son of God.

As you think of his pain, couple it with the thought that he bore all that agony voluntarily.
He said, "I *gave* my back to those who strike, and my cheeks to those who pull out the beard."
He also said, "I lay down my life for the sheep. No one takes it from me, but I lay it down of my
   own accord" (John 10:15, 18).

No one could have scarred that blessed back of his without his permission.
No one could have pulled out his beard unless he had allowed it to be pulled.

In addition to the pain, notice the contempt that Jesus endured.

The pulling of his beard was proof of the malicious contempt of his enemies;
   yet they still went further and spit in his face.
Spitting is regarded as the most contemptuous thing that one person can do to another;
   yet, the vile soldiers gathered around him and spit on him!

Oh, the utter uselessness of human speech
in trying to describe this scene!

We can never fathom this mystery—
that he, the Creator of heaven and earth,
did not hide his face from disgrace and spitting!

Oh, the splendor of voluntary condescension and of marvelous love
on the part of him before whom nations are as a drop in the bucket
and to whom time is but a span compared with his own eternity!

He is the exact image of his Father,
yet he bows to disgrace and spitting.

From sermon no. 2827, *The Redeemer Described by Himself*

A NEVER-ENDING TESTIMONY

Yes, he is altogether lovely.
SONG OF SOLOMON 5:16 NKJV

With these five words the bride gives us a summary of her Lord.
　She had just delivered a tenfold discourse concerning him, describing in detail his various beauties.
Now, after having surveyed him from head to foot,
　she gathers up her commendations in this sentence: "Yes, he is altogether lovely."

As in this allegorical song the bride sums up her witness in these words,
　so have all the patriarchs, all the prophets, all the apostles, all the confessors.
Yes, and the entire body of the church has left us with no other testimony.

Whatever the type, or symbol, or obscure oracle, or open word in which they bore witness,
　that witness all amounted to this: "Yes, he is altogether lovely."
And since the canon of inspiration has closed, all the saints continue to confirm the declaration.

From the sighs and the songs arising from the dying beds of saints,
　we hear this note, supreme above all others: "He is altogether lovely."
Wherever saints are and whatever their condition may be, we always hear this one master note.

Oh, there is no fear of exaggeration
when we speak of the loveliness of Christ!

Lay on, ye people of eloquence; spare no colors,
for you can never depict him too highly!

And sing aloud, ye blood-washed throng,
for all your praises fall short of the glory due to him!

Think of his name. It is Jesus, the Savior.
Is that not lovely?

Think of his work. He came to seek and to save the lost.
Is that not lovely?

Think of what he has done. He has purchased our souls with blood.
Is that not lovely?

Think of what he is doing now. He is pleading before the throne of God for sinners.
Is that not lovely?

Under every aspect Jesus is attractive.

From sermon no. 1001, *Altogether Lovely*

COMFORT FOUND AT CALVARY

The place called Calvary.
Luke 23:33 nkjv

The hill of comfort is the hill of Calvary.
The house of consolation is built with the wood of the cross.
The temple of heavenly blessing is founded on the riven Rock—riven by the spear that pierced his side.

No scene in sacred history ever cheers the soul like that scene on Calvary.

Nowhere does the soul ever find such consolation as on that very spot ...
    where misery reigned,
    where woe triumphed,
    where agony reached its climax.[1]

Light now shines from the midday-midnight of Golgotha,
    and every flower of the field blooms sweetly beneath the shadow of that once accursed tree.
In that place of thirst, grace has dug a fountain that ever gushes with waters, clear as crystal—
    each drop capable of alleviating the woes of mankind.

You who have had your seasons of conflict will confess that it was not at Olivet,
    nor on the hill of Sinai, nor on Tabor, that you found comfort.
Rather, it was at Gethsemane, at Gabbatha, and at Golgotha that your heart found true solace.

The bitter herbs of Gethsemane have often taken away the bitters of your life.
The whip of Gabbatha has often scourged away your cares.
The groans of Calvary have put your groans to flight.

We would never have known Christ's love
in all its heights and depths if he had not died,
nor could we have guessed the Father's deep affection
if he had not given his Son to die.

The common mercies we enjoy all sing of love,
just like the seashell we put to our ear whispers of the ocean.

Yet if we desire to hear the ocean itself,
we must not look at everyday blessings,
but at the transactions of the Crucifixion.

He who would know love,
let him go to Calvary and see the Man of Sorrows die.[2]

[1]From sermon no. 1261, *Justification by Grace*
[2]*Morning and Evening*, April 10 (M)

THE BAPTIST'S MESSAGE

*The next day he saw Jesus coming toward him, and said,
"Behold, the Lamb of God, who takes away the sin of the world!"*
JOHN 1:29

It is the preacher's principal business,
    and I think I might say his only business, to cry, "Behold, the Lamb of God!"
It was for this reason that John was born and sent into the world.

If the Baptist had been the most eloquent preacher of repentance;
if he had been the most earnest denouncer of the sins of the times,
he would have missed his life-work if he had forgotten to say, "Behold, the Lamb of God!"

He did well when he baptized the repenting crowd;
he spoke nobly when he faced the Pharisees;
he was a true hero when he rebuked Herod,
but still, his chief errand was to herald the Messiah, to bear witness to the Son of God.

What we have said of John, we may say of every God-sent minister.
    He is sent to bear witness to the Christ of God.
Whatever else he may do, if he does not do this continually, habitually, and earnestly,
    he is not fulfilling the errand on which his Master sent him.

> *As the stars called "the Pointers"*
> *always point to the Pole star,*
> *so we must always point to the Redeemer.*

John thoroughly discharged his life-work, for he was always saying, "Behold, the Lamb of God!"
Paul knew nothing among the Corinthians, except Jesus Christ and him crucified (1 Corinthians 2:2).
The crucified Christ is an essential subject for all of the saved, as well as for the lost.

> *No subject is more sweet, more refreshing, more sanctifying to the saint*
> *than the cross of our dying Lord.*

> *The sinner needs it if he would be saved,*
> *and the saint requires it if he would persevere, advance, and conquer.*[1]

Along with the Baptist, I, too, would concentrate my thoughts upon Christ and his atoning death.
I would lift up my voice in this wilderness, bearing witness to the Lamb of God.

The years may be short in which to guide this flock,
    but around the cross will be the place of green pastures,
and from the sacrifice of our Lord will flow the still waters.[2]

[1]From sermon no. 1060, *Behold the Lamb*
[2]From sermon no. 1987, *Behold the Lamb of God*

LOVED TO THE UTTERMOST END

Having loved his own who were in the world, he loved them to the end.
JOHN 13:1

These few words are a brief but complete summary of the Savior's conduct toward his disciples.
    He always loved them; no word or action of his was contrary to the rule of love.
We must remember, however, that this display of love for the disciples
    is a miniature of Jesus, the Lover of souls, who loves each individual he counts among his own.

Our Savior's faithfulness to the small band he had selected is very remarkable.

While he was denying himself in order to do his Father's will,
    they were asking to sit on his right hand and on his left hand in his kingdom.
They would have taken him and forced on him a crown, while he sought only a cross.
    Had they dared, they would have thwarted, rather than assisted him in his self-sacrificing mission.

Still, having loved them, neither their worldliness nor their stupidity—nor their lack of sympathy—
    could prevent him from loving them to the end.
Even with all of their failings they could not break out of the magic circle of his affection.

> *Yet, all of his loving actions put together*
> *cannot amount to such an overwhelming proof of love as this:*
> *After having lived out his love,*
> *the Lord Jesus then died to exhibit it even more.*

> *From Gethsemane to Golgotha—*
> *all along that blood-sprinkled road—*
> *you see the proof of his love for his very own*
> *and that he loved them to the very end.*

All the pains of death could not shake his firm affection for his own.

They may bind his hands, but they cannot restrain his heart of love.
They may flog him, but they cannot drive out of him his affection for his beloved.
They may slanderously revile him, but they cannot compel him to say a word against his people.
They may nail him to the tree, but they cannot tempt him to forsake his work of love.

> *In that tragedy on Calvary,*
> *Jesus indeed went to the bitter end*
> *when, having yielded up comfort, reputation, and liberty,*
> *he even gave up his last rag of covering and then resigned his breath.*

The cross of Jesus reveals love to the uttermost end.
It is a grand display of the immutability and invincibility of the affection of our Savior's heart.

From sermon no. 810, *The Faithfulness of Jesus*

A SEPARATE PLACE

A garden locked is my sister, my bride, a spring locked, a fountain sealed.
SONG OF SOLOMON 4:12

On the surface of this text, you see not only secrecy, but *separation.*

There is a garden but it is a garden locked up—completely shut off from the surrounding area.
There is a gate through which the great husbandman himself may enter, but it is also a gate that
    shuts out all those who would only rob the husbandman of his rightful fruit.

There is also separation in the spring, for it is not a common spring where everyone may drink.
It is so preserved that only one lip may touch it; only one eye may even see its secret.
The fountain as well is not a general fountain, but it stands alone by itself.

So it is with the spiritual life. It is a separate thing.
As God's people we are separated from the world around by the life of God in our souls.

Yes, and there are sacred seasons when we will not be at ease in any society, however select,
    because our souls will pine for sweet solitude, secret communion, hidden embraces.
We will be compelled to walk alone with Christ.

If your soul has been renewed, there will be times …
    when the face of man will disturb you,
    when only the face of Jesus can satisfy you.

At times, you will be a garden locked up …
    when you must enter your room and shut the door,
    when even the society of your dearest friend is an impediment.

> *Go not abroad, O my heart,*
> *but stay at home with Jesus,*
> *your lover, your Lord, your all!*
>
> *Shut up your gates, O my heart,*
> *to all company but his!*
>
> *O my sweet well-spring of delights,*
> *be shut up to every lip but his!*
>
> *O thou fountain of the issues of my heart,*
> *be thou sealed only for him,*
> *that he may come and drink, and drink again,*
> *and take sweet solace in you,*
> *your soul being his, and his alone!*

From sermon no. 431, *A Secret and Yet No Secret*

THE BLOOD OF JESUS

He has appeared once for all at the end of the ages
to put away sin by the sacrifice of himself ...
Christ, having been offered once to bear the sins of many.
HEBREWS 9:26, 28

The Jews slew a lamb every morning and every evening, for there was a continual mention of sin.
The blood of the lamb could not put it away.

The lamb availed for today, but there was the sin of tomorrow, so what was to be done with that?
Why, a fresh victim must bleed!

But oh, our greatest joy is that the blood of Jesus has been shed once,
    and he has said, "It is finished" (John 19:30).
There is no longer a need for the blood of bulls or of lambs, or of any other sacrifice,
    for his one self-sacrifice "has perfected for all time those who are being sanctified" (Hebrews 10:14).

Trembling sinner, come to the cross.
Your sins are heavy and many, but the Atonement for them is completed by the death of Christ.
Look then to Jesus and remember that he needs nothing to supplement his blood.

The road between God and man is finished and open.
The robe to cover your nakedness is complete, without a rag of yours.
The bath in which you are to be washed is full; nothing else needs to be added.

Nothing will hinder you from being saved if you are willing to believe in Jesus Christ.
He is a complete Savior, full of grace for an empty sinner.

Your deeds, your prayers, and your tears cannot save you.
Sacraments, however well they may be attended to, cannot save you.

> *Nothing but thy blood, O Jesus,*
> *can redeem us from the guilt of sin!*

> *Nothing but the blood of Jesus*
> *has in it the slightest saving power.*

God forbid that a word should be said against ordinances, but keep them in their proper places.
If you make them the basis of your salvation, you will find them to be lighter than a shadow.
We must repeat: There is not the slightest atom of saving power anywhere but in the blood of Jesus.

> *The blood—his blood—stands out in solitary majesty,*
> *the only rock of our salvation.*

From sermon no. 228, *The Blood*

LESSONS LEARNED AT GETHSEMANE

Then Jesus went with them to a place called Gethsemane,
and he said to his disciples, "Sit here, while I go over there and pray."
Matthew 26:36

The Savior went to Gethsemane, and there he poured out his soul in agonizing prayer to his Father.
So let us go to Gethsemane as well, so that we may view our Savior there and learn how to imitate him.

The first thing we will learn as we linger there is that our blessed Master sought seclusion
    when he was about to enter upon the great struggle of his life.

It was when Judas was about to give the traitor's kiss;
it was when scribes and Pharisees were about to hound him to the cross—
it was then that he felt he must get away to Gethsemane and be alone in prayer with his Father.

> *Some of us pray when we are, as it were, at Calvary, but not at Gethsemane.*
> *We pray when the trouble comes upon us, but not when it is on the road.*

> *Yet our Master teaches us here that in order to conquer at our Calvary,*
> *we must commence by wrestling at our Gethsemane.*

Also, when we pray in the presence of a great trouble, we should pray earnestly and repeatedly.
    Our Savior prayed with great intensity because his heart was bursting with anguish.
The throbs of his heart were so mighty that the canals overflowed their banks,
    and the red streams came bursting down in bloody drops—drops that even fell down to the earth!

We should also imitate Christ in the matter of our prayers.
No doubt he softly whispered the request: "My Father, if it be possible, let this cup pass from me."
But he must have said with all his might: "Nevertheless, not as I will, but as you will" (Matthew 26:39).

In the presence or in the prospect of a great crisis,
    we should make this our prayer to God: "Your will be done."
And having asked the Lord to screen us if it should seem good in his sight,
    we should resign ourselves into his hands, and say, "Nevertheless, not as I will, but as you will."

It is prevailing prayer when we get to that point.
We are prepared to die when we are able to present that petition.

> *O Christian, that is the best preparation*
> *for any cross that may come upon your shoulders!*

> *You can die a martyr's death*
> *and clap your hands even in the midst of the fire,*
> *if you can with all your soul really pray as Jesus prayed,*
> *"Not as I will, but as you will."*

From sermon no. 2767, *Jesus in Gethsemane*

LESSONS LEARNED AT THE CROSS

When they came to Jesus and saw that he was already dead, they did not break his legs.
But one of the soldiers pierced his side with a spear, and at once there came out blood and water.
JOHN 19:33–34

In the type of the Passover lamb it was strictly forbidden for even one bone to be broken.
   The people could kill it, sprinkle its blood, roast it and eat it, but they could not break its bones.
In effect, God says, "There is my Son. You may bind him, flog him, spit on him, crucify him;
   but he is the Lamb of my Passover and you must not break any of his bones."

See how Christ is identified here as "the Lamb of God, who takes away the sin of the world."
Not even one of his bones was broken.

Also, notice the last act of men towards their Redeemer.

They had already spit on him, and cried, "Crucify him, crucify him!" (John 19:6);
   they had nailed him to the cross and mocked his agonies until he died;
      and finally, their last act toward him is to pierce him through.
His experience at the hands of our race is summed up in the fact that they pierced him to the heart.

Oh, that is what men did to their Lord!
They have so despised and rejected him that he dies pierced to the heart.
Even when he is dead, they must insult his corpse with a spear-thrust.

Besides seeing our deep depravity, we must also learn *what Jesus did for us in this final act.*

In his life he had bled for us—drop by drop, the bloody sweat had fallen to the ground.
   Then the cruel scourges and the nails drew from him purple streams;
      but as a little store of lifeblood was left near his heart, he poured it all out before he went his way.
His body has gone into glory, but the purifying aspects of the blood and water are left behind.

Yes, blood and water from the heart of God's own dear Son
have fallen down on this dark and defiled planet,
thus sealing it as his own.

Our dear Lord, when he had given us his all—
even resigning his life on our behalf—
then parted with a priceless stream from the fountain of his heart.

Oh, the kindness of Christ's heart,
that not only for a blow returned a kiss,
but for a spear-thrust returned streams of life and healing!

Take all the types of the Old Testament together, and you will gather that the purification of sin
   was typically represented by blood and water.
Christ's side is pierced to give sinners the double cure of sin—the taking away of its guilt and power.

From sermon no. 1956, *On the Cross after Death*

July 24

A GLORIOUS VISION

**And the Word became flesh and dwelt among us,
and we have seen his glory.**
JOHN 1:14

We have seen Christ's glory in his *motive* for undertaking his great work of grace.

That motive was love—
    love for insignificant creatures,
    love for rebels who could never repay his love,
    love for men who crucified the Lord of glory.
There is a glory in this love that could never be found elsewhere.

And we have seen the glory of his *self-sacrifice.*
We have seen him giving up everything for us.

We have seen him laying aside his crown, his scepter, his royal robes, and his splendor.
We have seen him leaving his Father's house, his palaces, his honor, and becoming a man.

A man, did we say?
Yes, a poor man, a despised and afflicted man.
Yes, a man who became "obedient to the point of death, even death on a cross" (Philippians 2:8).

Throughout history we have never seen a self-sacrifice that could equal his.
These words reveal his whole history: "He saved others; he cannot save himself" (Matthew 27:42).

*O glorious Lord Jesus,
while you were being rejected by men
we have seen your great glory!*

We have seen, as well, the glory of his *endurance.*

We see him mocked yet never reviling.
We see him spit on yet never spitting back—even with a word of venom.
We see him accused yet silent before the judgment seat.
We see him enduring to the very end—until he could say, "It is finished," and giving up his spirit.

Where has there ever been a martyr like our Savior?
Who has endured like he has?
Who has ever borne such opposition?

*O Jesus! O Great God!—for such you are—
Great God, there is none like you in the omnipotence of your endurance!
We have seen your great glory even when you dwelt among men.*

From sermon no. 414, *The Glory of Christ Beheld!*

PRAISING OUR GOD AND KING

I will extol you, my God and King,
and bless your name forever and ever.
Psalm 145:1

David personally comes before his God and King
  and utters the deliberate resolution that he will praise the Divine Majesty forever.
He himself was a king according to the ways of earth, but to him God alone was King.

Our King is no tyrant—no maker of cruel laws—and he demands no crushing tribute or forced
  service.
His ways are ways of pleasantness and all his paths are peace.
His laws are just and good, and in the keeping of them there is a great reward.

> *Let others exult that they are their own masters.*
> *Our joy is that God is our King!*

> *Let others yield to this or that passion, or desire.*
> *We find our freedom in complete subjection to our heavenly King!*

Note that David also praises the Lord while claiming him as his own: "I will extol you, *my* God."
Ah! "My God" is as high a note as even an angel can reach!
Even though others claim God as theirs, he is also my God, and I will extol him.

> *To us there are Father, Son, and Holy Spirit;*
> *but these are one God, and this one God is our own God.*

> *Let others worship whom they will,*
> *but my soul adores and loves this God!*
> *Yes, claims him as her personal possession!*

Oh, do not be slow in his praise since he has been so swift in his grace!
Your very first breath was a gift from God, so spend it now to the Creator's praise.

With penitents and martyrs extol him!
With prophets and apostles extol him!
With saints and angels extol him!

Great is the Lord, and greatly to be praised!

> *Bless the Lord, for he is better than we could ever imagine!*
> *He is the crown of delight, the climax of goodness, the sum of all perfection!*

> *As often as we see the light, or feel the sun,*
> *we should bless the name of the Lord.*

From sermon no. 1902, *The Happy Duty of Daily Praise*

LOVE FOR JESUS

You whom my soul loves.
SONG OF SOLOMON 1:7

Why should we love Jesus?
Our hearts give their reasons for why they must love him: it is because of his infinite loveliness.

Setting aside the benefit we have received from his dear cross—
    which, of course, must ever be the deepest motive of love—
there is such beauty in Christ's character, such loveliness in his self-sacrifice that one must love him!

> *O Jesus, can I look into your eyes*
> *and not be smitten with your love?*

> *Can I gaze on your thorn-crowned head*
> *and not feel the thorn in my own heart?*

> *Can I see you in the fever of death*
> *and not be aroused with a passionate love for you?*

You cannot be in your Savior's company and not love him.

Go and kneel by his side in Gethsemane's garden,
    and each drop of blood as it falls on the ground
will be an irresistible reason for loving him.

Go and kneel by his feet at Calvary's cross
    and hear him as he cries, "My God, my God, why have you forsaken me?" (Matthew 27:46),
and you will find the greatest reason for loving him.

When you read the history of great men, there is much to admire, but nothing to win attachment;
    but when you read and learn about Jesus, you not only look up, you are also drawn up.
You do not admire so much as love; you do not adore so much as embrace.

> *His character enchants, subdues, overwhelms,*
> *and with an irresistible impulse of its own sacred attraction—*
> *it draws your spirit right up to him!*

As our life ebbs away, we may lose many mental powers, but memory clings to the name of Jesus.
The agonies of Christ have burnt his name into our innermost hearts.

We cannot stand and see him mocked by Herod's men of war;
we cannot behold him tortured, ridiculed, and spit on by vulgar lips;
we cannot mark him in the extreme agonies of his awful Passion
without saying, "Since you suffered all this for me, then I must love you, dear Savior."

From sermon no. 338, *Love to Jesus*

THE SINNER'S FRIEND

"A friend of tax collectors and sinners!"
MATTHEW 11:19

Our Lord proved himself to be the Friend of sinners,
    and what better proof could he give than to be numbered with them?
He even made his grave with the wicked!

Yes, God's fiery sword was drawn to smite a world of sinners!
Yes, that sword must fall in due time!

So what is to be done?
By what means can sinners be rescued?

Then suddenly—swifter than the lightning flashes, the sword descends!
It falls—but where?

It does not fall on the neck of sinners.

It is not the sinner's neck that is broken by its cruel edge.
It is not the sinner's heart that bleeds beneath its awful force.

No, the "friend of sinners" has put himself in the sinner's place.
As if he had been a sinner—though in him was no sin—he suffers, bleeds, and dies.

It was no ordinary suffering!
It was no ordinary bleeding!
It was no ordinary death such as mortals know!

It was a death in which the second death was comprehended!
It was a bleeding in which the very veins of God were emptied!
The God-man divinely suffered!

It was more than mortal agony, for the divine strengthened the human;
    the man was made mighty to endure because he was God.
Being God and man, Christ endured more than all men put together could suffer,
    and he endured the penalty that all of them ought to have suffered.

"Greater love has no one than this,
that someone lays down his life for his friends" (John 15:13).

This Christ has done, proving himself to be the Friend of sinners.

From sermon no. 556, *The Sinner's Friend*

TEARS OF HOLY PENITENCE

"When they look on me, on him whom they have pierced,
they shall mourn for him."
ZECHARIAH 12:10

Let us see that great sacrifice on Calvary so that we may bedew our Lord's cross with penitential tears.

Look as the soldiers rudely strip him, cruelly fling him down, and savagely pierce his hands and feet.
See them lift up his cross with a jolt, dislocating every bone, as the cross is fastened in the earth.
Notice them sitting down and looking at him in derision and gloating over his pain.
Watch now as in his extremity, Jesus cries, "I thirst," and they thrust vinegar into his mouth.

Finally, his agonies have become so intense that they must not be seen by any onlookers,
    so a thick darkness forms a secret chamber wherein he might do battle with his direst griefs.
At last, the storm passes, and he shouts, "It is finished"; bowing his head, he gives up his spirit.

Have we no tears for such sorrows as these?
Will we have no mourning for such griefs?

How is it that if we read the story of a common man suffering by his own folly we freely weep?
    But here on Calvary, where the King of heaven is tormented with sorrows so tremendous
        that they surpass all other griefs—as a mountain exceeds the molehills—
we are like flints of steel, scarcely feeling compassion move.

O God, pour out on us the spirit of grief and commiseration,
for Jesus Christ hangs on that tree, slain by our sins!

Had we never sinned, never rebelled,
there would have been no need of a Savior;
no need of a sword of vengeance to pierce his heart.

Now remember, as you continue at the foot of the cross, that Jesus Christ suffers all this *for you.*
Those wounds are *for you.*
That mangled frame lying in the tomb, motionless in the grasp of death, is *for you.*

Does this not urge you to no longer harbor the lusts that are the enemies of Christ?
Does this not make you cast out of your soul all the cruel foes that made the Savior bleed?

Come, thou heart of steel
and be melted in the furnace of his divine affection.
Come as you are—feeling or unfeeling—and look up to Jesus.

There is life in a look, and the first sign of life
will be a real and intense sorrow for sin.

From sermon no. 575, *The Pierced One Pierces the Heart*

JOY IN GOD THROUGH CHRIST

We also rejoice in God through our Lord Jesus Christ,
through whom we have now received reconciliation.
Romans 5:11

This joy in God is said to be through our Lord Jesus Christ,
    because we have *received reconciliation through him.*
No one can rejoice in an unreconciled God.

If you think that God is bound by the justice of his nature to punish you for your sin,
    you will not be able to find delight in him, but will be filled with dread.
But if by faith you see Christ making a full atonement for your sins,
    you will have the assurance that you have been reconciled to God.

God, apart from Christ, must be the object of dread to the guilty;
    but God, in Christ Jesus, on the throne with the covenant rainbow round about him—
that God becomes our joy and delight.

Furthermore, we only rejoice in God being reconciled to us
    when we ourselves have been viewing the Lord Jesus Christ.
Can anything make us love God like the sight of Christ?

A person may love God
for all his goodness in creation and in providence,
but the heart is never truly tuned to love
until it comes to Calvary.

The waves of love never rise to Atlantic billows
until the wind blows from Calvary.

When I behold him, who is the beloved of the Father, an infant in his mother's arms;
when I behold him as a sorrowing man, toiling over the rough roads of Palestine;
when I behold him as a bound victim led to the slaughter and willingly yielding up his life
    in a cruel and shameful death in order to redeem us from the curse of the law,
then my heart clings to the heart of God like a child clings to its mother.

Blessed be God the Father,
since we have beheld God the Son!

We now rejoice in God through our Lord Jesus Christ!

There is no joy in God unless you see Jesus Christ intimately knit with him.
Approach God by no other way than through the golden gate of his Son's great sacrifice.

From sermon no. 2550, *Joy in God*

THE GIFT OF GOD'S SON

For God so loved the world, that he gave his only Son,
that whoever believes in him should not perish but have eternal life.
JOHN 3:16

Let us consider God's *gift* to us: it was *"his only Son."*

When God gave his Son, he gave himself, for in his eternal nature Jesus is equal with God. *When God gave God for us, he gave his all, for he gave himself.* What more could he give?

Consider, you fathers, how you love your sons.
Could you give them to die for your enemy?

The highest proof of Abraham's love for God
    was when he did not withhold from God his son, his only son Isaac, whom he loved.
And the greatest display of the Eternal Father's love for us
    was when he gave his one and only Son to die for us.

If you desire to see the love of God in this great procedure, you must consider *how he gave his Son.*

He sent him down to yonder manger, united with a perfect manhood, in the form of an infant.
He sent the heir of all things to toil in a carpenter's shop.
He sent him down among scribes and Pharisees whose cunning eyes watched him, and where cruel
    tongues scourged him with base slander.
He sent him down to hunger and thirst, to poverty so dire he had nowhere to lay his head.
He sent him down to be crowned with thorns, to give his back to the plowers and his cheeks to those
    who pull out the hair.
At length he gave him up to death—a felon's death—the death of the crucified.

> *Behold that cross and see the anguish of he who dies on it,*
> *and mark how the Father has so given him to us that he hides his face from him.*

> *"Lema sabachthani?" tells us how fully God gave his Son to be our ransom.*
> *He gave him to be made a curse for us;*
> *he gave him to die, "the righteous for the unrighteous," to bring us to God.*

Could you even think of giving your child to die a felon's death,
    cursed by those whom he seeks to bless, stripped naked in body, and deserted in mind?
Would you not cry, "Why should my son be put to a cruel death for such abominable beings,
    who even wash their hands in the blood of their best friend?"

Remember that our Lord Jesus died what was considered to be an accursed death.
It was a death that contained all the elements of pain, disgrace, and scorn.
"God shows his love for us in that while we were still sinners, Christ died for us" (Romans 5:8).

From sermon no. 1850, *Immeasurable Love*

AS A LAMB

Then I looked, and behold, on Mount Zion stood the Lamb.
REVELATION 14:1

Observe the figure in which Christ is represented in heaven.
"I looked, and behold … the Lamb."

Now you know that Jesus is often represented in Scripture as a lion—
    he is that to his enemies—
but in heaven he is in the midst of his friends so he looks like a lamb.

Why would Christ choose to appear in heaven in the figure of a lamb?

Because it was as the Lamb that he fought and conquered;
it was as the Lamb that he died and defeated death;
it was as the Lamb that he redeemed his people;
therefore, it is as a Lamb that he will appear in paradise.

Ah, believer, you must not be afraid to come to Christ, for he is a Lamb.
You must be afraid to come to a Lion-Christ—but the Lamb-Christ?

O little children, have you ever been afraid of lambs?
O children of the living God, why hesitate to pour your griefs into the breast of one who is a Lamb?
Let us come boldly to the throne of grace, seeing that the Lamb sits on it.

If we could rend the veil, if we were now privileged to see inside the gates of heaven,
    there would be no sight so enthralling as the simple sight of the Lamb in the midst of the throne.
If a single glimpse of him on earth affords us such profound delight,
    it must be a very sea of bliss—without a bottom or a shore—to see him as he is.

> *Oh, to be lost in his splendors*
> *as the stars are lost in the sunlight!*
>
> *Oh, to hold fellowship with him*
> *as did John the beloved*
> *when he leaned his head on his bosom!*[1]
>
> *What must it be to lie in those arms forever;*
> *to be pressed to his bosom throughout a whole eternity;*
> *to feel the beatings of his ever-faithful heart;*
> *to drink his love;*
> *to be satisfied forever with his favor*
> *and filled with the goodness of the Lord!*[2]

[1]From sermon no. 110, *Heavenly Worship*
[2]From sermon no. 188, *The Redeemer's Prayer*

LOVED AND WASHED

To Him who loved us and washed us from our sins in His own blood.
REVELATION 1:5 NKJV

Christ loved us while we were dead in trespasses and sins.
He loved us, not because we were lovely, but because he is loving;
not because we were gracious, but because he is full of grace.
He loved us out of free, rich, sovereign grace.

*Tell out this glorious gospel, all you who know the glad tidings,
and let men and angels hear it again and again:*

*"Christ loved us while our sin was yet upon us,
and that is why he washed us
and made us white through his own blood!"*

With or without a word, God could have made another race of creatures and left sinful men to die;
and yet he loved us and stooped down to wash us from our defilement.

Oh, when you see the Christ of God,
taking a towel, a basin, and a pitcher of water;
when you see him pouring water on his disciples' feet
and taking foot after foot into his own dear hands and washing them,
you see a great act of love.

But when he opens his own side;
when he gives his hands and feet to be sacred fountains of blood,
and we are cleansed through his agony and death,
this is compassion like only our God possesses;
this is a sight that neither heaven nor earth has ever seen!

Well might we sing praises "to Him who loved us
and washed us from our sins in His own blood."

The priests could only cleanse with the blood of bulls and goats,
but Christ has washed us from our sins "in His own blood."

Men are willing enough to shed the blood of others.
How readily they will enter into war!
But Christ was willing to shed his own blood,
to pour out his soul to death in order to save us.

No language can ever fully portray this marvelous mystery!

From sermon no. 2230, *Loved and Laved*

THE OVERCOMER OF THE WORLD

"Take heart; I have overcome the world."
JOHN 16:33

If you look at this claim of Jesus without the eye of faith, it would appear to be ridiculous.
How could the betrayed man of Nazareth, say, "I have overcome the world"?

We can imagine Napoleon saying this when he had crushed the nations beneath his feet
    and had shaped the map of Europe according to his will.

We can imagine Alexander saying this when he had rifled the palaces of Persia
    and had led her ancient monarchs captive.

But who is this, who speaks such words?

It is a Galilean who wears a peasant's garment
    and who consorts with the poor and the fallen.
        He has neither wealth, nor worldly rank, nor honor among men.
And yet he says, "I have overcome the world."

He is about to be betrayed by his own base follower into the hands of his enemies
    and then he will be led out to judgment and to death.
And yet he says, "I have overcome the world."

He is casting an eye to his cross with all its shame
    and to the death that ensues from it.
And yet he says, "I have overcome the world."

He "has nowhere to lay his head" (Luke 9:58);
he does not even have one disciple to stand up for him, for he has just said, "You will be scattered,
    each to his own home, and will leave me alone" (John 16:32);
he is to be charged with blasphemy and sedition;
he is to be given up to brutal soldiers to be mocked and scourged and spat on;
his hands and his feet are to be nailed to a cross, so that he might die a felon's death.
And yet he says, "I have overcome the world."

How amazing are these words, and yet how true!
Jesus did not speak according to the natural flesh and the natural sight of the eye.

We must use faith's optics here and look within the veil,
and then we will see not only the despised body of the Son of Man,
but also the indwelling, noble, all-conquering soul
that transformed shame into honor and death into glory.

From sermon no. 1327, *Christ, the Overcomer of the World*

THE SWEETEST NAME

"She will bear a son, and you shall call his name Jesus."
MATTHEW 1:21

When a person is loved, everything connected with him also becomes lovely.
  And Jesus is so precious to believers that everything about him is inestimable and beyond all price.
David said, "Your robes are all fragrant with myrrh and aloes and cassia" (Psalm 45:8),
  speaking as if his Savior's garments were so sweetened by his person that he must love even them.

Certainly, there is no place where that hallowed foot has walked;
there is no word that those blessed lips have uttered;
there is no thought that his loving Word has revealed;
that is not precious beyond all price!

This is also true of the *names* of Christ—they are all sweet in the believer's ear.

Whether he is called the Husband of the church, her Bridegroom, her Friend;
whether he is styled the Lamb slain from the foundation of the world;
whether he is declared to be the King, the Prophet, or the Priest;
whether he is called Shiloh, Emmanuel, Wonderful Counselor—
every name of our Master is like the honeycomb dripping with honey.

But if there is one name sweeter than any other in the believer's ear, it is the name *Jesus!*
Jesus! It is the name that moves the harps of heaven to melody.
Jesus! He is the life of all our joys.
Jesus! If there is one name more charming and more precious than the others, it is that name!

That name is woven into the very fabric of our psalms!
Many of our hymns begin with it,
and scarcely any that are good end without it.

It is the sum total of all delights!

Jesus is the music that makes the bells of heaven ring.
Jesus is a song in one word.
Jesus is an ocean for comprehension, though a drop for brevity.
Jesus is a matchless oratorio in two syllables.
Jesus is all the hallelujahs of eternity in five letters.[1]

Jesus! The name that charms our fears,
That bids our sorrows cease,
'Tis music in the sinner's ears,
'Tis life, and health, and peace.[2]

[1]*Morning and Evening*, February 8 (M)
[2]Charles Wesley

THE FRUIT OF THE VINE

*"I will not drink again of this fruit of the vine
until that day when I drink it new with you in my Father's kingdom."*
MATTHEW 26:29

Such words would not have been spoken by our Lord Jesus unless they had deep significance.
So let us try to understand their meaning.

First, our Lord was renouncing from that moment on all the joys and comforts of life.
Putting aside that cup, filled with the juice of the vine, he was bidding farewell to earthly cheer.
The small comforts that he had enjoyed were now ended.

He had never been rich, often having nowhere to lay his head.
His clothing had always been that of a simple peasant.
His rest had been scanty and he had enjoyed little luxury.
Yet, he is now willingly, before his disciples, renouncing all worldly good.

Why will our Lord "not drink again of this fruit of the vine"?
When he departs from that table, he will be going out to finish his work of grace on this earth.

He had to sweat the bloody sweat.
He had to stand accused before Pilate and Herod.
He had to bear his cross through Jerusalem's heartless and scornful crowds.
He had to give his hands to the nails and his feet to the cruel iron.

Our Savior, out of love for us, had given up everything.

He was "God over all, blessed forever" (Romans 9:5), yet a manger held him and a cross upheld him.
From the highest throne in glory, he stooped to become a Man of Sorrows.

In saying that he would no longer drink of the fruit of the vine,
    our Lord was bidding farewell to his disciples and to this earth on which he had lived.
His words contained his anticipation of death and of the future life
    because he expected happier and brighter days, fairer banquets, fresher wine, and purer joys.

Yes, a day is coming …
    when the marriage banqueting-table will be spread,
    when all the redeemed will sit at that table with Christ seated at its head,
    when the glorious wine-cup of the New Jerusalem will be passed from lip to lip.

*Then will be fulfilled the saying of the Master,
"I will not drink again of this fruit of the vine
until that day when I drink it new with you in my Father's kingdom."*

From sermon no. 3526, *The New Wine of the Kingdom*

THE HEAVENLY RACE

So run that you may obtain it.
1 CORINTHIANS 9:24

What are we running for in this race?
Eternal life, justification by faith, forgiveness of sin, acceptance in the Beloved, glory everlasting.

Oh, make sure work of eternity!
Never be content with anything less than a living faith in a living Savior.

In running the race, seek a love that will increase—and continue to increase—
    until your heart is swallowed up therein
and the name of Jesus is the sole object of your affection.

> *Christian, run onward, always keeping in mind*
> *who is standing at the winning post!*

You are to run onward, always looking to Jesus (Hebrews 12:2).
You are never to look backward, but always forward.

Are you loitering?
See Jesus with his open wounds.

Are you about to leave the course?
See Jesus with his bleeding hands.

Will that not constrain you to devote yourself to him?
Will that not impel you to speed your course and never loiter until you have obtained the crown?

> *Your dying Master cries,*
> *"By my agony and bloody sweat,*
> *by my cross and by my Passion, onward!*
>
> *"By my life, which I have given for you,*
> *by the death which I endured for your sake, onward!"*

And see! He holds out his hand, laden with a crown, sparkling with many stars.
He is saying to you, "By this crown, onward!"

> *O Lord, draw us and we will run after you,*
> *and the glory will be yours!*
>
> *The crown of our race will be cast at your feet,*
> *and you will have the glory forever and ever!*

From sermon no. 198, *The Heavenly Race*

THE GREAT CROSS-BEARER

And he went out, bearing his own cross.
JOHN 19:17

Come closer to the Savior. Break through the crowd and look on *his burden.*

We are told by John that our Savior "went out, bearing his own cross."
  We know from other accounts that Simon the Cyrenian had also carried the cross,
    but here we see that Jesus bore his own cross at the beginning of that awful pilgrimage to Calvary.
It was a custom of the Romans to make felons bear their own gibbet.

It appears to have also been the Roman custom
  for criminals to be bound with cords to the cross they were doomed to carry.
If this is the case, you may picture our Lord with his cross bound to his shoulders,
  and hear him say, "Bind the festal sacrifice with cords, up to the horns of the altar!" (Psalm 118:27).

Now it was important for our Savior to carry his cross—even part way—
  so that we might see Isaac typified in this scene.
When Isaac went to Mount Moriah to be offered up by his father,
  he carried the wood for his own sacrifice (Genesis 22:6).

You would think that a Jew, full of hate for the Lord Jesus Christ, would have said, "Do not let him
  carry his cross because that will be too much like Isaac carrying the wood."
But no, even knowing the type, they wantonly fulfilled it!

> *Come ye saints and sinners;*
> *come and see your Great Isaac carrying the wood*
> *with which he is to be offered up by his Father.*

> *Oh, come and see how your Savior—in perfect obedience—*
> *is carrying the heavy load of your disobedience!*

> *The cross, which is called the curse,*
> *for "cursed is everyone who is hanged on a tree" (Galatians 3:13),*
> *is borne on Christ's blessed and bleeding shoulders.*

> *Oh, come and see your Lord bearing his cross,*
> *and at the same time, try to see him carrying all your sin!*

It is believed that the cross was eventually laid on Simon because Jesus fainted under the heavy load.

He had been in anguish all night in the garden, even sweating great drops of blood.
He had been before the Sanhedrin, before Herod, and twice before Pilate.
He had endured scourging, mocking, and beating by the soldiers, so it would be a great wonder if his
  body had not shown some signs of exhaustion.

From sermon no. 1683, *The Great Cross-Bearer and His Followers*

INCOMPARABLE INCENSE

Moses said to Aaron, "Take your censer,
and put fire on it from off the altar and lay incense on it
and carry it quickly to the congregation and make atonement for them,
for wrath has gone out from the LORD; the plague has begun."
NUMBERS 16:46

As the atoner, Aaron is to *bear in his censer that which is necessary for the atonement.*
As God's high priest, he must put fire in it from off the altar and lay incense on it.

With the censer in his hand, Aaron is safe,
   but without it he might have died with the rest of the people.
Aaron's qualification lay partly in the fact that he had the censer,
   and it was full of sweet odors that were acceptable to God.

Behold, then, Christ Jesus as the Atoner for his people!
He stands this day before God with his censer, its smoke rising up towards heaven.

Yes, behold the Great High Priest.
See him now with his pierced hands and his scarred side.
Mark how the marvelous smoke of his merits goes up forever and ever before the eternal throne.
It is he, and he alone, who puts away the sins of his people.

His incense consists first of all of his positive obedience to the divine law.
He kept his Father's commands; he fully kept the whole law of God and made it honorable.

Then mixed with this is his blood—an equally rich and precious ingredient.

The bloody sweat,
the blood from his head, pierced by the crown of thorns,
the blood of his hands and feet as they were nailed to the tree,
the blood of his very heart—richest of them all—
this blood, mixed with his merits, make up the incense—an incense that surpasses all others.

All the odors that ever rose from tabernacles or temples could not stand in rivalry with this,
   for the blood of Christ always prevails in bringing down pardon and mercy.
Our faith is fixed on perfect righteousness and complete atonement,
   which are as sweet frankincense before the Father's face.

O sinner, are you standing today beneath the shelter of the cross?
Are you covered by the purple robe of Christ's atonement?
Are you hiding in the wounds of Jesus?
Have you crept into his side—sheltered there until the tempest is past?

From sermon no. 341, *The High Priest Standing Between the Dead and the Living*

THE GREATEST DELIVERANCE

"He trusts in God; let God deliver him now, if he desires him.
For he said, 'I am the Son of God.'"
MATTHEW 27:43

Consider the test, which is the essence of the taunt: "Let God deliver him now, if he desires him."
Consider, too, that such a test will come to all believers.

God does not deliver according to the translation put on the word "deliverance" by the heartless crowd,
nor does he deliver according to the interpretation put on "deliverance" by our shrinking flesh.
He delivers, but it is in his own way.

If God delivers us in the same way that he delivered his Son, we will have no reason to complain.
Well, what kind of deliverance was that?

Did the Father tear up the cross from the earth?
Did he proceed to draw out the nails from the sacred hands and feet of his dear Son?
Did he place in Christ's hand a sword of fire with which to smite his adversaries?

No, nothing of the kind!
Jehovah did not interpose to spare his Son a single pang; instead he let him die.
Jesus went through with his suffering to the bitter end.

This may be God's way of delivering us.
We have trusted in God to deliver us,
and the true rendering of his promise is that he will enable us to go through with it.
We will suffer to the last and triumph in so doing.

Yes, God's way of delivering those who trust in him is *always the best way*.
If the Father had taken his Son down from the cross, what would have been the result?
Jesus would have returned to heaven with his life-work unfinished.

That would not have been deliverance but defeat!

It was much better for our Lord Jesus to die.
He paid the ransom price, and having accomplished the great purpose of atonement,
he slept a short while in the heart of the earth.
And after that he rose and ascended to his throne in the endless glories of heaven.

This was deliverance of the fullest kind!

From the pangs of Christ's death has come the joy of life to his redeemed.
It is not God's will for every mountain to be leveled,
but for us to be stronger by climbing the hill of difficulty.
God will deliver; he must deliver; but he will always do it in the best possible manner.

From sermon no. 2029, *"Let Him Deliver Him Now"*

MADE SIN FOR US

He made him to be sin who knew no sin,
so that in him we might become the righteousness of God.
2 CORINTHIANS 5:21

Jesus Christ "knew no sin." He was not sin; he was not sinful; he was not guilty;
but he was treated by his Father as if he had not only been sinful, but as if he had been sin itself.
God looked on him as if he were that noxious, that God-hating, that soul-damning thing called sin!

When the Judge of all the earth, asked, "Where is Sin?" Christ presented himself.
He stood before his Father as if he had been the accumulation of all human guilt,
and since the holy God looked on Christ as being sin, he had to be taken outside the camp.
Sin cannot be borne in God's Zion; it cannot be allowed to dwell in God's Jerusalem.

Take him away, take him away, ye crowd!
Hurry him through the streets and bear him to Calvary!
Take him outside the camp!

As the beast that was offered for sin must be taken outside the camp, so must Christ;
and now, being sin, he must bear sin's punishment.
The most fearful of deaths is exacted at his hand, because God cannot have pity on him.

Jesus prays, but heaven shuts out his prayer.
He cries for water, but heaven and earth refuse to wet his lips except with vinegar.

Oh, solemn necessity, what else could God do with sin but forsake it? Can his smile rest on sin?
No, it cannot be, and so it is, that he who is made sin must bemoan desertion and terror.
God cannot touch him, cannot dwell with him, cannot come near him.

He is abhorred! He is cast away!
"It was the will of the Lord to crush him;
he has put him to grief"(Isaiah 53:10).

At last he dies, and is it not the best thing in the world for sin to be buried?
Lo! As if he were sin, Jesus is put away—out of the sight of God and man as a thing obnoxious.

What a grim picture: sin gathered up into one mass—
murder, lust, rape, adultery, and all manner of crimes—all piled together in one hideous heap!
And God looked on Christ as if he were that mass of sin.

O Christian, your sins cannot condemn you
for they have been slain and buried!
Jesus Christ—who knew no sin—was made sin for you.

From sermon no. 310, *Christ—Our Substitute*

NOT BY PHYSICAL FORCE

And behold, one of those who were with Jesus stretched out his hand and drew his sword
and struck the servant of the high priest and cut off his ear.
Then Jesus said to him, "Put your sword back into its place.
For all who take the sword will perish by the sword."
MATTHEW 26:51–52

Jesus made no use of carnal force.

No doubt the priests and scribes were sometimes afraid to oppose him for fear of the people,
    but they had no need to fear for he asked neither the rich nor the strong nor the many to protect him.
No one could ever accuse Jesus of meeting force with force.

In Gethsemane, our Lord might have summoned legions of angels to the rescue, but he agonized alone.
No seraph came from the throne to drive away the son of perdition or the bloodthirsty priests.
No destroying angel smote the men who spit in his face.
No devouring flame burned up those who flogged him.

The force of his life was the omnipotence of gentle goodness.
Jesus did not even lay his little finger upon the minds of men to compel them to involuntary subjection.

Think of what he might have done.
Think of what we would have done, having such work to do amidst such opposition.

Jesus had no curses for his foes,
and he had no blows for his enemies.

The only time our Lord used the semblance of violence was when he took the whip of small cords
    and chased the buyers and the sellers out of his Father's house—
a deed in which the awe inspired by his presence seems to be the principal instrument employed.

Such was his gentleness
that when he might have shaken the earth
and rocked the thrones of tyrants,
he exerted no physical power.

He stood still with melting heart and tearful eye,
inviting sinners to come to him—
using no lash but his love,
no battle-ax and weapon of war but his grace.

Jesus relied upon the power of the Spirit and the force of love.
He would have people won to him by the sword of the Spirit, and bound to him by bands of love.

From sermon no. 1147, *The Gentleness of Jesus*

A SACRED MEDICINE

Twisting together a crown of thorns, they put it on his head.
MATTHEW 27:29

We have before us, in our Savior's crown of thorns, *a sacred medicine.*

Those blood-sprinkled thorns are plants of renown, precious in heavenly surgery.
    Take but a thorn from that crown and use it as a lancet,
        and it will release the hot blood of passion and abate the fever of pride.
He who sees Jesus crowned with thorns will loathe to look on self, except through tears of contrition.

Yes, that thorn-crown cures us of the desire for the vainglories of this world.
    It takes the glitter from our gold, and the luster from our gems
        when we see that no imperial purple can equal the glory of Christ's blood.
How can all the gem-studded crowns of this world ever rival Jesus' crown of thorns?

> *Show and parade cease to attract the soul*
> *when the superlative excellencies of the dying Savior are discerned.*

That thorn-crown also cures us of our selfish love of ease.
If Christ wears a crown of thorns, will we covet a crown of laurel?

Why this reclining on couches when Jesus hangs on a cross?
Why this soft raiment when he is naked?
Why these luxuries when he is so cruelly abused?

> *Neither the delights of the flesh nor the pride of life*
> *have any charms for us while the Man of Sorrows is in view.*

And that thorn-crown cures us of all love of sin.
Can we see our Beloved in such agony and shame and yet play with the sins that pierced him?

I have seen a hedge of blackberry thorns,
    and yet right in the center of it was the pretty nest of a little bird.
The creature placed its habitation there because the thorns sheltered it from harm.

So I would urge you to surround yourself with a hedge of thorns.
Yes, I would urge you to build your nest within the thorns of Christ.
It is a safe place for sinners where neither Satan, sin, nor death can reach you.

> *O guilty one, gaze on your Savior's sufferings,*
> *and you will see sin atoned for!*

> *Fly into his wounds! Fly, you timid, trembling doves!*
> *There is no resting-place so safe for you.*

From sermon no. 1168, *The Crown of Thorns*

OUR SAVIOR'S GRIEF

Yet it was the will of the L<small>ORD</small> to crush him; he has put him to grief.
I<small>SAIAH</small> 53:10

For a moment, picture in your mind a martyr. He is enchained in prison, but he sings even though he knows that he is about to be burned at the stake. Mark the serenity on his face as he is being marched to the place of his execution, and he says to the bystanders, "It is a sweet thing to die for Christ!"

See how he calmly steps on the stack of sticks. Even as the fire begins to ascend, he speaks boldly. But listen! He sings while the sticks are crackling and his body begins to burn. He sweetly chants a psalm of old: "God is our refuge and strength, a very present help in trouble. Therefore I will not fear" (See Psalm 46:1–2).

Now picture another scene.

There is the Savior going to his cross, all weak and wan with suffering.
When they nail him to the tree, there is no song of praise.
When he is lifted up in the air, there is no shout of exultation.

There is a terrible expression on his face as if unutterable agony is tearing his heart,
    as if Gethsemane is experienced again on the cross.
It is as if his soul is still saying, "My Father, if it be possible, let this cross pass from me."

But listen! He speaks. Will he not sing a sweeter song than that which has come from a martyr's lips?
Ah no! It is an awful wail of woe: "My God, my God, why have you forsaken me?"

The martyrs did not say that. Confessors of old did not cry in this way when they came to die.
They shouted in their fires, and praised God on their racks!
Why this? Why does the Savior suffer so terribly?

It was because the Father crushed him.
    The sunshine of God's countenance that has cheered dying saints was withdrawn from him.
The consciousness of acceptance with God—which has made many espouse the cross with joy—
    was not granted to our Savior; therefore, he suffered in the thick darkness of mental agony.

> *Underneath the church are the everlasting arms,*
> *but underneath Christ there were no arms at all.*
> *Instead, he was heavily weighed down by his Father's hand.*

> *The upper and lower millstones of divine wrath crushed and bruised him,*
> *and not one drop of joy or consolation was afforded him.*

"It was the will of the Lord to crush him; *he* has put him to grief."
This was the climax of the Savior's woe: His Father turned away from him, and put him to grief.

From sermon no. 173, *The Death of Christ*

SPITTING IN HIS FACE

They spit on him.
MATTHEW 27:30

When we see Adam in the midst of comfort, putting out his hand to take that one forbidden fruit,
  we indeed see sin, arrogance, and daring assumption.
But we do not see the levity and lawlessness that is apparent in the creatures who spit on their Creator.

> *O God, our hearts are heavy and smitten with grief*
> *when we think of how evil man has become!*
> *Why did you not sweep him from the world*
> *and let his name be remembered with hissing and scorn?*

But, bad as man is, he was never so bad—or rather, his badness was never exhibited so fully—
  as when gathering all his spite, his pride, his lust, and his abominable wickedness into one mouthful,
  he spat in the face of the Son of God himself!
Oh, this is an act that transcends every other!

The soldiers who drove the nails into the Savior's hands were ordered to do so,
  but this was a voluntary act, issuing from the base wickedness of their own hearts.
Sin saw Perfection in its power, and so it had to spit on Perfection's cheek!

Now while you blush over human nature, you must recollect that this is the nature of us all.
We are of the same nature as those who insulted our Lord.
We have not spit on him literally, but we have often been as rude and as wanton as they were.

> *O ye ministers of Christ,*
> *how our hearts have despised you!*

> *And ye lowly in heart,*
> *who follow Christ in the midst of an evil generation,*
> *how often we have mocked your piety and laughed at your prayers!*

In all this, have we not spit on Christ? Yes, but mercy of mercies, he has not spit on us!
No, he kisses us with his love, saying, "I have blotted out your transgressions" (Isaiah 44:22).

> *Melt, then, ye eyes, and stream down these cheeks, ye briny tears,*
> *remembering that he whom I once despised has not despised me;*
> *and though I hid, as it were, my face from him,*
> *he has not hidden his face from me.*

> *Here I am, a forgiven sinner,*
> *though once I assailed him with indignity and scorn*
> *as gross as those who spit in his beloved face.*

From sermon no. 3404, *A Gross Indignity*

THE LILY AMONG THORNS

Like a lily among thorns, so is my love among the daughters.
SONG OF SOLOMON 2:2 NKJV

Christ calls the church, "my love," as if his love has all gone out and become embodied in her.

This love is a distinguishing love, for in its light one special object shines like a lily,
   while the rest, "the daughters," are like thorns.
Christ's love reaches out to all people, but there is a special and peculiar love that he bears to his own.

"Like a lily," says he, "among thorns, so is my love."

She was at first no better than a thorn herself,
   but his grace made her different from the briars surrounding her.
As soon as he had put his life and his grace into her, though she dwelt among the ungodly,
   she became like the lily and he could not help but notice her.
The thorny hedge could not hide his beloved from his loving eye.

A preacher friend of mine once told the story of seeing a certain lily growing among thorns,
   but in trying to extricate the lily he sadly lacerated his hands.
Now try to picture the luxuriant, velvety softness of this lily
   with the withered, tangled hedge of thorns surrounding it.

Ah, believer, you know who it was, who in gathering your soul,
lacerated not only his hands, but also his feet, and his head, and his side—
yes, and also his heart and his innermost soul!

He noticed us, and said, "Yonder lily is mine, and I will have it";
but the thorns were a terrible barrier; our sins had gathered round about us,
and the wrath of God sharply blocked the way.

Jesus agonizingly pressed through all that we might be his;
and now when he takes us to himself he does not forget
the thorns that girded his brow and tore his flesh for our sakes.

This then is part of our relationship to Christ, that we cost him dearly.
He saw us where we were and he came to our deliverance;
and now, even as Pharaoh's daughter called the young child "Moses"
"because," said she, "I drew him out of the water,"
so Jesus calls his own "a lily among thorns"
because such she was when he came to her rescue.

Never will he forget Calvary and its thorns,
nor should his saints ever allow that precious memory to fade.

From sermon no. 1525, *The Lily Among Thorns*

THE TREE OF LIFE IN WINTER

On each side of the river stood the tree of life,
bearing twelve crops of fruit, yielding its fruit every month.
REVELATION 22:2 NIV

Let us look at this Tree of Life in the wintertime without its fruit.

This is a description of *Jesus in his sufferings,* in his dark winter days ...
when he hung on the cross, bleeding and dying,
when he had no honor and no respect from humanity,
when even God the Father hid his face from him for a season as he was made sin for us.

You will never see the Tree of Life aright
unless you first look at the cross.

It was there that this Tree gathered strength
to bear its life-giving fruit.

It was there that Jesus, by his glorious merits
and his wondrous work achieved on the cross,
obtained power to become the Redeemer of our souls,
and the Captain of our salvation.

Notice that our Savior's death on the cross was *an accursed death.*
Death comes to us in various ways, but only one death is pronounced by God to be accursed.
It is written, "Cursed is everyone who is hanged on a tree" (Galatians 3:13).

It was *a shameful death,* for the Roman law subjected only felons and slaves to it.
The Jews counted Jesus worthy to be sold as a slave, and then they put him to a slave's death.
The people also added their own ridicule. See them mocking and shaking their heads at him.

The death of the cross is also *exceedingly painful.*
It must be a fearful way in which to die when the tender hands and feet are pierced,
and when the bones are dislocated by the jarring of the cross when it is erected.
Then fever sets in and the mouth becomes as hot as an oven.

But now, we come to the most important point of all.
That death is the only hope for sinners; those wounds of Jesus are the only entrance to heaven.
The sufferings and the agony of Immanuel are the only expiatory sacrifice for human guilt.

Yes, Jesus Christ hanging on the cross
is the Tree of Life in its wintertime;
so you who would be saved, turn your eyes there.

From sermon no. 3251, *Christ the Tree of Life*

THE TREE OF LIFE IN SUMMER

On each side of the river stood the tree of life,
bearing twelve crops of fruit, yielding its fruit every month.
REVELATION 22:2 NIV

Now we will look at that selfsame Tree of Life when it has blossomed and yielded its fruit.

There he stands—Jesus, still the same Jesus, and yet how changed!—
    the same Jesus, but now clothed with honor instead of shame.
He is now "able to save to the uttermost those who draw near to God through him" (Hebrews 7:25).

The text says that this tree bears "twelve crops of fruit."
This probably signifies that all human necessities are perfectly and completely found in Christ.

The Tree of Life is a source of food, and Jesus Christ is the food of his people.
    What satisfying food, what plenteous food, what sweet food;
        what food, precisely suitable to all the wants of the soul, is Jesus!
How richly we are fed, for the flesh of Jesus is the spiritual food of every heir of heaven!

Jesus also gives his people drink.
    There are some tropical trees that, as soon as they are tapped,
        yield liquid as sweet and rich as milk, and many drink and are refreshed by them.
Now the blood of Jesus is the exhilarating and refreshing wine of all his people.

Jesus is a Tree of Life that yields clothing as well.
    Adam went to the fig tree for his garments, but we come to Christ;
        and we find, not fig leaves, but a robe of righteousness that is matchless in its beauty.
It is one that will never wear out, and it completely covers our nakedness from head to foot.

This is a Tree that also yields a shelter from the storm.
    Other trees are dangerous when the tempest howls, but he who shelters beneath his Savior
        will find that all the thunderbolts of God will fly right by him and he will not be harmed.
He who clings to Jesus cannot be hurt.

O ye ungodly ones, who have been roaming throughout the world,
looking to find the tree that will supply all your wants—
you must stop here!

There is comfort, joy, peace, and safety,
beneath those outstretched boughs.

Oh, do not fill yourself with the sour grapes of this world
while the sweet fruit of Christ's love is waiting to refresh and satisfy you!

From sermon no. 3251, *Christ the Tree of Life*

THE BEST POSITION FOR A PENITENT

At His feet.
LUKE 7:38 NKJV

This is a very helpful position for a weeping penitent.

> *"Behold, a woman in the city who was a sinner,*
> *when she knew that Jesus sat at a table in the Pharisee's house,*
> *brought an alabaster flask of fragrant oil,*
> *and stood at His feet behind Him weeping."*
> *Luke 7:37–38* NKJV

Do not go and stand at Moses' feet, for you will never repent there.
    To stand at the foot of Sinai and tremble may have its uses,
        but gospel repentance does not spring from legal terror.
Gracious tears are wept at Jesus' feet.

If you would have your heart broken until the rock gushes with rivers of repentance,
    stand at Jesus' feet and think of how those feet were pierced.
This woman could not see that for the deed was not yet accomplished,
    but you can see it and mark where the nail has bored each blessed foot.

"At his feet" is the best place for a penitent because it encourages faith.
    Seeing those dear feet, you will think, *He is God, but he became a man in order to suffer for me;*
        those precious feet were pierced so that my heart might be delivered from death.
You will find faith springing up in your soul at the sight of the great Substitute.

Standing at his feet, you will see him turn to you and say what he said to the penitent woman,
    "Your sins are forgiven … Your faith has saved you; go in peace" (Luke 7:48, 50).

> *O weeping penitent, get away to Jesus' feet*
> *for there your love will flow out to him,*
> *and there you will think of doing something for him who has blotted out your sin!*
>
> *Did this woman not unbind the luxuriant tresses of her head to make a towel?*
> *Did she not use the fountain of her eyes,*
> *aye, the fountain of her heart with which to bathe his feet?*
> *And then for ointment she broke the alabaster flask and kissed and kissed again*
> *the dear, dear feet of him who had brought salvation to her.*
>
> *O penitents, do not stand outside on the cold porch with Moses,*
> *but come indoors, where Jesus welcomes you!*
> *Stand at his feet, and he will give you that blessed, godly repentance*
> *that will bring you peace and will nourish life in your soul.*

From sermon no. 2066, *Our Place: At Jesus' Feet*

A HUMBLED PRIEST

"He is to put on the sacred linen tunic, with linen undergarments next to his body;
he is to tie the linen sash around him and put on the linen turban.
These are sacred garments."
LEVITICUS 16:4 NIV

The Jews had many striking ceremonies that marvelously depicted the death of Jesus Christ
as the great expiation of our guilt and the salvation of our souls.
One of the most important of these was the Day of Atonement, which happened only *once a year,*
teaching us that Jesus Christ would only have to die once.

It is interesting to note that on this day the high priest was a humbled priest.
On other days he wore what were called the golden garments.
He had the turban with a plate of pure gold around his brow and tied with brilliant blue.
He had the breastplate, studded with gems, adorned with pure gold, and set with precious stones.
He also had the glorious ephod, the tinkling bells, and all the other ornaments.

But on the Day of Atonement the high priest wore none of these.
He simply wore the sacred linen tunic, the linen undergarments, the linen sash, and the linen turban.

Even so, Jesus Christ was a humbled priest when he made atonement for us.
He did not make atonement while arrayed in all the glories of his ancient throne in heaven.

He wore no diadem on his brow—only the crown of thorns.
He wore no purple robe—only the one he wore for a while in mockery.
He held no golden scepter in his hand—only the reed that was thrust on him in cruel contempt.
He had none of those splendors that would make him mighty and distinguished among men.

He came out in his simple body—aye, in his naked body—
for they had even stripped him of the common robe.
They made him hang before God's universe naked—to his shame and to man's disgrace.

> *O my soul, adore your Savior, who when he made atonement,*
> *humbled himself and wrapped about him a garb of your inferior clay!*
>
> *O angels, you have an understanding of what glories he laid aside!*
> *O thrones and principalities and powers, you can tell of the diadem*
> *and of the robes he laid aside to wrap himself in earthly garb!*
>
> *But men, you can scarcely tell how glorious your High Priest is now,*
> *and you can scarcely tell how glorious he was before.*
> *But oh, adore him, for on that day it was the simple, clean linen of his own body,*
> *of his own humanity in which he made atonement for your sins!*

From sermon no. 95, *The Day of Atonement*

THE OVERFLOWING CUP

My cup overflows.
PSALM 23:5

Why does our cup overflow?

Our cup overflows because—having Christ—*we have all things in him.*
Through his living labors and his dying love, we have passed from death into life.

Oh, our hearts must overflow with thanksgiving and praise as we gaze at the beauty of our Savior!
Oh, is Christ not good? Is he not beautiful?

You have heard that when Henry the Eighth married Anne of Cleves, Holbein was sent to paint her.
    The king was charmed, but when he saw the original, his judgment was very different
        and he expressed disgust instead of affection.
The painter had deceived him.

But no such flatteries can ever be paid to our Lord Jesus Christ,
    because the painters—preachers—all fall short.
They have no faculty with which to depict beauties so inexpressibly charming;
    so beyond all conception of mind and heart!

The best words that have ever been sung by adoring poets,
    written by devout authors, or expressed by seraphic preachers
all fall far below the surpassing excellence of our Redeemer.

But there is also another reason why our cup overflows: it is because *the infinite God himself is ours.*
He is as much our own God as if there were no one else in the world to claim him.

> *Stand back ye angels and archangels, cherubim and seraphim,*
> *and all ye people redeemed by blood!*
> *Whatever may be your rights and privileges,*
> *you cannot lessen my inheritance.*
>
> *Assuredly, all of God is mine—*
> *all his fullness, all his attributes, all his love, all of him;*
> *all, all is mine—for he has said, "I am your God."*
>
> *O believer, see here your boundless treasure!*
> *What cup can hold your God?*
>
> *When you know that the Father, the Son, and the Spirit*
> *are all your own in covenant,*
> *your cup must overflow!*

From sermon no. 1222, *The Overflowing Cup*

THE AWAKENED SWORD

"Awake, O sword, against my shepherd,
against the man who stands next to me," declares the LORD of hosts.
ZECHARIAH 13:7

You will notice that the very wording of the text indicates the sharpness of Christ's sufferings,
for it says, "Awake, O sword," as if the sword of God had previously been asleep.
Yet we have read of Pharaoh and his hosts being destroyed at the Red Sea
and of Amalek cut off from before the Lord and of Sennacherib's vast army slain in a single night.

Was the sword of the Lord not awake then?

No, it was only, as it were, stirring in its sleep.
The sword of divine justice was stirring in its scabbard, but God's long-suffering was pushing it back.

But lo! He now cries, "Awake, O sword! End your slumbering!
Human sin has startled you many times,
but I have said, 'Sleep on; my patience must finish its work, so wait';
but now, leap out of your scabbard, O sword, for your victim is before you!

"He has come, the One whom you are to strike,
for I have laid on him the iniquity of all my people!"

It is obvious that this sword was awakened by the voice of God himself.

We can imagine the cry that arose to God's sword when the world was corrupt and full of sin in the
days of Noah, and man's sin cried aloud, "Awake, O sword!"
We can understand how the groans and tears of the children of Israel, when they were in Egypt in
cruel bondage, said, "Awake, O sword!"
We can imagine the unutterable abominations of the Canaanites crying, "Awake, O sword!"
Yet God did not allow that sword to awaken to the fullest extent, even in those dreadful times.

But, at last, God spoke! God, the Lord of Hosts, spoke: "Awake, O sword!"
Now the sword must awake because it is God who calls it.
And when God himself bids the sword of divine justice strike his Son,
he knows as we cannot what those blows would be!

The bruising of the Roman scourge was terrible, but the Father's bruising was far worse!
Neither Jew nor Gentile could have put Christ to grief as the Father did.
That was the keenest agony of all that made him cry, "My God, my God, why have you forsaken me?"

So it was God who awakened the sword,
and it was God who struck the Shepherd with omnipotent power.
And if Christ had not also been omnipotent, it would have utterly destroyed him!

From sermon no. 3088, *The Storm and the Shower*

HOW JUSTICE IS SATISFIED

That he might be just and the justifier of the one who has faith in Jesus.
ROMANS 3:26

Consider the terrible agonies that Christ endured in the sinner's place.
When you mark those agonies, you will see why Justice does not stand in the sinner's way.

Does Justice come to you today and say, "Sinner, you have sinned, so I will punish you"?
Then answer: "Justice, you have punished my sins. My Substitute suffered what I ought to suffer."

But if Justice still accuses and conscience clamors, take Justice with you to Gethsemane.

O Justice, do you see that man kneeling over there, wrapped in a sheet of his own blood?
Do you hear his groans, his earnest intercessions, his strong crying and tears?
Do you see him in the desperate agony of his spirit, crushed and bruised beneath your feet, O Justice?

Is that not enough, O Justice? Are you still not satisfied? Come then to the hall of Pilate.

See that man over there, arraigned, accused, charged with sedition and blasphemy!
See him taken to the guardroom, spit on, buffeted with hands, crowned with thorns, robed in mockery!

O Justice, look closely at that man; he is "God over all, blessed forever" (Romans 9:5),
   and yet he endured all this to satisfy your demands.
What! Are you not content with that? Do you still frown? Then come, let me show you even more.

See how he is stripped! Listen to those scourges as they fall on his back, making deep furrows there!
See strips of his quivering flesh torn from his poor bare back!

O Justice, if you are still not content, what will satisfy you?
"Nothing," says Justice, "but his death."

Come with me then, O Justice, and you will see that feeble man hurried through the streets!
See him driven to the top of Calvary, hurled on his back and nailed to the transverse wood!

O Justice, can you see his dislocated bones now that his cross is lifted up?
Stand with me, O Justice, and hear his agonizing cry, "My God, my God, why have you forsaken me?"
Come, listen O Justice, while you hear him cry, "I thirst," and see the burning fever devouring him.
And lastly, O Justice, do you see him bow his head and die? Are you now satisfied?

"Yes, I am perfectly satisfied. I have nothing more to ask. All my demands have been fully met."

Yes, and my soul is content and satisfied too.
By faith I cast myself at the foot of the cross and cling to it.
This is my only hope, my shelter, and my shield.

From sermon no. 255, *Justice Satisfied*

HIS BLOOD-RED ROBE

Then I saw heaven opened, and behold, a white horse!
The one sitting on it is called Faithful and True, and in righteousness he judges and makes war.
He is clothed in a robe dipped in blood, and the name by which he is called is The Word of God.
Revelation 19:11, 13

Gazing into the open door of heaven, John had a brief glimpse of his blessed Master.
Among other things, John noticed that he was "clothed in a robe dipped in blood."

Oh, this is the loveliest thought regarding our Master—
wherever he may be—
he is ever a red man wearing the bloody garment!

As the atoning sacrifice, he is always at his best.

Yes, he bled, and this is the greatest thing that can be said of him.
His life was glorious, but his death transcends it.

A living Christ, a reigning Christ—we are charmed as we think of this;
    but oh, the bleeding Christ, the bleeding Christ for us!
As the blood is the life, his blood is life to us; it is the life of the gospel, the life of our hopes.

We find great delight in the thought that even though Jesus now rides the white horse,
    he has never stripped off the bloody shirt in which he won our redemption.
He still looks like a Lamb that has been slain, and he still wears his priesthood.
    Whenever he goes out to conquer, it is with this robe on—this robe dipped in blood.

Oh, preach him, ye servants of Christ!
Preach him in his blood-red robe!

If you would see souls saved,
you cannot portray him in any other coat.
Some take his own garment from him and put on another,
and pretend they are making him more illustrious.

His blood is his beauty and his triumph.
Let him come before us in that
and our hearts will crown him with loudest acclaim!

Oh, how beautiful, how glorious, how mighty is the Son of God,
    as we contemplate him "clothed in a robe dipped in blood,"
and riding triumphantly on his white horse of victory!

From sermon no. 1452B, *The Rider on the White Horse and the Armies with Him*

LOVED OUT OF THE PIT

You have lovingly delivered my soul from the pit of corruption.
Isaiah 38:17 NKJV

See how we lay by nature in the grave of death—and even more, in the pit of corruption!
We were so destroyed by sin that we were like people who had rotted in a pit,
for sin is a foul putrefaction of our nature.
But through grace, those who have believed in Jesus have been delivered from the horrible pit.

Think of it! The Lord loved us
even when we were in that loathsome condition!

To love us when there was no good in us, but only evil;
to love us when we were unlovable, and even hateful—
this is unlike the ways of man,
but is only worthy of the infinite heart of God!

Now we know that this ancient, primeval love devised the way of delivering us from the pit.
The plan was made for us to be delivered by substitution, by the sacrifice of another in our place.
And since love planned this admirable method of mercy,
love also supplied all the provisions necessary for carrying out the plan.

Love brought the Savior to the cross, and love made him bear our sins in his own body.
Love led him to give up his precious life on our behalf and to become a hostage in the tomb.
Love sent the Holy Spirit to quicken us, to illuminate us, to strengthen us, and to dwell in us.
Love found the materials for our redemption, and love applied the redemption when it was completed.
Love has regenerated us, love has supported us until this day, and love will keep us to the end.

We have been delivered out of the horrible pit,
but we have not been drawn out of it by force;
we have not been driven out of it by terror;
we have been loved out of it by God's love.

"You have lovingly delivered my soul from the pit of corruption."

We are *loved into grace.*
When we realize that it was God who hung there on the cross, we are compelled to love.

This love is also the cause of all our advances in the divine life.
We have escaped from the love of sin and its enchantments because God has loved us out of them;
he has loved us away from the allurements and temptations of sin.
As Jesus becomes lovely in our eyes, sin becomes dark and hideous and abhorrent.

From sermon no. 1110, *Miracles of Love*

DINING WITH JESUS

Jesus said to them, "Come and eat breakfast."
JOHN 21:12 NKJV

With these words, the believer is invited into a holy *nearness to Jesus.*
"Come and eat" implies the same table and the same food.
Yes, and it sometimes means to sit side by side and lean our head on the Savior's bosom.

"Come and eat" gives us a vision of *union with Jesus*
   because the only food that we can feast on when we dine with Jesus is *Jesus himself.*

Oh, what a union this is!
It is a depth which reason cannot fathom![1]

Jesus said, "Whoever feeds on my flesh and drinks my blood abides in me, and I in him" (John 6:56).
To feed on Jesus means to meditate on him, to keep him in our thoughts.

There are many doctrines in the Bible that we make our own by reading, marking, and learning,
   for they are parts of the great circle of truth revealed by God.
But we are never so comforted, strengthened, and sustained
   as when we deliberately consider Jesus Christ's precious death and atoning sacrifice.

His sacrifice is the center of the circle, the focus of the light.
There is a charm, a divine fascination, about his wounds.

O sacred head, once wounded!
We could forever gaze, admire, and adore!

There is no beauty in all the world
like that which is seen in the countenance
"marred, beyond human semblance" (Isaiah 52:14).

There is no sustenance to the heart
like the sustenance that comes of his flesh and his blood,
given up in anguish and in death to work out our redemption.[2]

What enlightenment, what joy, what consolation, what delight of heart
   is experienced by those who have learned to feed on Jesus, and on Jesus alone!
Yet our understanding of Christ's preciousness, in this life, is imperfect at best.
   As an old writer says, "'Tis but a taste!"[3]

[1] *Morning and Evening*, October 16 (M)
[2] Source Unknown
[3] *Morning and Evening*, July 20 (M)

REMEMBERING YOUR LOVE

We will remember your love more than wine.
SONG OF SOLOMON 1:4 NKJV

We will remember your love, O Jesus, as it was manifested to us in your holy life.
We will track you from the cradle to the grave
for every word and every deed of yours was love.
Wherever you walked you scattered loving-kindness with both your hands.

And especially, O Jesus, we will remember your love for us in your Passion and death!

We will view you coming from the garden of your agony and from the hall of your scourging.
We will look into your pain-filled eyes as the thorns pierce your brow.
We will gaze at the love you manifested through your poor bleeding hands and feet and side.
We will watch you bending downward to the grave, in order to lift us upward to heaven.

We will also remember this love of yours, O Jesus,
until it invigorates and cheers us "more than wine"—
the love that you have exercised since your death.

Yes, we will remember the love that prompts you
to continually intercede for us before your Father's throne.

And we must sing of your love, O Jesus, passing all measure,
that has taken our soul and washed it in your precious blood
and then has clothed it in your spotless robe of righteousness.

We will never forget those chambers of fellowship where you have unveiled yourself to us.
As Moses had his cleft in the rock where he could see the back parts of God,
we also may have our clefts in the rock
where we can see the glorious splendors of the godhead in you.

*O Christian, can you remember
the sweet exchanges between you and your Lord
when you have left your griefs at his feet and have borne away a song?*

*Can you remember some happy seasons
when you went to him empty and came away full?*

*Can you remember the times when Jesus has linked his arm in yours
and has walked along the rugged pathway with you?*

*Can you remember the times when your head has rested on his bosom
and you could feel his very heart beating with warm love for you?*

From sermon no. 2794, *A Refreshing Canticle*

LOVING WITH GOD'S LOVE

"I made known to them your name, and I will continue to make it known,
that the love with which you have loved me may be in them, and I in them."
JOHN 17:26

Jesus prays for God's love to be transplanted into our hearts, and this becomes our love for Jesus.
How wonderful it is that God's own love for Jesus should dwell in our hearts!

All true love, such as the Father delights in and accepts at our hands,
is nothing but his own love,
which has come streaming down from his heart into our hearts.

You must try to understand the love of the Father for his Son.
Otherwise, you will not love him as you should for the sacrifice he made in giving up his Son to die.

Think of what it cost him …
to tear his Well-beloved from his heart and send him here to be "despised and rejected,"
to nail his Son to yonder cross and then forsake him because he had laid all our sins on him.

Now think of *the love he had for us* when he made his Son become a curse for us.

We cannot believe that God the Father does not love us as much as he loves Jesus
because the point can be settled by the grandest event that ever took place.
When there was a choice between Jesus and his people—which of the two should die—
the Father freely delivered up his own Son so that we might live through him.

What a meeting there must have been of the seas of love that day
as God's great love for us came rolling in like a glorious springtide,
and his love for his Son came rolling in at the same time!

If they had met and collided, we cannot imagine the result;
but when they both rolled together in one mighty torrent,
what a stream of love that was!

Our Lord Jesus sank so that we might rise,
and now we are borne onward forever by the mighty sweep of infinite love.
We are borne into an everlasting blessedness that tongues and lips cannot fully express.

Oh! Be ravished with this love!
Let it carry you away completely.

The Father loves you as he loves his own beloved Son;
and in the very same way you are to love Jesus.

From sermon no. 1667, *"Love and I"—A Mystery*

OUR PATTERN IN SUFFERING

"He trusts in God; let God deliver him now, if he desires him.
For he said, 'I am the Son of God.'"
MATTHEW 27:43

It is very painful to picture our blessed Master in his death agonies,
    surrounded by a heartless multitude who watched him and mocked him.
They even made sport of his prayers and insulted his faith.

See what an evil thing sin is when the Sin-Bearer suffers so bitterly to make atonement for it.
See the shame of sin when even the Prince of Glory is covered with contempt.

The treatment of our Lord Jesus Christ is the clearest proof of total depravity.
Those must be stony hearts indeed that can laugh at a dying Savior and mock even his faith in God.

The Son of God, whom angels adore with veiled faces,
is pointed at with scornful fingers by men who shake their heads,
and mockingly exclaim, "He trusts in the LORD; let him deliver him;
let him rescue him, for he delights in him" (Psalm 22:8)!

While we thus see our Lord in his sorrow and in his shame as our substitute,
    we must not forget that he is also there as our representative.
That which appears to relate to David in many of the psalms refers to Jesus in the Gospels.

Occasionally we will have to disentangle the threads
    to mark off that which belongs to David and that which relates to the Son of God.
Frequently, they relate to both.
    This shows us that the life of Christ is a revelation of the lives of his people.

Jesus not only suffers for us as our substitute,
he also suffers before us as our pattern.

We also must be crucified to the world,
    and we may look for the tests of faith and taunts of derision that go with such a crucifixion.
We must experience the cross and its shame, not for the world's redemption,
    but in order to have God's purposes accomplished in our lives.

Let us read the text in the following light:
Here we see what Jesus suffered in our place, and thus we learn to love him with all our hearts.
Here, too, we see as in a prophecy what great things we will suffer for his sake at the hands of men.

May the Holy Spirit help us to ardently love our Lord, who suffered for us,
    and then arm ourselves with the same mind that enabled him to endure such enmity.

From sermon no. 2029, *"Let Him Deliver Him Now"*

OUR DEATH TO SIN

He himself bore our sins in his body on the tree,
that we might die to sin and live to righteousness.
By his wounds you have been healed.
1 PETER 2:24

We who have looked to Jesus bearing our sins in his body are dead to the reigning power of sin.
  We are dead to sin because another passion has engaged our hearts,
    and we have no eyes or ears for anything but for our dear Lord, who bled and died to redeem us.
We cannot dally with the sins that required the precious blood of the Son of God.

Now sin may charm, but we have the adder's ear;
  sin may put on all its allurements, but we are blind as bats to its beauty.
Another passion has absorbed our life, and our life of sin is all dried up.

Have you ever looked at the green field and thought how bright the sparkling dewdrops are?
  And have you then turned your eye on the sun and tried to stare it out of brightness?
If you have, you know that when you looked down at the landscape again you could not see it.
  You seemed to have lost your eyesight—the eye being blinded by the brightness on which it gazed.

So you may look on the world of sin and see some beauty in it until you look at HIM,
  and then the brightness of his glory blinds your eye.
The world is dark and black after that.

> *Let these eyes be forever sightless as the eyes of night,*
> *and let these ears be forever deaf as silence,*
> *rather than yield my spirit to the charms of sin.*
>
> *Let nothing take up my heart except the Lord of love,*
> *who bled to death in order to redeem me.*

The death of Christ becomes the death of sin; we see him bleed, and then we put our sin to death.
It seems as if the last sentence of our text told us this—"by his wounds you have been healed."

The welts, the blue marks of his scourging—these will take out the lines of sin.
The wounds, the sweat, the death throes of the Savior—these will cure you of sin's disease.

Some think that the cure for sin is to give something, to do something good.
But in truth, the cure for sin is "Take."
Take what?

Take your dear Lord's wounds and trust in them;
take his griefs and rest in them;
take his death and believe in it;
take him and love him, and by his wounds you are healed.

From sermon no. 1143, *Death for Sin, and Death to Sin*

THE INEXPRESSIBLE GIFT

Thanks be to God for his inexpressible gift!
2 CORINTHIANS 9:15

Our Lord Jesus is the sum and substance of God's inexpressible gift to us.

Consider, first, that Christ is inexpressible *in his person.*
    No tongue of seraph, or of cherub, can ever describe the full nature of him,
        whose name is "Wonderful Counselor, Mighty God, Everlasting Father, Prince of Peace" (Isaiah 9:6).
He was the Creator of all things, yet he "became flesh and dwelt among us" (John 1:14).

> *Soul, God gave God to redeem you! Do you hear it?*
> *How great the wonder of this inexpressible gift!*

Christ is also inexpressible *in his condescension.*

What a stoop of condescension that is when he who is infinite becomes an infant;
when he who is the Ruler of the universe is in the carpenter's shop, obedient to his parents;
when he who owns all things is so poor that he "has nowhere to lay his head" (Luke 9:58).

> *He, before whom all the hosts of heaven veiled their faces,*
> *actually came here among men and dwelt among the poorest of the poor.*

> *Such a Savior surpasses all human thought!*
> *What an inexpressible gift!*

But if Christ is inexpressible so far, what can be said of him *in his death?*

Who can speak adequately of Gethsemane and the bloody sweat, and of the Judas kiss?
Who can describe the false accusations, the slanders and the blasphemies that were heaped on him?
Who can portray the thorn-crown, the shame and sorrow he endured as he was thrust out to execution?
Who can depict his pain as he is nailed to the gibbet and ridiculed by the whole mob of Jerusalem?

Yes, degraded men struck him!
Even dying thieves reproached him!

His eyes were dim with blood!
His throat was dry with thirst!

Finally, he cried, "It is finished," and he bowed his head.
The glorious Victim had yielded up his life to put away his people's sin!

> *O ye saints and sinners!*
> *This is God's gift to you—divine, inexpressible!*

From sermon no. 2247, *Praise for the Gift of Gifts*

REJOICING IN OUR KING

Let the children of Zion rejoice in their King!
PSALM 149:2

We follow our King joyfully as we think of *his deeds of love for us.*
Well may we rejoice in him, since his loving-kindness has exceeded all bounds.

The true splendor of kings lies not in what their people do for them,
    but in what they do for their people.
Herein our Lord excels all the princes who have ever lived.

He took our nature and was born a baby in Bethlehem.
He lived among us, bearing the brunt of poverty, hunger, homelessness, contempt, and treachery.
He died for us.

How royal was his love when the cross was his throne!
How royal was his crown when it was made of thorns!
How royal was his scepter when it was held in the pierced hand!

This is real kingship!
Everything else is merely stage-play.

Come and behold your King, who not only bleeds beneath the lash of man,
    but also bows beneath the bruises of his Father's justice.
Hear him as he cries, "My God, my God, why have you forsaken me?" (Matthew 27:46).

> *O loyal hearts, by the bitterness of your King's agony, be joyful in him!*
> *Since he loved you so much, can you refuse to rejoice in him?*

> *Yes, our acclamations will all be given to him*
> *who has proved his greatness and his goodness,*
> *not by gifts of gold, but by the gift of himself!*

In due time our King will remove our Zion and all its inhabitants
    to the land of cloudless days and unfading flowers.
We will soon be translated to the place where there is no more death, neither sorrow nor sighing.

Our King has great things in store for his church.
In him we possess earth and heaven, time and eternity.

> *Oh, let the children of Zion rejoice in their King,*
> *for all things are theirs in him!*
> *All heaven lies at their feet!*

From sermon no. 1968, *Jubilee Joy, or, Believers Joyful in Their King*

WHAT WAS IT TO SEE HIS FACE?

They will see his face.
REVELATION 22:4

What a delight for spiritual eyes to have seen Christ's face while he was here on earth!
What joy must have flooded Mary's heart when for the first time she gazed on that holy face!

That manger held an unrivaled form of beauty,
  and painters may very well strain their art to paint the wondrous child,
    for the spectacle brought shepherds from their flocks, sages from afar, and angels from heaven.
Both heaven and earth were intent on seeing his face.

It would have been a great joy to see the face of Jesus in the years of his maturity,
  and to have basked in the radiance of a sinless smile.
What a vision to have seen his face—so spiritual, so refined, so heavenly, so divine!

Have you sometimes wished that you could have gazed into the face of the Man of Sorrows?
Have you wished to see that blessed brow, plowed with the deep furrows of grief?
Have you wished to see those eyes—those founts of pity, those wells of love, those springs of agony?

What must it have been to look into his face …
  when it was covered with crimson sweat,
  when his brow was girded with the crown of thorns,
  when the foul drops of spittle followed each other down those bruised cheeks,
  when, in bitterest anguish, he cried, "My God, my God, why have you forsaken me?"

No, we have never seen our Lord's face under such conditions,
  but the accounts inspire us with a holy longing
    to behold his face forever and ever with our very own eyes!

The paradise of God is not the Elysium of imagination, the Utopia of intellect, or the Eden of poetry.
  Instead, it is the heaven of intense spiritual fellowship with the Lord Jesus—
    a place where it is promised to faithful souls that "they will see his face."
They will literally and physically, with their risen bodies, look into the face of Jesus!

They will not see the skirts of his robe as Moses saw the back parts of Jehovah,
  and they will not be satisfied to only touch the hem of his garment,
    or to sit far down at his feet where they can only see his sandals.
The promise is sure: "They will see his face."

Yes, they will see their Lord clearly, and they will see him always,
  for that is what the text implies, when it says, "They will see his face."
Not even for a moment, will they unlock their arm from the arm of their Beloved.

From sermon no. 824, *The Heaven of Heaven*

A GLORIOUS AND EVERLASTING NAME

To make for himself an everlasting name ...
to make for yourself a glorious name.
ISAIAH 63:12, 14

This text speaks of God as making for himself a great and glorious name in redeeming Israel;
but even though God has made for himself a great name at the Red Sea,
he has done much more through the great works of salvation *in the gift of Jesus.*

Ah! Here Egypt is eclipsed,
and the destruction of Pharaoh is no longer remembered!

Sin took us captive, but God brought us out
with a high hand and an outstretched arm!

However, for our redemption, it was necessary for God to become a man.

Would he come to Bethlehem's manger?
Would he who is infinite come robed as an infant?
Yes, he came, making all heaven to wonder and all the angels to sing.

And being here "in human form" (Philippians 2:8), he had to bear the wrath of God on our behalf.

There must be a scourging of those sacred shoulders!
There must be a piercing of those dear hands and feet!
There must be a rending open of that loving and holy heart!

Will it be done?
Will the Lord of glory give his back to the smiters and his cheeks to those who pull out the beard?
Will he yield his face to shame and spitting?
Will he, can he, die?

Death, you have slain your millions,
will you also slay the Son of God?

It must be so if we are to live.
He must die, or we must die, or justice must die.
Jesus solves the problem; he condescends to die.

As we see him bow his head, and cry, "It is finished,"
we know that God made for himself an everlasting name, a glorious name!

The Son of God was condemned, slain, and in the grave.
And all of this for us!

From sermon no. 2229, *God's Glorious and Everlasting Name*

GOING IN TO THE WEDDING

*"Those who were ready went in with him to the marriage feast,
and the door was shut."*
MATTHEW 25:10

As soon as the bridegroom appeared,
  "those who *were ready went in with him* to the marriage feast."
The manifestation of our Lord Jesus will be the glorification of his people,
  and he himself will escort us to our place in glory.

> *Ah, how else could we go in to the marriage if we did not go in with him—
> hidden behind him, covered with his righteousness, washed in his blood?*

Even the pure and holy God will not question our entrance if we enter with his Son.
All the demands of divine justice will be fully met by the fact that we go in *with him.*

Covered with his righteousness,
  adorned with his beauties,
  inseparably united to his person,
  the beloved of his heart,
we will go in *with him* to the marriage, and none will think of having us excluded.

We will go in with Christ to the marriage—
  not as mere spectators of his joy,
  not as friends of the Bridegroom who rejoice exceedingly in his gladness,
but we will go in *with him* to share his bliss.

> *Oh, matchless word!*

> *You, believer, will go in with him to the heavenly marriage feast;
> you will be part of that wondrous bride, the Lamb's wife,
> who is to find her bliss forever consummated with her glorious Husband.*

Even on earth, we always associate the highest degree of joy with a marriage.
Our greatest joy here, as beings of flesh and blood, is on our wedding day.
Imagine then what heaven will be to the people of God.

It is a marriage, a perpetual festival.
It is a banishment of everything that is sorrowful.
It is a gathering together of all that is joyous.

A marriage on earth—well, we know what that is.
But a marriage in heaven!—who can describe that?

From sermon no. 2500, *Entrance and Exclusion*

THE CHRIST OF PATMOS

I saw seven golden lampstands, and in the midst of the seven lampstands One like the Son of Man,
clothed with a garment down to the feet and girded about the chest with a golden band.
His head and hair were white like wool, as white as snow, and His eyes like a flame of fire;
His feet were like fine brass, as if refined in a furnace, and His voice as the sound of many waters;
He had in His right hand seven stars, out of His mouth went a sharp two-edged sword,
and His countenance was like the sun shining in its strength.
REVELATION 1:12–16 NKJV

This symbolic picture of Christ is a representation of *the same Christ who suffered for our sins.*
John calls him the Son of Man, that sweet and humble name that Jesus used to describe himself.

That he was the same identical person is very clear,
  for John speaks of him as being *like* the Son of Man.
He probably means that he perceived—even in his majesty—
  a likeness to the One whom he had known in his shame and suffering.

He did not see the thorn-crown, but he knew that brow.
He did not see the nail-print, for the seven stars had taken its place, but he knew that hand.
Despite Christ's glories, John knew that Person who had previously suffered inconceivable grief.

Christian, look with reverence, for there is your Lord …
  the Christ of the manger,
  the Christ of the wilderness,
  the Christ of Capernaum and Bethsaida,
  the Christ of Gethsemane.
The Christ of Golgotha is there, and it is important for you to turn aside and see this great sight!

This picture reveals to us what Christ is now, and is therefore of extreme value.
What he was when he was here on earth is all-important, but what he is now is also important.
We want to know today—in the midst of present strife and present pain—what Jesus Christ is now.

Yes, and there is also another reason why we should turn aside and see this great sight.
When John saw it, he was overwhelmed and fell at Christ's feet as though dead (Revelation 1:17).
Even though this is not a desirable condition physically, it should be coveted spiritually.

It is a great thing to be truly emptied, stripped, and slain before the Lord.
The death of all that is within us that is of the flesh and of the fallen nature is wholly desirable.

Oh, may the two-edged sword that comes out of Christ's mouth smite all our besetting sins.
May the brightness of his face scorch and burn up in us the very roots of evil.
May he mount his white horse and ride through our soul, conquering and to conquer, casting out
  of us all that is of the old Dragon, and bringing every thought into subjection to him.

Yes, we would lie at his dear conquering feet, slain by his mighty grace!

From sermon no. 357, *The Christ of Patmos*, and sermon no. 1028, *The Glorious Master and the Swooning Disciple*

THE BRUISING OF HEEL AND HEAD

"I will put enmity between you and the woman,
and between your offspring and her offspring;
he shall bruise your head, and you shall bruise his heel."
GENESIS 3:15

God promises that there will arise in the fullness of time a Champion, who, though he suffers,
will smite in a vital part the power of evil and will bruise the Serpent's head.

You know how our Champion came, and you know how throughout his whole life,
his heel—that is, his lower part, his human nature—
was perpetually made to suffer, for he carried our sickness and our sorrows.

But the bruising came mainly …
when in both body and mind his whole human nature was made to agonize;
when his soul was "very sorrowful, even to death" (Matthew 26:38);
when his hands and feet were pierced and he endured the shame and pain of death by crucifixion.

Come and behold your Master and your King on the cross,
all disdained with spit, and blood, and dust!

It was there that his heel was cruelly bruised.

When he was taken down from the cross, prepared for burial, and laid in Joseph's tomb,
his followers wept as they handled that precious body in which the deity dwells.
Yes, the heel of their Champion had been terribly bruised by Satan.

The Devil had let loose Herod and Pilate and Caiaphas and the Jews and the Romans.
They were his tools, used on him whom he knew to be the Christ,
and so Christ was bruised by the old Serpent.
However, that is all. It is only his heel—not his head—that is bruised.

Lo, the Champion rises again!
Jesus only retains a scar in his heel, and he bears that to the skies as his glory and beauty.
He looks like a Lamb that has been slain, but in the power of an endless life he reigns with God.

The figure represents the Dragon as inflicting an injury to the Champion's heel.
But at that same moment—the Champion with that very same heel—crushes the Serpent's head.

The day will come when our Champion
will cleanse the whole earth of the Serpent's slimy trail.

Satan thought this world would be the arena of his victory over God,
but instead, it is the grandest theater of divine wisdom, love, and grace.

From sermon no. 1326, *Christ the Conqueror of Satan*

THE BRONZE SERPENT LIFTED UP

So Moses made a bronze serpent and set it on a pole.
And if a serpent bit anyone, he would look at the bronze serpent and live.
NUMBERS 21:9

This particular remedy of a serpent lifted on a pole was exceedingly instructive.

As you would take a sharp pole and drive it through a serpent's head to kill it,
    so this bronze serpent was exhibited as killed and hung up as dead before all eyes.
It was the image of a dead snake.

> *Wonder of wonders, that our Lord Jesus Christ*
> *would condescend to be symbolized by a dead snake!*

The bronze serpent had no venom of itself, but it took the form of a fiery serpent.
    Christ is no sinner, and in him is no sin,
        but even as the bronze metal was made into the likeness of a serpent,
    so was Jesus sent forth by God "in the likeness of sinful flesh" (Romans 8:3).

He came under the law and sin was imputed to him;
    therefore, he came under the wrath and curse of God for our sakes.
He was made to be sin "so that in him we might become the righteousness of God" (2 Corinthians 5:21).

If you will look to Christ Jesus on the cross ...
    you will see that sin is slain and hung up like a dead serpent;
    you will see death put to death and life and immortality brought to light (2 Timothy 1:10);
    you will see the curse ended forever because he became "a curse for us" (Galatians 3:13).

Sin, death, and the curse are like dead serpents now.
They are hung on the cross as a spectacle to all beholders—all slain by our dying Lord.

> *Oh, what a sight!*
> *If you can see it, what joy it gives you!*
>
> *Had the Hebrews understood the meaning*
> *of the dead serpent dangling from a pole,*
> *it would have prophesied to them*
> *the glorious sight that our faith now beholds*
> *as it gazes at Jesus slain,*
> *and sin, death, and hell slain in him.*

The dying thief beheld that bronze serpent as he saw Jesus hanging at his side, and it saved him.
And we, too, may look and live since Jesus died in the sinner's place.

From sermon no. 1500, *Lifting Up the Brazen Serpent*

THE ONLY WAY TO GOD

"No one comes to the Father except through me."
JOHN 14:6

There is now a highway, a way of holiness, wherein the redeemed can walk to God.
It is the King's highway, Jesus Christ, "the way, and the truth, and the life" (John 14:6).

Who is there who does not desire to go to God in heaven?

Is there anyone with a soul so dead that he never pants for a better world?
Is there a heart so seared that it never longs to be at rest?
Is there an eye so blind that it never looks to the hereafter?

The wild untutored savage of the woods looks to another world,
    so how can we shut our eyes to the future—we who are living in a Christian country?
Are not most people looking and longing for a better world?

O world of woe, what are you if you are not a stepping-stone to a world of bliss?
O land of graves and shrouds, what are you if we did not dive through you into the land of light?
O vale of tears, what are you if you are not the pathway to the Mount of Transfiguration?

> *But there is no way to heaven, whatever our hopes may be,*
> *except through our Lord and Savior, Jesus Christ.*

O guilty one, the only way to the gates of pearl is through the bleeding side of Jesus!
These are the gates of paradise: Christ's bleeding wounds.

If you would find your way to God's bright throne, first find your way to Jesus' shameful cross.
If you would know the way to happiness, find that path of misery that Jesus trod.

What! Do you say that you are attempting another way?

Do you think you can rend the posts and bars and gates of heaven from their perpetual places and
    force your way in by your finite strength?
Do you think you can purchase with your riches and your gold a foothold in paradise, where the streets
    are made of gold, the gates of pearl, the foundations of jasper, and the walls of precious gems?
Do you think you can get there by your own merits?

> *O sinner, your admittance into the Father's presence is through Jesus Christ,*
> *and your admittance into heaven is only through him!*

> *Jesus alone holds the keys of heaven!*

From sermon no. 245, *The Way to God*

CHRIST'S INTERCESSION FOR US

Who is to condemn?
Christ Jesus is the one who died—more than that, who was raised—
who is at the right hand of God, who indeed is interceding for us.
ROMANS 8:34

How does Christ intercede today in heaven?

It has been stated this way: When God in his justice rose from his throne to strike the Guarantor (see Hebrews 7:22), he would make no concession, so the Guarantor paid the total debt.

Then the Judge said, "I will not come down to earth to receive the payment. You must bring it to me."

Therefore, the Guarantor groped through death, fighting his way up to the eternal throne. Mounting aloft by a glorious ascension, he dragged his conquered foes behind him. And scattering mercies with both hands, like Roman conquerors who scattered gold and silver coins in their triumph, he entered heaven.

He came before his Father's throne, and said, "There it is! The full price! I have brought it all."

God would not go down to earth for the payment. It had to be brought to him. This was pictured by the high priest of old. The high priest had the blood of the sacrifice, but he did not take the mercy seat outside the curtain and carry it to the blood. No, the blood must be taken to the mercy seat.

So, the high priest takes off his royal robes and puts on the garments of the minor priest.
He then goes behind the curtain and sprinkles the blood on the mercy seat.

Even so, our Lord Jesus Christ took the payment and bore it to God—
took his wounds, his rent body, his flowing blood.
He took them before his Father's very eyes,
and there he spread his wounded hands and pleaded for his people.

Now here is the proof that the Christian cannot be condemned:
The blood is on the mercy seat.

The blood is not poured out on the ground;
it is on the mercy seat;
it is on the throne.
It speaks into the very ear of God, and it must prevail.

Also, one of the sweetest proofs that the Christian cannot be condemned is this:
Who Christ is and with whom he intercedes.

If I had to intercede for my brother with my father, I know that I would have a safe case,
and this is exactly what Jesus has to do.
He has to intercede with his Father, and yes, with our Father too.

From sermon no. 256, *The Believer's Challenge*

SEEING GOD'S SALVATION

He took him up in his arms and blessed God and said,
"Lord, now you are letting your servant depart in peace,
according to your word; for my eyes have seen your salvation."
LUKE 2:28–30

Here is God in human flesh: the divine nature is in mysterious union with the human.
     He who now lies in Simeon's arms as an infant is also the infinite God;
          he who is feeble in his humanity is also omnipotent in his deity.
This child is both the Son of Man and the Son of God.

When we think of God coming down to our low estate and espousing our nature,
     we are ready to burst out with Simeon: "My eyes have seen your salvation."
We are sure that we will be lifted up to heaven now that heaven has come down to us.

Our Lord was not merely a child, he was also a poor child.
     He was so poor, that when his mother had to redeem him, she could not afford to bring a lamb;
          she presented the poorer offering—a pair of doves or two young pigeons.
So she came as a poor woman, and he was presented to the Lord as a poor woman's child.

When the Prince of Glory and the Lord of angels stoops so low—
     so low that a poor woman bears him in her arms and calls him her baby—
surely there must be salvation for the lowest, the poorest, and the most destitute.

But why has Mary brought him to the temple?

She has brought him in order to redeem him.
He was her firstborn, so he must be redeemed.

Was he then under the law?
Yes, for our sakes he was under the law, and he who redeemed us had to be redeemed as well.

> *When we think of the twelve and sixpence, or thereabouts,*
> *that his mother paid as redemption money,*
> *what a contrast arises before our eyes!*

> *Christ has redeemed us to God by his blood,*
> *and yet as Mary's firstborn child*
> *the price paid for him was a few silver coins.*

Yes, this wondrous stoop of deity to lowly humanity,
     and this marvelous honoring of the law in our nature by one who is Immanuel, God with us,
has brought salvation to our poor fallen race.

From sermon no. 1417, *"Thy Salvation"*

THE SOUL'S FOOD AND DRINK

"For my flesh is true food, and my blood is true drink."
JOHN 6:55

Let us try to feed spiritually on the two doctrines to which the words "flesh" and "blood" refer;
    namely, the incarnation of the Son of God and his death as man's substitute.
Man had broken God's righteous law and had so offended him that he was driven from his presence;
    but, in order to redeem man, Jesus Christ, the Son of God, became a man.

Whatever Jesus did as a man, he did as the great Representative of man.
    He kept the law of God perfectly, and his obedience was reckoned as man's obedience.
As Adam's sin was imputed to all who were in him as their federal head,
    so Christ's obedience was imputed to all who were in him as their federal Head.

The condemnation of our Substitute was our condemnation too.
When he was taken away and put to death, we were crucified with him.
When he was laid in the grave, we were buried with him.
When he rose from the dead, we rose with him, and we were justified by his resurrection.

Christ's resurrection is the guarantee of our resurrection.
Best of all, he has gone back to heaven as the Representative of his people.

That very flesh that was pierced by the nails,
that very flesh that the soldier's spear went through to his heart—
that very flesh he carried right up to the throne of God!
In so doing, we who are in him were carried up there as well, and we now sit in heavenly places.

When Jesus says that his "blood is true drink," it means that his redeeming sacrifice is soul-
    satisfying.

Man had sinned, and God was willing to forgive;
    but the inflexible law of the universe is that sin must entail punishment.
It is such a good and righteous law that altering it would be ruinous.

There must be punishment for sin, but Jesus endured the punishment that was due to his people.
    He took upon himself our flesh, and that flesh was made to bleed—
        even to death—in the accomplishment of that purpose.
All who believe in him may know that their sins were transferred from them and laid on him.

You who want to find the highest joy that can be found on earth, here it is!

In Emmanuel—God with us, born at Bethlehem and dying on Calvary—
in his incarnation and in his atoning sacrifice,
you will find that true food and drink
that gives the loftiest spiritual exhilaration to all who feed on them!

From sermon no. 3192, *The Soul's Meat and Drink*

HATRED WITHOUT CAUSE

"They hated me without a cause."
JOHN 15:25

No being has ever been lovelier than the Savior;
   and yet, lovely as he was, no being has ever met with hatred so early in life.
No creature has ever endured such continual persecution.

As soon as he was ushered into the world, the sword of Herod was ready to cut him off.
   The innocents of Bethlehem, by their horrible massacre,
      gave a sad foretaste of the sufferings that Christ would endure
and of the hatred that would be poured upon his devoted head.

From his first moment of life to the cross,
   except for the temporary lull while he was a child,
it seems as if the whole world was in league against him and all men sought to destroy him.

> *Christ was the hated One,*
> *the slandered and the scorned.*

> *He was "despised and rejected by men;*
> *a man of sorrows, and acquainted with grief"(Isaiah 53:3).*

What caused him to be rejected and scorned?
Should any of the reasons why he came from heaven cause indignation and scorn?

Christ came to earth to reclaim the wanderer—is there anything in that to make men hate him?
If he came to reform the drunkard, to reclaim the prostitute, to gather in the sinners, and to bring
   prodigals to their Father's house again—is there anything in that to cause hatred?
He came to heal the diseases of the body—is that a legitimate object for hatred?
Will I hate the physician who goes about gratuitously healing all manner of diseases?

Christ came to earth to die, so that sinners might not die. Was that a cause for hatred?
Should I despise him who allowed his Father's flaming sword to be quenched in his own vital blood?
Should I look with indignation upon the Substitute who takes my sins and griefs upon himself?
Should I hate and despise the man who loved me better than he loved himself; who loved me so
   much that he visited the gloomy grave for my salvation?

> *Never does sin appear so exceedingly sinful*
> *as when we see it pointed at the person of Christ,*
> *whom it hated without a cause.*

Man put to death his God—he slew his Savior—
   and that is the essence of all sin, the masterpiece of crime, the very pinnacle of mortal guilt.
Man outdid himself when he put his Savior to death.

From sermon no. 89, *Hatred without Cause*

THE BLOOD IS CONSPICUOUS

"It is the blood that makes atonement by the life."
LEVITICUS 17:11

All through Holy Scripture we constantly meet with the mention of "blood."

"Without the shedding of blood there is no forgiveness of sins" (Hebrews 9:22).
"The blood of Jesus his Son cleanses us from all sin" (1 John 1:7).
"You were ransomed … with the precious blood of Christ" (1 Peter 1:18–19).

But what does "the blood" mean in Scripture?

It not only means suffering, which may be typified by blood,
    but it also means suffering to death; it means the taking of a life.
To put it very briefly, a sin against God deserves death as its punishment,
    and what God said by the prophet Ezekiel still holds true, "The soul who sins shall die" (18:4).

The only way in which God could fulfill his threatening sentence—and yet forgive guilty people—
    was for Jesus Christ his Son, to come into the world and offer up his life in our place.
We are now saved through the sufferings of Jesus Christ, even to death.

> *All the sacrifices under the law, when their blood was poured out,*
> *were typical of the life of Christ, given up for men as a sacrifice—*
> *given in the place of those who had offended God's law and were doomed to die.*

The only way of salvation is by faith in the substitutionary sacrifice of Jesus Christ.
    There is no hope of entering heaven unless we are resting on his precious blood.
It is worth noting that in the death of Christ there was much shedding of blood,
    as if to direct our minds to the types of the Mosaic Law.

Jesus was scourged, and there was no scourging without blood.
His temples were pierced and lacerated with a crown of thorns.
His hands and feet were nailed with iron to the cross.
His side was opened by the soldier's spear and there flowed out blood and water.

There are many ways in which people may die without the shedding of blood,
    but Christ had to die a death in which the shedding of his blood was very conspicuous.
Thus he is linked forever with those sacrifices that were types and symbols of his great atoning work.

> *O Christian, keep before you the image of Jesus on the cross!*
> *Behold him pouring out his precious life's blood*
> *in order to bear away your guilt—*
> *dying for you so that you might live forever.*

From sermon no. 2369, *Blood Even on the Golden Altar*

HIS PRECIOUS CHEEKS

His cheeks are like beds of spices, mounds of sweet-smelling herbs.
SONG OF SOLOMON 5:13

Why are the cheeks mentioned?
Perhaps it is because every feature of Christ is inexpressibly delightful.
Take any portion of his countenance and you will find that it has surpassing beauty.

Though we cannot as yet see the majesty of our Savior's brow as King of kings and Lord of lords;
though we cannot perceive the brightness of his eyes that are like flames of fire;
though we cannot imagine the glory of his Second Advent;
    yet, if we can but see the cheeks that he gave to the smiters;
    if we can but know something of him as the suffering Savior,
then we will find inexpressible delight in him, and will also say, "His cheeks are like beds of spices."

I believe the saints see great loveliness in those parts of Christ that have been most despised,
    and the cheeks are part of Christ's body that were exposed to special shame.
Isaiah foretold his agony: "I gave my back to those who strike, and my *cheeks* to those who pull
    out the beard; I hid not my face from disgrace and spitting" (50:6).

Oh, if we could but see him now! If we could but gaze on his face as it is in glory!

If we were there, what a subject for meditation it would be …
    to think that the spittle of cruel mockers ran down those sacred cheeks;
    to think that brutal men disgraced the holy face of the Son of God by pulling out his beard;
    to think that such infinite loveliness was insulted with inconceivable contempt.

Oh, glorious love!

Our Lord stooped to this terrible depth of disgrace
in order to lift us up to dwell with him on high!

The followers of Christ have an intense admiration—an almost infinite love—
    for those parts of Christ's body by which they are able to commune with him.
Perhaps that is another reason why his cheeks are mentioned.
    The cheek is the place of fellowship where we may exchange tokens of love.

Just think of it!
The Son of God actually had a cheek
for the lips of love to approach and to kiss!

What a blessed privilege it was and will be again,
for loving hearts to express their affection for Christ in this way!

From sermon no. 2479, *Spices, Flowers, Lilies, and Myrrh*

BEAT YOUR BREAST

And all the crowds that had assembled for this spectacle,
when they saw what had taken place, returned home beating their breasts.
LUKE 23:48

By faith, place yourself at the foot of the little knoll of Calvary
   and there you will see on the center cross, between two thieves, the Son of God made flesh.
He is nailed by his hands and feet and is dying in inexpressible anguish.

Look steadfastly and devoutly for you are watching the death of the Destroyer of death.
It is he who was worshiped by angels who is now dying for the sons of men.

O believer, as you sit down and watch, beat your breast
as you remember that you are seeing in the Crucified your own sins!

Now look closely at your Lord and see how vile they have made him.

The mean-spirited soldiers have stained his holy cheeks with spittle.
They have lashed his shoulders with a felon's scourge.
They have dealt him a death that was awarded only to the lowest Roman slave.
They have stripped him naked and have left him without even a rag to cover him.

See here, believer, the shame of your sins.
See how disgraceful and abominable they are.
See how they aggravate Christ's sorrows.
It was not enough to crucify him; they also insulted him.

O believer, beat your breast that the pure and holy Christ
must be so disgraced and shamed for you!

Look even closer at your Savior—look into his face.
See the lines of anguish that indicate the deeper inward sorrow that far transcends bodily pain.

God, his Father, has forsaken him.
God has made him a curse for us.

What thunderbolts, what coals of fire, what indignation and wrath from the Most High
   would have been our portion had Jesus not interposed!

O believer, beat your breast as you see Christ bearing your curse!
Yes, beat your breast as you fall down and wash with tears his pierced feet!

From sermon no. 860, *Mourning at the Sight of the Crucified*

A MYSTIC CORONATION

Twisting together a crown of thorns, they put it on his head.
MATTHEW 27:29

We have before us a *mystic coronation.*

The coronation of Christ with thorns was symbolic, bearing great meaning,
   for it was to him *a triumphal crown.*
Our Savior had fought with sin all his earthly life and had conquered it,
   and as a witness that he had gained the victory he seized sin's crown as a trophy.

> *What was the crown of sin? Thorns.*
> *They sprang from the curse.*

> *"Cursed is the ground because of you …*
> *thorns and thistles it shall bring forth for you" (Genesis 3:17–18).*

> *This was the coronation of sin,*
> *and now Christ has taken away its crown*
> *and placed it on his own head.*

> *He has spoiled sin of its richest regalia*
> *and he wears it himself.*

And what if I say that the thorns also constituted *a mural crown?*[1]

Paradise was surrounded with a hedge of thorns so sharp that none could enter it,
   but our Champion leaped upon the bristling rampart
      and bore the blood-red banner of his crown into the heart of that better new Eden.
Thus he won it for us, never to be lost again.

> *Jesus wears the mural crown,*
> *which denotes that he has opened paradise.*

He wore a wrestler's crown for he did not wrestle with flesh and blood, but with principalities and
   powers, and he overthrew his foe.
He wore a racer's crown, for he had run with the mighty and outstripped them in the race.
He wore a crown rich with glory despite the shame that was intended by it.

Jesus is also the Prince of Martyrs.
He leads the vanguard among the noble army of suffering witnesses.
He—the faithful and true witness, *with the thorn-crown and the cross*—stands at the head of them all.[2]

[1]A golden crown bestowed by the ancient Romans on him who mounted the wall of a besieged place and
   lodged a banner
[2]From sermon no. 1168, *The Crown of Thorns*

"A MAN OF SORROWS"

A man of sorrows, and acquainted with grief.
ISAIAH 53:3

There are men of pleasure, others of wealth, but Jesus was "a man of sorrows."
Our Lord is called the "man of sorrows" because this was his special mark.

We might call him "a man of holiness" since there is no fault in him.
We might call him "a man of eloquence" since "no one ever spoke like this man!" (John 7:46).
We might call him "a man of love" since no love has ever been greater than his.

Still, conspicuous as all these and many other excellencies were,
    Jesus' most striking characteristic was his sorrows.
His countenance was "marred, beyond human semblance" (Isaiah 52:14).

All men have a burden to bear, but his was the heaviest of all.
His cup was more bitter, his baptism much deeper than the rest of the family.

> *Ordinary mourners may be content to rend their garments,*
> *but he himself was rent in his affliction.*
>
> *We sip at sorrow's rim, but he drained it dry.*

Because our Savior's heart was so big, it was inevitable that he would become "a man of sorrows."
    He was not only afflicted with the sight of sin and saddened by perceiving its effect on others,
        but sin was actually laid on him, and he himself was numbered with the transgressors.
In the last crowning sorrows of his life there came upon him the penal afflictions of God.

He was arrested in Gethsemane where he had wrestled until bloody sweat dripped from every pore.
He went from there to be treated with mingled scorn and cruelty before the judgment seat.
Pilate's soldiers almost murdered him with scourging; then they brought him forth and Pilate
    said, "Behold the man!" (John 19:5).

Still, their malice was not satisfied.
They must go further yet and nail him to the cross and mock him while fever parches his mouth.
He calls for drink and is mocked with vinegar.

Yet, we must remember that as bad as his bodily sufferings were,
    the sharpest scourging and the severest griefs were all within,
while the hand of God bruised him and the iron rod of justice broke him.

> *Child of God, turn to your bleeding Savior—gaze on him—*
> *and you will find the "man of sorrows," your Lord and your God.*

From sermon no. 1099, *The Man of Sorrows*

OUR EVERLASTING SONG

*"Worthy is the Lamb who was slain, to receive power
and wealth and wisdom and might and honor and glory and blessing!"*
REVELATION 5:12

What delight will seize the minds of the redeemed when they finally arrive in heaven;
and oh, how God will be glorified then *for every wound of Jesus will cause an everlasting song!*
As we circle around his throne rejoicing, this will be the very summit of all our harmony: "You were
slain, and by your blood you ransomed people for God" (Revelation 5:9).

We will be even better servants than the angels for we will be filled with deeper joy and gratitude.
They have not experienced evil, but we have; and yet we will be perfectly free from it.
They have not experienced pain, but we have known pain, grief, and death; and yet we will be immortal.

*Oh, how we will sing!
How we will praise the Lamb in the midst of the throne!*

It will be an inexhaustible theme for melodious joy and song …
that he became a man,
that he sweat great drops of blood,
that he died and rose again.

When the angels are singing, "Hallelujah! Hallelujah! Hallelujah!"
we will bid them stop their song a moment
while we say, "He whom you love and adore was once covered with bloody sweat!"

Then we will cast our crowns at Christ's feet,
and we will say, "He was once despised and rejected by men!"

Lifting our eyes and saluting him as "God over all, blessed forever" (Romans 9:5),
we will remember the reed, the thorns, the vinegar, the nails.
We will remember the awful depths of the grave into which he descended.

Amid all the splendors of heaven we will never forget the agony and misery and dishonor of earth;
and even when the loudest sonnets of God's love and power and grace are sung,
we will sing this after all, and before all, and above all—that Jesus the Son of God died for us.

This will be our everlasting song—

*"He loved us and gave himself for us,
and we have washed our robes,
and made them white in the blood of the Lamb."*

From sermon no. 478, *Christ—Perfect through Sufferings*

THE IMMUTABILITY OF CHRIST

Jesus Christ is the same yesterday and today and forever.
HEBREWS 13:8

It is well that there is One who remains the same.
It is well that there is one stable rock amid the changing billows of this sea of life.
All things have changed and are changing, but Jesus Christ is the same yesterday, today, and forever.

Yes, Jesus is still the same *in his person.*
Our youth fades away into the weakness of old age, but Jesus still has the dew of his youth.

Christ Jesus, whom we adore, you are as young as ever!
Your matchless beauty is unimpaired!
You are still the fairest among ten thousand, the altogether lovely!

If he came to earth to visit us again, we would find him to be the same Jesus—
as loving, as approachable, as generous, as kind.
He would still be the same person, unchanged by all his glories, triumphs, and joys.

We bless you, O Savior, that amid your heavenly splendors,
you are still the same; your nature is unaffected!

Believer, do you ever wonder how much Christ will love you when you are in heaven?
Do you ever think of how he will reveal his love to you when you are without spot or blemish?

Well, pause and remember that he will not love you one atom more when your head wears a crown
than he does right now amidst all your sin and care and woe.
Believe that saying of Jesus: "As the Father has loved me, so have I loved you" (John 15:9).

The Father loves his Son infinitely, and in this very same way, the Son of God loves you.
He cannot love you more; he will not love you less.

O my soul, if Jesus is the same today as yesterday,
do not set your affections on our changing things!
Set your heart on him.

Put your treasure where you can never lose it—put it in Christ.
Put all your affections in his person,
and all your trust in his efficacious blood.

My soul, cast all your cares on him who can never be taken from you,
even "Jesus Christ ... the same yesterday and today and forever."

From sermon no. 170, *The Immutability of Christ*

PRECIOUS TO GOD AND BELIEVERS

You come to him, a living stone rejected by men
but in the sight of God chosen and precious.
1 PETER 2:4

Our Lord is all the more precious to us when we see that he is despised and rejected by men.

Did they call the Master of the house Beelzebul (Matthew 10:25)?
Then we will heartily salute him as Lord and God!

Did they charge him with drunkenness, madness, and with being a friend of tax collectors and sinners?
Then we will bow down at his feet with reverence and love!

Did they spit on him? Did they scourge him? Did they blindfold him and then mock him?
Ah! Then he is to our souls all the worthier of adoration!

He is as the sun at noonday when nailed to the cross and reviled by the hard-hearted crowd.
He is glorious in our eyes when scribes and Pharisees ridicule and scorn him and he dies in agony.

Worship him, all ye angelic host!

Yet, we feel that the worship due to him on the throne
does not reach the height of the worship due to him on the tree.
Here our praise would rise far above that of angelic adoration!

Precious is our Lord Jesus as we see him on the tree,
bearing all our sins in his own body!

Precious is he when forsaken by God
and discharging all our debt by his awful sacrifice!

He also becomes inconceivably precious to us when we view him as chosen by God.

God has chosen the man Christ Jesus to be our Savior.
He says, "I have exalted one chosen from the people" (Psalm 89:19).

O glorious Christ, chosen by God, may you also be chosen by us!
If your Father's heart is set on you, so must ours be.

Even heaven itself cannot be compared with you!
You are incomparably, immeasurably, inconceivably precious!
All good things meet in you even to superabundance!

From sermon no. 2137, *Christ Precious to Believers*

A SERVANT OF ALL

"I am among you as the one who serves."
LUKE 22:27

When the twelve apostles came together to the Last Supper,
  there was no servant present to wash their feet.
And since none of them were willing to stoop to such a lowly position,
  they all took their places around the table with soiled feet.

Then the Master himself rose from their midst, poured water into a basin
  and went to each one of them and washed their feet.
He said to them in effect, "I am among you as a slave, as a domestic who does the most menial work."

That evening, Jesus literally did for his disciples what he had always been doing.

The disciples had always been, as it were, sitting at a table
  and Jesus had been feeding them with heavenly and spiritual food.
He was all the while their servant, washing their feet—
  bearing with their ill manners, kindly correcting their mistakes, patient with their ignorance.

Jesus could truly say, not only of that night but of his whole life,
"I am among you as the one who serves."

A servant is one who must patiently endure some hardship—sometimes misjudgment and harshness—
  but this blessed Servant bore cold and nakedness and hunger and even death in his servitude.
He was despised, abused, and slandered by the very people whom he sought to help.

Who could ever have imagined that he who now sits on the highest throne in glory
  would have been among us here below as the Servant of his own servants!

O gracious Master, you were humble indeed!
Despite your ineffable glory, you were like a slave to Peter and James and John,
taking their soiled feet into your pure hands and washing them clean.

Our blessed Lord was so full of love for us that nothing seemed like a stoop to him.
  For the joy of blessing his people, he "endured the cross, despising the shame" (Hebrews 12:2).
He seemed to say, "Will I wash their feet? That is a small thing *for I will soon wash them completely in my heart's blood,* and I will indeed be among them as the One who serves!"

It was love—wondrous love, excessive love—
that would not let Jesus stay in heaven amid the splendors of his royalty.
He came to earth amid the sorry surroundings of poverty and grief
in order to die for us and thus save us.

From sermon no. 2514, *Servus Servorum*

SCENES OF SHAMEFUL CRUELTY

When he learned that he belonged to Herod's jurisdiction,
he sent him over to Herod.
Luke 23:7

Away they go again, but this time it is to Herod!

Oh, I think I see that blessed Lamb of God hounded again through the streets!
Have you ever read such a story? No martyr has ever been harried like our Savior was.

We must remember that Christ's agonies were not all confined to the cross.
They were also endured in those streets—in those innumerable blows and kicks and strikes of the fist.

They took Jesus before Herod, and since Herod had heard of his miracles,
   he hoped to see some wonders performed.
But when Jesus refused to speak, Herod treated him with contempt.

Can you picture the scene? Can you see Herod and all his men mocking the Savior?

"A pretty king," they seem to say. "Better yet, a miserable beggar!"
"Look at his cheeks, all bruised. Is that the complexion of royalty?"
"Look," they say. "He is emaciated and covered with blood as though he has been sweating blood
   all night. Is *that* the imperial purple?"

Then Herod said, "Bring out that costly white robe. If he is a king, let us dress him up like one!"
And so the white robe is put on him—not a purple one, for that was later put on him by Pilate.

Jesus has two robes put on him—one is put on by the Jews and the other one by the Gentiles.
   This reminds us of that text in the Song of Solomon: "My beloved is white and ruddy" (5:10 NKJV).
Our beloved Savior is white with the splendid robe that marked him King of the Jews,
   and he is red with the purple robe that marked him King of the Gentiles.

Herod and his men of war—after treating Jesus as shamefully as they could—then return him to Pilate.
Oh, can you see him? It takes no great imagination to see how he is dragged back to Pilate.

It is another journey along those same streets.
It is another scene of shameful tumult, bitter scorn, and cruel hitting.

Oh, he must have died a hundred deaths!

It is not only one,
but it is death upon death that the Savior bears
as he is dragged from tribunal to tribunal!

From sermon no. 495, *The Greatest Trial on Record*

BETTER THAN WINE

Your love is better than wine.
Song of Solomon 1:2

Nothing gives the believer so much joy as fellowship with his Lord Jesus Christ.

Like others, he has enjoyment in the common pleasures of life,
    and he finds happiness in the gifts and works of God.
Yet in all of these—separately or all together—
    he does not find such substantial delight as in the matchless person of his Lord Jesus.

He has wine that no vineyard on earth has ever yielded;
he has bread that all the cornfields of Egypt could never produce.

Where can such sweetness be found
as we have tasted in communion with our Beloved?
In our opinion, the joys of earth are no better than husks
when compared to Jesus, the heavenly manna.

We would prefer one taste of Christ's love
and one sip of his fellowship
than a whole world of carnal delights.

What is the chaff to the wheat?
What is an imitation gem to the true diamond?
What is a dream to the glorious reality?

What is time's greatest enjoyment
when compared to our lovely Lord Jesus
in his most despised condition?

All earthly pleasures are simply earthy, but the comforts of Christ's presence are like him: heavenly.

When we review our fellowship with Jesus there are no disappointments.
There are no dregs in his wine.
There is no contamination in his ointment.

The joy of the Lord is solid and enduring.
In time and in eternity it is worthy to be called "the only true delight."

For nourishment, consolation, exhilaration, and refreshment,
no wine can rival the love of Jesus.

Morning and Evening, January 8 (E)

ALONE WITH GOD IN PRAYER

In these days he went out to the mountain to pray,
and all night he continued in prayer to God.
LUKE 6:12

If any person might have lived without prayer it was our Lord Jesus Christ.
    To us poor, weak, erring mortals, prayer is an absolute necessity,
        but you would not think that would be the case with he who is the Son of God.
He was "holy, innocent, unstained, separated from sinners" (Hebrews 7:26).

Obviously, there are certain aspects of prayer in which our Lord took no part.

He did not have to confess his sins,
    nor did he have to begin each day praying for strength to resist temptation and sin.
He was free from the weaknesses and the tendencies to evil that we all bear,
    yet no one has ever prayed with such intensity and fervency as he did.

To his disciples, his prayers must have made an even deeper impression than his sermons,
    for they did not say, "Lord, teach us to preach," but they said, "Lord, teach us to pray."
They felt that Jesus was the Master of that heavenly art, and they desired to sit at his feet
    and learn how to move heaven and earth with sacred wrestlings.

O Christian, since our sinless Lord was so mighty in prayer,
does this not say to you with an irresistible and persuasive voice,
"Watch and pray that you may not enter into temptation" (Matthew 26:41)?

Notice that our Lord sought the solitude of a mountain.
    In every city and village he was never free from innumerable followers,
        and the mountain was superior to a room with locked doors.
There, he was far from the din of the city and the noise of those who advertised their merchandise.

Believer, if you would draw near to God in an extraordinary way,
carefully seek a perfect solitude
where you can shut out the thoughts and sounds of the outer world.

Jesus sought a place far away from everyone so that he might, in his Father's presence,
    pour out his entire soul—groaning, struggling, wrestling, or rejoicing.
In order to prevent interruptions and to freely express his feelings, he went to the mountain.

The Son of God entered God's own glorious temple of nature when he wished to commune with heaven.
    Nothing could have equaled the glory of nature's midnight.
There the stars—like the eyes of God—looked down upon the worshiper
    and the winds seemed to bear the burden of his sighs and tears upon their willing wings.

From sermon no. 798, *Special Protracted Prayer*

A MODERNIZED QUESTION

"Will you not tell us what these things mean for us, that you are acting thus?"
EZEKIEL 24:19

Let us approach our divine Master and, looking at him in his wondrous Passion,
   earnestly ask him, "Will you not tell us what these things mean for us, that you are acting thus?"

Do you see him amid the dark shadows of the olive trees, bending low and pleading with God?
He pleads and pleads and pleads again until he is covered with sweat.
Sweat, did I say? It is blood, and it is so plentiful that it falls to the earth.

Dear Master, while that bitter cup is held to your lip,
can you tell us what this means for us, that you are acting thus?

"Sin is an exceedingly bitter thing and it is costing me soul agony to remove it.
I have cried, 'If it be possible, let this cup pass from me,'
but if I would save you, it is not possible."

But now, do you see the lanterns twinkling through the trees?
Evil men are coming with torches, lanterns, and clubs to take the blessed pleading One.

Dear Master, while the traitor's kiss is still wet on your cheek
and you are bound and led away to Caiaphas,
tell us what all this means. What has this to do with us?

"Sin has bound you! Sin has hampered and crippled you!
You are bond-slaves of Satan and I must be bound to set you free!"

But now, see this! They are scourging him! They are crowning him with thorns!
They are mocking him, blindfolding him, and then striking him with the palms of their hands!

Blessed One, will you tell us what these things mean for us?

"I must be put to shame, for sin is a shameful thing!
No scorn is too great for sin!
It deserves to be loathed and treated with contempt!"

And now, we see him walking the *Via Dolorosa*, staggering beneath the load of the cross.
We see him nailed to that cross and then lifted up as a gazing stock for guilty men.

Why, oh, why, thou Son of God, are you lifted up like the brazen serpent of Moses?

"I am lifted up so that I might draw all people to myself.
I hang here, the righteous for the unrighteous, to bring them to God."

From sermon no. 2286, *An Ancient Question Modernized*

CONSTRAINING LOVE

Love the LORD, all you his saints!
PSALM 31:23

Since the Father loves the Lord Jesus, should we not love him as well?

Jesus has always been dear to his Father's heart, but he is especially loved as our Mediator.
He is loved for the obedience he perfected, for the sufferings he endured, and for the ransom he paid.

When the Son of God became the Man of Sorrows, there was one eye that always followed him closely;
there was one heart that always understood his pains,
and one face that was always filled with celestial delight when he overcame his enemies.
Yes, God gave up his Son for us all, but how his heart followed him! How his soul yearned for him!

O Father, do you love the Lord Jesus, and will my heart refuse to love him?
Should not the object of your love be the darling of my heart too?

What you delight in will be my delight!
Where you see beauty, my eye will gaze with rapture!
Where your heart finds solace, there my heart will find repose and joy!

Does Christ lie in your bosom? Then he will lie in mine.
Is his name engraved on your heart? Oh, let it be engraved on mine too!

Do you love him so much that you could not possibly love him more?
Let me love him like that, with all the vehemence of my ransomed nature!

Remember that the angels also love our Lord; it is their greatest pleasure to serve him.
When he came to earth to suffer, you know how they watched over him and ministered to him.
You know how joyously they formed his escort when he returned to the realms of heaven.

Do the angels love him—the angels who had no need to be washed in his blood—
and will I not love him with all my heart?
Do these spirits, these spotless ones, cry, "Worthy is the Lamb!"
and will my heart not echo back in even louder strains?

Stand back, ye angels, and give us the first place in love!
You may adore, but you cannot love as we love
for he is our Brother—bone of our bone and flesh of our flesh.
He did not take the nature of angels, but the seed of Abraham.
He is ours more than he is yours, for he is man.

O Jesus, our souls must love you!
Even angels cannot be our rivals here.

From sermon no. 325, *Constraining Love*

"GOD WITH US"

"Behold, the virgin shall conceive and bear a son,
and they shall call his name Immanuel" (which means, God with us).
MATTHEW 1:23

This glorious word "Immanuel" means that God in Christ is in close union with us.
He must be for he has taken upon himself flesh, blood, bone—everything that makes a body.
Christ Jesus was the Man of men, the Second Adam, the Representative of man.

Being with us in our nature, God was with us in *all of life's pilgrimage.*
You can scarcely find a path in the march of life that Christ has not traversed.
From the gate of entrance, even to the door which closes life's way, his footprints may be traced.

Were you in the cradle? He was there.
Were you a child under parental authority? Christ was also a boy in the home at Nazareth.
Have you entered life's battle? Your Lord did the same; and though he did not live to an old age, yet
through incessant toil and suffering, he bore the marred countenance that attends a battered old age.

Wherever you may find yourself—on the hilltop or in the valley, on the land or on the sea—
wherever you are, you will discover that Jesus has been there before you.
There is no pang that rends the heart or disturbs the body but that Jesus has been with us in it all.

Do you feel the sorrows of poverty? He had "nowhere to lay his head" (Luke 9:58).
Do you endure the griefs of bereavement? Jesus "wept" at the tomb of Lazarus (John 11:35).
Have you been slandered for righteousness' sake, and has it vexed your spirit? He said, "Reproaches
have broken my heart" (Psalm 69:20).
Have you been betrayed? He also had his familiar friend who sold him for the price of a slave.

There is no glen of adversity so dark, so deep, apparently so pathless,
but that in stooping down you may discover the footprints of the Crucified One.
In the fires and in the rivers, in the cold night and under the burning sun
he cries, "I am with you! Be not dismayed for I am both your Companion and your God!"

It is mysteriously true that when we will come *to the last, the closing scene,*
we will find that Immanuel has been there; he felt the pangs and throes of death.
He endured the bloody sweat of agony and the parching thirst of fever,
and he knew the separation of the tortured spirit from the poor fainting flesh.

Yes, and he knew the grave, for there he slept.
That new tomb in the garden makes him God with us until the resurrection calls us from our beds
of clay—to find him "God with us" in newness of life.

We will be raised up in his likeness, and our first sight will be the incarnate God.
As long as the ages roll, he will be "God with us."

From sermon no. 1270, *"God with Us"*

GREAT FORGIVENESS FOR GREAT SIN

In Him we have redemption through His blood, the forgiveness of sins,
according to the riches of His grace.
EPHESIANS 1:7 NKJV

The sins spoken of in our text are great sins,
    and if you really want to know how great a thing sin is,
remember what it cost Christ to be able to forgive it.

Go to Gethsemane and see what it cost Christ to bear our sin.
The sin that covered him with a bloody sweat was no trifle.

Then follow him to Pilate's hall and hear the cruel whips falling on his shoulders.
See the soldiers taking him away and nailing him to the cross.
There he hangs, dying for guilty sinners amid untold anguish.

There could never have been forgiveness of sin
    if there had not been all this suffering on the part of the sinner's Substitute.
Yes, sin is a great thing, but as you have just seen, we have a greater Savior;
    and if we will put our trust in him, even our darkest sins will be forgiven.

Luther once said, "Jesus Christ is not a sham savior for sham sinners, but he is a real Savior
    who offers a real atonement for real sin, for gross crimes, for shameless offenses."
And a far greater one than Luther has said, "Though your sins are like scarlet, they shall be as
    white as snow; though they are red like crimson, they shall become like wool" (Isaiah 1:18).

Though your sins are like great mountains towering above the clouds,
    the floods of divine mercy can roll over them and drown them all.
They are all wiped away because of Christ's substitutionary pains and death.[1]

Oh, what a joy! What bliss to be a perfectly pardoned soul!
My soul dedicates everything to him who, because of his love,
became my substitute and redeemed me through his precious blood.

Oh, when I think of how great my sins were,
of how dear the precious drops were that cleansed me from them,
and of the gracious act that sealed my pardon,
I am filled with wondering, worshiping affection!

I bow before the throne that absolves me!
I clasp the cross that delivers me!
I serve the incarnate God through whom I am a pardoned soul![2]

[1]From sermon no. 2862, *Great Forgiveness for Great Sin*
[2]*Morning and Evening*, November 27 (E)

A RESOLUTION TO FOLLOW CHRIST

Ittai answered the king, "As the LORD lives, and as my lord the king lives,
wherever my lord the king shall be, whether for death or for life,
there also will your servant be."
2 SAMUEL 15:21

Let us also make this resolution: Wherever our Master, the Son of David, the King shall be,
  there will we also be as his servants, whether for life or for death.
Jesus deserves from every one of us who has tasted of his marvelous grace
  faithful service and unswerving allegiance at all times and under all circumstances.

Who else has ever done for us what Jesus has done?
Our mother brought us into this sinful world, but he will take us out of it—into a perfect world.
We have had many kindnesses from friends, but he has redeemed us with his own precious blood.

Think of these three words and try to measure what they mean: Gethsemane, Gabbatha, Golgotha.

Let those three words awaken your adoring memories—
  Gethsemane, with its garden and bloody sweat—for you.
  Gabbatha, with its flogging, its mocking, its shame, and its spitting—for you.
  Golgotha, with its cross and the five flowing wounds and the torment of death itself—for you.

The blood of Christ has uplifted us from the ruin of sin,
  so let us consecrate ourselves to him, following the Lamb wherever he goes.
His cross is despised, so let us be despised with it for he bore shame for us.

Sometimes it has required the loss of all things to defend his cause;
  so let it be ours, if need be, to lose all things for him who gave up all for us.
Our Savior lost the bliss of heaven—and life itself—so that he might redeem our souls.

Even if we placed our feet in his exact footsteps and walked up to Calvary itself, it would be our duty.
We cannot do better than to keep close to every step that Jesus has taken.

We must cleave to Jesus, for what is there in the world that could repay us for leaving him?
We would lose the joy of life.
We would lose our support in tribulation.
We would lose heaven itself to inherit nothing but death.

There is no bribe heavy enough to weigh against him.
There is no honor bright enough to compare with him.
There is no disgrace dark enough to compare with the disgrace of deserting him.

Blessed Master, we will cling to you in life and in death
so that where you are, there we may also be.

From sermon no. 3504, *Following Christ*

A TRUE SIGHT OF SIN

Make me know my transgression and my sin.
JOB 13:23

I have seen my sins in many different ways.

I saw them once by the blazing light of Sinai;
    and, oh, my spirit shrank within me, for my sins seemed to be exceedingly dark.
But alas, I had not seen enough of sin to make me loathe it, so I continued to play with sin.

I beheld another sight one day when I perceived the purity of God's character;
    and as I compared myself with him, I thought I saw how evil I was.
But alas, though I had seen enough to make me worship for a moment,
    my gladness disappeared and I went on my way, forgetting what manner of man I was.

Then there came to me another view as I beheld God's loving-kindness to me.
    I looked on my sin in the light of his grace, and said, "O sin, how vile you are!"
I cursed sin from my inmost heart and thought I had seen enough of it;
    but alas, that sense of gratitude passed away and I found myself still prone to sin, still loving it.

But, oh, there came a thrice-happy, yet thrice-mournful hour!

One day, in my wanderings, I heard a cry, a groan such as does not come from mortal lips,
    for it had in it such unutterable depths of grief and anguish.
I turned aside, expecting to see a great sight, and indeed it was!

Lo, there on a cross, all bleeding, hung a man.
I marked the misery that was making his flesh quiver on his bones.
I beheld the dark clouds rolling down from heaven, and I perceived that his heart was as full of the
    gloom and horror of grief as the sky was full of blackness.
I seemed to look into his soul and saw there torrents of inexpressible anguish, wells of torment of
    such an awful character that no lip can ever describe!

I said, "Who is this mighty sufferer? Is he the greatest of all sinners, the worst of all blasphemers?"
Then, from above, I heard a voice saying, "This is my beloved Son, but he has taken the sinner's
    sin upon himself, and he must bear its penalty."

Truly, I had never seen my sin until that hour …
    when I saw it tearing Christ's glory from him,
    when it seemed to even withdraw from him the loving-kindness of his Father,
    when I saw him covered with his own blood and plunged into the uttermost depths of grief.

    Then I said, "Now I know what you are, O sin!"

From sermon no. 2656, *The Death of Christ for His People*

A JOYFUL DOXOLOGY

To Him who loved us and washed us from our sins in His own blood,
and has made us kings and priests to His God and Father,
to Him be glory and dominion forever and ever. Amen.
REVELATION 1:5–6 NKJV

John had barely begun to deliver his message to the seven churches
when he felt that he must lift up his heart in a joyful doxology.
He could not sit down coolly to write even what the Spirit of God dictated;
but he must rise, he must fall on his knees, he must bless and magnify and adore the Lord Jesus!

This text is the upward burst of a great geyser of devotion.
John's spirit has been quiet for a while,
but all of a sudden the stream of his love for Jesus springs up like a fountain!
It rose so high that it must have bedewed heaven itself with its sparkling column of crystal love!

Now in the matter of spontaneous devotion, John is only one among the rest of the apostles.
Their love for their Master was so intense that they had but to hear his footstep and their pulse raced.
And if they heard his voice, they were carried away completely—
whether in the body or out of the body they could not tell.

Oh, that our hearts could also be fired with adoring praise
by just one glimpse of our Redeemer's eyes,
or by just one touch from that dear pierced hand!

Notice that this man of doxologies, from whom praise flashes forth like light from the rising sun,
is first of all a man who has realized the person of his Lord.
He says, "To *him* who loved us," rather than "to *the love* of him."
It is sweet to sing of love, but sanctified hearts find more delight in singing, "To him who loved us."

We could also sing of pardoning mercy forever and ever if we have been cleansed from sin,
but the center of the joy is to adore him who has "washed us from our sins in His own blood."
He cleansed us, not by some process outside of himself, but by the shedding of his own blood.

The value of the blood-washing rises to the highest degree in our hearts …
when we look into the wounds from which the Atonement flowed;
when we gaze on that face so sadly disfigured, that brow so grievously scarred;
when we peer into the heart that was pierced by the spear for our double cleansing.

The disciples were bound to love the hands that took the basin and then poured water over their feet,
but how can we praise our Savior enough for washing us in his own blood?
Well may we sing the new song, "Worthy are you … for you were slain,
and by your blood you ransomed people for God" (Revelation 5:9).

From sermon no. 1737, *John's First Doxology*

HEAVENLY LOVE-SICKNESS

I adjure you, O daughters of Jerusalem,
if you find my beloved,
that you tell him I am sick with love.
SONG OF SOLOMON 5:8

This love-sickness may be seen in a soul longing for a view of Jesus in his glory.
    Since it cannot as yet be in Christ's presence, cannot behold him on his throne,
        and cannot worship him face to face, it is sick until it can.
It loves him so much that it cannot endure being away from him.

A heart so set on Christ would traverse highway and byway, resting nowhere until it finds him.
    As the needle once magnetized will never rest easy until it finds the pole,
        so the heart once Christianized will never be satisfied until it rests on Christ.
It must rest on him in the fullness of that glorious vision before the throne.

What am I sick with love for? For the pearly gates?
No, but for the pearls that were formed in my Savior's wounds.

What am I sick for? For the streets of gold?
No, but for Christ's head that is like "the finest gold" (Song of Solomon 5:11).

What am I sick for? For the heavenly manna?
No, but for Christ himself, who is the food and drink of his saints.

Himself! Himself! My soul pines to see him!
Oh, what a heaven to gaze upon!

What bliss to talk with the man—the God—crucified for me,
to weep my heart out before him,
to tell him how I love him
for he loved me and gave himself for me.

What bliss to read my name written on his hands and on his side!
Yes, and to let him see that his name
is written on my heart in indelible lines.

Oh, to embrace him!

What an embrace that will be
when the creature will embrace his God,
to be forever so close to him
that not a doubt, nor a fear, nor a wandering thought
can come between my soul and him forever.

From sermon no. 539, *Heavenly Love-Sickness!*

October 1

THE MAJESTIC VOICE

The voice of the Lord is full of majesty.
Psalm 29:4

Yes, and so it should be! Should that voice not be full of majesty that comes from majesty? God is the Ruler of the whole earth. Should he speak with a voice below his own dignity? *Truly, from the very essence of God we might infer that his voice would be full of majesty!*

In a sense, Jesus Christ may be called the voice of God,
   for he is frequently called the Word of God in Scripture (see John 1:14).
And we are sure that this Word of God "is full of majesty."

The voice and the Word are very much the same thing.
God speaks and it is his Son.
His Son is the Word; the Word is his Son, and the voice is his Son.

Ah! Truly the voice, the Word of God, "is full of majesty."

Angels! You can tell what sublime majesty invested his glorious person
   when he reigned at his Father's right hand!

You can tell of the glory he laid aside to become incarnate;
   you can tell how sparkling was that crown,
      how mighty was that scepter,
   how radiant were those robes bedecked with stars!

You who saw him when he stripped himself of all his glories—
   you can tell of his great majesty!

And oh, you who saw him ascend on high, leading captives in his train—
you beloved songsters who bow before him and unceasingly sing his praise—
   you can tell how full of majesty he is!
High above all principalities and powers you see him sit,
   and the mightiest monarchs are like creeping worms beneath his throne!

High there, where God alone reigns, there he sits—
   not merely majestic, but full of majesty!

Christian, adore your Savior; adore the Son of God; reverence him;
   and remember in all seasons and at all times
   that no matter how little you may feel yourself to be,
   your Savior, with whom you are allied—the Word of God—
   is essentially full of majesty!

From sermon no. 87, *The Majestic Voice*

JESUS IS GOD'S SALVATION

"My eyes have seen your salvation."
LUKE 2:30

Long ago, before the world was created, God in his foreknowledge knew that man would sin,
    but Jesus—the Second Person of the Trinity—entered into a covenant with his Father.
He promised that in the fullness of time he would stand in the sinner's place and pay the sinner's debt.

Oh, the grandeur of that day when the angels came singing that the Baby was born in Bethlehem!

Ah, Simeon, what you see there is not merely a baby! It is the Word incarnate.
He who lies there is the Word that was with God when he fixed the sockets of the universe.
The Son of Mary is also the Son of God, and by seeing God in human flesh you see God's salvation.

Now with eyes of love follow that baby when he becomes a man.
    See his obedience to his father Joseph, handling the hammer and the saw in his carpenter's shop.
    See him during the three years of his public ministry toiling arduously, perfectly, and willingly.
In his active obedience, you see God's salvation for he rendered a recompense to the broken law.

But, ah! Let your eyes swim with tears as you follow him from his active to his passive obedience.

There he is in yonder garden among the olives. Do you hear his sighs, his deep-hearted groans?
Do you mark his sweat that "became like great drops of blood falling down to the ground"?
Do you see him hurried away to Caiaphas, Pilate, and Herod—scorned, flouted, and scourged?

Into that face, which angels look at with hushed awe, they spew their accursed spittle.
They strike him and cry, "Hail, King of the Jews!" (Matthew 27:29).
They mock his royalty with a crown of thorns, and they mock his priesthood by binding his eyes
    and then saying, "Prophesy to us, you Christ! Who is it that struck you?" (Matthew 26:68).

Remember that he who is in this shameful condition is God's salvation.

Jesus came down from heaven's glory to all those depths of shame
in order to lift us out of our shame and uplift us to supreme glory.

Finally, the patient Sufferer gives his hands and feet to the nails and he dies a felon's death.
    But the worst was this: God hid—as it were—his face from him,
        and that bitterest of all cries went up, "My God, my God, why have you forsaken me?"
There he was, the Forsaken One, and yet he was God's salvation.

Wherever we see Jesus, we see God's salvation!

Whether in Bethlehem's manger,
or on Calvary's cross, or on yonder throne—
wherever we see him—we see the salvation of God.

From sermon no. 3177, *Christ Seen as God's Salvation*

October 3

THAT LOOK OF COMPASSION

Immediately, while he was still speaking, the rooster crowed.
And the Lord turned and looked at Peter.
And Peter remembered the saying of the Lord, how he had said to him,
"Before the rooster crows today, you will deny me three times."
And he went out and wept bitterly.
LUKE 22:60–62

Can you picture Jesus there in the hall, up yonder steps, before the high priest and the council,
    while Peter is down below, warming his hands at the fire?
Can you see the Lord Jesus turning around and fixing his eyes intently on his erring disciple?

Jesus is bound, he is mocked and reviled, and he has just been struck on the face,
    but his thoughts are not concentrated on his own personal sufferings.
Our blessed Master is thinking of Peter and his eye seeks him out in wondrous love and compassion.

Blessed be his name,
Jesus always has an eye on his people,
whether he is in his shame or in his glory!

Though he now reigns in glory,
he still looks steadily on his own.

What tender wisdom we see here: "The lord turned and looked at Peter."

He had spoken to Peter before and that voice had called him to be a fisher of men.
    He had given Peter his hand before and saved him from a watery grave when he was sinking,
        but this time he gives him neither his voice nor his hand.
He gave him that which was equally effectual and intensely suitable—he lent him his eye!

How wise Christ is in the way he chooses to express his affection and to accomplish our good!
    If he had spoken to Peter then, the mob would have assailed him,
        or at least they would have remarked on the sorrow of the Master and the treachery of the disciple.
Our gracious Lord will never needlessly expose the faults of his people.

No words could ever express all that was portrayed in that look of compassion.
    A volume as big as the Bible was contained within that look of Jesus.
His glance was a divine hieroglyphic, full of unutterable meanings,
    conveyed in a clearer and more vivid way than words could ever have done!

The Lord looked, and Peter wept bitterly.
Oh, the power of Jesus!

If there was such power about him when he was bound,
what is his power now that he dwells in heaven and intercedes for us there?

From sermon no. 2034, *Peter's Restoration*

THE EXCEEDING RICHES OF GRACE

So that in the coming ages
he might show the immeasurable riches of his grace
in kindness toward us in Christ Jesus.
EPHESIANS 2:7

God's grace is above all observation.
The little grace we have seen bears no proportion to the glorious whole.
It is like someone standing on the beach, who thinks he can see the entire ocean.

No one has fully beheld the vast, majestic ocean in all its length and breadth and depth.
No one can see it in all its far resounding shores and hollow caves.
Such are the "immeasurable riches" of God's grace—unsearchable, passing knowledge!

This grace is *above all expression*—even inspired expression.
Paul, though filled with the Holy Spirit, could only say, "Thanks be to God for his inexpressible gift!"

Furthermore, the immeasurable riches of God's grace are *above all our sins.*
You can only sin as a human, but God can forgive as God.
You sin as a finite creature, but the Lord forgives as the infinite Creator.

We will never sin so that grace may abound, because that is detestable.
But what a blessed text this is: "Where sin increased, grace abounded all the more" (Romans 5:20).

Dwell for a moment on that last phrase: "In kindness toward us in Christ Jesus."

That is the channel through which all spiritual blessings come to us.
The riches of God's grace come to us through our Mediator.

O people, you can see the mark of the cross
on every spiritual blessing the Father has bestowed!

It seems to make every covenant blessing more and more precious
    because it is brought to us by the hand of the Beloved.
By his atonement it is procured to us, and by his matchless intercession it is bestowed.

Christ Jesus is the golden pipe of the conduit of eternal love.
He is the window through which grace shines.
He is the door by which it enters.

"The immeasurable riches of his grace in kindness toward us in Christ Jesus"—
this is an anthem worthy of the celestial choirs!

Sing it, O ye saints, while you are waiting to ascend his holy hill!

From sermon no. 1665, *The Exceeding Riches of Grace*

SAVED BY LOVE

"I am not doing this for your sake, declares the Sovereign Lord.
Be ashamed and disgraced for your conduct, O house of Israel!"
Ezekiel 36:32 niv

There are two sins that are bred in the bone and that continually come out in the flesh.
One is self-dependence and the other is self-exaltation.

It is very hard, even for the best of people, to keep themselves from the first error.
We must continually be reminded that salvation is God's work, from first to last, and is not of man.
How often the old error rises up that we can do something in the matter of salvation!

If we would dwell at the cross of Christ, it would help us to remember
     that the only reason Jesus gave up his life for us was because he loved us.
Nothing within us could have caused the boundless, the bottomless, the shoreless love of God.

Stand at the foot of the cross, ye who delight in your own works, and answer these questions:

Do you think the Lord of life and glory could have been brought down from heaven to be fashioned
     like a man—so that he could die—because of your merits?
Could his sacred veins have been opened with any sword less sharp than his own infinite love?
Do you believe that your poor merits, such as they are, could be so effectual as to nail the Savior
     to the tree and make him bend his shoulders beneath the enormous load of the world's guilt?

You may believe that coral insects can build rocks by their great multitude, and by their many works;
     but you cannot believe that all the accumulated merits of humanity (if there is such a thing)
          could bring the Eternal from the throne of his glory and bow him to the death of the cross.
No, from the cross comes the cry, "I am not doing this for your sake, O house of Israel!"

None of us possess anything that could recommend us to God.
He is not moved to do anything for us by anything that we do for him.
His motive for blessing us lies wholly in the depths of his own bosom.

The day is coming when all the blood-bought, blood-washed children of God will walk the golden streets.

Their hands will bear the palm branches.
Their ears will be delighted with celestial melodies.
Their eyes will be filled with the transporting vision of God's glory.

But, the only reason they will be there is because of God's love and not because they deserve it.

When we enter heaven, our song will be,
"Not unto us, not unto us, but unto thy name be all the glory!"

From sermon no. 233, *Free Grace*

October 6

NUMBERED WITH TRANSGRESSORS

He ... was numbered with the transgressors;
yet he bore the sin of many.
Isaiah 53:12

Christ was numbered with transgressors in the census of the Roman empire and in the courts of law,
    and the Jewish people also numbered him with transgressors.
They actually declared him to be a more abominable transgressor than a thief and a murderer.
    Barabbas is placed in competition with Christ, when they say, "Not this man, but Barabbas!"

He is numbered with the transgressors when he bears the transgressor's scourging.
He is tied to the whipping post and the plowers make deep furrows down his back.

He is numbered with the transgressors when he bears the felon's cross.
He comes into the street carrying his own gibbet upon his raw and bleeding shoulders.
He comes to Calvary and there he is hoisted upon the cross.

But Jesus is pure and holy! Surely he will be taken down from the cross before he dies!

Death is the curse of sin; it only comes upon transgressors.
    It is impossible for the innocent to die—
        as impossible as it is for immortality to be annihilated.
Surely God will deliver his Son at the last moment, after he has been tried in the furnace!

Not so! He must become "obedient to the point of death, even death on a cross" (Philippians 2:8).

> *Yes, he who was numbered with the transgressors,*
> *having worn the transgressor's crown of thorns,*
> *lies in the transgressor's grave.*

"They made his grave with the wicked and with a rich man in his death,
    although he had done no violence, and there was no deceit in his mouth" (Isaiah 53:9).
Jesus had no sin; he was "holy, innocent, unstained, separated from sinners" (Hebrews 7:26),
    but he bore the fullness, vileness, and condemnation of sin upon his shoulders.

Our Savior allowed himself to be "numbered with the transgressors"
    so that we, who are guilty, might be numbered with the holy.
All that we have goes to Christ—sin and all.
    And all that Christ has comes to us—his righteousness, his blood, everything.

> *Trembling sinner, place your trust in Christ.*
> *Cast your soul upon his perfect righteousness;*
> *wash in his cleansing blood and he will make you whole,*
> *and will present you faultless before his Father's face.*

From sermon no. 458, *The Friend of Sinners*

ALL LAID DOWN FOR US

He laid down his life for us.
1 JOHN 3:16

Nothing produces in us such a sense of gratitude as does the cross of our Lord Jesus Christ.

This we know, whether we look back to the decrees of eternity
  or look forward to all the splendors that God has prepared for his beloved children,
we can never see our Father's love so clearly as when we look at Christ dying on the cross.

We can read the love of God in the letters engraved on the rock of the eternal covenant
  and in the blazing letters of heaven hereafter.
But, it is in those crimson lines—those lines written in blood—
  that we have the most striking revelation of God's love.

Ah, here it is that you learn love: Christ "laid down his life for us."
He laid down his glorious life for poor, sinful creatures.

He stripped himself of all his splendors,
  then of all his happiness,
  then of his own righteousness,
  then of his own robes.

Yes, even his one poor garment, all stained with blood,
  he laid down for his beloved people.
And then when he was naked to his own shame,
  he laid down what he had come to earth to give us—his life.

Oh, love insatiable!

He had given up one hand to cancel sin,
and then he gave up the other hand to reconcile us to God.

He had given up one foot so that our sinful feet might be transfixed—
nailed and fastened, never to wander—
and then he gave up the other foot
so that our feet might be free to run the heavenly race.

When there was nothing left but his poor heart,
he gave up his heart too,
and they split it apart with the spear,
loosening precious streams of blood and water.

From sermon no. 2656, *The Death of Christ for His People*

RESPONDING TO LOVE

We love because he first loved us.
1 John 4:19

Why do we love Jesus?

We love him because he gave himself for us (Galatians 2:20).
We have life through his death and peace through his blood.

And we also love Jesus because of his excellence.
    We are filled with a sense of his beauty, a consciousness of his infinite perfection.
His goodness, greatness, and loveliness combine in one resplendent ray to enchant the soul
    until it is so ravished that it exclaims: "Yes, he is altogether lovely" (Song of Solomon 5:16 NKJV).[1]

> *Nothing will contribute more in making you see Jesus as admirable and lovely*
> *than a right apprehension of his love for you.*

> *This is the constraining, ravishing, engaging, and overwhelming consideration*
> *that will infallibly steep you in a sea of love for him![2]*

Oh, strong and deep love of Jesus,
    come in like the sea at high tide!

Cover all my powers!
Drown all my sins!
Wash away all my cares!

Lift up my earthbound soul
    and float it right up to my Lord's feet!

There let me lie,
    a poor broken shell
        washed up by his love,
            having no virtue or value of my own
    and only venturing to whisper to him
        that if he will put his ear to me,
            he will hear within my heart the faint echoes
                of the vast waves of his own heart—
    love that has brought me
        where it is my delight to lie,
    even at his feet forever![3]

[1]*Morning and Evening*, September 3 (M)
[2]*The Saint & His Saviour*
[3]*Morning and Evening*, April 12 (M)

A PRICELESS TREASURE

He who did not spare his own Son but gave him up for us all,
how will he not also with him graciously give us all things?
ROMANS 8:32

Think of God's love for his one and only Son.
　The heart of God is filled with fathomless oceans of eternal affection,
　　and this affection has always been fixed on his Son.
What must it have cost him to give up his Son to die for us—a Son so near and so dear to him?

Well then, since God has given up his beloved Son,
how can he deny anything to you who believe in him?

Do you feel anxious about the bread that perishes?
Is that worthy to be compared with God's only Son?

Are you concerned about how you are going to get food and clothing?
How can God deny you such trifles as these when he has given you his Son?

Perseverance in grace—is that what you ask?
Even that is but a crumb under the Master's table compared with his Son.

All the wants of all people put together could only make one little drop
　in comparison with the tremendous ocean of benevolence that flowed out of God's heart
　　when he did not spare his own Son but gave him up for us all.
As we look at Christ—God's gift to us—we must believe that we will be given everything we need.

Yes, it is a wonder that God gave us his Son, but we must also consider who his Son really is!
Jesus said, "Before Abraham was, I am" (John 8:58), claiming the very name of the Eternal Jehovah.
He was indeed God; he was one with the Father even while he was man.

Who can describe the preciousness of this gift?

This gift of God's Son is so precious
that even if heaven and earth could be sold,
their united price could not buy another treasure like Jesus!

Since God has given you this priceless treasure, will he not give you everything else that you need?
If someone gave you ten thousand dollars, would you doubt his willingness to give you a dollar?
If he gave you a liberal income for life, would you doubt his willingness to give you a penny?

God is yours, and Christ is yours to the fullest extent possible; there is no reservation.
So ask boldly, wait patiently, receive gratefully, and walk joyfully.

From sermon no. 3204, *The Saints' Riches*

THE GLORY OF DIVINE GRACE

His glorious grace.
EPHESIANS 1:6

In ancient times, all the attributes of God sat in solemn conclave *in the great council chamber,*
  devising a way by which God should be glorified.

Foreknowledge—as one of the attributes of God—prophesied that man, if made fallible, would sadly fall;
  but then, Justice arose and thundered forth his word that if man fell, he must be punished!
Grace, however, asked whether it would be possible for man to be saved,
  and yet for justice to be satisfied as well.

Infinite Wisdom answered the question, and God's own Son was the answer.
He promised that in the fullness of time, he would become a son for us
  and would bear the whole weight of Jehovah's justly merited wrath as our redemption.

Now while all the attributes displayed themselves in the council chamber,
  when our reverent soul dares venture into that once secret but now revealed will of the Most High,
we are compelled to admire all the attributes of God, but most of all his grace.

It appears that grace presided at this meeting,
that grace pressed man's redemption,
that grace inspired wisdom,
that grace defended man when justice might have spoken against him.

Grace was our advocate, and Christ Jesus—who is grace himself—
  long ago stood as the Wonderful Counselor and devised the plan.
He pleaded our cause and promised to work it out.

When the council was over, grace stepped forward to be glorified in another manner.
  It glorifies itself in its gifts, giving us blessings countless in number and priceless in value,
    scattering them along our pathway as if they were but stones.
Yet each one of them is so precious that heaven alone can tell their worth.

But finally, after giving man blessings through long ages,
  grace came up to Calvary and there gave its all—its grandest gift!
Grace gave up the incarnate Son of God to die.
  He gave up his own life, bowing his own head upon the cross.

Yes, grace in its highest form is best seen on Calvary!

Who can adequately declare the glory of that grace
seen in the dying Son of God on Calvary?

From sermon no. 2763, *The Glory of Grace*

THE BLOOD-SHEDDING

Without the shedding of blood there is no forgiveness of sins.
HEBREWS 9:22

Yes, there was a shedding of most precious blood.
 We will not deal here with the rivers of blood of goats and rams
  for there was a blood-shedding once that far outweighed all others!
It was a man—God—who shed his blood at that memorable season.

Come and see it! Here is a garden, dark and gloomy; the ground is crisp with the frost of midnight.
Between those gloomy olive trees we see a man and we hear him groaning out his life in prayer.

> *Harken angels! Harken people! And wonder!*
> *It is the Savior groaning out his soul!*
> *Come and see him! Behold his brow!*

> *O heavens! Drops of blood are streaming down his face and from his body!*
> *Every pore is open and they sweat, but not with the sweat that toils for bread;*
> *it is the sweat of One who toils for heaven—he "sweats great drops of blood."*

That is the blood-shedding, without which "there is no forgiveness of sins."

Follow that man farther as sacrilegious hands drag him to the hall of Pilate.
They seat him in a chair and a robe of purple is thrown over his shoulders in mockery.
And mark his brow where they have placed a crown of thorns.

> *Ye angels! Drops of blood are running down his cheeks!*
> *But look! Look also at his back!*
> *They have stripped him and are now tearing his flesh with the scourge,*
> *making rivers of blood run down his shoulders!*

That is the blood-shedding, without which "there is no forgiveness of sins."

This is not all! They fling him on the ground and nail his hands and feet to the transverse wood.
They hoist it in the air, dashing it into its socket. It is fixed, and there he hangs—the Christ of God!

> *Ye people! There is blood from his head, blood from his hands, blood from his feet!*
> *In agony unknown, he bleeds his life away!*
> *And then see! They pierce his side and blood and water pour out!*

This is the shedding of blood, sinners and saints;
this is the awful shedding of blood, the terrible pouring out of blood,
without which for you—and for the whole human race—"there is no forgiveness of sins."

From sermon no. 118, *The Blood-Shedding*

THE GLORY OF GOD

"Worthy are you, our Lord and God, to receive glory and honor and power."
REVELATION 4:11

Although the crucifixion of Jesus was intended to be a blow at the glory and honor of God,
  he has never received greater glory and honor than through the sufferings of his Son.
Satan thought that God was dishonored when in actuality he was more glorified than ever.

O nature,
  adoring God with your ancient and priestly mountains,
  extolling him with your trees that clap their hands,
  worshiping with your seas that in their fullness roar out Jehovah's praise,
you cannot glorify God as Jesus glorified him when he became obedient even to death!

O heaven,
  with all your jubilant angels,
  with your ever-chanting cherubim and seraphim,
  with your thrice-holy hymns,
  with your streets of gold and endless harmonies,
you cannot reveal the Deity as Jesus Christ revealed it on the cross!

O earth and heaven! O time and eternity, things present and things to come,
  you are dim mirrors of the Godhead compared with the bleeding Lamb!

O heart of God,
  I see you nowhere as at Golgotha where the Word incarnate reveals the justice and the love,
the holiness and the tenderness of God in one blaze of glory!

If any created mind desires to see the glory of God,
  he need not gaze at the starry skies;
  he need not soar into the heaven of heavens;
he has but to kneel at the cross and watch the crimson streams that gush from Immanuel's wounds!

If you would behold the glory of God,
  you need not gaze between the gates of pearls;
you have but to look beyond the gates of Jerusalem and see the Prince of Peace die!

If you would receive the noblest conception that ever filled the human mind
  of the loving-kindness and the pity of God—and yet the justice and the severity of God's wrath—
you have but to look into Christ's heart, all crushed, broken and bruised, and you have seen it all!

Oh, the joy that springs from the fact that God has triumphed after all!

From sermon no. 860, *Mourning at the Sight of the Crucified*

October 13

GOLDEN SILENCE

The high priest then questioned Jesus about his disciples and his teaching.
JOHN 18:19

Caiaphas, the high priest, questioned Jesus before the public trial, hoping to catch him in his speech. He asked him first about his disciples.

We do not know what questions he asked. Perhaps they went something like this:
"Who are you that you have twelve men attending you and calling you Master?"
"Are these men to be your lieutenants to raise up an army on your behalf?"
"Where are your gallant followers now? Why are they not here to witness for you?"

Our Lord Jesus, on this point, did not say a word.
Why? Because it is not for our Advocate to accuse his disciples.

He might have answered:
"You ask where my disciples are. When one proved to be a traitor the rest took to their heels."
"Look! There is one of them sitting by the fire—the same one who just now denied me with an oath."

But no, our Savior would not utter a word of accusation.
He whose lips are mighty to intercede for his people will never speak a word against them.

Satan slanders but our Savior pleads.

The Prince of Darkness is the accuser of God's children,
but the Prince of Peace is our advocate before the eternal throne.

When questioned about his teaching, Jesus boldly answered,
    but when it came to defending himself, he remained silent.
Perhaps nothing displays more fully the omnipotence of Christ than his power of self-control.

Behold, the Son of God does more
than just rule the winds and command the waves—
*he **restrains himself**!*

Just a word, a whisper, could have refuted his foes and sent them to their eternal destruction,
    but "he opened not his mouth" (Isaiah 53:7).
He who spoke up for his enemies, saying, "Father, forgive them" (Luke 23:34),
    would not utter even one word for himself.

If ever silence is golden,
it is this deep silence under infinite provocation.

From sermon no. 495, *The Greatest Trial on Record*

OUR SAVIOR'S LONELINESS

"You will be scattered, each to his own home, and will leave me alone."
JOHN 16:32

Note the loneliness of our Savior.

When he came to the hour of his agony, his humanity pined for sympathy, yet it was denied him.
In the bloody sweat and agony of Gethsemane he trod the winepress alone.
His three favored disciples might have watched with him, wept with him, and prayed with him,
but instead, they let his lone prayer ascend to heaven unattended by human sympathy.

Our Savior was alone, too, when facing his trial.

False witnesses were found to bear lying testimony against him,
but no one stepped forward to attest to the honesty, quietness, and goodness of his life.
He was "like a lamb that is led to the slaughter," but no voice was heard begging for his deliverance.

Though a few loving ones gathered at the foot of the cross,
they could offer him no assistance and probably dared not utter more than a tearful protest.
Perhaps the boldest one there was the dying thief who called him "Lord"
and also rebuked his fellow criminal, saying, "This man has done nothing wrong" (Luke 23:41).

Few, indeed, were the voices that were lifted up on behalf of the Man of Sorrows!

From the time when he bowed in agony amid the deep shadows of the Mount of Olives
until the moment when he entered the thicker darkness of the valley of death-shadow,
he was left to suffer alone.

Now there was a greater reason for our Savior's loneliness than appears on the surface.
Desertion was a necessary ingredient in that cup of suffering he had covenanted to drink for us.
We deserved to be forsaken; therefore, he must be forsaken.

Since our sins against man—as well as our sins against God—
deserved that we should be utterly forsaken by both,
Jesus, bearing our sins against God and man, is forsaken.
Sin is a separating thing, so when Christ is made the Sin-Bearer, his friends must all leave him.

O blessed Savior, you did not turn aside from the purpose of redeeming your people
even though they proved themselves unworthy of being redeemed!

Although they forsook you,
you fulfilled to each one of them your ancient promise,
"I will never leave you nor forsake you" (Hebrews 13:5).

From sermon no. 3052, *Christ's Loneliness and Ours*

THE GOSPEL OF CHRIST'S GLORY

The light of the gospel of the glory of Christ.
2 CORINTHIANS 4:4

The Anointed was, in Paul's view, the one subject of the glad tidings from beginning to end.
Christ is the author of the gospel, the subject of the gospel, and the end of the gospel.

The glorious Savior
is the substance of the glorious gospel.

Much of the glory of the gospel lies in the glory of Christ's person.
   The Son of God himself gloriously undertook the work of our salvation,
      and that is why he was made flesh and dwelt among us.
He who is able to save us is not merely a man; he is Immanuel, God with us (Matthew 1:23).

See how glorious Christ is in his incarnation.
It is the glory of Christ to us that he was born at Bethlehem and dwelt at Nazareth.

It looks like dishonor that he would condescend to be the carpenter's son,
   but throughout all the ages it will be the glory of the Mediator,
that he actually stooped to be a partaker of our flesh and blood.

There is glory in his poverty and shame!
There is glory in his homelessness!
There is glory in his weariness and hunger!

Surpassing glory springs from Gethsemane and the bloody sweat,
from Calvary and the death of the cross!

All heaven could not yield him such renown
as that which comes from the spitting and the scourging,
the nailing and the piercing.

A glory of grace surrounds the incarnate God. And this, to those convinced of sin, is the gospel.

When we see God in human flesh, we expect reconciliation.
When we see that he took our infirmities and bore our sicknesses, we hope for pardon and healing.

Did God himself cover his glory with a veil of our inferior clay?
Then he means only good to humanity.

In the Word made flesh we see the glory of God,
and noting how love predominates and condescending pity reigns,
we see in this a gospel of grace for all believing people.

From sermon no. 2077, *The Gospel of the Glory of Christ*

HONOR TURNED TO SHAME

O men, how long shall my honor be turned into shame?
PSALM 4:2

Everything about our Savior that was honorable was made the object of scorn.
Look at his glorious person and see how shamefully that was treated by the sons of men.

He was betrayed, but the betrayer was one of his own disciples.
> This was shameful cruelty on the part of Judas, not only to betray Jesus to his enemies,
>> but also to mock him by calling him "Master," and then to scorn him with a kiss.
There was shame even in the way he was arrested—with swords and clubs.

When Jesus was dragged before Annas and Caiaphas, Pilate and Herod,
> he was the constant object of abuse, ridicule, and scorn.
He could truly say, "I gave my back to those who strike, and my cheeks to those who pull out the beard;
> I hid not my face from disgrace and spitting" (Isaiah 50:6).

All of Christ's offices were also ridiculed.
> Remember how they mocked him as a prophet: "They also blindfolded him and kept asking him,
>> 'Prophesy! Who is it that struck you?'" (Luke 22:64).
The soldiers felt that Christ's prophetic office was only worthy of their jests and sneers.

Jesus claimed to be the King of the Jews, so with vulgar shouts, they cried, "A king! Bring here
> his throne and his royal robes and let him be fitly arrayed!"
So they threw over him a soldier's discarded cloak—this in mockery of the royal purple.
> Then they put a reed in his right hand as a mock scepter.

The only crown they thought him worthy to wear was made of thorns,
> and to show their contempt for his royalty, they mockingly bowed the knee before him.
Then they brought to him their gifts—cruel blows and coarse insults.

Christ's agonies on the cross provided further subjects for their contempt and scorn.

Our Savior could truthfully employ the language of the twenty-second Psalm: "All those who
> see Me ridicule Me; they shoot out the lip, they shake the head" (22:7 NKJV).
We read that those who passed by derided him, shaking their heads, and saying, "If you are
> the Son of God, come down from the cross" (Matthew 27:40).

Yes, at Calvary, the last expiring groans of our Savior
were met with cruel mockery by the heartless rabble around the cross.

How all this must have pained his sensitive spirit
and made him cry out with David,
"O men, how long shall my honor be turned into shame?"

From sermon no. 3276, *Christ's Glory Turned to Shame*

SORROW TURNED INTO JOY

"Truly, truly, I say to you, you will weep and lament, but the world will rejoice.
You will be sorrowful, but your sorrow will turn into joy."
John 16:20

The chief thought connected with our Redeemer's death should be that of grateful praise.

It is a natural cause of sorrow that our Lord Jesus Christ had to die on the cross,
   but sorrow is turned into joy when we discern the glorious fruit of his sufferings
      and know that he saved us on the cross and that he also triumphed in the deed.
We lament our sin, but our hearts rejoice in that death by which he has reconciled us to God.

By all means, let us mourn that Jesus had to die,
   but let us not make mourning the prominent thought in connection with his death.
The language of our text gives permission to weep, but only for a short while
   for it promises to turn the sorrow into joy.

Jesus told his disciples they would "weep and lament" while he was dying, dead, and buried;
   but their sorrow would be turned into joy.
Their grief would end when they saw him risen from the dead;
   and so it did, for we read, "Then the disciples were glad when they saw the Lord" (John 20:20).

The sight of the cross—to their unbelief—was sadness and only sadness;
   but now to the eye of faith, it is the gladdest sight that a human eye can rest upon!
The cross is as the light of the morning, ending the long and dreary darkness that covered the nations.

> *O wounds of Jesus, you are as stars, breaking the night of man's despair!*
> *O spear, you have opened the fountain of healing for mortal woe!*
> *O crown of thorns, you are a constellation of promises!*
>
> *Now eyes that were red with weeping*
> *sparkle with hope at the sight of you, O bleeding Lord!*
>
> *As for your tortured body, O Emmanuel,*
> *the blood that dripped from it cried from the ground*
> *and proclaimed peace, pardon, and paradise to all believers!*
>
> *Though laid in the grave by your weeping friends,*
> *your body, O divine Savior, is no longer in Joseph's tomb!*
> *You have risen from the dead,*
> *and we find in the songs of resurrection and ascension*
> *an abundant solace for the griefs of your death!*

From sermon no. 1442, *Sorrow at the Cross Turned into Joy*

October 18

POOR FOR OUR SAKES

Though he was rich, yet for your sake he became poor,
so that you by his poverty might become rich.
2 Corinthians 8:9

Who can comprehend the boundless riches of God?
Yet, there has never been a poorer man than Jesus Christ.

He who scattered the harvest over the broad acres of the world often hungered.
He who dug the springs of the ocean sat on a well and asked a woman for a drink of water.
He who had been waited on by angels became the Servant of servants, washing his disciples' feet.
He who was once honored with the hallelujahs of ages is now spit on, ridiculed, and despised.
He who was loved by his Father and had a wealth of affection now said, "He who ate my bread
    has lifted his heel against me" (John 13:18).

Oh, for words to picture the humiliation of Christ!

Who can measure the distance between
he who sat on the throne and he who died on the cross?

Who can measure the mighty chasm between
the heights of glory and the cross of deepest woe?

Follow him all along his journey, beginning with his temptations in the wilderness; see him fasting
    and hungering there, surrounded by wild beasts.
Trace him along his weary way as the Man of Sorrows, scorned and hooted at by the profane.
Follow him until at last you meet him in Gethsemane, sweating great drops of blood.
Follow him to Gabbatha, where rivers of blood run beneath the cruel whips of the Roman soldiers.

And finally, with weeping eye follow him to the cross of Calvary and see him nailed there.

Mark his poverty—
    so poor that they have stripped him naked from head to foot;
    so poor that when he asked for water they gave him vinegar to drink;
    so poor that his head is girded with thorns in death!

O thou Mighty Sufferer, what should we admire most—
your heights of glory or your depths of misery?

O Man slain for us, shall we not exalt you?
God over all, blessed forever, shall we not give you our highest praise?

You were indeed rich, yet for our sakes you became poor.

From sermon no. 151, *The Condescension of Christ*

FAITH IN CHRIST'S LOVE

I live by faith in the Son of God, who loved me and gave himself for me.
GALATIANS 2:20

The love of Jesus was *an ancient love.* The verb is in the past tense: "Who *loved* me."

Jesus loved me on the cross.
He loved me in the manger of Bethlehem.
He loved me even before the earth was created.

> *That Christ loves us at all is a great wonder,*
> *but that he loved us always is a wonder of wonders!*

Jesus could not give you any more than himself—he "gave himself."

He gave himself for you in the everlasting covenant when he stood as your Surety and Representative.
He gave himself for you throughout the long ages while he waited to come to earth to redeem you.
He gave himself for you when he became a man, becoming bone of your bone and flesh of your flesh.
He gave himself for you through a life of toil and righteousness.
He gave himself for you as your Substitute when he "bore our sins in his body on the tree."
He gave himself for you in the flogging, the shame, the spitting, the bloody sweat, the Crucifixion.

> *He gave himself to the utmost, the boundless, the inconceivable, the indescribable!*

> *There is a limit to everything else, but not to the love of God.*
> *You say to the sea, "This far you shall come, but no farther,"*
> *but you cannot say that to this boundless sea of divine love.*

You may drink and drink and drink again throughout a long life;
  and yes, throughout all eternity, you may go on receiving of this love;
    but you will never be able to measure its heights, and depths, and lengths, and breadths.
God stops nowhere in his love; it is as boundless and infinite as he is himself.

Saving faith is faith in a person—faith in the living, loving Lord, who gave himself for us.
If you trust him—wholly and alone—then you know that he loved you and gave himself for you.

> *For you the manger at Bethlehem,*
> *for you the cross at Calvary,*
> *for you the empty sepulcher,*
> *for you his pleading before the eternal throne.*

> *He loved you and gave himself for you.*

From sermon no. 2370, *"Christ First, Me Last: Nothing Between but Love"*

CHRIST'S RETURN FROM DEATH

Who is this who comes from Edom, in crimsoned garments from Bozrah,
he who is splendid in his apparel, marching in the greatness of his strength?
ISAIAH 63:1

It appears that the person asking the question knows where the Conqueror has come from
since the text says, "Who is this who comes from Edom, in crimsoned garments from Bozrah?"

Yes, our Redeemer has just returned from death.
The words of the psalmist are now fulfilled: "You will not abandon my soul to Sheol,
or let your holy one see corruption" (16:10).
He has loosed the bands of death and has returned from the land of the enemy.

Oh, how our Lord had fought
with all the adversaries of our souls!
It was a terrible battle!

How thick and fast the arrows flew
at the commencement of the fight!

The garments of our Hero had soon been rolled in blood.
He was literally covered with a bloody sweat.
And how sharp were the arrows that wounded him
when his friends proved to be cowards and one of them betrayed him!

And oh! How terrible were the blades that sheathed themselves in his body and mind!

His head was stabbed with thorns,
his back was cut with knotted whips,
his hands and feet were pierced with nails,
but our Savior did not cease his battle with the evil powers.

The cry was forced from him, "My God, my God, why have you forsaken me?"
but the victorious shout quickly followed, "It is finished."
And there and then he hurled his adversary headlong, crushing his head.

As we see our Lord coming back to us on this Resurrection Day,
we see his garments sprinkled with the blood of all who strove against us.
Our blessed Lord has fought with all the enemies of our souls,
and he has returned from the enemy's country, leading captivity captive.

O child of God, look to Jesus trustfully for his fight is over
and his enemies are crushed like grapes in the winepress.

Worship him this day as King of kings and Lord of lords.

From sermon no. 1947, *Who Is This?*

October 21

INEXPRESSIBLY LOVELY

Yes, he is altogether lovely.
SONG OF SOLOMON 5:16 NKJV

These words are evidently uttered by one who is under the influence of *overwhelming emotion.*
The sentence labors to express the inexpressible; it pants to utter the unutterable!

The bride begins somewhat calmly in her description: "My beloved is radiant and ruddy" (5:10).

She starts at the head and proceeds with various parts of the body of her beloved.
    As she proceeds, she warms, she glows, she flames—and at last the heat that has been repressed
        is like a fire within her and she bursts forth in flaming words!
Here is the live coal from off the altar of her heart: "Yes, he is altogether lovely."

This is the utterance of someone who is completely overcome with admiration
    and feels that in attempting to describe her beloved, she has undertaken a task beyond her power.
Lost in adoring wonder, she avoids description and cries with rapture, "Yes, he is altogether lovely."

This is the way it is with true saints when they are overpowered with the love of Jesus.
Their hearts burn within them!
They mount up with wings like eagles!

They feel what they cannot tell!
They experience what they cannot express!
They are completely enraptured with the sight they have of their all-beauteous Lord!

Lord, reveal yourself to us,
so that we may also be compelled to say,
"Yes, he is altogether lovely."

Oh, that our eyes might see the Lord Jesus
as he is seen by his bosom friends,
and to also sing of those beauties
that are the light and crown of heaven itself!

If you but touch the hem of his garment, you will be made whole. But will this always satisfy you?
    Is it not your desire to get beyond the hem and the garment—
        to get to Christ himself, to his very heart, and then to abide there forever?
Who desires to be forever a babe in grace with a half-awakened consciousness of the Redeemer?

May we never find a place to build our nest while our wing is wandering away from the Tree of Life.
    Like the dove of Noah, may we not find any rest for the sole of our foot
        on anything less than the ark, Christ Jesus, our Savior.
The happiest saints are the ones who are overwhelmed with a sense of the preciousness of Christ.

From sermon no. 1001, *Altogether Lovely*

THE GREAT WINDOW OF LOVE

By this we know love, that he laid down his life for us.
1 JOHN 3:16

There are many of his acts of which it might be said: "By this we know the love of God."
Yet many of us fail to perceive the love that lies behind the actions.

The love of God may be clearly seen in that *he has given us a wise and judicious law.*
   The law of the Ten Commandments is a gift of great kindness
     for it tells us of the wisest and the happiest way of living.
It forbids only that which is injurious to us, and it withholds nothing that is for our happiness.

We have also had *in the daily bounties of Divine Providence* abundant manifestations of God's love.

If our eyes were really opened we would see ...
   that every loaf of bread comes to us as a token of our Father's care,
   that every drop we drink comes as a gift from our Father's bounty.

Are we not clothed by his love?
Who places the breath in our nostrils, but our Creator?
Who preserves us in health, but our great Benefactor?

 If the Lord opened our eyes we would perceive his love in the bountiful gifts surrounding us,
   but still, this is not where we first perceive the love of God.
The cross is the window through which the love of God is best seen,
   and until that window is opened, all the bounties of God's care fail to convince us of his love.

     Perception comes to us through a stained glass window,
     the window that was stained crimson with the blood of Christ.

     There, we truly perceive the love of God
     because "he laid down his life for us."

There is no greater proof of love than for a person to lay down his life for the object of that love.
   All kinds of sacrifices may be made as proofs of affection,
     but the relinquishment of life is the supreme proof of love.
Our Lord Jesus Christ has proven his love for sinners by dying for them.

     The story has been written four times in the Gospels, but not once too often;
     the story of the Son of God, who for our sakes died a felon's death.
     He was barbarously nailed to the cross to bleed away his life.

     Read that story and see how he proved his love for us.

From sermon no. 2959, *God's Love to the Saints*

FELLOWSHIP WITH CHRIST

Fellowship with him.
1 JOHN 1:6

It is our Lord's desire to bring his disciples into union and communion with him;
    and we do hold communion with him by faith and in prayer.
But the most precious seasons of intimate fellowship with him
    are derived from *meditating on his sufferings.*

When we in thought …
    see Christ in Gethsemane and witness the blood-red drops bedewing the soil;
    behold him at Gabbatha, shamed and spit on, mocked and flogged;
    view him at Golgotha and hear his death-cry startling the darkness;
then our hearts are attracted to him, and we love him.

> *While he holds out his hands, and says,*
> *"These were pierced for you,"*
> *we hold out our hearts, and say,*
> *"Here are our hearts, Lord; take and seal them;*
> *they are yours for they are bought with your precious blood."*

Believer, have you experienced this kind of fellowship with your Savior?
If you desire personal communion with him you must find a place to sit down, and—

> *View the flowing*
> *of his soul-redeeming blood,*
> *with divine assurance knowing*
> *he has made your peace with God.*

As you meditate on Christ's sufferings and he descends to talk with you,
    your mind will be freed from the cares of this earth.
You will see your Savior's heart wide open, his hands open, his eyes open, his ears open.

Can you picture Jesus on the cross welcoming sinners?

He has his arms stretched out as though he has them wide open to take in big sinners.
His head is hanging down, as if he is stooping to kiss them.
His feet are pouring out streams of blood, as if his very blood is running after them,
    begging them to come and take it.

Truly, if you see your Savior by faith, each bleeding wound and quivering atom of his body,
    will say to you, "Come and welcome, sinner; come."
But they will also say to you, "Come to Jesus now and hold intimate fellowship with him."

From sermon no. 2572, *Fellowship with Christ*

October 24

DO YOU KNOW HIM?

That I may know him.
PHILIPPIANS 3:10

There are people who know the life of Christ but not Christ the Life.
 Some know Christ's doctrine, and others are delighted with Christ's example.
I find no fault with this, but I want more—I want to "know *him*."
 I love Christ's precepts, but I love *him* more.

The water from Bethlehem's well is sweet,
 and it is certainly worth the struggle of the armed men to win just a bucket from it.
But the well itself is better, and it deserves all of Israel's valor to defend it.

As the source is always more valuable than the stream,
 so Christ is much better than the best words of his lips or the best deeds of his hand.
I want to know him!

I love his works of suffering, of patience, and of holy charity, but I love even more …
 the hands that wrought those master-works,
 the lips that spoke those goodly words,
 the heart that heaved with that matchless love that was the cause of everything.

>*We must get further than Immanuel's achievements, however glorious.*
>*We must come to "know **him**."*

Most believers rest at ease knowing Christ's sacrifice.
 They see Jesus as the Great High Priest laying a great sacrifice on the altar for their sins,
  and with their whole heart they accept his atonement.
But others perceive that Christ not only offered a sacrifice, but was himself the sacrifice,
 and they love him as such—priest, altar, victim, everything.

When I see that he loved me and gave himself for me, it is not enough to know this fact.

I want to know him—the glorious Person who does and is all this.
I want to know the man who thus gave himself for me.
I want to behold the Lamb once slain for me.
I want to rest on that bosom that covers the heart that was pierced with the spear.

I love Calvary, that terrible scene of woe;
 but I love Christ better—the great object of that agony.
His cross and all his sufferings, dear as they are to my mind, only occupy the second place.

The first place is for him—his person, his deity, and his humanity.

From sermon no. 552, *Do You Know Him?*

THE LORD HAS RISEN

"Why do you seek the living among the dead?
He is not here, but has risen."
LUKE 24:5–6

Though Jesus is not dead now, he certainly was dead—he was crucified and buried.

No light remained in his eye.
Thought fled from his thorn-crowned brow.
Speech disappeared from his golden mouth.

They laid him in the sepulcher—a dead man—a fit occupant of the silent tomb.
Yet, as he is not there now but has risen, let us gather around the place where he slept.
In spirit, we will gather up the precious relics of the risen Redeemer.

First, he has left in the grave *the spices* in which his body had been wrapped.

That lowly bed in the earth is now perfumed with costly spices and decked with sweet flowers,
for on its pillow the truest Friend we have once laid his holy head.
We will not start back with horror from the chambers of the dead,
because the Lord himself has traversed them, and where he goes no terror abides.

The Master has also left his *grave clothes* behind.
When Peter went into the sepulcher he saw them carefully folded and lying by themselves.

Our Lord has risen from his couch and has left his grave clothes behind
as a pledge and as a reminder to us in our mortality.
He assures us that, just as he has cast aside the death garments, so will we.

Then, carefully folded up and laid by itself, Jesus left *the cloth* that was wrapped about his head.

Ye widows and ye fatherless children, all ye mourning people,
take this cloth that wrapped your Savior's face and wipe away your tears.
O mourner, just as our Savior rose from the grave, your loved ones will arise!

Lastly, he left behind him an *open passage* from the tomb—an otherwise doorless house of death.
The saints will sleep awhile, but they will surely rise because the stone is rolled away.
A mighty angel rolled it away—for it was very great—and then sat down on it.
As he sat on that stone, he seemed to say to death, "Roll it back again if you can!"

The Savior's empty tomb leaves us many sweet reflections,
which we will ever treasure in our hearts and minds.

From sermon no. 1106, *"The Lord Is Risen Indeed."*

THE SINNER'S SAVIOR

They all grumbled, "He has gone in to be the guest of a man who is a sinner."
LUKE 19:7

Jesus was indeed the guest of a sinner—not only once, but as often as he saw a need.
The object of Christ and the design of the gospel has always been the saving of sinners.

Jesus has not come into the world to save those who are keeping God's law perfectly
     and who are excellent and meritorious in themselves.
Why would he?

Christ does not come to offer needless services to those who are not sin-sick or needy.

Is a Savior needed for those who are not lost?
Do the rich need alms?
Do the healthy need medicine?
Do the innocent need pardon?
These are all needless things.

Gospel promises are addressed to the guilty.
Who else would need abundant pardon?

Gospel invitations are addressed to the sinful.
Who else would be entreated to wash but those who are foul?

Gospel blessings are for those who have transgressed and are under condemnation.
Who else would value forgiveness and justification?

Now the Lord Jesus did not even ask Zacchaeus to wash his little finger,
     before he said, "Hurry and come down, for I must stay at your house today" (Luke 19:5).

In the parable, did the Father not receive his returning son at once?
How many minutes did he wait before he kissed him?
How many times did the Prodigal Son wash his face before his father pressed him to his bosom?

The father did not even tell his son to wash his hands, though he had been feeding swine;
     but, there and then, he embraced him and kissed him.
Our Lord Jesus, not only has pity on sinners, he also treats them with love.
     He comes under their roof and brings salvation to their homes.

Blessed be the name of Jesus,
all this is true and we have no wish to conceal it:
"He has gone in to be the guest of a man who is a sinner."

From sermon no. 1319, *The Sinner's Savior*

HOLDING OUR BELOVED

I found him whom my soul loves.
I held him, and would not let him go.
SONG OF SOLOMON 3:4

Notice the steps in the bride's progress. The first one is, *"I love him."*
We can think of many, many reasons why we should love the Christ of Calvary.

Can we kneel at the cross and not kiss the feet of him who suffered and died for our sins?
Can we see him risen from the grave and not long, as Mary did, to cling to him?
Can we hear him saying, "Peace I leave with you" (John 14:27) and not feel delight in him?

Each one of us should be able to say, "I love him," "I sought him," and now, *"I have found him."*
The heart that seeks the King in his beauty will never be satisfied unless he is consciously enjoyed.

The least drop of Christ's love, consciously realized,
has more sweetness in it than all of heaven without it.

The love of Jesus is another word for heaven.

It is a marvel that even while we are here on this earth,
we are permitted to enjoy a bliss beyond what the angels know.
They have never tasted redeeming grace and dying love;
but that joy is ours if we can truly say, "I have found him."

After finding him, the bride says, "I held him."
How are we to hold Christ?

Well, you will hold him by making him your all in all.
You will have to walk as he would have you walk in careful holiness and earnest service for him.
If you want to walk with Jesus there must be harmony of heart.

Is there anything in this vile world that is fit to stand in rivalry with him?
Is there any gain, any joy, any beauty that can be compared to his gain, his joy, his beauty?

This must be our cry: "Christ for me! Go, harlot-world! Do not even come to the outside of my door,
   for my heart is with my Lord, and he is my soul's chief treasure."[1]

Thou Son of God made flesh for me,
you are all my salvation and all my desire!
I love you supremely, desiring to honor and obey you until death.

I hold you, thou Covenant Angel, and will not let you go![2]

[1]From sermon no. 2485, *Love's Vigilance Rewarded*
[2]From sermon no. 1035, *The Real Presence, the Great Want of the Church*

A TYPE AND ITS TEACHING

Abraham said, "God will provide for himself the lamb for a burnt offering, my son."
GENESIS 22:8

The old man, a kind and doting father, bears in his hands a sharp knife and hot coals of fire,
    while the younger man—possibly thirty-three years of age—
comes toiling up the hillside by his side, bearing a load of wood on his back.

The son knows that the wood is destined to burn a victim for his father carries the fire and the knife.
He knows they are about to worship God in a very solemn manner by a sacrifice of blood.

Along the way, wondering where the victim is, he asks one question,
    "Behold, the fire and the wood, but where is the lamb?" (Genesis 22:7).
With indescribable grief, Abraham tells him that God will provide for himself a lamb.

Little did Isaac realize that he was to be that lamb;
    and when they come to the appointed place,
no doubt Abraham tells his son what God has directed him to do.

The young man is strong, but the old man has lost some of his youthful vigor,
    so if the young man chooses to struggle, the intent would be frustrated.
But he, like his father, is ready to say to the sovereign command of God: "Here I am."

He allows himself to be bound by his aged father—no, helps to put himself on the altar—
    and there he lies a willing victim: willing to die, there and then, at God's command.
And here we have a picture of the Almighty One, whom we address as "our Father";
    and here we also see his Son, his only Son—his Isaac—who fills his heart with gladness.

He bears on his back the load of wood—the cross.
No, our blessed Jesus, the antitype of Isaac, bears a heavier load than the cross!
The sin of all his people lay heavily on his shoulders.

He turns upwards to the hill of Calvary. And there in the thick darkness the Father binds his Son
    while the Son lies there submissively, allowing himself to be fastened to the tree.
Then, the Omnipotent hand unsheathes the knife to slay his Son,
    and he does not draw back, but in sovereign vengeance slays him!

> *That picture of Abraham with the knife in his hand, about to execute Isaac,*
> *is a picture of God the Father about to smite his one and only Son on Mount Calvary.*

Now consider the emotions of the Father's heart.

Can you smite your own child without feeling more anguish than you inflict?
Yet, God smites even to death his only beloved Son.

From sermon no. 3523, *A Type and Its Teaching*

THE RAM OF GOD

Abraham said, "God will provide for himself the lamb for a burnt offering, my son."
GENESIS 22:8

You will remember that Jesus once said, "Abraham rejoiced to see My day" (John 8:56 NKJV).
When did he see it?
Why, it must have been on this occasion.

The venerable patriarch had seen in his son Isaac a vivid picture of the Son of God;
but when you see that his hand is stayed, you know at once that the portrait is incomplete.
A ram is caught in the thicket, and this ram is laid hold of and put in Isaac's place.

So far the delineation is accurate, for the ram dies;
it is really slain, even as Christ was sacrificed for us.
The vision changes its form—Isaac goes free, but not so the ram.

Isaac's blood still flowed in his veins, but that is not the case with the ram;
the knife keenly severs his arteries and the blood pours out.
There is the ram, laid on the wood, quickly glowing and smoking as a burnt offering.

Isaac gazes on that burning body—that body that should have been his—
and he knows that he owes his life to the victim that was presented as a substitute.

> *O Christian, look earnestly,*
> *gaze intently, linger fondly on the picture,*
> *for it represents your own salvation!*

> *See yourself standing there instead of Isaac*
> *for that is your place.*

Because our Lord Jesus Christ—the ram of God's burnt offering—
really did burn on the altar for us, we are spared.
I cannot tell you how Isaac felt when the cords were loosed and he narrowly escaped death;
nor can I tell you how I felt, when standing at the foot of the cross—

> *"I beheld the flowing*
> *Of my dear Redeemer's blood,*
> *With assurance, knowing*
> *He had made my peace with God."*

O Christian, there are no longer any cords binding Isaac because he was set free,
and neither are there any bonds on you.
You can say with David, "O Lord, I am your servant … You have loosed my bonds" (Psalm 116:16)

From sermon no. 3523, *A Type and Its Teaching*

ALL HAIL THE KING!

The LORD *is king forever and ever.*
PSALM 10:16

We have seen our well-beloved Monarch humiliated and wounded during his days on earth. "He was despised and rejected by men; a man of sorrows, and acquainted with grief" (Isaiah 53:3).

He whose brightness is as the morning
wore a sackcloth of sorrow for his daily dress.

Shame was his cloak and reproach was his garment.

Yet now, because he has triumphed over all the powers of darkness on the bloodstained tree, our faith beholds our "king in his beauty" (Isaiah 33:17), robed in the splendor of victory. We recognize him as King by divine right, and every believing heart would gladly crown him.

Yes, he shall reign! All hail to thee, King Jesus!

Go forth, ye virgin souls who love your Lord!
Bow at his feet!
Carpet his way with the lilies of your love
and with the roses of your gratitude!

Our Lord Jesus is King in Zion by right of conquest, for he has slain our enemies who held us in cruel bondage. In the Red Sea of his own blood our Redeemer has drowned the Pharaoh of our sins.

He has delivered us
from the iron yoke and the heavy curse of the law,
so will the Liberator not be crowned?

We are his portion, whom he has taken out of the hand of the enemy, and who will snatch his conquest from his hand? God has declared that he will give him a portion with the great, and that he will divide the spoils with the strong (Isaiah 53:12).

We are the spoils.
We are the trophies of his victory.
We are the treasure for which he laid down his life.

We, therefore, who have believed in Jesus, accept him as our King. We rejoice to see him established on the throne of his Father, on his holy hill of Zion.

From sermon no. 752, *The King in His Beauty*

WE SHALL SEE HIM

We shall see him as he is.
1 JOHN 3:2

All of us who love our Lord Jesus have an insatiable desire to behold him.
 Remember how Moses asked to see God, and Job said, "In my flesh I shall see God, whom I shall
  see for myself, and my eyes shall behold, and not another. My heart faints within me!" (19:26-27).
And the psalmist said, "I shall behold your face in righteousness" (17:15).

Oh, we rejoice to find a verse such as this,
for it tells us that our curiosity will be satisfied,
our desire consummated, our bliss perfected:

"We shall see him as he is."

Yes, we will see our Savior, not abased in his incarnation, but exalted in his glory.

We will not behold him subject to the weaknesses and sorrows and infirmities he once bore.
We will have no need to pity the man who had once wiped the hot sweat from his burning brow.
We will not see his eyes, wearied from lack of sleep.
We will not behold his hands, tired in labor, or his feet bleeding from arduous journeys.

We will see him, not with a peasant's garb, but with the empire of the universe upon his shoulders.
We will not see him mocked and spit on and insulted, but we will see him exalted.
We will no longer see Christ as the Man of Sorrows, but as Christ the God-man—
 radiant with splendor, clothed with rainbows, crowned with stars, the sun beneath his feet!

Oh, glorious vision!
How can we guess what he is?

Yet, with all his splendor unveiled, all his glories unclouded,
we shall see him as he is!

There will be no tempting devil near him for he has crushed the Dragon's head.
There will be no insulting people as the redeemed cast their crowns before him.
There will be no molesting demons as angels sound his lofty praise through every golden street.

Yes, we will see him—not abhorred, not despised and rejected—
 but worshiped, honored, crowned, exalted!
We will see him served by the redeemed and worshiped by cherubim and seraphim.

"We shall see him as he is."

From sermon no. 61, *The Beatific Vision*

HIS NAME IS "MIGHTY GOD"

And his name shall be called ... Mighty God.
Isaiah 9:6

Let us see how Christ has proved himself to be "Mighty God."

The passage from which the text is taken says, "To us a child is born."
    A child! A child totters in its walk; it trembles in its steps;
        and this is a newborn baby feeding at its mother's breast.
That! Can that child work wonders?

Yes, says the prophet, "To us a child is born,"
    but then it is added, "To us a son is given."
Christ was not only born, he was also given.

As man, he is a child born.
As God, he is a son given.
He comes down from on high and is given by God to become our Redeemer.

But here behold the wonder!
This child's name "shall be called Wonderful Counselor, Mighty God."

This child born—this son given—came into the world to enter into the battle with sin.
He had to wrestle with temptations more numerous and more terrible than we have ever known.

Adam fell when just a woman tempted him, and Eve fell when but a serpent offered fruit to her;
    but Christ, the Second Adam, stood invulnerable against all the shafts of Satan.
He thus proved himself to have the immaculate holiness of the Eternal One,
    before whom angels veil their faces, and cry, "Holy, holy, holy, Lord God of hosts!"

We can also see Christ as "Mighty God" when "he bore our sins in his body on the tree."

The heart of Christ became like a reservoir in the midst of mountains.
    All the tributary streams of iniquity, and every drop of sin,
        ran down and gathered into one vast lake, deep as hell and as shoreless as eternity.
All these met, as it were, in Christ's heart; and yet he endured them all.

With many signs of human weakness, but with convincing signs of divine omnipotence,
    Jesus was more than a conqueror, putting our sins to a public execution.
And he did even more, descending into the grave and being fettered fast with the cold chains of death;
    but when the appointed hour arrived, he snapped the bands of death as if they were but straw.

Who is the death of death, the plague of the grave, the destroyer of destruction, but God?
Christ has proved himself then to be "Mighty God."

From sermon no. 258, *His Name—The Mighty God*

CHRIST'S CARE FOR HIS DISCIPLES

Jesus answered, "I told you that I am he.
So, if you seek me, let these men go."
JOHN 18:8

Notice how Jesus cares for his disciples' safety even while the soldiers are seizing and binding him.
They will take him to prison and to death, but he has no word to say in his own defense.
His only thought is for his disciples.

It is even more remarkable that Jesus thought of his disciples, considering *his great agony.*
He had just come from the garden, all crimson with the bloody sweat.
Yet he revealed no care for himself—only for the safety of his followers.

That crimson sweat meant a heart flowing out at every pore with love.

Jesus had been brought to the lowest point of endurance;
yet his only thought was for his disciples.

Our Lord Jesus was already faint with agony, even though the heat of the battle had only begun.
He was also fully aware of the cruel death to follow; he knew all that was to be done to him.

He knew he would be mocked, spit on, and flogged.
He knew the crown of thorns would tear his temples.
He knew he would be led forth like a criminal, bearing the gibbet on his shoulders.
He knew his hands and feet would be nailed to the cross.
He knew his Father must forsake him because of the sin laid on him.

He knew all that. These huge Atlantic billows of grief were already casting their spray in his face;
   his lips were already salted with the brine of his coming grief, but he did not think of that.
His only thought was for his beloved disciples.

Until he dies, he will keep his eye on his sheep,
and he will grasp his shepherd's staff with which to drive off the foe.

Oh, the all-absorbing, self-consuming love of Christ!

Jesus continued to think of his disciples even when *he knew what they were.*
They had slept while he lay in anguish covered with a bloody sweat.
He knew that all of the eleven would forsake him and flee and that one of them would deny him.

You who love Jesus and yet often fail him, gather strength.
Even as Jesus cared for his disciples then,
he cares for his disciples now.

From sermon no. 2368, *The Living Care of the Dying Christ*

THE BLOOD OF THE COVENANT

"This is the blood of the covenant that God commanded for you."
HEBREWS 9:20

The Son of God covenanted with God on our behalf that he would vindicate the broken law
and that he would also keep the smallest dot and letter of the law for us.

As for the Father, he covenanted that because of the sacrifice the Son would offer
and the obedience he would render,
he would put away the sin of his people and they would be accepted in love.

How dreadfully in earnest was God the Father when he gave his Son!
How deeply in earnest was the Son when he gave his life!

The blood of the covenant is also a guarantee of its infinite provision.
"He who did not spare his own Son but gave him up for us all,
how will he not also with him graciously give us all things?" (Romans 8:32).
All our wants are very small compared to what we have already received in the gift of Jesus Christ.

Do you believe, O heart, that God will deny you anything that is necessary
when he has already given his Son to bleed for you?

If he had held back anything, it would have been the costly alabaster flask of his Son's body,
which contained the most precious ointment that ever perfumed earth or heaven;
but since he broke that precious body and poured out the priceless contents,
you may be sure that he will withhold nothing good from you.

God would break up heaven itself if you required it,
and he would pour out all creation at your feet if you needed it.

Already he has given you his angels to be your servants,
his courts to be your dwelling place,
and his throne to be your shelter!

Yet, if you ask for more, there is more provided for he gives you himself.
When he gave you his Son, he gave you all, for his Son is one with him.

Oh, the breadth and length, the height and depth of covenant provisions!
That scroll of love, which has for its seal this precious thing—the blood of Jesus—
must contain treasures beyond all estimation!

"God will supply every need of yours
according to his riches in glory in Christ Jesus" (Philippians 4:19).
The blood of Jesus secures this fact.

From sermon no. 1567, *The Blood of the Testament*

CLOTHED WITH RICHES

According to the riches of his grace.
EPHESIANS 1:7

A man's riches may often be judged by the way he dresses his family.
A poor man's children, though comfortably dressed, are not clothed like the children of princes.

Let us then look at God's children. In what type of garments are they clothed?

God's children are wrapped about with a robe—a seamless robe—
    a robe that neither earth nor heaven could ever buy, should it ever be lost.
For texture, this robe excels the finest linen of earth, and for whiteness it is purer than the snow.

No looms on earth could ever weave this robe,
    but Jesus spent his whole life, working my robe of righteousness.
There was a drop of blood in every throw of the shuttle,
    and every thread was made of his heart's agonies.

It is a robe that is divine, complete—
    a better one than Adam wore in the perfection of Eden.
He had but a human righteousness, though a perfect one,
    but we have a divinely perfect righteousness.

O my soul, what riches of divine grace there must be
in the God who clothes you so gloriously!

If you would know the full riches of divine grace …
    read the Father's heart when he sent his Son to the earth to die;
    read the lines on the Father's countenance when he pours out his wrath upon his beloved Son;
    read the mysterious handwriting on the Savior's flesh and soul while he quivers on the cross in agony.

If you would know love …
    you must go to Gethsemane and see a man so full of pain that his head, his hair, and his garments
        are all dripping with blood;
    you must see the Omnipotent mocked by his creatures;
    you must hear the Eternal One groaning out his life and crying in the agonies of death, "My God,
        my God, why have you forsaken me?" (Matthew 27:46).

The riches of God's grace are infinite!
They are inexhaustible; they are all-sufficient!
There is enough to richly clothe every soul that comes to him.

From sermon no. 295, *The Treasure of Grace*

THE LAW FULFILLED

"This is the name by which he will be called:
'The Lord is our righteousness.'"
JEREMIAH 23:6

Jesus Christ is the Alpha and Omega of *the great law of God.*

Human nature cannot fulfill even a single letter of the law's demands.
We do not know its first letter: "You shall love the Lord your God with all your heart" (Matthew 22:37).
We also know very little of the next: "You shall love your neighbor as yourself" (Matthew 22:39).

But if you would see the law fulfilled, look to Jesus, our blessed Lord and Master.
Where will you find anything that will compare with his love for God?

And what love for man is always exhibited in him!
He is even better than the Good Samaritan!

The Samaritan had given of his wine and his oil and his pennies, but Jesus gives himself—
    gives his heart's blood instead of wine,
    gives the anointing of the Holy Spirit instead of oil,
    gives his own flesh and blood for us to feed on.

All the love that has ever gleamed in human hearts—
    if it could be gathered together—would be but a spark,
while his great love for us would be like a flaming furnace.

So, if you are in Christ Jesus, do not permit legal fears to distress you.
Do not fear that your failures in obedience will destroy your soul.

Seek holiness, but never put your trust in your holiness.
Seek virtue, but when you see your imperfections, do not despair.

Your saving righteousness is the righteousness of Christ.
    That in which God accepts you is Christ's perfect obedience.
The spirit of the law breathes through his whole life of holiness and service;
    and as for the letter of the law, he carried it out to its extremity.

The commandment may be exceedingly broad,
but not broader than the life of Christ.

The law may ask for perfection,
but it could not ask for greater perfection
than is found in the One whose name is
"The Lord is our righteousness."

From sermon no. 546, *Alpha and Omega*

THE CROWNING ACT OF SHAME

But one of the soldiers pierced his side with a spear,
and at once there came out blood and water.
JOHN 19:34

Our Lord was the object of inconceivable abuse and shame.

He was scourged like a felon.
He was spat on and mocked.
The thorn-crown, the scepter of reed, and the old scarlet cloak—who could have invented a more
   shameful insignia for One who was greater than all the kings of the earth?

And our Lord's death itself was a great part of his shame.
It was a shame for him to die, and it was a disgrace for him to die hanging on a cross.

But when Christ is actually dead, you would expect the scorn to cease;
      but no, since the brutal Roman soldiers are not very nice as to what they do with living bodies,
         you cannot expect them to be overly nice as to what they do with dead bodies.
Thus we see this soldier—in a wanton act of brutality—thrusting his spear into the Savior's heart!

This was the last kick of the old enemy.

It was, as it were, the last of the spittle
from the foul mouth of human slander and hatred.

It was the last vicious thrust that human malice could devise
against the Lord of life and glory.

In this brutal piercing of our Savior's heart,
we see the crowning emblem of the shame he endured.

When the soldier's spear found Christ's heart, it released a double flood of blood and water,
   and John explains this by saying that our Lord "came by water and blood" (1 John 5:6).
Christ came into the world by blood to take away sin's guilt, and by water to take away sin's power.
   He came by blood to remove the punishment of sin, and by water to remove the filth of sin.

O sinner, if you want to be doubly washed, go to Christ for the washing!

His blood can wash you from the accumulated filth of years,
and the water from his side can take away your propensities to sin.

It can change your nature and make you holy instead of filthy,
and it can make you pure in heart instead of polluted in spirit.

From sermon no. 3311, *The Water and the Blood*

THE RIDER ON THE WHITE HORSE

I saw heaven opened, and behold, a white horse!
The one sitting on it is called Faithful and True,
and in righteousness he judges and makes war.
REVELATION 19:11

John saw our Captain, the King of kings, in his glorious state.

While Jesus was here on earth, he was a foot soldier.
He had to plunge knee-deep through mire and dirt, walking as wearily as anyone else,
but now that he has ascended he fights in another manner.
Our Lord is described as sitting on a gallant white steed, which means that he is greatly honored now.

In royal state our Lord Jesus goes forth to war,
not as a weary, dusty, fainting footman
but as a glorious King royally mounted.

The horse in this vision also symbolizes power.

Jesus was crucified in weakness, giving his hands and his feet to the nails,
but there is no sign of weakness in him now.
He is now mounted on the horse of his exceedingly great power, and he rules in heaven and earth,
and none can stay his hand, or put him to dishonor, or dispute his will.

O ye who love your Lord, feast your eyes on him this day!

Let your eyes be satiated with the image of him
who was once despised and rejected,
now taking to himself his great honor and power.

The color of the horse denotes victory.
There is a pale horse in Revelation, and the name of him who sits on him is Death;
and there is a horse, red with blood, and yet another, black with judgment.
But this horse is white, signifying comfort and joy to all who know and love Jesus.

He comes to fight, but the fight is for peace.
He comes as a conqueror, but it is as a delivering conqueror, who breaks only the oppressor
but blesses the citizens whom he emancipates.

O ye who have wept at Gethsemane, lift up your eyes and smile
as you see that same Redeemer, who once lay groveling beneath the olive trees,
now riding on the white horse of victory!

Your Lord, at this moment, is no longer despised.
All the glory that heaven itself can devise is lavished on him.

From sermon no. 1452B, *The Rider on the White Horse and the Armies with Him*

CHRIST'S GREAT MISSION

"The Son of Man came not to be served but to serve,
and to give his life as a ransom for many."
MATTHEW 20:28

Though our Lord had set his heart on being the incarnate God, he had nothing to gain by it.
Gain! What could the infinite God gain?

Splendor? Behold the stars—far away they glitter beyond all mental count!
Servants? Behold angels in their squadrons—thousands of angels are the chariots of the Almighty!
Honor? The trump of fame forever proclaims him, King of kings and Lord of lords!

Who can add to the splendor of that diadem that makes the sun and moon grow pale in comparison?
Who can add to the riches or the wealth of the One who has all things at his disposal?

Christ comes then "not to be served but to serve."

You see him in the workshop, serving his earthly father.
You see him in his home, honoring his mother with filial obedience.
You see him in the midst of his disciples, much more their servant than their master.

As he kneels down and washes his disciples' feet, you can see the meekness of his disposition.
And soon after this, you see him giving up himself in order to serve us.

Behold! Behold and wonder! Behold and love! Behold and trust!

Jesus comes from the right hand of God
to the manger, to the cross, to the sepulcher—
not to be served but to serve the sons of men.

Jesus did not come to earth merely to be an example; he came purposely to give his soul as a ransom.

Our Lord Jesus gave up the very essence of his humanity in order to be a substitutionary sacrifice for us.
    His spirit was tortured with inexpressible anguish.
He was like a splendid cluster put into the winepress, and the feet of eternal vengeance trod on him
    until the sacred wine of his atoning blood streamed forth to save the sons of men.

Oh, that our eyes could gaze within the wounds of Jesus
and into that heart boiling like a cauldron with the wrath of God,
oppressed, burdened, tormented, and filled with inconceivable anguish!

He came from heaven to suffer all this
so that he could be the victim of a vengeance we deserved;
so that his sorrows and griefs might rescue us from destruction.

From sermon no. 3532, *Christ's Great Mission*

THE LOWLINESS OF OUR LORD

"I am gentle and lowly in heart."
MATTHEW 11:29

Think of the lowliness of our Lord when he came to this earth and veiled his godhead.
    His sojourn here was full of the truest greatness;
        but it was a grandeur, not of loftiness, but of lowliness; not of glory but of humiliation.
Our Lord has never been more glorious, in the deepest sense, than in his humiliation.

He showed his lowliness in that *he assumed our nature.*

A free spirit voluntarily encased itself in human clay;
a pure spirit willingly became a partaker of flesh and blood.
This is marvelous lowliness!

The strong was compassed with infirmity;
the happy assumed the capacity for suffering;
the infinitely holy became one with a race notorious for its iniquity.
This is a triumph of lowliness!

The great God, the Infinite of ages, united himself with a human body.
He was born into our infancy, grew up into our youth, toiled through our manhood.
This is a miracle of lowliness!

The angels must still gaze into these things and wonder at the Word made flesh.
They wondered that he would eat and drink and sleep and sigh and suffer—just like his creatures.
Surely they still talk of it now with hushed voices and astonished hearts.

To crown all, our Well-beloved *died.*
He laid down his life for us—dearest pledge of lowliness!

The decease that he accomplished at Jerusalem was no famous death in battle
    amid the roar of cannon and the blast of trumpet, shaking heaven and earth with tidings of victory.
His was no death amid the tears of a nation that prepares a royal mourning for its beloved prince.

No, he dies with criminals; he dies at the common gallows; he dies amid a crowd of scoffers
    where even felons cast contempt on him as he hangs between them.
Hear the scoffers challenging his deity: "If you are the Son of God, come down from the cross."

This lowliness was such as only our God could display.
Who else could bear such infamy and endure such scorn?

This we humbly admire and feebly imitate but never can equal.

From sermon no. 1861, *The Lowly King*

OUR SAVIOR'S PATIENCE

I waited patiently for the LORD; he inclined to me and heard my cry.
PSALM 40:1

Our Savior's conduct when he was under the smarting rod was that of waiting.
   He waited upon his Father all his life, and this was even more obvious in his Passion and death.
He went to Gethsemane and there he prayed earnestly, but with sweet submission,
   "Nevertheless, not as I will, but as you will" (Matthew 26:39).

He rose up from this prayer all crimson with his bloody sweat and went forth to meet his foes,
   delivering himself up voluntarily to be led as a sheep to the slaughter.
He did not unsheathe the sword as Peter did, nor did he flee like his disciples,
   but he waited upon the will of the Most High, enduring all things until he was given deliverance.

When they took him before Annas and Caiaphas, Pilate and Herod, hurrying him from bar to bar,
   how patiently he kept silent even though false witnesses appeared against him!
When they nailed him to the tree and there he hung—tortured, fevered, agonizing—
   his words were not those of murmuring or regret, but of pity, pain, patience, and submission.

> *Until he bowed his head and gave up his spirit,*
> *he bowed his whole being to his Father's will,*
> *awaiting his time and pleasure.*

Oh, if you would see patience, look at Jesus on the cross!
   Our blessed Lord gave himself up completely, without the slightest sign of agitation.
His murderers sat down around the cross and mocked him, jeered at him, insulted him,
   but he did not utter a single word of rebuke.

> *In our Savior's body on the tree,*
> *patience was written out in crimson characters.*

Now this was needful for the completion of his great work of atonement,
   because no expiation could have been made by an impatient Savior.
Only a perfect obedience could satisfy the law,
   and only an unblemished sacrifice could put away our sins.

> *There must be about our Substitute*
> *no trace of resistance to the Father's will.*

> *As a sacrifice, he must not struggle against the cords,*
> *nor turn his head away from the sacrificial knife.*

From sermon no. 1674, *Brought Up from the Horrible Pit*

OUR PLACE IS AT JESUS' FEET

At his feet.
LUKE 7:38

Whether we pray standing as Abraham did, or sitting as David did, or kneeling as Elias did,
  let us take care that the posture of the soul is carefully observed.
The best position for our heart is at Jesus' feet.

We may know Jesus as a man. But he is also God, and on his head are many diadems.
We cannot think of him without bowing in lowly adoration before him.

O Jesus, you are exceedingly glorious!

Behold, every tongue will confess that you are Lord,
and every knee will bow before you! (See Philippians 2:10–11.)
So with glad prostration of spirit we bow at your feet even now!

Well may we bow at his feet when we remember our unworthiness.
How can we aspire to a higher position when we think of our sinfulness?

Oh, if I may but sit forever at his feet
and look up and bless him
that he loved me and gave himself for me,
it will be an everlasting heaven to my spirit!

When John was on the Isle of Patmos and he saw his beloved Master,
  he did not attempt to place his head on his bosom.
Remember his words: "When I saw him, I fell at his feet as though dead" (Revelation 1:17).

Now if someone like John the divine lay there "at his feet," surely that is the best position for us too.

Oh, let us get there!
Down, down, down, high looks!
Down with you, proud thoughts!
Down with you, legal hopes and self-confidence!

Away, away, with everything that uplifts man,
and may Christ alone be exalted while we lie at his feet!

The Lord has "put all things under his feet" (Ephesians 1:22),
so let us put ourselves "at his feet."

From sermon no. 2066, *Our Place: At Jesus' Feet*

CHRIST IN BONDS

Annas then sent him bound to Caiaphas the high priest.
JOHN 18:24

Here we see Christ in bonds—a king in chains!

The captors bound him, perhaps fearing that he would break loose or in some way outwit them.
They also bound him, no doubt, to increase his shame.

Jesus said to those who came to arrest him in the garden, "Have you come out as against a robber,
    with swords and clubs to capture me?" (Matthew 26:55).
They bound him fast as though he were a thief, perhaps tying his hands with cords behind his back,
    to show that they regarded him as a felon.

This binding of the Savior also increased his pain.
    It was in Gethsemane that he was arrested and bound and led away to Annas,
        and there is no indication that Annas loosened his bonds or that he was granted any relief.
With the cruel ropes still binding him fast, he was sent off to Caiaphas.

O cruel persecutors, look into your Savior's face!

If you are resolved to lead him away to his death,
you may lead him like a sheep going to the slaughter.
He will not even open his mouth to criticize you!

There was no need to put cords on one so meek and gentle.

They tried to express their hatred by every conceivable method,
    both in the little details and in the great end to which they were aiming.
Their goal was to put him to a most painful death.

How shamefully our blessed Master was treated
in this cruel and inhospitable world!

Men were putting to death the Son of God himself;
but before they did it,
they heaped on him all the scorn and dishonor possible
so that he might die with disgrace as well as with pain.

We must remember that our Savior was bound with our bonds.
We had sinned against God, incurring the sentence of infallible justice, and now that sentence fell on him.

When he was made sin for us, we were made the righteousness of God in him (2 Corinthians 5:21).
When he died, then we lived; when he was bound, we were set free.

From sermon no. 2822, *Christ in Bonds*

HIS FAVORITE NAME

"For the Son of Man came to seek and to save the lost."
LUKE 19:10

No prophet or apostle needed to call himself by way of distinction the son of man.
It would be ridiculous for any man to speak of himself emphatically as the son of man.

Therefore, when we hear our Lord calling himself by this name,
   we are compelled to contrast it with his higher nature.
We see deep condescension when he chooses to be called the Son of Man instead of the Son of God.

O my soul, he who has come to save you is so plainly God
that he feels he must remind you that he is also the Son of Man.

It is no angel's arm that is stretched out for your salvation;
it is the arm of the One who created all worlds.

In speaking of himself as the Son of Man,
   our Lord is telling us that he has come to us in a *condescending character.*
Jehovah Jesus did not come down to us in his chariot of wrath, girded with the sword of vengeance.

He has come on his errand of mercy …
   as one who has lain on a woman's breast,
   as one who has known weakness, suffering, and want,
   as one who has known by personal experience the lowliness of our position.

O sinner, is it not a joy to know that the Son of God
has come to save you as the Son of Man?

"The Son of Man."
That also describes the *tenderness* of his character—a man can sympathize with a man.

He is not a judge of severe countenance, but Jesus, "a man of sorrows, and acquainted with grief."
He comes to us as our Brother, able to "sympathize with our weaknesses" (Hebrews 4:15).

O guilty one, you are dealing with an attractive Savior!

Jesus is your Brother; he is the Friend of sinners
for he received them and ate with them (Luke 7:34),
and it is he who "came to seek and to save the lost."

Go to him without fear
and pour out your broken heart at his feet.
Appeal to his manly heart—his brotherly sympathies—
and you will be tenderly received.

From sermon no. 1100, *Good News for the Lost*

ALL BEAUTIES UNITED IN ONE

Behold, you are beautiful, my beloved.
SONG OF SOLOMON 1:16

Just as all rivers meet in the sea, so all beauties unite in our Redeemer.

Take the character of any gracious person and you will find a measure of loveliness, but it has its limits.
    Peter has many virtues, but he also has many failings.
        John, too, excels, but in certain areas he is deficient.
Our Lord transcends all his saints; all human and divine virtues are harmoniously combined in him.

He is not this flower or that; he is the paradise of perfection.
He is not a star here or a constellation there; he is the whole heaven of stars.
No, he is the heaven of heavens! He is all that is fair and lovely, condensed into one.[1]

Jesus is a picture of beauty and a breastplate of glory.
    In him, all the "things of good repute" are in their proper places and assist in adorning each other.
Not one feature in his glorious person attracts attention at the expense of another,
    but he is perfect and altogether lovely.

His power, his grace, his justice, his tenderness, his truth, his majesty, and his immutability
    make up such a man—or rather such a God-man—as neither heaven nor earth has seen elsewhere.
His infancy, his eternity, his sufferings, his triumphs, his death, and his immortality
    are all woven in one gorgeous and seamless tapestry.

O Jesus, you are music without discord;
you are many, but not divided;
you are all things, but not diverse.

As all the colors blend
into one resplendent rainbow,
so all the glories of heaven and earth
meet in you.

They unite so wondrously
that there is none like you in all things.

If all the most excellent virtues
were bound in one bundle,
they could not rival you.

You are the mirror of all perfection.[2]

[1] From sermon no. 1001, *Altogether Lovely*
[2] *Morning and Evening*, June 21 (M)

BEARING OUR SCORN AND SHAME

The soldiers twisted together a crown of thorns and put it on his head
and arrayed him in a purple robe.
They came up to him, saying, "Hail, King of the Jews!"
JOHN 19:2–3

Come to Gabbatha and there behold your Lord bearing the ridicule and the insults of his creatures.

A crown of thorns was placed on his head and a purple robe was cast over his shoulders in mockery. The soldiers made our Lord a mimic monarch—a carnival king.

> *Behold, how he has left all the honor of his Father's house;*
> *and here he stands with a mock robe, a mimic scepter, and a thorny crown—*
> *the butt of ridicule, scoffed at by all!*

Yet this must be so because sin is a shameful thing and part of the penalty of sin is shame.
Shame fell on Adam when he sinned; then and there he knew that he was naked,
and now shame has come down in a tremendous hail upon the head of the Second Adam.
Being the Substitute for shameful man, he is covered with contempt.

It is hard to say whether cruelty or mockery had most to do with our Lord's sufferings at Gabbatha,
but by enduring these two things together he laid the cornerstone of his dominion of love and grace.
His sorrow secured his power to save and his shame endowed him with the right to bless.

Earth had been a vast prison and men a race of condemned criminals,
but he who stands before us at Gabbatha in all his shame and grief has delivered us.
Therefore, he who was made nothing for our sakes becomes everything to us.[1]

> *O Savior, you are indeed very precious to us!*
>
> *Dearest of all the names above, our Savior and our God,*
> *you are always glorious;*
> *but in our eyes you are never more lovely*
> *than when arrayed in shameful mockery!*
>
> *Neither the delights of the flesh nor the pride of life*
> *has any charms while the Man of Sorrows is in view!*
>
> *Oh, "worthy is the Lamb" (Revelation 5:12)!*
> *We worship you!*
> *We adore you!*
> *We bless you!* [2]

[1] From sermon no. 1353, *Ecce Rex*
[2] From sermon no. 1168, *The Crown of Thorns*

STERN JUSTICE

So that he might be just and the justifier of the one who has faith in Jesus.
ROMANS 3:26

Just pause and think of the relationship that Jesus had with the Great Judge of all the earth, and then you will understand why the law was fully satisfied.

We have heard of Brutus, the inflexible lawgiver, who, when he sat on the bench, made no distinction between individuals. His justice was greatly admired because even when the noblest Roman senator was convicted of a crime and condemned, without mercy he was taken away by the lictors[1] to his doom.

Now imagine Brutus' own son brought before him—and such was the case. See that son tried and condemned by his own father. See him tied up before his father's very eyes, while as the inflexible judge, that father bids the lictor lay on the rod and afterwards cries, "Take him away and use the ax!"

See how Brutus loves justice more than his own son. "Now," says the world, "Brutus is indeed just!"

Now if God had condemned each one of us, that would certainly have been a vindication of his justice. But lo! His own precious Son takes on himself the sins of the world, and he thus comes before his Father.

See how the Father condemns his Son!
He gives him up to the Roman rod.
He gives him up to Jewish mockery, to military scorn, and to priestly arrogance.
He delivers him up to the executioner and bids him nail his Son to the tree.

And since that is not enough—the creature cannot of itself
    bring down a full vengeance on its own substitute—
God himself smites his Son!

Are you staggered at such an expression?
It is scriptural: "It was the will of the LORD to crush him; he has put him to grief" (Isaiah 53:10).

When the whip had gone around to every hand—to Pilate and Herod, Jew and Gentile—
    it was very obvious that the human arm was not powerful enough to execute the full vengeance.
Then the Father took his sword and cried, "Awake, O sword, against my shepherd, against the man who stands next to me" (Zechariah 13:7), and then smote him sternly!

He smote his Son as if he had been his enemy!
He smote him as if he were the worst of criminals!
He smote him until that awful cry rang out, "My God, my God, why have you forsaken me?"

Surely justice has received more than its due when God smites his beloved Son.
Then the law received an honor such as it never could have received in any other way.[2]

[1] A Roman officer who attended the chief magistrates in public and whose insignia of office was a bundle of rods and an ax.
[2] From sermon no. 255, *Justice Satisfied*

THE LAMB IN GLORY

And between the throne and the four living creatures and among the elders
I saw a Lamb standing, as though it had been slain.
REVELATION 5:6

Jesus appears in heaven in his sacrificial character.
His attributes, achievements, and offices all concentrate their glory in his great sacrifice.

We read that he is "the Lion of the tribe of Judah" (Revelation 5:5),
    by which is signified the dignity of his office as King and the majesty of his person as Lord.
Like a lion, he is courageous. He is as terrible as a lion, for "who dares rouse him?" (Genesis 49:9).

If any come into conflict with him, let them beware; as he is courageous, so he is mighty!
He has the lion's heart and the lion's strength, and he comes forth conquering and to conquer!

This makes it even more wonderful that he would become a Lamb,
    that he would yield himself up to the indignities of the cross.
He was not only mocked with a thorn-crown, he was also spit on by the lowest of men.

> *Oh wonder, wonder, wonder, that the Lion of Judah,*
> *the offspring of David's royal house,*
> *would become like a lamb led forth to the slaughter!*

Further, it is clear that he is a champion:
"The Lion of the tribe of Judah, the Root of David, has conquered" (Revelation 5:5).

Oh, what battles he has fought!
What feats of prowess he has performed!

He has overthrown sin by meeting the Prince of Darkness face to face and overcoming him.
He has entered the dungeon of the sepulcher and conquered death.

The brilliance of his victories does not diminish our delight in him as the Lamb.
Oh no! He won these triumphs as a Lamb, by gentleness and suffering and sacrifice.
He won his battles by a meekness and patience unseen before.

> *Oh, what a Conqueror he has been on our behalf,*
> *and how astounding it is that he has won the fight by humiliation and death!*

> *Let us reflect on the thought that he still looks like a Lamb that has been slain.*
> *His prowess and his lion-like qualities display much more vividly*
> *the tender, lowly, condescending qualities of the Lamb of our redemption.*

From sermon no. 2095, *The Lamb in Glory*

SURVEYING GOD'S LOVE

The Lord appeared to us in the past, saying:
"I have loved you with an everlasting love;
I have drawn you with loving-kindness."
JEREMIAH 31:3 NIV

When as yet the sun and the moon and the stars were not—
    when they still slept in the mind of God like unborn forests in an acorn cup—
God had already inscribed your name on the heart and hands of your Savior, Jesus Christ.

O soul, does this not compel you to regard the love of God?

When you see that he loved you even before time began,
are you not drawn to give him all of your heart?

Since you have soared back into eternity, I would now urge you to take another flight.
I would urge you to soar back through your own experience.

Look back and think of how the Lord your God has led you in the wilderness,
    of how he has fed and clothed you every day,
    of how he has borne with your bad manners,
    of how he has put up with all your murmurings and all your longings for the flesh-pots of Egypt,
    of how he has opened the rock to supply you and has fed you with the manna from heaven.

Think of how his grace has been sufficient for you in all your troubles,
    of how his blood has been a pardon to you in all your sins,
    of how his rod and his staff have comforted you.

When you have thus looked back on the Lord's love, then let faith survey his love in the future.

Remember that Christ's covenant and blood have more in them than just the past.
He who has loved you and pardoned you will never cease to love and pardon.
He is Alpha, and he will also be Omega; he is the first, and he will be the last.

Therefore, remember …
    when you pass through the valley of the shadow of death, you need fear no evil, for he is with you;
    when you face the mysteries of eternity, you need not tremble; nothing can separate you from him.

O soul, is your love not refreshed?

A flight over those limitless plains of love must inflame your heart
and compel you to delight yourself in the Lord your God.

From sermon no. 229, *Love*

SELF-EXAMINATION

Come, my lover ... Let us go early to the vineyards to see if the vines have budded,
if their blossoms have opened, and if the pomegranates are in bloom—
there I will give you my love.
SONG OF SOLOMON 7:11–12 NIV

The Church desires to practice self-examination.
    She would go and see if the vines have budded and if their blossoms have opened.
It is of the utmost importance that we search ourselves to see if we are in the faith; and if, being in
    the faith, determine if our graces are growing, our faith increasing, and our love deepening.

> *Well does the bride suggest that she go and see if the vines have budded—*
> *if the grapes and the pomegranates are in bloom—*
> *for our spiritual vineyard needs perpetual watchfulness.*

While you are attending to this important business,
    you must also be diligent in maintaining communion with your Beloved.
It is only *when you see him* that you fully understand why self-examination is so important.

Go and see him fastened to the tree, wearing the thorn-crown, all set with ruby drops of blood.
Behold his awful agonies.
Listen to the heart-rending cry: "My God, my God, why have you forsaken me?" (Matthew 27:46).

> *Did Christ suffer all this so that souls might be saved?*
>
> *Then surely, my soul, it should be your chief business*
> *to see that you have an interest in him!*

When such a crimson stream from Christ's own heart is present to cleanse away sin,
    will I consider it a small matter as to whether I am cleansed or not?
When that head that was once reverenced by angels is crowned with thorns of cruelty,
    should I not use my head to find out whether I am one with Christ?

That cannot be a small heritage that Christ has purchased with such agonies.
Let me fear lest I should lose it.

That cannot be a slight evil that cost my Savior such grief.
Let me search myself to see whether I am delivered from it.

> *You cannot have a better candle*
> *to look into the secret recesses of your soul*
> *than a candle lit at the fire of Jesus' love.*

From sermon no. 605, *Good Works in Good Company*

THROUGH HIS BLOOD

*"If the anointed priest sins, bringing guilt on the people,
he must bring to the Lord a young bull without defect
as a sin offering for the sin he has committed."*
LEVITICUS 4:3 NIV

As soon as the bull was slain, the priest carefully collected the blood in a basin;
and then taking the blood of the sin offering, he entered the holy place.
After he had walked past the golden altar of incense, he proceeded to dip his finger in the basin
and to sprinkle the blood seven times toward the curtain that concealed the Holy of Holies.

The priest began there to show us that our communion with God is by blood.
The curtain was not yet torn, indicating that the way of access to God was not yet revealed.
The sprinkling of the blood showed that the only thing that could give access to God was blood—
that the blood, when it was perfectly offered (seven times sprinkled), would rend the curtain.

The blood of Jesus has to the letter fulfilled the type.

*When our Lord had sprinkled his own heart's blood on the curtain,
he said, "It is finished" (John 19:30),
and "the curtain of the temple was torn in two,
from top to bottom" (Mark 15:38).*

Through the perfect offering of the precious blood,
"we have ... obtained access by faith into this grace in which we stand" (Romans 5:2).
We who have faith in that blood have intimate communion with the living God.

After sprinkling the curtain, the priest went to the altar of incense, adorned with four horns of gold,
and dipping his finger in the basin, he smeared the horns with blood.
That golden altar of incense was typical of prayer and especially of the intercession of Christ;
and the blood on the horns showed that the power of all-prevailing intercession lies in the blood.

Oh, think of this: Christ's intercessory power with God lies in his precious blood,
and our power with God in prayer must lie in that blood too!
How can we ever prevail with God unless we plead the blood of Jesus?

*Child of God, if you would overcome in prayer,
tell the Lord of all the groans of his dear Son.
Use only arguments fetched from Jesus' wounds.*

*These are potent pleas with God—
the bloody sweat, the scourging, the nails, the spear, the vinegar, the cross.*

Oh, let the altar of your incense be smeared with precious blood!

From sermon no. 739, *The Sin Offering*

THE APPLE OF HIS EYE

He who touches you touches the apple of his eye.
ZECHARIAH 2:8

God esteems his people as much as we value our eyesight.
  He is as careful to protect us from injury as we are to protect the apple of our eye.
As the pupil of the eye is the tenderest part of the tenderest organ,
  so this text clearly depicts the inexpressible tenderness of God's love.

O God, how is it that you have chosen the debased,
rebellious creature called man?
"What is man that you are mindful of him,
and the son of man that you care for him?" (Psalm 8:4).

Since we cannot answer this inquiry,
we will weave it into our everlasting song,
and we will sing of your sovereign grace forever and ever!

We cannot reach the bottom of this divine mystery.

Yet, God's love that comes to us freely has so ennobled us in Christ
  that God's present esteem of us in Jesus is not without reason and justification.
Love without cause has imparted and imputed such loveliness to its objects
  that they are now suitable subjects for love's embrace.

All the people of God are the objects of *the dearest purchase* that has ever been known—
  not with corruptible things, like silver or gold, but with the precious blood of Christ.
Stand at the foot of Calvary and let the groans of Jesus pierce your heart.
  Behold his head crowned with thorns, and his hands and feet dripping with blood.

Think of the awful anguish, the unknown pangs Christ bore when he redeemed our souls to God;
  and you will readily conclude that a love so amazing—that could pay such a stupendous price—
    would not easily let go of that which it has so dearly purchased.
We who are God's people are precious monuments of Christ's Passion and conflict.

We think little of ourselves when we value ourselves at anything less than the price that Jesus paid,
  and we dishonor him when we think we are only fit to live to the flesh and to this poor world.
We are fitted for a heavenly world and for divine purposes,
  seeing that the Son of God shed his very heart's blood to redeem us from our sins.

When we think that God—our God—
has made his people the objects of his eternal thoughts,
it is but little wonder that he would guard them with jealous care,
even as men do the apple of their eye.

From sermon no. 452, *The Lord's Care of His People*

THE TRUE TABERNACLE

And the Word became flesh and dwelt among us, and we have seen his glory,
glory as of the only Son from the Father, full of grace and truth.
JOHN 1:14

Another translation says, "The Word was made flesh, and tabernacled among us."

The greatest glory of the Jewish people was that God *tabernacled* in their midst.
    They had the King himself—God—dwelling with them.
The tabernacle was a tent to which the people went when they wished to commune with God,
    and it was also the spot where God manifested himself when he wanted to commune with the people.

To use Matthew Henry's words, this was the "trysting place" between the Creator and the worshiper.
Here they met each other through the slaughter of a bull or a lamb that resulted in reconciliation.

Now Christ's human flesh is God's tabernacle,
    and it is in Christ that God meets with man,
and it is in Christ that man has dealings with God.

The Jew of old went to God's tent,
    that tabernacle in the center of the camp if he wanted to worship.
But we come to Christ if we wish to pay our homage.

If the Jew needed to be released from ceremonial uncleanness,
    he would have to perform the rites of washing.
Then he would go to the sanctuary of God in order to feel peace between his soul and God.

And we, having been washed in the precious blood of Christ,
    have access to God the Father through Jesus Christ.
He is *our* tabernacle and the tabernacle *of God* among men.

The tabernacle of old was full of image and shadow and picture, but Christ is full of substance.
He is not the picture, but the reality; he is not the shadow, but the substance.

> *Herein, O believer, you must rejoice with unspeakable joy,*
> *for you come to Christ, the real tabernacle of God!*
>
> *You come to One who is not the representative of grace,*
> *but the grace itself.*
>
> *He is not the shadow of a truth ultimately to be revealed,*
> *but the very truth by which your soul is accepted in the sight of God.*

From sermon no. 414, *The Glory of Christ Beheld!*

A VEHEMENT LOVE

You whom my soul loves.
SONG OF SOLOMON 1:7

In this text, the bride speaks with a firm assurance of her love for Christ.

A child of God possesses true happiness when he knows that he loves Jesus,
   when he is able to put his hand upon his heart and appeal to him,
      saying, "Lord, you know everything; you know that I love you" (John 21:17).
A Christian should never be satisfied until he can say with certainty, "You whom my soul loves."

Notice that the bride—the church—in thus speaking of her Lord,
   also directs our thoughts to the unity of her affections.
She has but one love; she has but one for whom her heart is panting.

She is not a worshiper of God and of Baal, too.
She is not like the prostitute, whose door is open for every passerby.
She is a chaste one; she sees none but Christ and desires none but her crucified Lord.

> She has gathered all her affections into one bundle,
> and has cast that bundle of myrrh and spices
> upon the breast of her Beloved.

> All her love is focused.
> It is all concentrated on the Altogether Lovely.

There is constancy in this love: "You whom my soul loves."

You will not see Love playing fast and loose with Jesus,
   pressing him to her bosom today and then turning aside to other distractions tomorrow.
No, she cannot; she will not pollute herself with sin at any time or in any place.

In our text you will clearly perceive a vehemence of affection.
The bride does not love her Lord with an ordinary passion, but in the deepest sense of that word.

You should see Love when her heart is full of her Savior's presence as she comes out of her chamber!
   Indeed, she is like a giant refreshed with new wine!
Even though she dashes down difficulties and treads on hot irons of affliction, her feet are not scorched.
   She even gives up all that she has for Christ—even to stripping herself—and yet seems to grow richer.

> O Christian, do you know this love?
> Can you say, "You whom my soul loves"?

From sermon no. 338, *Love to Jesus*

LOOK TO HIM AND BE RADIANT

Those who look to him are radiant,
and their faces shall never be ashamed.
Psalm 34:5

It may seem strange, but the more deeply the Savior dived into the depths of misery,
    the brighter the pearls were that he brought up.
The greater his griefs, the greater our joys, and the deeper his dishonor, the brighter our glories.

Come then, *you who are doubting God's mercy*, come now to Calvary's cross.
    There, on the summit of that little hill, outside the gates of Jerusalem—
        there where common criminals were ordinarily put to death—there stand three crosses.
The center one is reserved for one who is reputed to be the greatest of criminals.

See there! It is the Lord of life and glory, before whose feet angels delight to worship.
He has been nailed to the cross and he hangs there in mid-heaven, dying, bleeding, thirsty.
His enemies mock him and say, "He saved others; he cannot save himself" (Matthew 27:42).

Oh, see him now, before the curtain is drawn over agonies too awful for eyes to behold!

Has there ever been a face marred like that face?
Has there ever been a heart so big with agony?
Have there ever been eyes so pregnant with the fire of suffering?

Come and behold him!
You are invited to look to this scene
so that you may be radiant.

Whatever your doubts are,
you may find a kind and fond solution here.

If you are doubting God's mercy, can you look at Jesus on the cross and still doubt it?
If God was not full of mercy and compassion, would he have given his Son to bleed and die?
Would he have given his Son to suffer a shameful death for our sakes, and yet be merciless?

There must be mercy in the heart of God,
or else there would never have been a cross on Calvary.

Oh, that you would look to Jesus now, for there is nothing that so speedily kills all doubts and fears
    as a look into the loving eye of the bleeding, dying Savior!
You cannot contemplate the dying Savior, and then say, "I doubt that he is able to save me."

Would you rejoice in the Lord
with faith unmoved and confidence unshaken?
Then look to Jesus and you will be radiant.

From sermon no. 195, *Looking Unto Jesus*

THE BELIEVER'S CHALLENGE

Who is to condemn?
Christ Jesus is the one who died—more than that, who was raised—
who is at the right hand of God, who indeed is interceding for us.
ROMANS 8:34

The Christian can never be condemned because Christ has died.
In Christ's death, a full penalty has been paid to divine justice for all the sins of all believers.

The whole shower of divine wrath was poured upon Christ's head.
   The black cloud of vengeance emptied itself upon the cross;
      therefore, the believer's sins are no longer recorded in the Book of God.
Not even a particle of punishment can be exacted at the hand of one who believes in Jesus.

Jesus has been punished to the full for every believer.
He has suffered, "the righteous for the unrighteous, that he might bring us to God" (1 Peter 3:18).

Yes, we may find a secure shelter
beneath the bloodstained tree of Calvary.

How safe we are there!

We may indeed look around at all our sins and defy them to destroy us.
This will be an all-sufficient argument to shut their clamorous mouths: "Christ has died."

Ah! There comes one, even now, and he cries, "You have been a blasphemer!"
Yes, but Christ died a blasphemer's death and he died for blasphemers.

"But you have stained yourself with lust!"
Yes, but Christ died for the lustful.

"But you have resisted his grace and the warnings of God for a long time!"
Yes, but Jesus died, so say what you will, O conscience, this will be my sure reply: "Jesus died."

The Christian may indeed gather courage as he stands at the foot of the cross.

There is not only a sea—a Red Sea—in which to drown his sins,
   but the very tops of the mountains of his guilt are also covered.
There is enough to bury and to hide his sins from sight forever.

Yes, the eternal arm of God, nerved with strength—
   now released from the bondage in which justice held it—
is able to save to the uttermost those who come to God through Christ.

From sermon no. 256, *The Believer's Challenge*

CONFORMED TO CHRIST'S IMAGE

Those whom he foreknew he also predestined
to be conformed to the image of his Son.
ROMANS 8:29

In moral virtues, the Christian is to be conformed to Christ,
   but there is one thing so linked to Christ that you cannot think of him without it—that is, *his cross.*
You do not see all of Christ until you see his cross,
   and if we are to be conformed to him, we must also bear his cross.

Do you see him, Christian, as he is despised and rejected by men?
Do you see him passing through the midst of a crowd as they yell and hoot at him?

See the men—those he had blessed—now cursing him!
See the lame men he had healed, now running after him to scorn him!
See the lips that had once been dumb, now venting blasphemies on him!
See the world as it cries, "Away with him, away with him! He is not fit to live!"

See there, O Christian, an image of yourself if you are to be conformed to Christ's likeness.

You must bear the cross of suffering.
You must bear the shame and spitting of ungodly men.
You must be crucified to the flesh with its affections and lusts.

Today, we see Christ,
not only as the bearer of the cross,
but also as the wearer of the crown.

And this will also be the Christian's experience.

If we are cross-bearers, we will be crown-wearers.
If the hand feels the nail, it will grasp the palm branch.
If the foot is tightly fastened to the wood, it will one day be girded with the sandals of immortal bliss.

Fear not, believer!

You must first bear the image of the Sorrowful One
if you would bear the image of the Glorious One.

Christ himself did not come to his crown, except by his cross.
As the man-Mediator, he earned his dignity by his sufferings.

And we, too, must fight if we would reign.
We must endure if we would obtain the reward.

From sermon no. 355, *Portraits of Christ*

MOURNING BITTERLY FOR SIN

"When they look on me, on him whom they have pierced,
they shall mourn for him."
ZECHARIAH 12:10

What is there in a sight of Christ that makes us mourn over sin?

To answer this question, come with me to Golgotha's terrible mount of doom
   so that we may sit down and watch the death pangs of the great Lover of our souls.
There on the transverse wood bleeds the incarnate Son of God.

His head yields ruby drops where the thorn-crown has pierced it.
His face is marred with bruises and is filthy with the spittle of mockers.
His hair has been pulled from his cheeks, and his lips are parched with fever.
His hands and feet are flowing with rivulets of blood.

He hangs yonder in physical pain impossible to be fully described,
   while his soul—crushed beneath the wheels of the chariot of justice—bears a woe far more terrible!
His "soul is very sorrowful, even to death" (Matthew 26:38),
   while his body is like a sponge saturated with infinite misery.

Think of the greatness of this Sufferer; he who hangs there is none other than the Son of God.
Think of his character as man; in him was no sin, and his whole life was spent in doing good.
Think of how he did not spare himself for us, but now men do not spare him their worst cruelty.

O thou immaculate man,
can I see you bleed without feeling compassion?

O people, can we think of the beauty of our Lord
without our soul being filled with the bitterness he felt?

Those eyes that are like the eyes of doves (Song of Solomon 5:12)
were drowned in tears of blood.

Those cheeks that "are like beds of spices" (Song of Solomon 5:13)
were given to those who pull out the hair.

Those hands that are "set with jewels" (Song of Solomon 5:14)
were brutally pierced with nails.

All human eyes—if they were forever full of tears—could not express the woe
   that one so glorious, so pure, so loving, so condescending,
      would in his own world find no shelter, and among his own creatures find no friends.
In this world he is racked upon the cross, and among his creations he meets his murderers.

From sermon no. 575, *The Pierced One Pierces the Heart*

THE MANNER OF THE GIFT

Thanks be to God for his inexpressible gift!
2 CORINTHIANS 9:15

This gift is inexpressible since no one can ever depict the manner of this gift.

Jesus Christ is not only the Father's Son, he is God himself; he is one with God.
   The gift of the Son is virtually the giving of God himself to men.
There can be no separation between God the Son and God the Father.
   Jesus said, "I and the Father are one" (John 10:30).

Do not think of Christ as suffering and of the Father as scarcely participating in the sacrifice.
   We swim in mysteries when we speak of the Father and the Son.
How could God give the Son to die, he being one with himself? Can anyone explain it?
   Or, if he can explain the mystery, can he tell us what it cost the Father to give his Son?

Who can tell what the Father felt when he had to send his Well-beloved among the wicked tenants,
   who said, "This is the heir. Let us kill him" (Luke 20:14)?
Who can tell what the Eternal felt when "the exact imprint of his nature" (Hebrews 1:3) was bound
   like a felon, accused as a criminal, mocked as an imposter, and flogged as a transgressor?
Who can tell what he felt when he saw his Son hung up like a thief and made to bear infinite agony?

True, "it was the will of the Lord to crush him" (Isaiah 53:10),
   but not without great self-denial on his part.
All the agony of Abraham when he unsheathed the knife to slay his son
   is but a faint type of what it cost the Father when he gave his only Son to die for us.

You will also see how inexpressible this gift of God is
   as you try to measure our Lord's sufferings when he was made sin for us.
No one can declare the greatness of his sacrifice.

Think of the descent from heaven's majesty to Bethlehem's manger,
   from the throne of Jehovah to the breast of Mary.
Think of what it must mean that "the Word became flesh and dwelt among us" (John 1:14).
   Incarnation is but the first step, but of that first descent of love, who can declare the mystery?

Our Lord became a man so that he might go further yet and become man's substitute.

Try to picture the incarnate God having sin imputed to him, transgression laid on him.
Try to picture justice with its iron rod, bruising and pounding the innocent Son of God
   with inexpressible grief; all borne for us.

O Jesus, what a price it was that you paid for us!
The brightest spirit before your throne cannot tell what you endured!
Your grief and your groans are a gift inexpressible!

From sermon no. 1550, *The Gift Unspeakable*

HEAVEN'S SWEETEST EMPLOYMENT

"Father, I desire that they also, whom you have given me,
may be with me where I am, to see my glory."
JOHN 17:24

This is heaven's sweetest employment.

There will be many joys in heaven, such as seeing departed friends, apostles, prophets, and martyrs;
but still, the sun that will give the greatest light to our joy
will be the fact that we will be with our gracious Lord and Savior.
There may be other employments in heaven, but the chief one is that we will behold Christ's glory.

Oh, for the tongue of an angel! Oh, for the lip of cherubim
to depict the mighty scenes the Christian will behold
when he sees the glory of his Master, Jesus Christ!

Perhaps we will be struck with astonishment—
Is this the face that was marred beyond human semblance?
Are these the hands that were once torn by rude iron?
Is that the head that was once crowned with thorns?

Oh, how our admiration will rise to the very highest pitch
when we see him who was—

"The weary man, and full of woes,
the humble man before his foes,"

now King of kings and Lord of lords!

What! Are those fire-darting eyes the very eyes that once wept over Jerusalem?
Are those feet, shod with sandals of light, the feet that were torn by the rough acres of earth?
Is that the man who, scarred and bruised, was carried to his tomb?

Yes, it is he! And that will absorb our thoughts—the godhead and the manhood of Christ—
that he is God over all, blessed forever, and yet man, bone of our bone and flesh of our flesh.

The songs of all creatures will find a focus in him;
he will be the grand reservoir of praise.

As all the rivers run into the sea,
so all the hallelujahs will come to him,
for he is Lord of all.

From sermon no. 188, *The Redeemer's Prayer*

THE SONG OF SONGS

Sing, O heavens, for the LORD has done it; shout, O depths of the earth;
break forth into singing, O mountains, O forest, and every tree in it!
For the LORD has redeemed Jacob, and will be glorified in Israel.
ISAIAH 44:23

Let us listen to the song.

The angels sing for they have deep sympathy with the redemption of man.
The material heavens themselves also ring with the sweet music;
    and every star takes up the refrain and with the sun and moon praise the Most High.

Descending from heaven, the song charms the depths of the earth
    and the prophet calls upon the mountains and valleys, forests, and trees to join in the song.
And so they should, for the creature will also be delivered from the bondage of corruption.

> *What mountain is there that has not been defiled with idolatry?*
> *Lo, the altars of Chemosh and the high places of Baal!*

> *But sing, ye mountains, for the God of the hills is revealed,*
> *and he has purged you by the blood of Calvary!*

Sing, O Moriah, on whose summit the patriarch drew his knife to slay his son; the true Isaac has
    been offered up! God has provided for himself a Lamb.
Sing, O Sinai; the law proclaimed from thy awful summit has now been magnified and honored!
Sing, O Pisgah; now that Christ has died, from thy peak may be seen the Promised Land into which
    the servants of the Lord will not be denied an entrance!
Sing, O Tabor; the Messiah transfigured has become the image of the future race!

Shout, O Valley of Jordan; in thy river the Redeemer was baptized!
Shout, O Eshcol; thy richest clusters are outdone by the true vine, which the Lord has planted!
Oh ye wildernesses and solitary places, be glad; redemption will make you blossom as the rose!

Fruitful trees and all cedars, praise ye the Lord!
Oh, let every tree in the forest join in the song!

The meaning of the whole seems to be this: Wherever saints are, they ought to praise God
    for redeeming love—whether in the Alps or in the valleys, in the plains or in the woods.
Wherever they are, they should praise God for redeeming grace and dying love.

> *All ye who are born of a woman, praise the Redeemer of Israel!*
> *He has accomplished the salvation of his people.*

From sermon no. 1240, *The Song of Songs*

THE GREATEST SUFFERER

Christ also suffered for you.
1 PETER 2:21

Who can describe the greatness of Christ's sufferings as he paid the price of our salvation?

See him yonder! It is night, but he does not sleep; he is in prayer.
Listen to his groans! Has a man ever wrestled as he wrestles?
Hear his own words: "My soul is very sorrowful, even to death" (Matthew 26:38).
See him as he rises and is seized by traitors and dragged away.

Now, let us step to the place where he has just been engaged in agony.

O God, what is this we see? What is this that stains the ground?
It looks like blood, but from where? Did he have a wound that bled afresh through his dire struggle?
Ah no! "His sweat became like great drops of blood falling down to the ground" (Luke 22:44).

> *O agonies! O sufferings that surpass the words by which we name you!*
> *What were you, thus working on the Savior's blessed frame*
> *and forcing a bloody sweat to fall from his entire body?*

This is only the opening of the tragedy.
He is condemned and tried, and his sentence is pronounced: "Let him be crucified!"

His back is bared and the bloody scourge plows deep furrows down his back.
His eyes are bound and then they buffet him, saying, "Who is it that struck you?" (Luke 22:64).
They spit in his face; they twist together a crown of thorns and press it into his temples.

Then, with many a jeer and jibe, they force him through the streets;
   but emaciated through fasting and agony of spirit, he stumbles beneath his cross.
They raise him up, lay his cross on another man's shoulders and continue to urge him on,
   perhaps with many a spear-prick, until at last he reaches the mount of doom.

There, rough soldiers hurl him down on the transverse wood.
Nails are grasped and hammers drive the nails through the tenderest parts of his body.
The cross is then lifted up and dashed into its place.
Every bone is put out of joint by the dashing of the cross into its socket.

> *Oh, never has man suffered as this man suffered!*

> *This, however, was only the outward; the inward was far worse.*
> *What our Savior suffered in his body was nothing*
> *compared to what he endured in his soul.*

From sermon no. 181, *Particular Redemption*

KEEPING OUR FIRST LOVE

"I have this against you, that you have left your first love."
REVELATION 2:4 NKJV

Oh, what love I had for my Savior on that day when he had forgiven all my sins!
　　Oh, that happy hour when the Lord appeared to me, bleeding on his cross,
　　　　and he said to me, "I am your salvation; I have blotted out like a thick cloud your transgressions."
Oh, how I loved him then!

If, at that place where I first met him there had been a stack of blazing sticks,
　　I would have willingly stepped on them, glad to testify of my love for him.
Had he asked me to give all my possessions to the poor, I would have done it and thought myself rich.

I then understood the language of Rutherford when he said from his dungeon in Aberdeen,
　　"Oh, my Lord, if there were a broad hell between me and thee,
　　　　if I could not get at thee except by wading through it, I would not think twice,
　　but I would plunge through it all, if I might embrace thee and call thee mine."

Now it is that first love that we must sadly confess to losing to some extent.

How earnest we were! Every word in the Bible was considered to be most precious.
Every command of God was thought to be like purest gold.

Yes, we must go back to the place where our spiritual journey began.
　　It is by going back to the great foundation stone, the cross of Christ,
　　　　that we will be led back to our first love.
Have we not lost our first love by neglecting communion with our Savior?

Love for Jesus is dependent on our nearness to him.

It is just like the planets and the sun.
　　Why are some planets cold, and why do they move so slowly?
It is because they are so far away from the sun; but put them where Mercury is,
　　and they will be in a boiling heat, spinning around the sun in rapid orbits.

So, if we live near to Christ, we cannot help loving him.
But if we live days and weeks without real fellowship, how can we maintain love for a stranger?[1]

*Oh, keep your first love, and hold the first flame
with that soul-delighting, lovely Bridegroom, our sweet, sweet Jesus!*

*There is none like him.
I would not exchange one smile of his lovely face for kingdoms.[2]*

[1]From sermon no. 217, *Declension from First Love*
[2]Samuel Rutherford

THE APPROACHABLENESS OF JESUS

Now the tax collectors and sinners were all drawing near to hear him.
LUKE 15:1

The most depraved and despised classes of society formed an inner circle of hearers around our Lord. We gather from this that he was very approachable and that he encouraged human confidence.

When I see Christ in the manger where the horned oxen feed,
   or being obedient to his parents,
   or being "a man of sorrows, and acquainted with grief" (Isaiah 53:3),
   or being a poor man without a place to lay his head,
then I feel that he is indeed approachable and that I can freely come to him.

Jesus proclaims his approachability in such words as these:
"Come to me, all who labor and are heavy laden, and I will give you rest" (Matthew 11:28).
"If anyone thirsts, let him come to me and drink" (John 7:37).

All the invitations in Scripture may be said to be the language of Christ.
Our Master never spurned anyone who came to him.

> *But if you really want to see how approachable Jesus is, look yonder!*
> *The man who has lived a life of service at last dies a felon's death.*

Look at his head girded with the crown of thorns.
Mark his cheeks where they have pulled out his hair.
See the spittle from those scornful mouths staining his marred countenance.
Mark the crimson rivers that are flowing from his back where they have scourged him.
See his bleeding hands and feet, pierced with the nails.
See that face so full of anguish as he cries, "I thirst."

As you see him expiring there, can you see him spurning anyone who seeks him?
As you see him turn his head to the dying thief by his side, and saying, "Today you will be with me in Paradise" (Luke 23:43), can you doubt that you may approach him?

You will outrage your reason if you doubt Christ crucified.
The cross of Jesus should be the hope, the anchorage of faith.

> *Filthy, vile, hellish sinner, you may come to him and have life,*
> *even as the dying thief had it when he said, "Jesus, remember me."*

> *Never be afraid to approach the One who went to Calvary for sinners.*

From sermon no. 809, *The Approachableness of Jesus*

THE BRIDEGROOM IS A LAMB

Blessed are those who are invited to the marriage supper of the Lamb.
REVELATION 19:9

Since Christ was the Lamb suffering for sin, and because he delights in being our sacrifice,
    he is seen in that capacity in the day of his heart's gladness.
He links the memory of his grief with the manifestation of his glory;
    and as he was a Lamb to redeem us, so he appears as a Lamb in the marriage supper of his glory.

We cannot imagine our Lord Jesus as ever being less than infinitely glorious,
    but if there is a time when the splendor of his character is more fully revealed,
it is when he dies on the cross to redeem his people.

Do not tell us of all the glory that surrounds him now in the midst of the throne.
    We cannot imagine any glory exceeding in brightness the glory of his self-denial.
What glory can exceed Christ's lowliness when he took upon himself the form of a servant
    and became "obedient to the point of death, even death on a cross" (Philippians 2:8)?

The glory of men consists in what they are prepared to suffer for others,
and Christ's glory is best seen in his sacrifice for sinners.

"Greater love has no one than this, that someone lays down his life for his friends" (John 15:13).
Yes, but Christ has done more than that. He has laid down his life for his enemies.

When he put on the bloody shirt in Gethsemane,
when he bedecked himself with the five bright rubies of his wounds,
when he was adorned with the crown of thorns,
when he was decorated with that robe of blood as the soldier pierced his side,
then he was more illustrious than at any time—before or since—in the eyes of his people.

Ah, it is very appropriate for Christ to appear in glory as a Lamb
    because it is as a Lamb that he most fully displayed his love for his church.
The marriage supper is a feast of love, and in order to reveal his love the most effectively,
    Jesus appears as a bleeding sacrifice on the day of his love's triumph.

We rejoice in knowing that in the day
when Jesus takes his church by the hand
and leads her home to his Father's house,
he will appear in that character in which he most fully revealed his love!

We see most of his love when we see most of his grief,
and when we see most of his condescension,
so he will appear in that character at his marriage supper.

From sermon no. 2428, *The Marriage Supper of the Lamb*

OUR CHAMPION

*Samson lay till midnight, and at midnight he arose
and took hold of the doors of the gate of the city and the two posts, and pulled them up, bar and all,
and put them on his shoulders and carried them to the top of the hill that is in front of Hebron.*
JUDGES 16:3

You remember when our Samson—our Lord Jesus—came down to the Gaza of this world,
   leaving the delights of heaven in order to live among the Philistines, the sons of sin and Satan.
But when it is rumored among men that the Lord of glory is in the world,
   they immediately look for ways in which they might slay him.

Herod slays all the males two years of age and under, thinking the newborn Prince cannot escape.
Afterwards, scribes and priests and lawyers hunt him and hound him.
Death also pursues him, for he has marked him as his prey.

At last, the time comes when his foes surround him, capture and bind him.
They drag him before Pilate where they cruelly scourge and torture him.
His blood drips on the streets of Jerusalem as they drag him to the place called Calvary.
There they pierce his hands and feet, lifting him up, a spectacle of suffering and shame.

And then, when he closes his eyes, and cries out, "It is finished,"
   sin, Satan, and death all feel they have the Champion safe in their grasp.
There he lies silently in the tomb.

*O thou Great Deliverer of the world,
there you lay, as dead as a stone!*

*Surely your foes have led you captive,
O thou Mighty Samson!*

Yes, he sleeps for a short while, and then our Samson awakes; he comes forth from the tomb.
   He has defeated death and has pulled up the posts of the grave and taken away its doors and bars;
      and as for sin, he treads that beneath his feet for he has utterly overthrown it.
He has also broken the old Dragon's head and has cut his power into pieces forever.

Oh, I think I see him now as he goes up that hill that is in front of Hebron, the hill of God,
   bearing on his shoulders the uplifted doors of the grave, the tokens of his victory over death.
Doors and posts and bars and all—he is bearing them all up to heaven
   and in sacred triumph is dragging all his enemies behind him.

*O ye angels, praise him!
Exalt him, cherubim and seraphim!*

*Our mightier Samson has gained the victory,
and he has cleared the road to heaven for all his people.*

From sermon no. 3009, *Our Champion*

SALVATION IN JESUS CHRIST

*There is salvation in no one else, for there is no other name under heaven
given among men by which we must be saved.*
ACTS 4:12

O sinner, you have been trying to find the road to heaven, but you have missed it.
    A thousand dazzling cheats have deceived you,
        and you have not found a solid ground of comfort for your poor, weary foot.
Encompassed by your sins, you are unable to look up and cry for pardon.

Poor soul! Come to the cross and you will see something there that will remove your unbelief.

Do you see that man nailed to yonder tree? Do you know his character?
    He was no thief that he should die a felon's death;
        he was no murderer or assassin that he should be crucified between two criminals.
No, he was pure and holy; his hands were full of good deeds, and his feet were swift in acts of mercy.

O sinner, there must be merit in the death of such a man as that!
God is not a tyrant that he would crush the innocent; he is not unholy that he would punish the righteous.

Christ suffered, then, for the sins of others.

*Come sinner, with your blackness, and look at his whiteness;
come with your defilement, and look at his purity.*

*As you look at that purity, like the lily,
and as you see the crimson of his blood overflowing it,
let this whisper be heard in your ear: "He is able to save you."*

Remember, that man who is dying on the cross is no less than the everlasting Son of God.

Those hands that are nailed to the tree are hands that could shake the world.
Those feet that are pierced could make the mountains melt beneath their tread.
That head, bowed in anguish, has the wisdom of God and its nod could make the universe tremble.

He who hangs on yonder cross is the Creator of all things.
He who died for you is "God over all, blessed forever" (Romans 9:5).

How can there not be power to save in such a Savior as this?

*O sinner, if Christ was just a man, I would not urge you to trust him;
but since he is none other than God himself, incarnate in human flesh,
I beseech you to cast yourself on him since he is able and willing to save you.*

From sermon no. 209, *The Way of Salvation*

OUR GREAT SHEPHERD

"And when he has found it, he lays it on his shoulders, rejoicing."
LUKE 15:5

The shepherd searches for his lost sheep, and when he has found it he lays it on his shoulders;
  and there it is with all its weight, carried by powerful shoulders.
And that is what the Savior does for poor, weary sinners.
  He carries the weight of their sins—aye, the weight of themselves!

> *Now you have before you one of the loveliest portraits imagination can sketch:*
> *the Great Shepherd of the sheep, King of kings and Lord of lords,*
> *bearing on his shoulders a burden he delights to carry—*
> *the sheep that had gone astray.*

> *Oh, that you may lie on those broad shoulders,*
> *those shoulders of omnipotence bearing up your weakness—*
> *the mighty Savior bearing you and all your sin and all your care!*

The shepherd "lays it on his shoulders, rejoicing,"
  because he is glad to carry this burden, happy to carry his lost sheep home.
And we love to picture the joy in the heart of Christ,
  "who for the joy that was set before him endured the cross, despising the shame" (Hebrews 12:2).

Now, whenever he finds a lost sheep to carry home he rejoices.
With a thankful heart he gets hold of his lost sheep and places it on his shoulders.

He takes us just as we are, and instead of driving us back by his law, he carries us home by his love.
Instead of urging us to go home, he becomes the great Burden-Bearer of his redeemed.[1]

> *Oh, what sorrow was on Christ when our load was laid on him!*
> *But oh! What joy he knew when he had recovered us from our lost condition!*

> *His love for us made it a joy to feel every lash of the scourge of justice;*
> *it made it a delight to have the nails pierce his hands and feet,*
> *and to have his heart broken by the absence of his Father, God.*

> *Can a shout of triumph exceed that cry of grief, "Eli, Eli, lema sabachthani?"*
> *Yet, for the sins of his people, our Lord enjoyed even the forsaking of his Father.*

> *Oh, who can understand it, except in a very feeble measure—*
> *the Maker of heaven and earth bowing his shoulders to bear the weight of sinners!*[2]

[1]From sermon no. 2065, *Our Great Shepherd Finding the Sheep*
[2]From sermon no. 1801, *Parable of the Lost Sheep*

THE WAY TO GOD

And a highway shall be there, and it shall be called the Way of Holiness.
ISAIAH 35:8

This text reveals the great truth that *there is a way to God and heaven.*

Note that there is only one highway, one way—not two highways or two ways.
Many roads lead to ruin, but only one road leads to salvation.

We learn here what that "way" of salvation is: "Jesus said … 'I am the way, and the truth, and the life.
   No one comes to the Father except through me'" (John 14:6).
When we find Jesus, we find the way of truth, the way of life, the way of peace, the way of holiness.

There is only one Christ,
so there is only one way of salvation.

God has given us a way to himself
in the person of his Son Jesus Christ.

We might gather that this highway was built at great expense,
   since building a road over a long and rugged country is a costly business.
Engineering has done much to tunnel mountains and bridge abysses,
   but the greatest feat of engineering has made a way from sin to holiness—from death to life.

Who could make a road over the mountains of our iniquities but Almighty God?

None but the God of love would have wished it.
None but the God of wisdom could have devised it.
None but the God of power could have carried it out.

It cost the great God the Jewel of heaven: He emptied out the treasury of his own heart
   when he "did not spare his own Son but gave him up for us all" (Romans 8:32).
In the life and death of the Well-beloved, infinite wisdom laid a firm foundation
   for the road by which sinners may journey home to God.

The highway of our God is such a masterpiece that even those who travel it every day
   often stand and wonder and ask how such a way could have been planned and constructed.
And even though it has lasted thousands of years, it is still in good traveling condition.

Our text also tells us the name of this highway: "It shall be called the Way of Holiness."
The way to God by Jesus Christ is the Holy Road.

This highway is reserved for those upon whom a miracle of grace has been performed,
   upon whom the Messiah has laid his healing hand, and they find delight only in holy things.
They cannot be driven from this Way of Holiness, so the pure in heart will see God (Matthew 5:8).

From sermon no. 1912, *The Holy Road*

CHRIST DIED FOR SINNERS

Christ Jesus came into the world to save sinners.
1 TIMOTHY 1:15

There is a vague notion abroad that Christ's Passion benefits only the good,
    that Christ came into the world to save the righteous.
You will clearly see, if you will but open an eye,
    how inconsistent such a supposition is with the whole teaching of Scripture.

For whom did Christ shed his blood?
For whom did he agonize in the garden?
For whom did he cry on the cross, "Father, forgive them" (Luke 23:34)?
For the perfect? Surely not!

> *The fact that Jesus Christ bled for sin on the cross*
> *bears, on its very surface,*
> *evidence that he "came into the world to save sinners."*

A moment of thought will be enough to convince us that the plan of salvation is for sinners.
Indeed, it is only when we have a clear view of this that *we see Jesus in his glory.*

When does the shepherd appear most lovely?

It is a fair picture to portray him in the midst of his flock,
    feeding them in green pastures and leading them beside the still waters.
But if my heart is to leap for joy,
    give me the shepherd pursuing his stray sheep over the mountains.

Let me see him bringing that sheep home upon his shoulders, rejoicing.
Let me hear him call his friends and neighbors to rejoice with him because he has found the lost sheep.

When does our God look most like a loving and tender Father?

He truly looked blessed when he divided his inheritance among his sons,
    but I have never seen him so resplendent in his fatherhood
        as when he ran out to meet the prodigal, threw his arms around him, and kissed him.
Hear him crying, "My son was dead, and is alive again" (Luke 15:24).

Indeed, for some of Christ's offices, a sinner is an absolute necessity.
Why is a priest needed, if not for the sins of the people?
Christ's priesthood is a mockery, and his sacrifice is a sham, unless he came to save sinners.

How is he a Savior if not to the lost?
How is he a Physician if not to the sick?
How is he like the brazen serpent if he does not save the sin-bitten?

From sermon no. 458, *The Friend of Sinners*

WONDERFUL IS HIS NAME

And the angel of the LORD said to him,
"Why do you ask my name, seeing it is wonderful?"
JUDGES 13:18

Gather up your thoughts and center them all on Christ and see how wonderful he is.
First of all, consider the wonders of his incarnation.

O world of wonders, what is that I see?
The Eternal of the ages, whose hair is like wool—as white as snow—has become an infant!

O wonder of wonders!
Manger of Bethlehem, you have miracles poured into you!
This is a sight that surpasses all others!

See, he who is infinite is an infant—he is eternal and yet is born of a woman;
he supports the universe—and yet he needs to be carried in a mother's arms;
he is the King of angels—and yet he is called the son of Joseph;
he is the heir of all things—and yet he is the carpenter's despised son.

Wonderful art thou O Jesus,
and that shall be thy name forever!

Trace the Savior's course and all the way he is wonderful.
Is it not marvelous that he submitted to the taunts and jeers of his enemies?
Do you not wonder at his patience when he was blasphemed by foes?

But see him die!

Come ye children of God and gather around the cross.
Can you understand this riddle: God was manifest in the flesh and crucified by men?

My Master, how could you stoop your head to such a death as this—
taking from your brow the coronet of stars that shone resplendent there,
and permitting the thorn-crown to gird your holy head?

How could you cast away the mantle of your glory, the azure of your throne,
and be stripped naked to your shame, without a single covering?

Truly your name is wonderful! Oh, your love for me is wonderful!
No other love has ever opened the floodgates of such grief.

You have now come to the summit of everything that may be wondered at!
There is no astonishment, no admiration that ever equals what we feel when we behold Christ!

From sermon no. 214, *His Name—Wonderful*

HOPE LAID UP IN HEAVEN

Because of the hope laid up for you in heaven.
COLOSSIANS 1:5

The hope that is laid up for us in heaven is a *marvelous hope.*
This is especially so, considering it is because of a great act of grace that sinners even have a hope.

When sin lay heavily upon our conscience,
    Satan came and wrote over the lintel of our door, "NO HOPE".
And the grim sentence would have remained there had not a loving hand taken the hyssop
    and by a sprinkling of precious blood removed the black inscription.

Now, though we are sinners, we have a hope.
Ever since we looked to Jesus on the cross, a hope full of glory has filled our hearts!
We now have a hope that anticipates heaven and a happiness that surpasses all earthly—all carnal—joy.

We know a little of heaven's happiness because the Lord has revealed it to us by his Spirit;
    yet what we do know is only a meager taste of the marriage feast.
It is only enough to fill us with longing for the whole banquet.

If it is so sweet to preach about Christ, what will it be to see him and to be with him?
If it is so delightful to hear the music of his name, what will it be to lean on his bosom?
If these few clusters of Eshcol[1] that are now and then brought to us are so sweet, what will it be to
    abide in the vineyard where all the clusters grow?

Oh, this is our hope—
the hope of everlasting fellowship with our Redeemer!

We would give ten thousand worlds
to have even one glimpse of that dear face
that was so marred with grief and sorrow for our sake.

What a heaven it will be to sit at our Lord's feet and look up into his glorious face!
    Oh, matchless joy to be as holy, harmless, and undefiled as our beloved Lord,
        and know that we will never, never grieve his tender heart again!
What joy to also participate in all his triumphs and glories forever and forever!

And we will also have fellowship with all his saints
    in whom he is glorified, and by whom his image is reflected.
Thus we will behold fresh displays of his power, fresh beams of his love.

Oh, the noblest intellect and the sweetest speech
cannot convey to you even a thousandth part of the bliss of heaven![2]

[1]The valley where the Israelites spying out the promised land found a large cluster of grapes (Numbers 13:23).
[2]From sermon no. 1438, *The Hope Laid Up in Heaven*

December 12

FAITH IS HIDING IN GOD

*Be merciful to me, O God, be merciful to me,
for in you my soul takes refuge;
in the shadow of your wings I will take refuge,
till the storms of destruction pass by.*
PSALM 57:1

Trusting in God—that is, faith—is the same thing as hiding
or taking refuge in the shadow of God's wings.

Take a look at this figure as it relates to birds hiding beneath their mother's wings.

There is a hawk in the sky, and the hen seeing it, begins to give her warning "cluck."
Can you see the hen crouched close to the ground with her wings outspread,
calling and calling until every one of her chicks comes and hides beneath her wings?
They are now out of sight of the bird of prey.

If that hawk comes down at all,
it will have to attack the hen and kill her before it can reach her chicks.
The pecking of its bill and the tearing of its talons must be first upon the mother bird
because her little ones are all hidden beneath the covert of her wings.

Now that hiding is an illustration of faith.
Here is Christ, our Savior, and we hide beneath him.

The justice of God must smite the sinner
or one who is able and willing to suffer in the sinner's place.
It is the law of the universe that sin cannot go unpunished.

As Justice approaches with drawn sword,
we find Christ coming and interposing between us and the sentence of the law.
And if the Avenger seeks us we hide under Christ, and all the blows delivered are inflicted on him.

Yes, we will never forget how our Savior was wounded, rent, and torn
so that all of us hiding beneath him might escape!

*I have taken refuge, O Justice,
in the shadow of my Savior's wings,
so your dealings are not with me but with my dying Savior!*

*I interpose between your wrath and my guilty head
the sacrifice he presented on the cross
when he bowed his head and said, "It is finished."*

From sermon no. 2335, *Three Texts, But One Subject—Faith*

ALL FOES DESTROYED

He said, "It is finished."
JOHN 19:30

When he said, "It is finished," *Jesus had destroyed the power of sin, of Satan, and of death.* For our soul's redemption, our Champion fought against all our foes.

First, our Champion met Sin.

Horrible, terrible, all-but-omnipotent Sin nailed him to the cross;
  but in that deed, Christ also nailed Sin to the tree.
There they both hung together—Sin and the Destroyer of Sin.
  Sin slew Christ, and by that death, Christ destroyed Sin.

Next came the second enemy, Satan, who assaulted Christ with all his hosts.
  He had called them from every corner and quarter of the universe.
He said to them, "Awake, arise, or be forever fallen! Here is our great enemy
  who has sworn to bruise my head. Now let us bruise his heel!"

They shot their hellish darts into his heart!
They poured their boiling cauldrons on his brain!
They emptied their venom into his veins!
They spat their insinuations into his face!
They hissed their devilish fears into his ear!

He stood alone, the Lion of the tribe of Judah, hounded by all the dogs of hell;
  but using his holy weapons, he struck back with all the power of God-supported manhood.
Standing foot to foot with the Enemy, he smote him with divine fury,
  until, having despoiled him of his armor and crushing his head, he cried, "It is finished!"

At that very same moment, our Champion also vanquished Death.

Death had come against him, as Christmas Evans[1] puts it, *with his fiery dart,*
  which he struck right through the Savior, until the point was fixed in the cross;
    but when he tried to pull it out again, he left the sting behind.
What more could he do? He was disarmed.

Then Christ set some of his prisoners free. Many of the saints arose and were seen by many.
He then said to Death, "You must exist for a short while in order to be the warder of those beds
  in which my saints sleep, but now, O Death, I take from you your keys."

And lo! The Savior stands today with the keys of death in his possession,
  and he waits for the hour when he will say, "Let my captives go free."
Then the tombs will be opened in virtue of Christ's death,
  and the saints will rise and live again, in an eternity of glory.[2]

[1]Christmas Evans (1766–1838) was regarded as one of the greatest preachers in the history of Wales.
[2]From sermon no. 421, *"It Is Finished!"*

ONLY VINEGAR TO DRINK

Knowing that all was now completed, ... Jesus said, "I am thirsty."
A jar of wine vinegar was there, so they soaked a sponge in it,
put the sponge on a stalk of the hyssop plant, and lifted it to Jesus' lips.
JOHN 19:28–29 NIV

How great was the love that led to such condescension as this!

We must not forget the infinite distance between the Lord of glory on his throne
    and the Crucified who was dried up with thirst.
"The river of the water of life, bright as crystal" (Revelation 22:1), flows from the throne of God,
    and yet our Lord once condescended to say, "I am thirsty."

He is the Lord of fountains and of all ocean depths, but not even a cup of cold water was placed to his lips.
    He placed himself into a position of shame and suffering where none would wait upon him;
        but when he cried, "I am thirsty," they gave him vinegar to drink.
Glorious humiliation of our exalted Head!

> *Jesus came to save, and man denied him hospitality.*
>
> *At first there was no room for him at the inn,*
> *and at the last there was not even a cup of water for him to drink.*
> *When he thirsted they gave him vinegar to drink.*
>
> *This is man's treatment of his Savior.*
> *Universal manhood—left to itself—*
> *rejects, crucifies, and mocks the Christ of God.*
>
> *O Lord Jesus, we love and worship you!*
> *We would lift your name on high in grateful remembrance*
> *of the awful depths to which you descended!*

While we admire our Lord's condescension, let us also turn with delight to his sure sympathy.
    If Jesus said, "I am thirsty," then he knows all about our frailties and woes.
The next time we are in pain or are suffering from a broken heart,
    we will remember that our Lord understands it all, because he has had practical experience.

In all our sufferings, we are never deserted by our Lord; his line runs parallel with ours.
The arrow that has lately pierced us was first stained with his blood.
The cup that we now have to drink, though it is very bitter, bears the mark of his lips about its brim.

> *Our Savior has traversed the mournful way before us,*
> *and every footprint we leave in the sodden soil*
> *is stamped side by side with his footprints.*

From sermon no. 1409, *The Shortest of the Seven Cries*

A VEIL THAT CONCEALS

From the sixth hour there was darkness over all the land until the ninth hour.
MATTHEW 27:45

Christ is hanging on yonder tree, and I can see the thieves on either side.
  I look around and sorrowfully mark that diverse group of citizens from Jerusalem,
    and scribes, priests, and strangers from different countries, mingled with the Roman soldiers.
They turn their eyes and gaze with cruel scorn on the Holy One who is hanging on the center cross.

It is an awful sight as they all unite in dishonoring the meek and lowly One.

The pain involved in crucifixion was immeasurable,
  but there was more than that kind of anguish experienced at Calvary.
Those jests, those cruel gibes, those mockeries—what can we say of these?

Let us thank God for bidding the darkness cover all the land, bringing an end to that shameful scene.
  Jesus must die; there must be no alleviation from his pains;
    and there must be no deliverance from his death.
But the scoffers must be silenced, and their mouths were effectually closed by the dense darkness.

How it must have grieved the heart of the Eternal God
  to see the teachers of the people rejecting his Son with such cruelty and scorn;
  to see the offspring of Israel, who should have accepted Christ as their Messiah,
casting him out as a thing to be despised and abhorred!

Thank God for providing a pavilion of thick clouds in which to shelter our King in his time of misery.
  It was too much for wicked eyes to gaze so rudely on that immaculate person.
Had not enemies stripped him naked and cast lots for his robe?
  Therefore, it was right that the holy manhood should find suitable concealment.

It was not fitting for brutal eyes to see the lines made on that holy form by the engraving tool of grief.
It was not proper for revelers to see the contortions of that sacred frame while it was being broken
  beneath the iron rod of divine wrath on our behalf.
It was right that God should cover him so that none could see all that he did and all that he bore while
  he was being made sin for us.

Oh, bless God devoutly for thus hiding away our Lord!

He was screened from eyes that were not fit to see the sun,
  much less look upon the Sun of Righteousness.

From sermon no. 1896, *The Three Hours' Darkness*

December 16

THE SINGLE-HANDED CONQUEST

*"I have trodden the winepress alone,
and from the peoples no one was with me."*
ISAIAH 63:3

In the toil of redemption, Christ worked alone.
No one could help him since he alone could bear his people's guilt.

How lonely Jesus must have been in this world during the years of his ministry!
He talked with his disciples, but even they could not sympathize with him.

Who were so pure that they could match his unsullied purity?
Who were so wise as to talk with the Wonderful Counselor?
Who were so farseeing as to be able to commune with the Prophet of all the ages?
Who were so sorrowful as to be fit companions for the Man of Sorrows?

His loneliness increased as his sorrows increased.
When he was in the Garden of Gethsemane, he trod the winepress alone.
What heavy drops of bloody sweat flowed from him in his agony!

Yet, he clung to the three disciples, Peter, James, and John, as if he wanted some companionship.
He went to them three times, but each time he found them asleep.
Finally, he says to them, "Rise, let us be going; see, my betrayer is at hand" (Matthew 26:46).

Surely, they will rally around him now;
    but, no, "all the disciples left him and fled" (Matthew 26:56).
He is then taken prisoner by men who are armed with swords and clubs.

*O earth, has he no friend?
O heavens, have you no friend for Jesus?*

*There is no one to be with Jesus; no one to help him.
He is taken before the council,
but there is no one there to declare his innocence.*

And now he goes up to Calvary, and still there is no one with him.
When he is hanging on the cross, he is completely alone, alone—alone in thick, impenetrable gloom!
Hear him cry, "My God, my God, why have you forsaken me?" (Matthew 27:46).

Then he truly cried, "I am treading the winepress alone, and from the peoples no one is with me."

*Ah, Christian, never associate anyone with Jesus in the work of redemption.
Jesus has trodden the winepress alone; therefore, he is all in all.*

From sermon no. 2567, *The Single-Handed Conquest*

THE SHAMEFUL SUFFERER

Who for the joy that was set before him endured the cross, despising the shame.
HEBREWS 12:2

The cross was regarded as the most terrible and frightful of all punishments.
    Here was the death of a villain, of a murderer, of an assassin—a death painfully protracted,
        one that cannot be equaled in all inventions of human cruelty for suffering and shame.
And Christ himself endured this!

The shame of the cross, however, was intensified in our Savior's case,
    since he was crucified during Passover when people of all nations were present to behold the spectacle.
        All were there to unite in scoffing and in increasing the shame.
He was also crucified between two thieves as if to say he was viler than they were.

Now, let us go to the cross—the cross! The cross!

The rough wood is laid on the ground and Christ is grabbed and hurled down!
Soldiers seize his hands and feet, and his flesh is rent with the accursed iron!
Bleeding profusely, he is lifted into midair, and the cross is dashed into the ground!
Every limb is dislocated and every bone is put out of joint by the terrific jolt!

There he hangs—the hands and feet are pierced where the nerves are the most tender and numerous—
    and there is the iron rending and tearing its fearful way.
The weight of his body drags the iron up his feet, and when his knees are too weary to hold him,
    then the iron begins to drag through his hands.

That is a terrible spectacle, but you have only seen the outward; there is also the inward.
Jesus had lost that which is the martyr's strength, because he had lost his Father's presence.

There was Jesus, forsaken by God and man,
left alone to tread the winepress.

No, he was left alone to be trodden in the winepress
and to dip his robe in his own blood!

All the billows of the Eternal dashed upon this Rock of our salvation!
He must be bruised, trodden, crushed!
His soul must be exceedingly sorrowful, even to death!

Notice that Christ despised the shame;
    but the sufferings of the cross were too awful for him to despise—that he endured.
The shame he could cast off, but the cross he must carry, and to it he must be nailed.
    He "endured the cross, despising the shame."

From sermon no. 236, *The Shameful Sufferer*

OUR CONQUERING KING

He said to the Jews, "Behold your King!"
JOHN 19:14

"Behold your King" so that you may see him *subduing his dominions.*
Dressed in robes of scorn, and with a face marred with pain, he comes forth conquering and to conquer.

He is not arrayed like a man of war and has no sword on his thigh nor bow in his hand.
He speaks no threatening words, nor does he even speak with eloquent persuasion.
He is unarmed, yet victorious; he is silent, but yet conquering.

In this garb he goes forth to war:
His shame is his armor and his sufferings are his battle-ax.

How can it be so? Talk to missionaries and they will tell you.

When they have told the heathen of the greatness and justness of God, they have listened unmoved;
   and even when they spoke of Christ's second coming, there was still no response.
But when they spoke of God's love in giving his only Son, and of the matchless griefs of Immanuel,
   then the deaf ears heard and the blind eyes glistened. Christ crucified is the conqueror.

He does not subdue the heart in his robes of glory, but in his garments of shame.
He does not at first gain the faith and the affection of sinners while sitting on his throne,
   but while bleeding, suffering, and dying in their place.

"Far be it from me to boast," said Paul, "except in the cross of our Lord Jesus Christ" (Galatians 6:14).
Every theme connected with the Savior should play a part in our ministry, but this is the master theme.
The cross is the mighty battering ram with which to shatter the brazen gates of human prejudice.

Christ coming to be our judge alarms,
but Christ the Man of Sorrows subdues.

The crown of thorns has a royal power in it that compels allegiance.
The scepter of reed breaks hearts better than a rod of iron.
The robe of mockery commands more love than Caesar's imperial purple.

No royalty is so all-commanding as that which has for its insignia
   the crown of thorns, the reed, the red cloak, and the five wounds.
Other sovereignties are superficial compared with the sovereignty of "the despised of men."

Fear or custom makes men courtiers elsewhere, but fervent love crowds the courts of King Jesus.
His marred countenance is the most majestic ever seen!

From sermon no. 1353, *Ecce Rex*

SEEING EXTRAORDINARY THINGS

"We have seen extraordinary things today."
LUKE 5:26

The human mind craves novelties and when it finds them, it makes "much ado about nothing."
It whips itself up into an intense excitement over matters that have no importance.

But no one has ever spent a day with the Lord Jesus
  without being filled with the sight of extraordinary things.
No one has ever entered into communion with him
  without being delighted with wonders of love, of mercy, of grace, of truth, and of goodness.

Though the gospel of our Lord Jesus Christ is the old, old gospel,
it is continually fresh and new.
It never grows stale.

When John saw our Lord, as recorded in the book of Revelation, he says, "The hairs of his head
  were white like wool, as white as snow" (1:14) to denote his antiquity.
And yet the bride said of him, "His locks are wavy, black as a raven" (Song of Solomon 5:11)
  as if to indicate his perpetual youth, his unfailing strength, and his unfading beauty.

If you want to see that which is truly extraordinary,
  you must get into that spiritual realm where Christ is owned as King.
You must wait "for new heavens and a new earth in which righteousness dwells" (2 Peter 3:13).

Dear child of God, if you want to be astounded, amazed, filled with holy awe,
you must become familiar with the Savior—his person, his work, his offices!

When you have become familiar with everything that has to do with him,
you will be forced to say continually:

"I have seen extraordinary things today!
My Lord has seemed to outdo himself!
His mercy has appeared to go deeper than ever before,
even though it has already gone deeper than the abyss itself!"

He who enters this spiritual world where Christ is adored as God and King
  has unlocked a cabinet of marvels—
marvels that will astonish him throughout his lifetime on earth, and even throughout eternity!

Oh, spend your time in the company of the great Wonder-Worker,
and you will be able to say every day, "I have seen extraordinary things today!"

From sermon no. 2614, *Strange Things*

THE VICTORIOUS ASCENSION

You have ascended on high, You have led captivity captive;
You have received gifts among men.
PSALM 68:18 NKJV

Our Savior *descended* when he came to the manger of Bethlehem, a baby;
and descended further when he became "a man of sorrows, and acquainted with grief."
He descended still lower when he was "obedient to the point of death, even death on a cross";
and yet further when his dead body was laid in the grave.

Long and dark was the descent—
there were no depths of humiliation, temptation, and affliction that he did not fathom.
Because he stood in the place of sinners,
he went as low as justice required of sinners who had violated God's law.

The utmost abyss of desertion heard him cry, "My God, my God, why have you forsaken me?"
Low, low in the depths of the grave he lay!

But on the third day he left the couch of the dead
and he commenced his glorious ascent by rising to the light of the living.
And he later declared his victory by ascending to the Father's throne.

Yes, his descent had ended.

There was no need for him to remain amidst the men who despised him.
The shame and suffering, blasphemy and rebuke are far beneath him now.
He is far above the reach of sneering Sadducees and accusing Pharisees.

The traitor cannot kiss him again.
Pilate cannot scourge him.
Herod cannot mock him.

He who trod the weary ways of Palestine now reigns as King in his palace.
He who sighed and hungered and wept and bled and died is now above all heavens.
He who was earth's scorn is now heaven's wonder.
The Christ who was buried here, now sits on his throne.

We rejoice in your ascension, O Savior, for it is the ensign of your victory!

If you had not led captivity captive, you would never have ascended on high;
if you had not won gifts of salvation for us, you would still be here suffering.
You would never have relinquished your chosen task if you had not perfected it.

The voice of the ascension is, "It is finished."

From sermon no. 2142, *Our Lord's Triumphant Ascension*

A VISION OF THE CROSS

"And I, when I am lifted up from the earth, will draw all people to myself."
He said this to show by what kind of death he was going to die.
JOHN 12:32–33

Notice that Christ went to his death with a clear understanding of what it entailed.
Men who go into battle have no idea beforehand of what it is to be wounded to death,
but our Lord took stock of his death, and he looked it square in the face.
He not only speaks of his death, but he also describes it: "I, when I am lifted up from the earth."

In his own mind Jesus had already gone through the nailing to the wood
and to the uplifting of that wood into the air and the fixing of its socket into the ground.
In spirit he already felt himself to be hanging there, lifted up from the earth.

Though our Savior knew the bitterness of his death, he read its issues in another light.
"I, when I am lifted up," did not merely mean to him that he would be lifted up on the cross.
It also meant another kind of uplifting—it meant that he would be exalted.

Jesus looked to his death as one might look into an opal—
looking until he sees wondrous rainbows and flames of fire in the precious stone.
So Jesus looked into his Passion, into the ruddy depths of that blood-cup until he saw his glory.
He saw that he was being lifted up, even though men saw him as being cast down.

His cross was his throne for with his outstretched hands he ruled the nations.
With his feet fixed there, he trampled on the enemies of men.

> *O glorious Christ, when I had a vision of your cross,*
> *I saw it at first like a common gibbet,*
> *and you were hanging on it like a felon.*
>
> *But, as I have looked, I have seen it rise and then tower aloft*
> *until it had reached the highest heaven.*
> *By its mighty power it lifted up myriads to the throne of God.*
>
> *I have seen its arms extend and expand*
> *until they embraced the whole earth.*
>
> *I have seen its foot go down—deep, deep down—*
> *as deep down as our helpless miseries.*
>
> *What a vision I have had of your magnificence,*
> *O thou Crucified One!*

From sermon no. 2338, *The Crisis of This World*

BEHOLDING CHRIST'S GLORY

His face shone like the sun.
MATTHEW 17:2

Notice the circumstances in which Christ revealed his glory to his three disciples.
It was in a lonely spot; they were "on a high mountain by themselves."

Learn from this that if we would see Jesus in his glory, we must depart from the multitude.
  He may come to us when we are with his people as he came to the disciples in the Upper Room,
    but there was a form of loneliness and seclusion even there.
The world was shut out and none were there but his own followers.

Our Lord delights to talk to his beloved ones when they are alone;
  so leave the servants at a distance from the secret meeting place, even as Abraham did,
    and go up to the top of the hill alone, or with some specially chosen companion.
We may even walk the fields in the evening, like Isaac, and hold secret communion with God.

> *The best visits from Christ*
> *are like the best visits we have from those we love—*
> *not in the busy marketplace, or in the crowded street,*
> *but when we are alone with them.*

We are far too often like Martha "distracted with much serving" (Luke 10:40).
  We need to be more like Mary, sitting at the feet of Jesus
    and looking up into his dear face while listening to his gracious words.
The active life will have little power if it is not accompanied by contemplation and prayer.

Something may be learned from the fact that Jesus revealed his glory to only a few of his disciples.
  All who believe in Jesus have found salvation through him,
    but there are many who are partially blind and cannot see afar.
There are only a few who have seen our Lord Jesus Christ as distinctly as he may be seen.

I hunger and thirst to see as much of him as can be seen while dwelling on this earth.
Why should we not all do so?

> *Eyes are meant to see light,*
> *and spiritual eyes are intended to see Christ;*
> *and they are never so fully used for their true design*
> *as when they are continually fixed on him.*

> *All lower lights are forgotten and permitted to burn out*
> *while he becomes the one great Light in which we bask and revel.*

From sermon no. 2729, *Christ's Transfigured Face*

ALL IS VANITY

*I have seen everything that is done under the sun,
and behold, all is vanity and a striving after wind.*
ECCLESIASTES 1:14

Nothing can ever satisfy our hearts except the Lord's love and presence.
Solomon experimented with life for us all and did for us what we dare not do for ourselves.

Here is Solomon's testimony in his own words:
"So I became great and surpassed all who were before me in Jerusalem … And whatever my eyes
   desired I did not keep from them. I kept my heart from no pleasure, for my heart found pleasure
   in all my toil … Then I considered all that my hands had done and the toil I had expended in
   doing it, and behold, all was vanity and a striving after wind, and there was nothing to be gained
   under the sun" (Ecclesiastes 2:9–11).

Solomon even begins Ecclesiastes by saying, "Vanity of vanities! All is vanity."
What! Everything is vanity?

O favored king, is there nothing of worth in all your wealth?
Is there nothing in all your wide land that reaches from the river to the sea?
Is there nothing in all your music, dancing, wine, and luxury?
"Nothing," he replied, "but weariness of spirit."

This was his verdict after he traveled the whole globe of pleasure.
To embrace our Savior, to dwell in his love, and to be fully assured of union with him—this is all in all.

*O believer, you do not have to try other lifestyles
to see if they are better than the Christian way of life!*

*If you roam the world,
you will see no sights like the Savior's face.*

*If you could have all the comforts of life
but lost your Savior,
you would be utterly wretched.*

*But if you have Christ,
then even if you live in obscurity or die from famine,
you will be satisfied with God's favor
and filled with the goodness of the Lord.*[1]

Those who know his love must feel his spell on their affections, holding them captive.
There is none like him among the sons of men. His beauties ravish the heart!
If Jesus would lift the veil and let us see him for a moment, our hearts would melt within us.[2]

[1]*Morning and Evening*, December 2 (E)
[2]From sermon no. 1553, *Faith Working by Love*

DAY BY DAY WITH THE BEST OF SPURGEON

THE BELIEVING THIEF

And he said, "Jesus, remember me when you come into your kingdom."
And he said to him, "Truly, I say to you, today you will be with me in Paradise."
LUKE 23: 42-43

The salvation of the dying thief is a constant witness of the power of Christ to save.
　　We must remember that Jesus—at the time he saved this criminal—was at his lowest state.
His glory had been ebbing away in Gethsemane, and before Caiaphas, Herod, and Pilate,
　　but it had now reached its lowest point.

Stripped of his garments and nailed to the cross,
　　our Lord was mocked by a heartless crowd, and was dying in agony.
He was then "numbered with the transgressors" (Luke 22:37), and treated like the worst of criminals.
　　Yet, while in that condition, he achieved this marvelous deed of grace.

Behold the wonder wrought by the Savior
when he was emptied of all his glory,
and was on the very brink of death!

If a dying Savior could save the thief,
　　surely he can do even greater wonders now—now that he lives and reigns.
Can anything at this present time surpass the power of his grace?

Now consider the thief who is looking at Jesus hanging in agony on the cross.
Could you readily believe him to be the Lord of glory who would soon come into his kingdom?
That was no small faith which, at such a moment, could believe in Jesus as Lord and King!

Remember, also, that our Lord was surrounded by scoffers.
　　This man heard the priests, in their pride, ridiculing him,
　　　　and he also heard the great multitude of common people, with one consent, scorning him.
Yet through God's grace, he believed in the Lord Jesus in the face of all that awful scorn.

Oh, the glory of divine grace!
It gave the thief such faith and then freely saved him.

See how glorious the Savior is,
who at such a time could save such a man;
who could give him such great faith,
and then so perfectly and speedily prepare him for eternal bliss!

Behold the power of that divine Spirit
who could produce such faith on soil so unlikely,
and in a climate so unfavorable!

From sermon no. 2078, *The Believing Thief*

IN A MANGER

She gave birth to her firstborn son and wrapped him in swaddling cloths
and laid him in a manger, because there was no place for them in the inn.
LUKE 2:7

Come to the stable at Bethlehem and see this great sight: The Savior lying in a manger.

We are told that Mary laid Jesus in a manger, "because there was no place for them in the inn,"
   but this is not the only reason why Jesus is laid in a lowly manger.
Besides revealing our Savior's poverty and humility,
   he is giving an invitation to the most timid and needy to come to him.

O sinner, you might tremble to approach a throne,
but there is no fear in approaching a manger!

No being has ever been more approachable than Jesus Christ of Nazareth.

No rough guards were present to push poor petitioners away.
No meddlesome friends were allowed to hold back the imploring widow.
No one resisted the man who clamored that his son might be made whole.
The hem of Christ's garment was always trailing where sick folk could reach it.

Jesus always had a hand ready to touch any disease
   and an ear ready to catch the faintest accents of misery.
Like the light of the sun, his soul went forth everywhere in rays of mercy.

By being laid in a manger, Jesus proved himself to be a priest taken from among the people,
   one who has suffered like his brethren and therefore can sympathize with their weaknesses.
Of him it was said, "This man receives sinners and eats with them" (Luke 15:2).
   Even as an infant—by being laid in a manger—he was shown to be the sinner's friend.

So, come to him, you who are weary and burdened.
Come to him, you who despise yourselves and are despised by others.
Come to him, idolater and prostitute, thief and drunkard.

In the manger there he lies,
unguarded from your touch and unshielded from your gaze.
Bow the knee and kiss the Son of God.

Accept him as your Savior.
He puts himself into that manger
so that you may approach him.

The throne of Solomon might awe you,
but the manger of the Son of David must invite you.

From sermon no. 485, *No Room for Christ in the Inn*

NO LONGER REMEMBERED

As far as the east is from the west,
so far does he remove our transgressions from us.
PSALM 103:12

The people who believe in Jesus feel a deep peace in their souls.
They know that he died in their place and that their sins are put away.

That is why they love to gaze upon their crucified Lord.

They stand and hug the cross;
they kiss those bleeding feet;
they look up to that dear face bedewed with drops of grief;
they observe that dear brow, crowned with thorns,
 and they say:

> *"You are my Savior!*
> *Dear Lover of my soul, I rest in you!*
>
> *"Your side, split open for me, yields me my pardon.*
> *Your death is my life.*
> *Your life in heaven is the guarantee of my immortality."*

Happy are they who can stand at the cross-foot
 and know that even as far as the east is from the west,
so far has God removed their transgressions from them.

This means that the Lord has *forgotten* their transgressions.
He says, "I will forgive their iniquity, and I will remember their sin no more" (Jeremiah 31:34).

What inconceivable love!
What force and pathos!
What grace there is in every syllable: "I will remember their sin no more"!

Has he not said, "I have blotted out your transgressions like a cloud" (Isaiah 44:22)?
Has he not said, "Though your sins are like scarlet, they shall be as white as snow; though they
 are red like crimson, they shall become like wool" (Isaiah 1:18)?

> *O child of God, realize the fact that your sins are now gone—*
> *effectually, completely, perfectly gone—*
> *through the precious sacrifice of Jesus Christ.*

From sermon no. 1108, *Plenary Absolution*

RESTING FROM LABOR

"They may rest from their labors."
REVELATION 14:13

Our Savior has labored in his love, but now he rests.

Love fetched him from his throne in heaven.
Love disrobed him of his glories.
Love laid him in Bethlehem's manger.
Love led him through this weary world for thirty-three years.
Love took him to Gethsemane where it oppressed him until he sweat great drops of blood.
Love made him stand erect when he was the focus of the war, and every arrow of the enemy
　　found a target in his heart.
Love made him bow his head and die so that he might redeem his people from their sins.

And now that our Redeemer is more than a conqueror,
he has risen to heaven and he rests in his love.

Oh, what a wondrous rest that is!

If rest is sweet to a laboring man, how much sweeter …
　　to the bleeding man,
　　to the dying man,
　　to the crucified man,
　　to the risen man!

If rest is sweet after toil,
　　how sweet must be the rest of Jesus
after all the toils of life and death, the cross and the grave!

If victory makes the soldier's return joyous,
　　how joyous must have been the return of that conquering Hero
who led a host of captives and gave gifts to men (Ephesians 4:8)!

The very thing that drove him to labor now makes a pillow for his head.
That which made him strong in the day of battle makes him joyous in the hour of victory.
That is the love that he bears to his beloved people.

Lo! As our Lord Jesus sits down in heaven, he must think to himself:

"I have done it! I have finished the work of my people's redemption.
God's vengeance cannot fall on them now, for it has all fallen on me.
I have borne their curse and have delivered them from it forever."

From sermon no. 2720, *The Savior Resting in His Love*

PERPETUAL PRAISE

Yes, he is altogether lovely.
SONG OF SOLOMON 5:16 NKJV

This is not only rare praise, it is also perpetual praise.
You may say of Christ whenever you look at him, "Yes, he is altogether lovely."

All the while he lived on earth, what moral perfections, what noble qualities,
    and what spiritual charms encompassed his sacred person!
His life among men is a succession of charming pictures.

And he was lovely in his bitter Passion when the thick darkness was overshadowing his soul
    and he prayed in an agony of desire, "Not my will, but yours be done" (Luke 22:42).
The bloody sweat did not disfigure him, but rather, it adorned him.

And oh, was he not beautiful when he died?
What a sight to see him bleeding on the tree and, at the same time, see our sins rolling into his sepulcher!

He is lovely in his resurrection from the dead—beyond description lovely!
Yes, and he will be lovely forever when our eyes will eternally find their heaven in beholding him!

Oh, no tongue of man, no tongue of angel can ever depict Christ's unutterable beauties!
    When we have summoned up all that our poor tongues can express,
        we must not say, "Now we have described him."
Oh no, we have but held a candle to this glorious Sun!

But the day will soon dawn and usher in the everlasting age when Christ will be better seen,
    for every eye will see him and every tongue confess that he is Lord.
The whole earth will one day be sweet with the praises of Jesus.

Earth did I say?

The sweetness of our Lord's person will rise above the stars and perfume worlds unknown.
It will fill heaven itself!

Eternity will be occupied with declaring the praises of Jesus!

Seraphs will sing it!
Angels will harp it!
The redeemed will declare it!

Earth is too narrow to contain him!
Heaven is too little to hold him!

Eternity itself is too short for the utterance of all his praises!

From sermon no. 1446, *The Best Beloved*

SPRINGS OF LIVING WATER

For the Lamb in the midst of the throne will be their shepherd,
and he will guide them to springs of living water.
REVELATION 7:17

The description of the heavenly life has this conspicuous feature: The leading of the Lamb.
"The Great Shepherd of the sheep" will personally minister to us.

We will hear his voice;
we will see his face;
we will be fed by his hand;
we will follow at his heel.

How gloriously he will guide and feed us!
How restfully we will lie down in green pastures!

Drinking at the springs—this is the secret of heaven's ineffable bliss.
"The Lamb ... will be their shepherd, and he will guide them to springs of living water."

We are now compelled to thirst at times like the poor flocks
    driven through the streets of London on their way to the slaughter.
Alas! We stop at the puddles by the way and there we try to refresh ourselves.

This will never happen to us when we reach the land where the Water of Life flows.
    There the sheep will not drink of stagnant waters or bitter wells,
        but they will be satisfied at the springs of living water.
The enthroned Lamb, who is the source of all bliss, will be the fulfillment of all our desires.

We may say of the wells of earth, "Whoever drinks of this water will thirst again,"
    but when we go beyond temporary supplies and live on God,
        then the soul receives a truer and more enduring refreshment.
In heaven we will not live on bread, which is the staff of life, but on God, who is life itself.

When I am close to God and dwell in the overflowing of his love,
    I feel like the cattle on a hot summer's day
        when they wade into the brook that ripples up to their knees.
There they stand, filled, cooled, and sweetly refreshed.

Such is heaven!
We will have bliss within and bliss all around us.
We will drink at the source of all bliss and will dwell by the Well-head forever.

Heaven is God fully enjoyed.

From sermon no. 2128, *Heaven Above, and Heaven Below*

HE "MUST"

He must reign.
1 Corinthians 15:25

"He *must* reign."
Yes, but there was also another "must" that Christ's disciples were slow to learn.

Much of our Lord's teaching to his apostles was concerning the necessity that he must suffer,
   but this notion could not be drilled into them.
Their very spirits seemed to revolt against it.

And do you wonder?

If you had actually lived with our dear and blessed Lord, and had known the marvels of his person,
   could you have endured the thought that he must be shamefully abused?
Could you have accepted the idea that he must be spit on and then nailed like a felon to a gibbet?

Oh, it was such a cruel "must" that Jesus must die!

Even after he had died and all the prophecies concerning his death had been fulfilled,
   it was still a bewilderment to his disciples.
The two who walked to Emmaus with Christ were still in a maze concerning it.

That first "must" cost the people of God much agony before they learned it,
   but we now know that the price of our pardon was Christ's suffering and death.
There was no other method by which the lost inheritance could come back to us
   except by the ransom price that was found in the pierced heart of Christ.

And now there is another "must" that is almost as difficult to learn.

It appears almost impossible that the crucified Christ will yet be the universal Conqueror;
   that the man of Nazareth will yet mount his white horse and lead his conquering armies to victory.
Yet, as surely as it was true that he must suffer, just as surely "he must reign."

Yes, Jesus must reign.

Delay there may be, but the victory must come.
The second necessity will be as certainly fulfilled as was the first.

> *Oh, let heaven ring with the anticipation of it: "He must reign"!*
> *Let earth resound with the prophecy of it: "He must reign"!*

> *And let each Christian feel revived and quickened by the joyful sound*
> *that he who had to die must surely reign!*

From sermon no. 2940, *"He Must Reign"*

OUR COMING KING

Your eyes will behold the king in his beauty.
ISAIAH 33:17

By faith, we have had as it were a telescopic view of Christ, but we have yet to see him face to face.
Even a distant sight of him ravishes the heart, but what must it be to see him without a veil between!

Our eyes can never gaze on anything in this world with complete satisfaction.
    The most charming vision of sea or land or sky never satisfies the spirit.
But when our "eyes will behold the king in his beauty," we will exclaim, "It is enough, Lord!
    Our eyes have at last found the one object upon which they can rest forever!"

We will behold the King himself—
    that King who was once the Baby in Bethlehem,
    that carpenter at Nazareth who went about doing good, preaching the gospel, healing the sick,
    that same Jesus who agonized in Gethsemane and died on Calvary.

*Yes, we will behold the King
in all the glory of his combined deity and humanity—
very God of very God, yet just as truly man.*

The beauty of a king—his glory—also consists of his official robes, jewels, and ornaments.
    Glorious vision! Our "eyes will behold the king in his beauty"—
    not as people beheld him when his ruby robe was formed from his own blood,
and when his only diamonds were his tears, and his only crown was made of thorns.

*Pilate mockingly said to the Jews,
"Behold your King!" (John 19:14).*

*But the heavenly heralds, with the sound of trumpets,
will cry in a far different manner,
"Behold your King!"*

Words cannot fully express all that this vision of the King will be.
It will be a ravishing sight, a rapturous, ecstatic, entrancing, transporting vision!
Heaven will be a place of many surprises, but the vision of our glorified King will astonish us forever![1]

*Oh! Thick veils and clouds hang between our souls and their true life!
When will the day break and the shadows flee away?
When will we leave the glass in which we see our Beloved dimly
and see him face to face?*

Oh! Long-expected day, begin![2]

[1]From sermon no. 3238. *A Vision of the King*
[2]From sermon no. 752, *The King in His Beauty*